ARTIFICIAL NEURAL NETWORKS

THEORY AND APPLICATIONS

ARTIFICIAL NEURAL NETWORKS

THEORY AND APPLICATIONS

DAN W. PATTERSON

Institute of Systems Science
National University of Singapore

PRENTICE HALL

Singapore New York London Toronto Sydney Tokyo

First published 1996 by
Prentice Hall
Simon & Schuster (Asia) Pte Ltd
Alexandra Distripark
Block 4, #04-31
Pasir Panjang Road
Singapore 118491

Cover photograph by Art Matrix, Ithaca, New York

Library of Congress Cataloging-in-Publication Data

Patterson, Dan W., 1930-
    Artificial neural networks: theory and applications/Dan W. Patterson.
      p.   cm.
    Includes bibliographical references and index.
    ISBN 0-13-295353-6 (pbk.)
    1. Neural networks (Computer science)   I. Title.
    QA76.87.P39 1995   95-30355
    006.3--dc20   CIP

Printed in Singapore

1 2 3 4 5   99 98 97 96

ISBN 0-13-295353-6

Prentice Hall International (UK) Limited, *London*
Prentice Hall of Australia Pty. Limited, *Sydney*
Prentice Hall Canada Inc., *Toronto*
Prentice Hall Hispanoamericana, S.A., *Mexico*
Prentice Hall of India Private Limited, *New Delhi*
Prentice Hall of Japan, Inc., *Tokyo*
Editora Prentice Hall do Brasil, Ltda., *Rio de Janeiro*
Prentice Hall, Inc., *Upper Saddle River, New Jersey*

Dedicated to Grace, Joseline and Adrian

Acknowledgements

I owe a debt of gratitude to the many researchers in neural networks from whom I have learned over the past ten years and to my students whose unceasing quest for knowledge has been a continual challenge and inspiration to me. I also want to thank the director of the Institute of Systems Science, Dr. Juzar Motiwalla and the assistant director, Mr. Lim Swee Cheang for their support. I wish to acknowledge the assistance and support given to me by the Prentice Hall editors and to the anonymous reviewers. Finally, I want to thank my family for their unending support and encouragement throughout the course of writing this manuscript.

Dan W. Patterson
February 1995
Singapore

CONTENTS

◇ PART II   Early Neural Networks and Developments

◇ PART III   Multilayer Feedforward Neural Networks and
             Backpropagation

◇ PART IV   Dynamic Recurrent and Stochastic Neural
              Networks

◇ PART V   Other Neural Network Architectures

◇ PART VI   Networks Based on Unsupervised Learning

◇ **PART VII   Conclusion**

PREFACE

This textbook is written for newcomers to the field as well as for those who have already acquired some basic knowledge. For the newcomer, the first few chapters provide introductory material on simple neural computing elements and basic learning algorithms. These chapters also review historical developments in the field and give some biological motivation for the artificial network architectures which follow. Early neural networks are then presented as a further step to more sophisticated architectures. For the already initiated, the book covers basic theory and operation of more than 22 network architecture types with a comprehensive treatment of all important learning algorithms. The most recent advances relating to each architecture are covered including design guidelines for specific applications. For both the initiated and the newcomer, the book presents a generous number of applications spanning a wide variety of fields.

When I first started writing the book, I was looking for a reference text on neural networks for students in my postgraduate program in knowledge engineering (KE). This is an intensive, ten-month full-time (two-year part-time) program in KE offered by the Institute of Systems Science, National University of Singapore. At that time there were only a few texts available. Although some were excellent texts, none offered the balance between theory and applications that I was looking for. Since then, a number of additional books have appeared on the market, but still, in my opinion, none have met the criteria I had established for my program. I believe this text has.

During the course of writing the manuscript I was fortunate enough to gain a new son, Adrian. Watching his development over the next several months made me acutely aware of the complexity (and beauty) of natural, biological neural networks. It also made me cognizant of the real challenge that researchers face in this field when trying to understand and model these complex products of nature. Evolution has provided us with a powerful start on life at birth. Billions of neurons are prewired and put in place, ready for development through further connectivity and refinement. The learning process that follows seems slow. After all, it is carried out at multiple levels and in parallel paths concurrently (motor control, vision, language, cognition, and a host of others) over a period of 30 years or more. Of course, this whole process would not be possible without some prewired networks. They include the networks that generate the powerful sense of curiosity in a child and an uncanny drive to mimic the behaviors of others. One can only wonder if we shall ever be able to match the capabilities of these natural networks with our simple, synthetically crafted ones.

I have been an active scholar and researcher in the field of artificial intelligence since the early 1980s. This was a time when knowledge-based expert systems were gaining popularity, and the generally accepted approach to modeling intelligent systems was through logic-based representations and symbolic computations. The immediate following years marked the turning point in this attitude. Conventional AI had not "delivered." There was little real progress being made beyond the limited, smart problem solver types of expert systems. Mastering more complex tasks such as natural language processing and vision were found to be too difficult, too elusive. A new approach was clearly needed. The most promising (and obvious?) alternative came with a resurgence of interest in neural networks at this same time. This rebirth of interest began in the mid-1980s and quickly mushroomed into a virtual explosion of research activity that cut across many disciplines: physics, engineering, computer science, neuroscience, psychology, and cognitive science. Numerous important advances were made during the ten-year period following. But, with all the effort, we are still far from achieving real artificially intelligent systems. Much work remains, but the natural, biological approach toward AI is likely to be the correct one. Of course, we must still learn to model more accurately what nature has been perfecting for millions of years. The technology advances described in this manuscript represent only a first step in this direction. I believe it is one of the more important steps taken in the twentieth century and certainly one of the most exciting fields of scientific study.

Prerequisites and Organization of the Text

There are no prerequisites for the text except a basic knowledge of calculus and a general maturity in mathematics. For those whose mathematics is a bit rusty, a reference chapter (Chapter 3) covering the necessary topics has been included. Basic definitions and operations for topics such as vector and matrix algebra, differential and integral calculus, differential equations, probability and statistics, information theory, fuzzy sets and fuzzy logic and nonlinear system dynamics with chaos are provided.

The book could serve as a course text or reference book for a one-semester course at the upper division (third or fourth year) undergraduate level or at the first year graduate level. The book is organized into six parts as follows. Part I is introductory covering simple neural computing, biological neural concepts, historical background, and neural network taxonomies. Part II covers early neural network systems and learning algorithms. Part III is devoted to multilayer feedforward networks (multilayer perceptrons) with error backpropagation learning. Part IV covers general recurrent networks, networks with feedback connections. Part V is devoted to other important architectures, including self-growing networks. Part VI covers networks that learn without a teacher or unsupervised learning. The final part, Part VII is a concluding chapter.

Part I

Introduction, Background and Biological Inspiration

1
Introduction to Artificial Neural Networks

In this introductory chapter, we describe the basic operation of a simple neural network and the types of computations they can perform. We also discuss characteristics of biological neural systems and how they have served as an inspiration for researchers in building models of neural networks, the so-called artificial neural networks. This is followed by some historical background to show how the field has progressed over the past 50 years. Finally, we present a description of some general application tasks for which neural networks have been successfully employed. The chapter should serve to define the basic parts and functioning of a simple neural network and the types of tasks they can learn and be expected to perform. Background and historical details will also help to relate progress made in neural network research to other fields involved in cognitive systems development.

1.1   Introduction

Artificial Neural Networks (ANNs) are simplified models of the central nervous system. They are networks of highly interconnected neural computing elements that have the ability to respond to input stimuli and to learn to adapt to the environment. It is believed by many researchers in the field that neural network models offer the most promising unified approach to building truly intelligent computer systems; and, that the use of distributed, parallel computations as performed in ANNs is the best way to overcome the combinatorial explosion associated with symbolic serial computations when using von Neumann computer architectures. The human neural network system provides a strong argument in favor of this thesis. Biological networks are able to process millions of input stimuli in milliseconds even though

1

the processes are electrochemical in nature, and therefore propagate at relatively slow millisecond rates. This is several orders of magnitude slower than the high speed picosecond operations performed in conventional serial digital computers. In spite of this wide divergence in signal propagation and unit processing speed, conventional state-of-the-art computer systems, such as vision systems, fall far short of the performance exhibited by biological systems in their processing ability.

ANNs have been shown to be effective as computational processors for various tasks including pattern recognition (e.g. speech and visual image recognition), associative recall, classification, data compression, modeling and forecasting, combinatorial problem solving, adaptive control, multisensor data fusion and noise filtering. They exhibit a number of desirable properties not found in conventional symbolic computation systems including robust performance when dealing with noisy or incomplete input patterns, a high degree of fault tolerance, high parallel computation rates, the ability to generalize, and adaptive learning.

In this introductory chapter, we describe simple neural network systems to illustrate how they function as a parallel processor and examine the basic notions of ANN learning methods. We also present a summary of biological neuron properties and how the living neuronal networks have inspired the development of simulated networks as well as hardwired very large scale integration (VLSI chip) networks. We give an overview of important historical events in neural network research that have brought us to the level of sophistication found in modern day architectures. We conclude the chapter with a description of some generic ANN applications. (Subsequent chapters present numerous ANN applications in more detail.)

1.2   Basic Concepts in Neural Computing

Although ANN architectures differ in several characteristic ways, a typical ANN neuron or computing element is basically a comparator that produces an output when the cumulative effect of the input stimuli exceeds a threshold value. In Figure 1.1, a single ANN neuron is illustrated with three inputs and a single output.

Each input link i ($i = 1, 2, 3$) has an associated external input signal or stimulus x_i and a corresponding weight w_i, a sort of filter which is part of the linkage connecting the input to the neuron. The input x_i values can be real ($+$ or $-$), binary (0, 1), or bipolar ($-1, +1$). The weights, which model the synaptic neural connections in biological nets (see Section 1.3), act to either increase (excitatory input) or decrease (inhibitory input) the input signals to the neuron. The weights can also be binary or real-valued, but are usually assumed to be real (positive for excitatory and negative for inhibitory links). The output from the ANN can also be real-valued or binary or bipolar. A schematic black box equivalent of the neuron is illustrated in Figure 1.2.

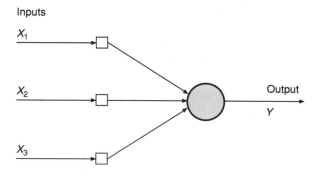

Figure 1.1   A Simple Artificial Neural Network

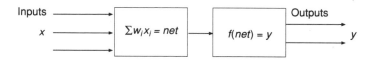

Figure 1.2   Schematic Diagram of a Single Neuron

The neuron behaves as an activation or mapping function $f(\cdot)$ producing an output $y = f(net)$, where net is the cumulative input stimuli to the neuron and f is typically a nonlinear function of net. For example, net is often taken as the weighted sum of the inputs

$$net = x_1 w_1 + x_2 w_2 + x_3 w_3 = \Sigma_i x_i w_i$$

and f is typically a monotonic nondecreasing function of net. Of course, the number of inputs to a network will often be much larger than three. In such cases, we use the index n to denote that there are an arbitrary number of inputs.

Some examples of commonly used activation functions $f(net)$ are depicted in Figure 1.3. Note that a threshold term θ is sometimes included in the definition of net, but this can be replaced by placing a fixed bias input of $+1 \times w_0$ on one of the input links and setting the value of $w_0 = -\theta$.

The use of vector and matrix notation is used extensively in the literature on ANNs since it greatly simplifies the descriptions for computations. Consequently, we use vector and matrix notation frequently in subsequent chapters. Vectors and matrices are denoted by bold letters, and all vectors will be regarded as column vectors unless the transpose is given ($\mathbf{v}^T$ is the transpose of $\mathbf{v}$) in which case the

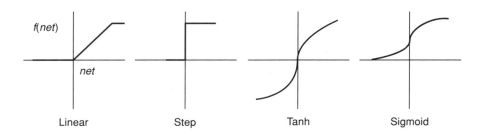

Figure 1.3   Typical Neural Network Activation Functions

vector is regarded as a row vector. (Vectors and Matrices are reviewed in Chapter 3.)

A simple ANN such as that depicted in Figure 1.1 can compute a two-class membership grouping of input stimuli patterns. The components of the input vector **x**, given by x_1, x_2, ..., x_n, are the individual stimuli values. They correspond to the features or attributes of the input. For example, x_i may be visual properties of objects (light intensity) in the field of view, characteristics of speech waveforms (e.g. power spectra for different frequencies), physical values of some process variables (temperature, humidity, flow rates, and so on), values which determine the financial profile of a loan applicant (age, income, monthly obligations, credit history), physical values which characterize today's weather (so the network can forecast tomorrow's weather) or observed and measured symptoms from a sick patient. The output might correspond to the presence of a visual object or word of text, fluid flow control rate, risk level of a loan applicant, predicted weather state (fair/rain) or the health status of a patient (ill/fit).

In computing a two-class membership for inputs, a single ANN neuron behaves like a predicate that computes concept or class membership. The weight vector value **w** defines a separating hyperplane in n-space which divides the input values into two regions or classes, class-1 and class-2, accordingly, as the weighted sums, $\mathbf{x}^T\mathbf{w} = \Sigma_i x_i w_i$ are greater than or less than zero (or some other threshold value θ):

$$\text{If } \mathbf{x}^T\mathbf{w} = \sum_{i=1}^{n} x_i w_i > 0 \qquad \text{then } \mathbf{x} \text{ belongs to class-1}$$

$$\text{If } \mathbf{x}^T\mathbf{w} = \sum_{i=1}^{n} x_i w_i \leq 0 \qquad \text{then } \mathbf{x} \text{ belongs to class-2}$$

The classification regions are easily depicted for the two-dimensional case, $n = 2$ as illustrated in Figure 1.4. Typically, a constant bias input of $x_0 = +1$ is included with an adjustable weight w_0. The bias input weight w_0 together with the other weights, determine the location of the separating line for the two-class regions. This is easily seen when the net input equation is viewed as the equation of a line in two-dimensional space $x_1 \times x_2$

$$net = w_0 + x_1 w_1 + x_2 w_2 = 0$$

In this form, we easily find the slope of the line to be just $-w_1/w_2$ and the offset of the line from the origin is determined by the value of the bias weight w_0, so the location and orientation of the line separating the two-class regions in two-space is completely determined by the values of $\mathbf{w}$. Input values of $\mathbf{x}$ for a fixed $\mathbf{w}$, will then be classified as belonging to class-1 when they result in a value of $net > 0$, and classified as class-2 when they result in a value of $net \leq 0$. Thus, we see that by choosing a specific set of weights, we can define an arbitrary separating boundary for input patterns $\mathbf{x}$. This is important because it is the key to autonomous learning in ANNs. By adjusting the weights $\mathbf{w}$, a separating boundary for a set of patterns can be found that satisfy some desired classification criteria. In subsequent chapters, we will explore different ways in which ANNs can learn mappings, such as separating class boundaries, through a process of weight adjustment driven by a set of training examples.

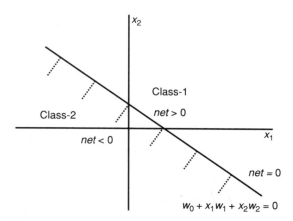

Figure 1.4 The Separating Plane for Two-Class Membership

Regions or classes which can be partitioned into two or more spaces using linear boundaries such as a line, plane or hyperplane given by $\mathbf{x}^T\mathbf{w}$, are said to be linearly separable. Regions bounded by curves that overlap one another or surround each other cannot, in general, be separated with linear hyperplanes (Figure 1.5). More general nonlinear (or piecewise-linear) boundary functions will be required to separate such regions.

Each output element of a one-layer feedforward linear network of the type considered above (one layer of input elements connected through weights to one output layer of elements) is capable of separating a space only into linearly separable classes. Computing more complicated class membership relationships requires that more layers be added, or that nonlinear combining functions be used either in the same layer or in additional cascaded layers. In later chapters, we will explore more general ANN architectures which overcome the above limitations.

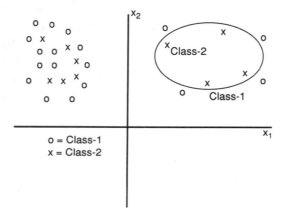

Figure 1.5   Class Regions Which Are Not Linearly Separable

1.3   Biological Systems: Biological and Cognitive Aspects

Much of the research work in ANNs has been inspired and influenced by our knowledge of biological nervous systems. Our knowledge of the mammalian nervous system is far from complete, but some important facts have been learned by neuroscientists and others, particularly over the past few decades. The basic computing element in biological systems is the neuron. A neuron is a small cell that receives electrochemical stimuli from multiple sources and responds by generating electrical impulses that are transmitted to other neurons or effector cells. There are something like 10^{10} to 10^{12} neurons in the human nervous system and each is capable of storing several bits of "information". The total weight of an average brain is 1.5 kg, so an average neuron weighs something less than 1.5×10^{-9} g.

Neurons receive inputs from sensory or other types of cells and send outputs to other neurons or effector organs such as muscles and glands. About 10% of the neurons are input (afferent) and output (efferent). The remaining 90% are interconnected with other neurons which store information or perform various transformations on the signals being propagated through the network. Although many different types of neurons have been identified, they all share some common characteristics.

Neurons are complex cells that respond to electrochemical signals. They are composed of a nucleus, a cell body, numerous dendritic links providing input "connections" from other neurons through synapses, and an axon trunk that carries an action potential output to other neurons through terminal links and synapses (Figures 1.6 and 1.7).

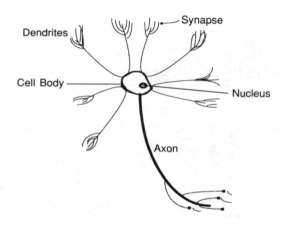

Figure 1.6   A Typical Neuron

A single neuron may be connected to hundreds or even tens of thousands of other neurons (Figure 1.8). The connections are made through two general types of synapses: excitatory and inhibitory (Figure 1.9). Neuronal activity is related to the creation of an internal electric potential called a membrane potential. This potential may be increased or decreased by the input activity received from other cells through the synapses. If the cumulative inputs raise the potential above a threshold value, the neuron "fires" by propagating a sequence of action potential spikes down the axon to either excite or inhibit other neurons. The pulses cause a chemical neurotransmitter substance to be released at the terminating synapses which, in turn, can excite or inhibit other neurons. The rate of pulse propagation ranges from

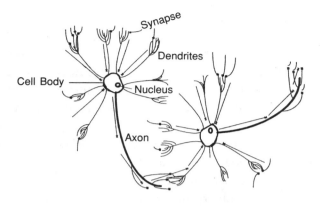

Figure 1.7   Signal Transmission Among Neurons

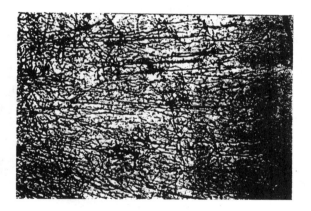

Figure 1.8   A Slice of Neurons in the Cerebral Cortex
(From *Mechanics of the Mind*, p. 84, by C. Blakemore, 1977, Cambridge, England: Cambridge
University Press. Copyright 1977 by Cambridge University Press. Reprinted by permission.)

about 5 to 125 ms^{-1}, and the time required for a stimulus to "traverse" a synapse
is about 1 ms. Following the firing, there is a refractory period lasting about
10 ms during which the neuron cannot fire again. The activity of a neuron is
measured by the firing frequency of the potential analog spikes which it generates.
They range from about 50 to a few hundred spikes per second.

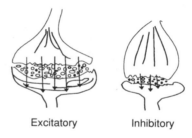

Figure 1.9   Two General Types of Synapses

Although we know little about the learning processes within the brain, it is believed that some form of metabolic growth takes place in neurons as a result of increased cell activity. This growth, it is believed, is responsible for memory and learning. It affects the potential charge a synapse produces and is thought to be roughly equivalent to the weights used in ANNs. The size (areas) of synapses, which may be related to learning, vary by a factor of more than ten. Synapses with larger surface areas are believed to be excitatory, while those with smaller surface areas are inhibitory. Donald Hebb was the first to suggest that such a process is related to learning in biological systems (Hebb, 1949). He reasoned that "When an axon of cell A is near enough to excite a cell B and repeatedly or persistently takes part in firing it, some growth process or metabolic change takes place in one or both of the cells such that A's efficiency, as one of the cells firing B, is increased." The process Hebb refers to could be realized in various ways including synaptic growth as he suggested. The reinforcement could be realized, for example, through either chemical or electrochemical (ionic) processes. In any event, the rule has been the inspiration for many different learning models in ANNs over the years.

We summarize some of the important characteristics of human neural networks in Table 1.1.

1.4   History of Neural Network Research

The more recent history of ANNs most likely begins with the work of McCulloch and Pitts (1943) with their important paper describing the properties of a simple two-state binary threshold type of neuron that has both excitatory and inhibitory inputs. Through proper choice of threshold levels, these units can be shown to perform any of the finite basic Boolean logic functions (inclusive OR, AND, NOT, and so on). Networks of these units were then thought to be representative models of the brain.

Table 1.1   Gray Matter Statistics

Number of Neurons	10^{11}–10^{13}
Number of Connections	10s to 10,000s
Number of Afferent (input)	10%
Number of Efferent (output)	90%
Storage Capacity	10^{13}–10^{15} bits
Utilization Factor	10%
Average Brain Weight	1.5 kg
Average Neuron Weight	1.2×10^{-9} g
Signal Propagation Rate	5–125 ms^{-1}
Synapse Traverse Time	1 ms
Refractory Period	10^{-2} s
Firing Frequency	50–100 spikes/s
Synapses (general types)	Excitatory and Inhibitory
Membrane Potential	Triggers Firing
Synapse Area (variance)	Factor of 10
Operation Mode	Asynchronous (some rhythm imposed)

Another early result was published by Hebb (1949), who was one of the first to suggest a plausible process for neural learning as pointed out in the preceding section. Even today, many of the learning models used by researchers are some form of "Hebbian" learning. We examine various forms of Hebbian learning in subsequent sections. Hebb had also reasoned that many distributed cell assemblies were used to represent knowledge, one of the first suggestions of the *connectionist* architecture.

Probably the first computer simulations of ANNs were reported by Rochester and colleagues (1956) at the Dartmouth summer conference now recognized as the official beginning date of Artificial Intelligence (AI). In conducting simulations of Hebb's model, this group discovered that some changes were essential before cell assemblies could be formed to exhibit certain properties predicted of the model. They generalized the model to include inhibition as well, so that active cells could inhibit others from becoming active. They also introduced normalization of weights to prevent unbounded growth in some synapse weights, and a form of "fatigue" so that firing cells were less likely to fire in the immediate future. Although their work was not too conclusive, it was important as a forerunner of many simulation studies which followed.

One of the most sensational research accomplishments of the period was Rosenblatt's work on perceptrons (Rosenblatt, 1958, 1961). Rosenblatt was a psychologist who believed the brain functioned as a learning associator that computed classifications in response to stimuli. He developed several variations of the networks he called perceptrons and studied different forms of learning. The basic perceptron network was a threshold logic unit made up of three layers: an input (photo) sensory layer that was randomly connected to an association layer that was, in turn, connected to an output response or classification layer. If the cumulative inputs from the sensory layer to an associative layer exceeded some threshold, that unit fired and passed on an impulse to the response layer. The response layer would then produce an output of +1 (class-1) if the cumulative inputs exceeded some threshold and, an output of 0 (non class-1) if not. These networks are described in some detail in Chapter 5. But, it is worth noting here that many of the ideas and concepts studied by Rosenblatt then are still objects of research today. In spite of Rosenblatt's work, the excitement of perceptron networks was later seriously dampened when Minsky and Papert (1969) put forth strong arguments that perceptrons were too limited in their computational power to be of any real practical use.

The AI possibilities introduced by perceptrons brought about a flurry of research during the 1960s. This excitement continued until it became apparent that few new results were forthcoming. Then, toward the end of the decade, Minsky and Papert published their critical treatise on Perceptrons (Minsky and Papert, 1969). This book was an elegant mathematical analysis of the computational capabilities and limitations of perceptrons. It essentially showed what logical functions simple perceptrons could and could not compute. The book proved to be the final blow in killing most neural network funding for further research. Consequently, most research efforts were reduced or terminated. Only a few stalwart researchers continued their work, including James Anderson, Teuvo Kohonen, Stephen Grossberg, Bernard Widrow, Chr. von der Malsburg, Amari and a few others.

Bernard Widrow was one of the early researchers to develop practical applications of ANNs. He developed a simple neural element similar to the Perceptron called ADALINE (ADAptive LInear NEuron), and networks of ADALINEs he called MADALINE (Multiple ADALINEs). These types of units are in use today as adaptive echo suppressors for long distance telephone circuits and as noise suppressors for high speed MODEMS. Widrow and his collegues are also responsible for developing a supervised learning procedure known as the least mean square (LMS) or Widrow-Hoff learning method (Widrow and Hoff, 1960) used to learn input-output pair associations. LMS was important in its own right, but also because it served as a forerunner of the popular backpropagation learning method used in multilayer feedforward networks. ADALINEs and MADALINEs and the corresponding learning algorithms used in these networks are described in Chapter 5.

During the early 1970s, a number of investigations were conducted on associative memories by researchers such as Kohonen (1972), Anderson (1972) and others. The models used in this work were linear, single layer associators (described in Chapter 4). They used a form of Hebbian or correlative learning where pattern x_i is associated with pattern y_i. A set of associations are stored as "traces" $(x_1y_1, x_2y_2, ..., x_ny_n)$ for subsequent recall. The work of these researchers provided much insight into the behavior of linear associators and related phenomena such as "crosstalk" which is related to the storage of many nonorthogonal or interfering patterns.

James Anderson of Brown University and his co-workers (Anderson, 1968; Anderson et al., 1977) also developed content-addressable associative memory models based on Hebbian learning. Patterns were stored as the superimposition (the sum) of matrices and retrieved when sufficiently similar inputs were presented to the network. Anderson was also responsible for an extension of the linear associator models called the Brain-State-in-a-Box (BSB). In this model, the output is truncated to prevent unlimited growth as the model iterates to find a solution. The truncation values define a hypercube "box" which the output is contained within.

Stephen Grossberg is founder and director of the Center for Adaptive Systems and a professor of mathematics, psychology, and biomedical engineering at Boston University. He has been an active researcher in psychological and biological information processing and in the use of artificial neural networks to model human perception and cognition since the early 1960s. Grossberg's early work focused on cooperative-competitive learning systems leading to the creation of constructs such as the instar, outstar, and avalanche used in learning and recall of spatial-temporal patterns. Later work by Grossberg and his colleagues focused on the mathematical dynamic properties of ANNs. This work led to an important theorem on the global convergence of dynamic networks (Cohen and Grossberg, 1983). Grossberg is perhaps best known for the highly successful adaptive resonance theory networks (ART networks) which he invented. He and his colleagues, particularly Gail Carpenter, studied, generalized and characterized the ART networks extensively. These networks are described in Chapter 15.

In 1982, John Hopfield presented a paper at the National Academy of Science describing how an analysis of stable points could be performed for symmetrical recurrent crossbar networks. The analysis was based on the use of a Lyapunov energy function for the nonlinear equations. He showed that the energy function dissipated (decreased) and converged to a minima and remained there. Thus, patterns are stored in memory as dynamically stable attractors. The networks, which are now named after Hopfield, can be used as associative memory networks or in finding solutions to constrain satisfaction problems such as the "N Queens" or the "Traveling Salesman Problem." Hopfield, who is a Nobel prize winner in physics, has been credited with reviving interest in neural network research in the early 1980s.

One of the most important developments of recent neural network research is the discovery of a learning algorithm to adjust the weights in multilayer feedforward networks (also referred to as multilayer perceptrons). The algorithm is known as backpropagation since the weights are adjusted from the output layer backwards layer-by-layer to reduce the output errors. The method was discovered at different times by Werbos (1974), Parker (1985), and Rumelhart, Hinton and Williams of the Parallel Distributed Processing (PDP) Group (Rumelhart et al., 1986). This development opened the way for more general ANN computing by overcoming the limitations suffered by single-layer perceptrons. Such networks are able to learn to solve nonlinear problems such as the logic XOR function.

The Japanese researcher Kunihiko Fukushima is the founder of the cognitron and neocognitron networks (Fukushima, 1969; Fukushima and Myaki, 1982; Fukushima, 1988). The more recent network, the neocognitron, is a hierarchical feedforward network that learns through either supervised or unsupervised methods. The networks are modeled after biological visual neural systems. Fukushima and his colleagues have published results showing the neocognitron to be capable of handwritten character recognition, independent of scale, position and some deformation in the characters. One version of the system using a feedback path, is capable of identifying multiple characters by sequentially segmentating the characters while identifying them. One of the unique aspects of neocognitrons is the connectivity of the network layers. Layers are connected in such a way that low-level features are recognized and successively combined into a coherent whole for object identification.

The preceding events are summarized in Figure 1.10.

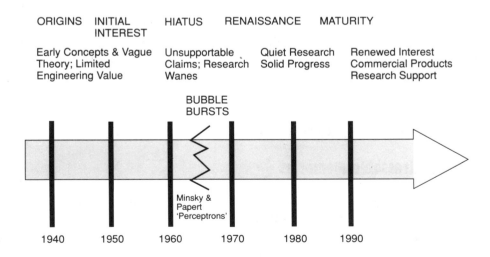

Figure 1.10   Significant Events in Neural Network Developments

1.5 Artificial Neural Network Applications

In this section, we describe some of the more common applications of neural networks to give the reader a general feeling for the variety and breadth of problems for which ANNs have been used. Our descriptions here are intentionally general, and hence generic. More specific application descriptions are given for each of the more important ANN architectures as presented in later chapters.

Constraint Satisfaction

Solutions to many types of problems require that the variables defining the system be restricted or constrained to take on only certain values. For example, acceptable solutions to job shop scheduling tasks typically require that subtasks be completed in a given order (cutting, grinding, polishing, painting, and so on) and only a single job can be assigned to a machine at one time. The n queens problem is another problem that requires satisfaction of several constraints. Two or more queens can never be placed on the chess board in the same row, in the same column, or in the same diagonal path of squares. And, all n of the queens must be placed on the $n \times n$ chess board to realize an acceptable solution. In the manufacture of printed circuit boards, it is often necessary to drill large numbers of accurately positioned holes in the boards. The total time spent in drilling is a function of the order in which the holes are drilled since this determines the total distance traveled (time spent) in positioning the board. This problem is similar to the Traveling Salesman Problem (TSP) which is both an optimization and constraint satisfaction problem. The constraints are that each hole position must be "visited" once and once only. Whereas the optimization part relates to the total time spent (distance traveled) in drilling each board. Generally, the time for each board should be a minimum to produce a least cost solution. Other manufacturing problems have similar constraints and optimization goals.

Solutions to all of the above named problems have been found using some type of ANN architecture. The details of each of the particular problems and corresponding solutions are given in subsequent chapters.

Content Addressable Memories

Some types of ANN architectures can learn to act as memories and store patterns that are retrieved when presented with an "associated" pattern. The retrieval pattern can be the same as the stored pattern, perhaps with some distortion (added noise or missing bits) or a different pattern altogether (a different index pattern). When the retrieval and stored patterns are the same, the process is called autoassociative retrieval. When the two patterns are different, the form of retrieval is known as heteroassociative. Such networks are also known as content addressable memories since they can be used to retrieve patterns using indices that are derived from the "content" of the stored patterns. These types of memories are presented in Chapter 5.

Control

ANNs have been used effectively in learning to control outdoor mobile robots, including driverless driving (autonomous land vehicles) tasks. They have been trained to learn the difficult task of backing up a trailer truck to a loading dock with minimal effort, even trucks with double trailers attached. They have also been used to efficiently control the positioning of huge electrodes in electric arc furnaces used by steel-making companies, saving the companies millions of dollars through reduced electricity consumption and extended life of costly equipment. They have been used to control and optimize chemical plant processes saving companies huge sums through better process control and material usage. Dozens of consumer products, especially those manufactured by Japanese companies, now use neural network technology for more effective and efficient control. The range of applications in the area of control seems unlimited.

Data Compression

Some network types are used to learn to compute a mapping that is a reduction of the input pattern space dimension and hence, to perform a sort of data compression. Patterns are transformed from n-dimensional space to m-dimensional space where $m < n$ by the assignment of "codes" to groups of similar patterns. The m-dimensional code words serve as prototypical patterns for whole clusters or groupings of similar patterns in n-dimensional space. Consequently, much shorter length patterns can be dealt with, thereby reducing the amount of transmission bandwidth required in data transmission applications and memory storage requirements when storing groups of patterns. Data compression is particularly important in applications where large amounts of data are being collected and processed as in the case of satellite image data processing.

Diagnostics

Diagnosis is a common ANN application for many fields: medicine, engineering, and manufacturing to name a few. This problem is essentially one of classification. It requires the correct association between input patterns that represent some form of symptom or abnormal behavior with the corresponding disease or equipment fault or other type of malfunction. Diagnosing complex systems, including ill people, is a popular expert system application. It is also a viable ANN application, and many diverse applications of diagnosis using some form of ANN architecture have been published in the literature. Specific applications of diagnosis are described in subsequent chapters.

Forecasting

Prediction is a common task in many fields. A consumer products company will want to know the growth in sales for a new product they plan to introduce. Meteorologists need to predict the weather. Banks want to predict the creditworthiness of companies as a basis for granting loans. Airport management groups want to know the growth in customer arrivals at busy airports, and power companies want to know customer demand for electric power in the future, and so on. ANNs have been shown to be successful as predictive tools in a variety of ways: predicting that some event will or will not occur, predicting the time at which an event will occur, or predicting the level of some event outcome. To predict with an acceptable level of accuracy, an ANN must be trained with a sizable set of examples of past pattern/future outcome pairs. The ANN must then be able to generalize and extrapolate from new patterns to predict associative outcomes. Many financial institutions are now using ANNs in a big way for foreign exchange trading, for stock selection and for portfolio management. Some organizations have developed sophisticated systems that require the training of hundreds or even thousands of ANNs on a weekly basis to predict stock market index movements as well as individual stock price behaviors.

General Mapping

One of the most salient characteristics of some ANNs is their ability to learn arbitrary functions from a set of training examples. This capability covers a diverse range of applications. In fact, one could argue that all ANN applications fall under the general heading of functional mappings, where an ANN learns to transform an n-dimensional input vector to an m-dimensional output vector according to some (not necessarily known) criteria. A considerable body of research results relating to ANN mapping capabilities has been published over the past few years. These results are described in subsequent chapters.

Multisensor Data Fusion

Sensor data fusion is the process of combining data from multiple sources in order to derive more information through combining than is possible through individual sources. The fusion process includes detection, association, correlation, estimation, and combination of data to achieve identity estimation and timely assessment of situations. During the 1980s advances in sensor technology have led to rapid expansion of multisensor fusion applications, including military (situation and threat assessment), process control, monitoring, robotics, diagnostics and others.

The most powerful example of large scale multisensor fusion is found in human and other biological systems. Humans apply fusion of the body's sensory data (touch, sight, sound, scent) to gain meaningful perception of the environment. Hundreds of thousands of sensors are collecting data in real-time for fusion and processing through successively higher levels of abstraction. The nervous system performs the fusion of sensory data through its massively interconnected network of neurons.

Artificial neural networks offer great promise in multisensor data fusion applications for the same reasons biological systems are so successful at these tasks. ANN architectures and processing capabilities make them a natural choice for many fusion applications. Indeed, in a sense, every ANN is performing a kind of data fusion to achieve some desired mapping of input to output signals.

An example of an ANN used in multisensor fusion is illustrated in Figure 1.11.

In subsequent chapters, we describe a number of multisensor data fusion applications using different ANN architectures.

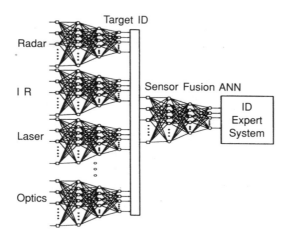

Figure 1.11 Multisensor Data Fusion with Neural Networks

Optimization

ANNs have been used for a number of problems that require finding an optimal or near optimal solution. Such problems typically require the satisfaction of some constraints and hence often overlap with constraint satisfaction applications described above. Some examples of optimization applications include the pricing and sale of passenger seats by airlines, the scheduling of manufacturing operations (sequencing of tasks to machines to meet some criteria), finding the shortest of all possible tours (distances of paths) through a large number of cities or other geographic points that must be traversed sequentially with a single "visit" per each operation, minimization of some cost function under a set of constraints, and so on. The range of optimization applications is limited only by the ingenuity of the implementor in defining the objective functions and building an accurate ANN model of the system. One of the earliest examples of ANNs in solving optimization problems was application of dynamic recurrent networks to the traveling salesman problem (Tank and Hopfield, 1987). This application is described in more detail in Chapter 4.

Pattern Recognition

In general, ANNs are good at learning perceptive type of tasks such as the recognition of complex patterns: visual images of objects, printed or handwritten characters, speech recognition, and other types of pattern recognition tasks. Increasingly, researchers and practitioners are publishing accounts of successful applications of ANNs in the areas of image processing, speech recognition, handwritten character recognition, automatic target recognition, robotics, process control and so on. This is in sharp contrast with conventional symbolic processing methods where the combinatorial explosion in computation time has limited further progress. Comparative studies made by researchers suggest that ANNs compare favorably with conventional statistical pattern recognition methods such as the popular Bayesian classifiers.

Risk Assessment

Risk assessment is a form of pattern recognition and generalization. The characteristics or profiles of known high-risk or low-risk situations (credit worthiness of individuals or companies, financial investment instruments such as stocks or bonds, company business ventures) represent patterns that ANNs can learn to differentiate and group. The learned pattern groupings or clusterings can then serve as a basis for prediction of new, unknown situations based on their similarity to the learned groupings. An extensive and diverse number of business applications have been and are still being developed for such applications. Banks, stock brokerage firms, consumer product companies, economists, econometricians, currency exchange dealers, meteorologists, engineers, utility companies, and many other organizations have investigated and implemented some form of ANN for such purposes, many reporting high success rates.

Summary

In this introductory chapter, we have introduced simple artificial neural networks consisting of a few interconnected neurons. For these networks, all neurons were contained within a single layer. We have described the basic ANN computation process and the types of linear separable mapping tasks that such networks can perform. We also suggested how ANNs can learn through weight adjustments until the decision space is separated into different class groupings. We went on to describe biological neural network characteristics and how our knowledge of these networks have inspired development of their artificial counterparts. A brief history of ANNs was given to provide background on the progression of ANNs as practical tools for various applications. Many of the principal researchers and their most noted work accomplishments were given for the period from the mid-1940s to the mid-1980s when ANN research resumed with full vigor. We concluded the chapter with descriptions of some 11 different generic ANN applications to illustrate the wide applicability they have found in research, business, and industry.

2
Characteristics of Artificial Networks

Having described a simple three-input network in the previous chapter, we look next at the basic building blocks of ANNs. We also consider some of their important characteristics and general classifications or taxonomies. We also discuss some general properties that characterize ANNs and present an overview of the different learning methods employed in training different ANN architectures. Several of the network types named in the taxonomies will have meaning only after being introduced in subsequent chapters. Therefore, the reader may wish to refer to this chapter again after reviewing several network types.

2.1 Introduction

In Chapter 1, we introduced one of the simplest ANN architectures, a single layer feedforward network. It is *single layer* because the input patterns are processed through a single layer of neurons only. An input pattern is propagated through neural synaptic weight connections to the neuron where a response is generated as the output activation. It is *feedforward* because signals propagate only in a forward direction, from the input nodes to the output node. No signals are allowed to propagate laterally or backwards among the neurons. Although we did not specify any order in which computations are performed and in which signals propagate, it should be noted that such networks can operate in either a synchronous (clocked) or asynchronous mode. In synchronous mode operation, the neuron's states are updated in accordance with a specific order and at specific times (e.g. all simultaneously). In asynchronous mode, the updating may be in any particular order and at nonspecific times. The order of update may be at random and/or the time between updates may be governed by a probability distribution. Thus, we see that to completely specify an ANN's behavior, one should give the number of neurons, how they are interconnected, the manner in which signals are combined at the neuron's input, the activation functions or mapping each neuron performs on its input, the order in which computations are performed and the way in which signals propagate from input to output. Finally, one should specify the dynamic equations governing the system's behavior and the form of learning method used to train the network.

In the following sections, we consider these issues in detail to gain a better appreciation of the types of networks that have been proposed and studied. We begin by describing the building blocks used to create different networks. Next, we consider some of the important properties peculiar to ANNs such as self adaptation, generalization, robust performance, and parallel processing. We also consider different ANN classifications or taxonomies and general learning paradigms. This will lay the groundwork needed to better understand different architectures and specific ANNs studied in subsequent chapters.

2.2 Neural Network Structures

To characterize a given ANN, it is necessary to specify the number of neurons, how they are interconnected and the processing that takes place throughout the network. While many variations are possible in the way signals can be combined and processed in a network, we restrict our discussion below to the more popular methods in use today. Even then, we will see that there are some 20 to 30 popular ANN types being studied and used for different applications today.

Neural Computing Elements or Cells

Every ANN is composed of a set of n simple neural computing elements (neurons, units, processing elements or PEs, cells) $C = \{c_i\}$ $i = 1, 2, ..., n$. Functionally, there are three types of cells: input, output and interior or hidden cells. Input cells are connected to some form of external stimuli which produce input signals either synchronously or asynchronously in time. The input signals, which may be real or discrete valued, are denoted by the n-dimensional vector $\mathbf{x}$. The inputs typically correspond to a set of object feature values, an environmental stimulus of some type or values defining some general concept. Output cells produce an output signal vector $\mathbf{y}$ of m dimensions. The output cells, which may also be real or discrete valued, are connected to effectors, displays or other output devices. Interior cells are connected to either input, output or other interior cells. When they receive inputs, these cells compute values that are then passed on to other cells for further processing. In general, these cells compute values that relate to arbitrary concepts or mappings between concepts. To characterize cells, it is necessary to specify the way in which input signals are combined at the cell's input, how the cell transforms its net input and any timing relationships among the inputs and outputs if relevant to the network's operation. For example, inputs are commonly combined linearly as described in Chapter 1 ($net = \mathbf{x}^T\mathbf{w} = \Sigma_i x_i w_i$) or sometimes as weighted cross products of input signals ($net = \Sigma w_{ij} \Pi x_{i1} x_{i2}...x_{ik}$). The latter form of combination is performed in units called sigma-pi units.

Rather than combining weighted sums or sums of cross products, some cell inputs are a measure of the distance d between the input vector $\mathbf{x}$ and the cell's weights $\mathbf{w}$, ($d[\mathbf{x}, \mathbf{w}]$). In such cases, the cell's weights might correspond to prototypical patterns or cluster centers of input pattern vectors. The distance metric d used for such networks can also vary (Hamming distance, Euclidean distance, vector norm).

Once the net input to a cell has been defined, one should specify the functional transformation the cell performs on the input, the cell's activation function. This can take one of several forms such as the monotonic nondecreasing functions depicted in Chapter 1 or other (linear clamped, step, S shaped or sigmoid) or some form of exponential function. Activation values can be positive, negative, real valued, binary, bipolar, or other form. Finally, it may be necessary to specify any timing constraints or order imposed on the computations within and among different cells.

Connectivity Pattern

The interconnections of all the processing elements and directions of signal flows within the network provide essential information on the basic system architecture. The input links connected to each cell c_i usually have an associated weight w_{ij} (noted above) which is a measure of the influence that an output cell c_j or input stimulus has on the cell. Positive weights have an excitatory influence whereas negative weight values have an inhibitory influence. Zero weight values correspond to no connection. Weights on the connections between two layers or groups of cells are specified by weight matrices $\mathbf{W}$. Such matrices completely determine the connectivity of networks and the direction of signal propagation. For example, the matrix element w_{ij} by convention, is used to denote the weight connecting the output of cell j to the input of cell i. (Some authors use w_{ij} to denote the opposite, that is, connection between cell i output and cell j input.) With this notation, signals can, in general, propagate forward, laterally, self-feedback or backwards. For such general network architectures, it is especially important to specify the timing or order in which signals propagate among the cells.

The values of weights on all interconnecting links correspond to neural synapse parameters. They establish the network's *stored,* distributed knowledge. In general, weights are real-valued numbers that can be modified through a learning process or other means.

System State

Once the cell's characteristics, the input combining rules, the interconnection patterns among cells, the activation functions and order of signal propagation have been specified, the system state can be determined at any time. The state of the system at some time t is the activation values (output values) over the set of all cells at time t. It is specified by an n-dimensional activation function vector. This vector captures what the network is representing at different times t.

Learning Process

Adaptive learning is an essential property of systems which must function in dynamic environments or which must compensate for variations in input stimuli (such as the speech or handwriting patterns generated by different people). Iterative learning procedures have been developed for a variety of ANN architectures. These procedures can require a considerable amount of computation resources for some classes of nets. Thus, it is important that efficient learning algorithms be developed, and particularly for those networks with multiple layers and massively large numbers of interconnections. This explains why much interest and research effort has focused on the learning efficiency problem over the past few years: Jacobs (1988), Giles and Maxwell (1987), Werbos (1988), Hinton (1989), Dahl (1987), Hinton and Sejnowski (1983). In Section 2.3, we present a brief survey of learning methods used in a number of the more important ANNs.

   Learning in ANNs is accomplished in one of the following ways: by the establishment of connections between nodes, adjustment of the weight values on the links connecting nodes (corresponding to synapse excitations or inhibitions in biological nets), adjustment of threshold values of node activation functions or combinations of the three operations. If a bias input is included with each of the nodes in a network and the number of initial nodes and interconnections is sufficient for the application, it is possible to learn through weight adjustments alone, since the bias weight can serve as the threshold value and the use of real-valued weights (including zero), can serve to model excitatory, inhibitory, and "no connection" conditions between nodes. The general learning problem then is to find a weight matrice **W** that satisfies the vector equations

$$\mathbf{y}^p = \mathbf{F}(\mathbf{x}^p, \mathbf{W})$$

for all input patterns $\mathbf{x}^p$, $p = 1, 2, ..., P$, where the vector function $\mathbf{F}$ is, in general, a nonlinear function.

Learning by weight adjustment can take one of several forms. The weights can be modified as a function of the input signal strengths, as a function of both the input and output signal strengths, as a function of the weights themselves, as a function of the difference between some target and computed pattern (the error), or combinations of these parameters. Weight adjustment can also be performed on the basis of probabilistic methods.

2.3   Characteristics of ANNs

Before looking at the capabilities of specific ANNs, it is useful to consider their general characteristics and limitations. Thus, we are interested in their general mapping capabilities, what they can or cannot learn and other properties such as robustness, processing speed and so on. We begin with a characterization of their mapping abilities.

Mapping Capabilities

A neural network can be regarded as a black box that transforms input vectors $\mathbf{x}$ from an n-dimensional space to an output vector $\mathbf{y}$ in m-dimensional space $\mathbf{F} : \mathbf{x} \rightarrow \mathbf{y}$. The types of mappings $\mathbf{F}$ a network can approximate depends on the particular ANN architecture. In general, the mapping $\mathbf{F}$ will be either autoassociative (mapping to an original pattern from a noisy or partially given input pattern) or heteroassociative (mapping from an input pattern to a different output pattern). We will see in subsequent chapters, however, that certain multilayer feedforward networks can approximate almost any reasonably well behaved functions $\mathbf{F}$ to any desired degree of accuracy. However, to implement such a network it may be necessary to use an unwieldy number of neurons if very high accuracy is desired.

Learning and Generalization

Generalization is the process of describing the whole from some of the parts, reasoning from the specific to the general case, or defining a class of objects from a knowledge of one or more instances. Generalization is an essential part of learning as it permits us to remember facts that apply to whole classes of objects rather than remembering many specific facts that apply only to individual members of the class. It serves as an efficient mode of memorization and storage. Without the ability to generalize, we would be compelled to remember and recall an unlimited number of specific events, facts, relationships and other details related to our experiences—an impossible task. In short, generalization is an essential trait of intelligent behavior.

ANNs generalize when they compute or recall full patterns from partial or noisy input patterns, when they recognize or classify objects not previously trained on, or when they predict new outcomes from past behaviors. The ability to classify objects not previously trained on is a form of interpolation between trained patterns. The ability to predict from past behaviors is a form of extrapolation. Both of these types of mappings are a form of generalization.

Most learning paradigms for ANNs, whether assumed to be supervised by a teacher or carried out without a teacher, are either a form of rote or inductive learning. Systems that learn by rote memorization are not very interesting. They are given precomputed weight values to perform their tasks. On the other hand, inductive learning is more interesting, and more challenging. It is the process of forming generalized concepts or rules from a number of specific instances or examples. In conventional artificial intelligence (AI) computation systems (also called symbolic computation systems), generalization is accomplished through the formation of classes of objects, the target classes. This amounts to partitioning a universe of objects into two groups, those objects belonging to the target class and those belonging to the complement class. In these conventional symbolic AI systems, such classes are defined with predicates which usually describe the training examples, and generalization is implemented in one of several ways: by substituting variables for constants in the predicates, dropping conjunctive terms in the descriptors, adding disjunctive terms in the descriptors, climbing a generalization tree or other like method (Patterson, 1990). For example, from the observations

bird(sparrow) & fly(sparrow)
bird(robin) & fly(robin)
bird(hawk) & fly(hawk)
bird(canary) & fly(canary)

one can *induce* the generalized implication "all birds fly" (for all x, if x is a bird, then x can fly) written as

$$(\forall x) \ bird(x) \rightarrow fly(x)$$

Note that generalization was implemented in this case by substituting the variable x for the constants "sparrow, robin," and so on to obtain the induced rule "all birds fly." Of course, inductive learning is not sound in a logical sense. It can be flawed.

For example, from bird(ostrich) and the above implication we conclude fly(ostrich). Even though induction is not a logically valid form of reasoning, it is useful in both learning and reasoning tasks as we will see.

In ANNs, generalization is also accomplished through the formation of classes. In this case, the classes are defined by the mapping function **F** as boundaries in weight space. Such boundaries delineate the object feature space values which satisfy the target and complement classes. The boundaries are formed through synaptic weight adjustments during the learning process. We say that accurate learning (generalization) occurs when the final class boundaries contain only the desired target examples and exclude all non-target examples. By target examples, we mean all patterns correctly belonging to the given concept classes, including those used in the training set and those not used. This is illustrated in Figure 2.1.

More formally, we can define generalization in the following way. Given input vectors $\mathbf{x}^p$, $p = 1, 2, ..., P$, with probability distribution $\rho(\mathbf{x})$, let $\mathbf{y}^p = f'(\mathbf{x}^p)$ be the computed network outputs corresponding to a given set of network weights **W**. We want f' to approximate the true desired mapping f as closely as possible for all values of $\mathbf{x}$ (not just at the training set points $\{(\mathbf{x}^p, \mathbf{t}^p) \mid p = 1, 2, ..., P\}$ where $\mathbf{t}^p$ is the desired or target output corresponding to the input $\mathbf{x}^p$), in the training set.

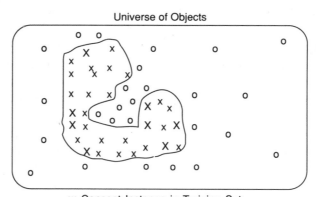

Universe of Objects

x: Concept Instance in Training Set
X: Concept Instance Not in Training Set
o: Non-concept Instance

Figure 2.1   Learning a Generalized Concept

In later chapters, it is shown that it is possible to overtrain some networks such that poor generalization results. The network becomes "specialized" and learns the training set too well. As a consequence, it is unable to recognize target-class patterns that were not included in the training set. Excessive or overtraining can occur when a limited training set has been used repeatedly too many times in the training process or even when a very large training set is used extensively. In attempting to more accurately learn the individual pattern mappings, the class boundaries become warped to more closely fit the individual training patterns. As a consequence, the boundaries exclude some patterns in the class that were not in the training set. This same phenomenon occurs in polynomial function fitting when the number of data points and degree of polynomial are not chosen well. A polynomial of degree n can be made to fit n data points exactly, but it may be at the expense of fitting a smooth, low-curvature graph that follows the trend of most of the points rather than the points themselves. Overtraining can also occur when excessive neurons are used in a network for some applications. The neurons "memorize" the training set patterns.

Learnability relates to the ability of a learning algorithm to find a set of weights that performs the desired mapping with a tolerable error rate. Mapping accuracy and learnability are closely related but they are not the same. For example, it may be possible to show that a given class of networks can perform accurate mappings but only if there is some learning algorithm A that is assured of finding a set of weights **w** that help to define the mapping. Learnability is currently a "hot topic" area of research. It is addressed in more detail in Chapter 7.

Robust Performance

ANNs typically are robust as computing systems. They continue to perform well when part of the network is disabled or when presented with noisy data. This is possible because the "knowledge" stored in an ANN is distributed over many neurons and interconnections, not just a single or a few units. Consequently, concepts or mappings stored in an ANN have some degree of redundancy built in through this distribution of knowledge. This aspect of ANNs is sometimes called fault-tolerance. It is in sharp contrast to conventional computers. The loss of a single transistor or other component in a serial (von Neumann) computer can result in complete system failure. Such systems are most intolerant of faults. One would expect the human brain to exhibit similar characteristics to ANNs. Indeed this is the case. A portion of the brain can be damaged or removed without seriously affecting the performance of an individual. And dealing effectively with noisy data is the norm for humans rather than the exception.

Parallel Processing

The high speed with which the brain and ANNs are able to process information is astounding. Consider the amount of computation needed to process a single visual image. If one restricts the image resolution to $1,000 \times 1,000$ receptors, a small number compared to the retina, over one million numbers (three million for color images) must be examined and several million computations performed in order that objects in the image are identified. Even at the nanosecond speeds of modern computers, this task can require several seconds in a conventional computer. And then the "recognition" may be marginal. In contrast, biological visual systems compute such tasks in milliseconds. This is possible even though signals propagate in millisecond, rather than nanosecond time frames, in biological systems. The reason for this disparity in performance is, of course, due to the massively parallel computations being performed in the brain. At any one time, tens of thousands of computations are being performed simultaneously within a biological NN.

Although ANNs share many salient features with biological networks, they do lack some characteristics, including the ability to forget (Zak, 1991).

2.4   Overview of ANN Learning Methods

Learning methods for ANNs can be classified as one of three basic types: supervised, reinforcement, or unsupervised. In supervised learning a teacher is assumed to be present during the learning process and each example pattern used to train the network includes an input pattern together with a target or desired output pattern, the correct answer. During the learning process, a comparison can be made between the computed output by the network and the correct output to determine the error. The error can then be used to change network parameters which result in an improvement in performance. The weight matrices connecting the layers are usually initialized by setting all weights to zero or to small random real-valued numbers. The input training pattern vectors $\mathbf{x}^p$, $p = 1, 2, \ldots$ are then presented to the network one at a time and a corresponding output pattern $\mathbf{y}^p$ is computed. This computed output pattern is compared to the desired or target output pattern $\mathbf{t}^p$ and an error $\mathbf{e}^p = \mathbf{y}^p - \mathbf{t}^p$ is determined. The resultant error is then used through some form of computation and feedback to adjust the individual weights to reduce the error for each training pair. After iteratively adjusting weights for all training patterns, the weight values may converge to a set of values needed to perform the required pattern recalls. Learning has been achieved when the errors for all training patterns ($p = 1, 2, \ldots, P$) have been reduced to some acceptable level for all new patterns not in the training set.

In reinforcement learning, a teacher is also assumed to be present, but the right answer is not presented to the network. Instead, the network is only presented with an indication of whether the output answer it computes is right or wrong. The network must then use this information to improve its performance. Typically, a reward is given by reinforcing weights on units which give the right answer and a penalty is imposed by reducing the weight values on those units giving the wrong answer.

In unsupervised learning, the network has no feedback on the desired or correct output. There is no teacher to present target patterns. Therefore, the system must learn by discovering and adapting to structured features in the input patterns, that is, by adapting to statistical regularities or clusterings of patterns from the input training samples. Such learning may be accomplished by strengthening selected node sensitivities (weights) to match central, prototypical training patterns that are representative of a group of similar patterns or clusters. Examples of these learning algorithms are found in the Hamming net (Lippmann, 1987), the Linsker model (Linsker, 1988), the Kohonen model (Kohonen, 1982), in the cognitron and neocognitron models of Fukushima (Fukushima, 1982) and the adaptive resonance theory (ART) models of Grossberg (Grossberg, 1988). Learning in these nets is accomplished by strengthening the weights on links to neural units which respond the most to the input training signals and ignoring or reducing weights on links to units with weaker responses. The unit responding the most may inhibit other units' outputs residing in the same layer (e.g. in Hamming, neocognitron and Kohonen nets) or inhibitions may be fed back from successive layers (e.g. in the ART nets). An important class of unsupervised learning methods are known as competitive learning (described below).

Although reinforcement learning has been studied by ANN researchers to some extent, it is not one of the more popular forms of learning. Consequently, we restrict our attention to supervised and unsupervised learning only in what follows.

Hebbian or Correlative Learning

Hebbian learning is a form of correlative weight adjustment (related to the pre- and post-synaptic strengths of a neuron). The basic theory was proposed by Donald Hebb (1949) who reasoned that "When an axon of cell A is near enough to excite a cell B and repeatedly or persistently takes part in firing it, some growth process or metabolic change takes place in one or both cells such that A's efficiency, as one of the cells firing B, is increased." Examples of Hebbian learning are those found in single layer associative memory nets (see Chapter 5) or nets that learn through unsupervised methods (see Chapter 14). Learning in this case is accomplished in a straightforward manner. The input patterns $\mathbf{x}^p$ and corresponding desired output patterns $\mathbf{t}^p$ are used to compute the weight matrix $\mathbf{W}$ as the sum of p superimposed pattern matrices $\mathbf{W}^p$ ($p = 1, 2, ..., P$), where each $\mathbf{W}^p$ is computed as the outer product or correlation matrix, $\mathbf{W}^p = \mathbf{x}^p(\mathbf{y}^p)^T$ (the superscripted T denotes vector transpose).

For autoassociative nets, such as the Hopfield net (Hopfield, 1982) and Brain-State-in-a-Box (BSB) (Anderson, 1983), $\mathbf{y}^p = \mathbf{x}^p$. For heteroassociative nets, such as the Bi-directional Associative Memory (BAM) (Kosko, 1985) and Hamming nets (Lippman, 1987), $\mathbf{x}^p$ and $\mathbf{y}^p$ in general are different. Numerous variants of the Hebbian rule have been proposed, including weight adjustment based on minimization of an energy or entropy function (Linsker, 1988). We study Hebbian forms of learning for various ANN architectures, and particularly in Chapter 14 where we look at several modified forms in some detail.

Competitive Learning

In competitive learning, the weights are adjusted to favor neurons that initially respond most strongly to given input stimuli. Weight adjustment is typically a modified form of Hebbian adjustment. Neurons in a given layer compete to represent an input pattern, but only a single unit wins ("winner-takes-all"). At the start of the learning process, the units in a layer will have small, but unequal weights. When an input pattern is presented to the network, one of the elements in the layer will respond more to the pattern than the other elements. This unit will have its weights reinforced or changed to more closely match the input pattern, and the weights of all other units in the layer remain unchanged. In some cases, the weights of neighboring units are also strengthened. Weights on inactive units may be reduced. In other words, weight is shifted from inactive to active input links of the winning element while the total sum of the weights linked to the element remains constant.

There are many variations on the competitive learning paradigm. Some examples are given in Chapters 14 and 15.

Stochastic Learning

Stochastic learning is accomplished by adjusting weights in a probabilistic manner. Examples of stochastic learning are found in simulated annealing as applied in Boltzmann and Cauchy machines where the states of all units are determined by a probability distribution. During the learning phase, the system is operated in two modes: clamped mode where input/output nodes are "clamped" to the values of associative pairs of binary patterns and in the unclamped (no inputs) mode. The network is allowed to operate in both modes until "thermal" equilibrium is reached at which time real-valued weights w_{ij} on the connections between nodes i and j are then adjusted on the basis of the difference between two state probabilities $p_{ij}(C)$ and $p_{ij}(U)$. Here, $p_{ij}(C)$ is the probability that the ith and jth elements are both on in the clamped mode while $p_{ij}(U)$ is the probability both units are on in the unclamped mode. Because of network symmetry it is possible to define an energy function for the system as

$$E = -\frac{1}{2}\sum_{i=1}^{n}\sum_{j=1}^{n}w_{ij}s_i s_j$$

where s_i is the binary state $(0, 1)$ or bipolar state $(-1, 1)$ of the ith unit. Equilibrium is reached when the energy function reaches a minimum.

Operation of Boltzmann machine networks with simulated annealing are described in Chapter 10.

Gradient Descent Learning

Several learning paradigms are based on the reduction of an error or cost function E, through the use of gradient descent methods. Such methods require that the activation functions f be differentiable as the weight updates are based on the gradient of the error which is defined in terms of the weights and activation functions. The form of the update rule is given as a solution to an equation such as

$$\Delta w_{ij} = \eta\frac{\partial E}{\partial w_{ij}}$$

where η is a learning rate parameter and w_{ij} is the weight on the connection between unit i and j. Examples of this type of learning include the Widrow-Hoff Delta Rule and the popular Backpropagation learning algorithm.

The Delta Rule learning procedure is in a sense optimal for single layer networks. It will find a weight matrix that produces perfect recall when the input patterns are linearly independent, or in general, for patterns which exhibit the highest correlations in a least squares sense. The procedure fails to produce a solution in multilayer networks, however. It does not specify how to adjust the weights for interior layer units during learning. In multilayer networks this is known as the "credit assignment" problem. There is no clear way in which to assign credit or blame to the internal layer unit weights for the reduction of output unit errors.

The credit assignment problem was solved using the error Backpropagation (BP) method. The BP method can be applied to any multilayer network that uses differentiable activation functions. It amounts to repeatedly adjusting the interior layer weights using the computed errors from the output-layer and propagating the error adjustments backwards layer-by-layer to the first interior layer. Convergence is not assured for BP as it is for the Delta Rule, however. The process may find a local minimum where it gets stuck.

The Delta Rule is derived in Chapter 4 and the Backpropagation algorithm is derived in Chapter 6. Both of these learning methods are studied in detail because of the great success with which they have been applied.

2.5   Neural Network Taxonomies

In this section, we present three different ANN taxonomies or classifications. Each gives a different perspective of ANNs in terms of the learning paradigm, the network architecture, and general area of application. We begin with classification by learning strategy which includes the broad classes of supervised, unsupervised, and reinforced. For each of these categories, an ANN will fall into one of four subcategories (or some combination of them) described above: (1) Hebbian or correlative, (2) gradient descent, (3) competitive, and (4) stochastic.

More than 22 ANN types are described in the following chapters. Although this is not an exhaustive treatment of types, it does cover what are considered to be the most important architectures at the time of writing this manuscript. The ANNs covered in the text include the following (not necessarily in the order given below):

ADALINE (Adaptive Linear Neural Element)
ART (Adaptive Resonant Theory)
AM (Associative Memories)
BAM (Bidirectional Associative Memory)
Boltzmann Machine
BSB (Brain-State-in-a-Box)
CCN (Cascade Correlation)
Cauchy Machine
CPN (Counter Propagation)
GRNN (Generalized Regression Neural Network)
Hamming
Hopfield
LVQ (Learning Vector Quantization)
MADALINE
MLFF with BP (Multilayer Feedforward Backpropagation)
Neocognitron
NLN (Neurologic Networks)
Perceptron
PNN (Probabilistic Neural Network)
RBF (Radial Basis Function)
RNN (Recurrent Neural Networks)

RCE (Reduced Coulomb Energy)
SOFM (Self-Organizing Feature Map)

In Figure 2.2, the types are illustrated by broad learning category. In Figure 2.3 typical networks are given for each of the two main categories by the general learning algorithm used. Note that some of the ANNs belong to more than one category (such as Hopfield). Although some ANN architectures have been studied for reinforcement learning, we do not cover these learning methods and architectures.

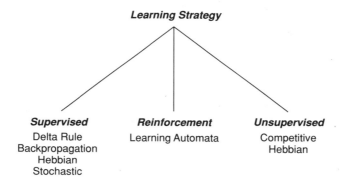

Figure 2.2   Typical Learning Methods for Basic Learning Strategies

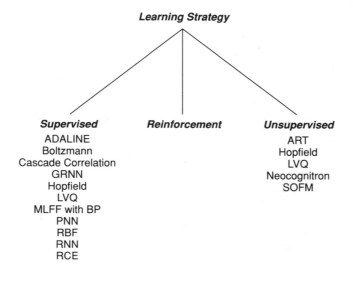

Figure 2.3   Categories of Network Types by Broad Learning Method

We also include a network type classification based on learning method. This is illustrated in Figure 2.4 where we have defined four types of learning methods: (1) error correction, which includes algorithms such as Perceptron learning, the Delta Rule and Backpropagation, (2) Hebbian learning including variants of Hebbian learning, (3) competitive learning and (4) stochastic learning.

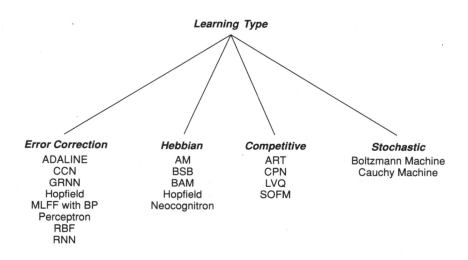

Figure 2.4   Categories of Network Types by Learning Method

The next classification of networks is by type of application, where we have grouped the networks into six areas of applications: associative memories, classification, pattern recognition, prediction optimization and general mapping. The taxonomy by application is illustrated in Figure 2.5.

Our final taxonomy of network types is based on network architecture. For this, we have defined three classes only: (1) single-layer feedforward networks, networks with a single layer of computational neurons that process input signals in a feedforward direction, (2) multilayer feedforward networks, networks with two or more layers of connections with weights that process the inputs in a forward direction, and (3) recurrent neural networks, networks that have feedback connections which propagate the outputs of some neurons back to the inputs of other neurons (including self-feedback connections) to perform repeated computations on the signals.

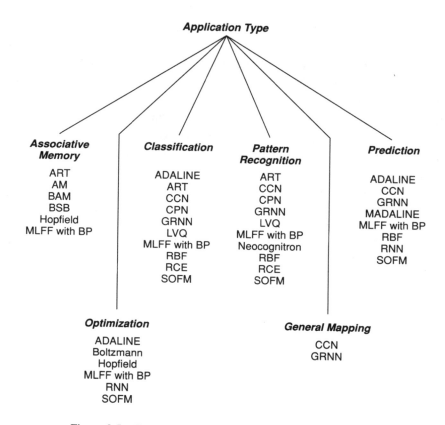

Figure 2.5   Categories of Network Types by Application Type

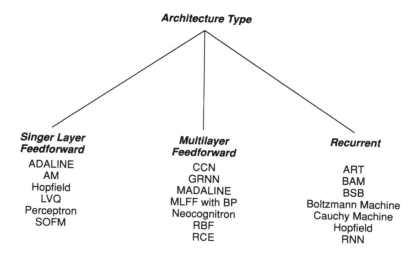

Figure 2.6   Categories of Networks by Architectural Type

Summary

In this chapter, we have considered the basic building components that make up neural network structures. We have also considered different architectures and different types of learning algorithms. We have looked at the capabilities and limitations of ANNs, including their ability to learn and generalize and their mapping capabilities. Finally, we have presented several different classifications or categories of networks, including a taxonomy of learning types, a taxonomy of architectures, and a taxonomy based on type of application.

3
Review of Mathematical and Statistical Concepts

In this chapter, selected topics in mathematics and statistics are presented as a prerequisite and supplement to material found in later chapters. In particular, we review vector and matrix algebra, calculus, probability and statistical concepts, information theory and fuzzy logic to the extent they are needed within the text. We also introduce some nonlinear systems theory and chaos as it relates to material on recurrent networks which are presented in Chapters 5, 9 and 15.

3.1 Introduction

The capabilities, limitations, and general behaviors of neural network systems cannot be fully appreciated without an understanding of the underlying functionality and dynamics of such systems. This requires that a minimal understanding of some basic mathematical theory be known. Consequently, in this chapter, we have included a brief review of selected topics in mathematics and statistics for those wishing to refresh their knowledge in these areas or for those who are simply seeking definitions to specific concepts. Our treatment is intentionally brief and limited only to those topics that are needed to better understand the theory and concepts presented in subsequent chapters. No attempt has been made to provide a comprehensive coverage of any subjects introduced and examples have been kept to a minimum. This chapter may be read selectively in part for specific topics of interest when needed, or skimmed or even skipped altogether for those readers who possess a strong background in mathematics.

3.2 Review of Vector and Matrix Algebra

The theory of vector spaces and linear algebra are mature branches of mathematics. Extensive papers and texts have been written on these topics so we make no attempt here to provide a comprehensive treatment of the fields. Instead, as a convenience to those readers who may have forgotten some of their vector and matrix algebra, we review a few of the more relevent topics needed in the sequel.

Vectors

A vector $\mathbf{x}$ (denoted by lower case bold letters) is defined as an n-tuple column of numbers,

$$\mathbf{x} = \begin{pmatrix} x_1 \\ x_2 \\ \vdots \\ x_n \end{pmatrix}$$

which may be regarded as defining a point in n-dimensional space. The transpose of a vector $\mathbf{x}^T$ (denoted with superscript T) is obtained by rotating the column to form a row of numbers $\mathbf{x} = (x_1, x_2, ..., x_n)$. The dot product (also called scalar product) of two vectors $\mathbf{x}$ and $\mathbf{y}$ is defined by the scalar quantity $\mathbf{x} \cdot \mathbf{y} = x_1 y_1 + x_2 y_2 + ... + x_n y_n = \Sigma_i x_i y_i$.

Let $\mathbf{x}$, $\mathbf{y}$, and $\mathbf{z}$ be vectors, $\mathbf{0}$ the vector of all zeros and c a number. Then the following vector operations hold:

$$\mathbf{x} \cdot \mathbf{y} = \mathbf{y} \cdot \mathbf{x}$$

$$\mathbf{x} \cdot (\mathbf{y} + \mathbf{z}) = \mathbf{x} \cdot \mathbf{y} + \mathbf{x} \cdot \mathbf{z} = (\mathbf{y} + \mathbf{z}) \cdot \mathbf{x}$$

$$(c\mathbf{x}) \cdot \mathbf{y} = c(\mathbf{x} \cdot \mathbf{y})$$

$$\mathbf{x} \cdot (c\mathbf{y}) = c(\mathbf{x} \cdot \mathbf{y})$$

$$\mathbf{x} \cdot \mathbf{x} = 0 \text{ if } \mathbf{x} = \mathbf{0}, \text{ otherwise } \mathbf{x} \cdot \mathbf{x} > 0$$

Two nonzero vectors $\mathbf{x}$ and $\mathbf{y}$ are orthogonal (perpendicular) if $\mathbf{x} \cdot \mathbf{y} = 0$. For example, the unit vectors $\mathbf{e}1$, $\mathbf{e}2$, and $\mathbf{e}3$ given by $(0, 0, 1)$, $(0, 1, 0)$, and $(1, 0, 0)$ respectively, are mutually orthogonal (Figure 3.1).

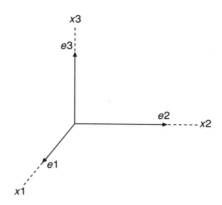

Figure 3.1 Orthogonal Unit Vectors in Three-Dimensional Space

The norm (length) of a vector is a scalar defined by

$$\|\mathbf{x}\| = (\mathbf{x} \cdot \mathbf{x})^{1/2} = \left(\sum_{i=1}^{n} x_i^2 \right)^{1/2}$$

The following properties are easily verified:

$\|c\mathbf{x}\| = |c|\,\|\mathbf{x}\|$ where $|\ |$ is absolute value
$\|\mathbf{x} - \mathbf{y}\| = [(\mathbf{x} - \mathbf{y}) \cdot (\mathbf{x} - \mathbf{y})]^{1/2}$ is the distance between vectors $\mathbf{x}$ and $\mathbf{y}$. If
$\quad \|\mathbf{x}\| = 1$ then x is a unit vector, and hence, if
$\quad \|\mathbf{x}\| = a$ then $(1/a)\mathbf{x}$ is a unit vector

If $c\mathbf{x} = \mathbf{y}$ then $\mathbf{x}$ and $\mathbf{y}$ have the same *direction*. Thus, $\mathbf{x}/\|\mathbf{x}\|$ is a unit vector in the same direction as $\mathbf{x}$ ($\mathbf{x} \neq 0$). The *projection* of a vector $\mathbf{x}$ along another vector $\mathbf{y}$ is the vector $c\mathbf{y} = \mathbf{y}(\mathbf{x} \cdot \mathbf{y})/(\mathbf{y} \cdot \mathbf{y})$. The angle θ between two vectors is given by the relationships

$$\mathbf{x} \cdot \mathbf{y} = \|\mathbf{x}\|\,\|\mathbf{y}\| \cos \theta \qquad \cos \theta = c\frac{\|\mathbf{y}\|}{\|\mathbf{x}\|} = \frac{\mathbf{x} \cdot \mathbf{y}}{\|\mathbf{x}\|\,\|\mathbf{y}\|}$$

An important relationship between any two vectors $\mathbf{x}$ and $\mathbf{y}$ is given by the Cauchy-Schwartz inequality which states that the square of the scalar product of two vectors is less than or equal to the product of the norms of the vectors,

$$(\mathbf{x} \cdot \mathbf{y})^2 \leq \|\mathbf{x}\|^2 \|\mathbf{y}\|^2$$

A set of vectors $\{x_1, x_2, ..., x_n\}$ are linearly *dependent* if there exists numbers $c_1, c_2, ..., c_n$ not all zero such that $c_1x_1 + c_2x_2 + ... + c_nx_n = \Sigma_i c_i x_i = 0$. If there do not exist such numbers, then the set of vectors are said to be linearly *independent*. In other words, the set of vectors $\{x_1, x_2, ..., x_n\}$ are linearly independent if and only if for constants $c_1, c_2, ..., c_n$ such that $\Sigma_i c_i x_i = 0$ then $c_i = 0$ for all $i = 1, ..., n$.

In n-dimensional space $\mathbf{R}^n$, there are at most n linearly independent vectors. Furthermore, any n linearly independent vectors in $\mathbf{R}^n$ can generate the space $\mathbf{R}^n$. That is, any vector in $\mathbf{R}^n$ can be expressed (generated) as a linear combination of the linearly independent vectors. Such vectors are said to form a *basis* for $\mathbf{R}^n$.

Matrices

A matrix is defined as a rectangular array of numbers consisting of m rows and n columns. Matrices are denoted by upper case bold letters, such as $\mathbf{A}$, or by the $m \times n$ array of numbers a_{ij}, for $i = 1, 2, ..., m$, and $j = 1, 2, ..., n$

$$\mathbf{A} = \begin{bmatrix} a_{11} & a_{12} & \cdots & a_{1n} \\ a_{21} & a_{22} & \cdots & a_{2n} \\ \cdot & \cdot & \cdot & \cdot \\ a_{m1} & a_{m2} & \cdots & a_{mn} \end{bmatrix}$$

or simply by the shortened notation $\mathbf{A} = (a_{ij})$. The zero matrix, $\mathbf{0}$, is the matrix with all elements equal to zero. The identity matrix, denoted $\mathbf{I}$, is the matrix with ones on the diagonal elements and zeros elsewhere,

$$\mathbf{I} = \begin{bmatrix} 1 & 0 & \cdots & 0 \\ 0 & 1 & \cdots & 0 \\ \cdot & \cdot & \cdot & \cdot \\ 0 & 0 & \cdots & 1 \end{bmatrix}$$

Note that the columns (rows) of an identity matrix are linearly independent vectors.

The addition (difference) of two matrices is possible only when they are of the same size. If $\mathbf{A}$ and $\mathbf{B}$ are each matrices, their sum (difference) is obtained by adding (subtracting) elements with the same subscript values such that $\mathbf{A} + \mathbf{B} = (a_{ij} + b_{ij})$.

A vector is a special $m \times 1$ matrix consisting of a single column of m

elements. A row vector is a $1 \times n$ matrix consisting of a single row. Some valid operations on matrices include multiplication of a matrix by a constant c, multiplication of two matrices $\mathbf{A}$ and $\mathbf{B}$, and the transpose of a matrix.

$$
c\mathbf{A} = \begin{bmatrix} ca_{11} & ca_{12} & \cdots & ca_{1n} \\ ca_{21} & ca_{22} & \cdots & ca_{2n} \\ \cdot & \cdot & \cdot & \cdot \\ ca_{m1} & ca_{m2} & \cdots & ca_{mn} \end{bmatrix} \quad \text{multiplying a matrix by a number}
$$

If $\mathbf{A}$ is an $m \times n$ matrix and $\mathbf{B}$ is an $n \times s$ matrix, the product $\mathbf{AB}$ is defined as the matrix with element ik given by

$$
\sum_{j=1}^{n} a_{ij}b_{jk} = a_{i1}b_{1k} + a_{i2}b_{2k} + \ldots + a_{in}b_{nk} \quad ik\text{th element of product } \mathbf{AB}
$$

If $\mathbf{A}_1, \ldots, \mathbf{A}_m$ are the row vectors of $\mathbf{A}$ and if $\mathbf{B}^1, \ldots, \mathbf{B}^s$ are the column vectors of $\mathbf{B}$, then the ik-coordinate of the product $\mathbf{AB}$ is equal to $\mathbf{A}_i \cdot \mathbf{B}^k$. Therefore, the matrix product can also be written as

$$
\mathbf{AB} = \begin{bmatrix} A_1B^1 & A_1B^2 & \cdots & A_1B^s \\ A_2B^1 & A_2B^2 & \cdots & A_2B^s \\ \cdot & \cdot & \cdot & \cdot \\ A_mB^1 & A_mB^2 & \cdots & A_mB^s \end{bmatrix} \quad \text{product matrix}
$$

The transpose of a matrix $\mathbf{A}$, denoted by $\mathbf{A}^T$ is obtained by exchanging columns and rows such that the first column is "rotated" to the first row position, the second column to the second row position and so on. Thus, if $\mathbf{A}$ is an $m \times n$ matrix $\mathbf{A} = (a_{ij})$,

$$
\mathbf{A}^T = \begin{bmatrix} a_{11} & a_{21} & \cdots & a_{m1} \\ a_{12} & a_{22} & \cdots & a_{2m} \\ \cdot & \cdot & \cdot & \cdot \\ a_{1n} & a_{2n} & \cdots & a_{mn} \end{bmatrix}
$$

If a matrix is equal to its transpose, $\mathbf{A} = \mathbf{A}^T$, the matrix is said to be *symmetric* and $a_{ij} = a_{ji}$. An *inverse* for a matrix, denoted $\mathbf{A}^{-1}$, is a matrix $\mathbf{B}$ such that $\mathbf{AB} = \mathbf{BA} = \mathbf{I}$. Clearly, $\mathbf{A}$ must be a square matrix ($n \times n$) to have an inverse. Not all matrices have inverses, but if one does exist, it is unique, there is only one and $(\mathbf{A}^{-1})^T = (\mathbf{A}^T)^{-1}$.

The *rank* of a matrix is the number of linearly independent column vectors. If the rank of a matrix is r, the matrix will have r linearly independent columns and r linearly independent rows as well.

A matrix can be regarded as a linear mapping M from n-dimensional space to m-dimensional space, $M : \mathbf{R}^n \rightarrow \mathbf{R}^m$. For example, if $\mathbf{A}$ is an $m \times n$ matrix, $\mathbf{x}$ is an $n \times 1$ matrix (a column vector), then the product $\mathbf{Ax} = \mathbf{y}$ is an $m \times 1$ matrix (a column vector), a linear mapping from $\mathbf{R}^n$ to $\mathbf{R}^m$.

The *outer product* of two vectors is a special type of mapping. The outer product of $\mathbf{x}$ (an $n \times 1$ matrix) and $\mathbf{y}$ (a $1 \times m$ matrix) is the $n \times m$ matrix $\mathbf{A}$ with ij-coordinate a_{ij} where $a_{ij} = x_{i1}y_{1j}$. This is essentially how the correlation matrix is formed from two jointly distributed random variables.

Pseudo-inverse

Not all matrices have an inverse. But every matrix has a *pseudo*-inverse, a modified limit form of the original matrix. The pseudo-inverse provides an alternative approach to the solution of a system of simultaneous equations. It arises in the context of minimizing a sum of squares. In neural networks the sum of squares to be minimized is typically the errors in the network output. The errors are the difference between a target output $\mathbf{t}$ and the actual output $\mathbf{y}$ computed by the network over a set of training patterns $\{(\mathbf{x}^p, \mathbf{t}^p), p = 1, 2, \ldots, P\}$, where $\mathbf{x}^p$ is the pth input training pattern. The $\mathbf{x}$ vectors are n-dimensional while the $\mathbf{y}$ and $\mathbf{t}$ vectors are both m-dimensional. The total error has the form

$$E = \sum_{p=1}^{P} E^p = \sum_{p=1}^{P} \sum_{j=1}^{m} \left(t_j^p - y_j^p\right)^2 \tag{3.1}$$

where E^p is the sum of the squared errors for pattern p over all output units and the output vector $\mathbf{y}^p$ is some function of the weights. For example, if the jth component of the $\mathbf{y}^p$ vectors is a linear function of the weights

$$y_j^p = \sum_{i=1}^{n} w_{ij} x_1^p$$

then, to minimize the total error E with respect to the weights, requires that the partial derivatives of equation (3.1) be set equal to zero

$$\frac{\partial E}{\partial w_{ij}} = \frac{\partial}{\partial w_{ij}} \left(\sum_{p=1}^{P} \sum_{j=1}^{m} \left(t_j^p - \sum_{i=1}^{n} w_{ij} x_1^p \right)^2 \right)$$

$$= -2 \sum_{p=1}^{P} \left(\sum_{i=1}^{n} t_j^p - w_{ij} x_1^p \right) \cdot x_1^p = 0 \tag{3.2}$$

In matrix notation this may be written as

$$\mathbf{WXX}^T = \mathbf{TX}^T \tag{3.3}$$

where $\mathbf{W}$ is an $m \times n$ matrix with components w_{ij}, $\mathbf{X}$ is an $n \times p$ matrix with components x_1^p and $\mathbf{T}$ is an $m \times p$ matrix with components t_1^p. In general, equation (3.3) cannot be solved for $\mathbf{W}$ directly since $\mathbf{XX}^T$ may not have an inverse. This will be the case if $\mathbf{XX}^T$ does not possess m linearly independent rows. Hence, because of the noninvertibility of $\mathbf{XX}^T$, $\mathbf{W}$ will, in general, possess a family of solutions. To restrict the solution to a single one, an extra condition can be placed on the error expression to be minimized. The condition is to simultaneously limit the weights by minimizing the error plus a term containing the squared sum of all the weights

$$E + \lambda \sum_{i=1} w_{ij}^2$$

where λ is a positive constant. Minimizing this new expression as before, leads to the modified matrix solution

$$\mathbf{W}(\mathbf{XX}^T + \lambda \mathbf{1}) = \mathbf{TX}^T \tag{3.4}$$

It can be shown that for every $\lambda > 0$, the matrix $(\mathbf{XX}^T + \lambda \mathbf{1})$ has an inverse. Therefore, post multiplying both sides of (3.4) by the inverse $(\mathbf{XX}^T + \lambda \mathbf{1})^{-1}$ and taking the limit of the resultant expression as $\lambda \to 0$, we obtain the pseudo-inverse needed

$$\mathbf{W} = \lim_{\lambda \to 0} \left[\mathbf{TX}^T (\mathbf{XX}^T + \lambda \mathbf{1})^{-1} \right] = \mathbf{T}\tilde{\mathbf{X}}.$$

$\tilde{\mathbf{X}}$ is the pseudo-inverse of the matrix $\mathbf{X}$, and there is always at least one solution. If there are more solutions, the pseudo-inverse solution is the one with the smallest sum of squares of matrix values. Furthermore, when $\mathbf{X}$ does have an inverse, $\mathbf{X}^{-1}$, then $\tilde{\mathbf{X}} = \mathbf{X}^{-1}$.

The following definition is generally given for the pseudo-inverse $\tilde{\mathbf{X}}$ of a general rectangular matrix $\mathbf{X}$ of rank k. The pseudo-inverse of the matrix $\mathbf{X}$ is defined as one which satisfies the following conditions:

1. $X\tilde{X}X = X$

2. $\tilde{X}X\tilde{X} = \tilde{X}$

3. $X\tilde{X}$ and $\tilde{X}X$ are Hermitian matrices.

A Hermitian matrix is a matrix which equals the complex conjugate of its transpose. For a real matrix, the Hermitian condition simply means the matrix is symmetrical.

Eigenvectors

Let A be a square $n \times n$ matrix and x an n-element non-zero vector. Then x is called an *eigenvector* of A if there exists a number λ such that $Ax = \lambda x$. Eigenvectors of a matrix are vectors that when multiplied by the matrix, give the same vector multiplied by a constant. The constant λ is called an *eigenvalue* of A associated with the eigenvector x. An $n \times n$ matrix has n eigenvectors and associated eigenvalues. Some of the eigenvalues may be equal, some zero and some imaginary, depending on the matrix A. If x is an eigenvector of the matrix A, then so is kx. So eigenvectors are unique to within a multiplicative constant only. An example of an eigenvector x and its eigenvalue $\lambda = 6$ are as follows:

$$\begin{bmatrix} 6 & 2 & 1 \\ 2 & 6 & 1 \\ 1 & 1 & 7 \end{bmatrix} \begin{bmatrix} 1 \\ 1 \\ -2 \end{bmatrix} = \begin{bmatrix} 6 \\ 6 \\ 0 \end{bmatrix}$$

$$A \qquad x \quad = \quad \lambda x$$

The other two eigenvectors for A are $(1\ -1\ 0)$ and $(1\ 1\ 1)$. The corresponding eigenvalues are easily found.

The equation $Ax = \lambda x$ can be written as $(A - \lambda I)x = 0$, called the characteristic equation of the matrix. One way to find the eigenvalues for A is to find the n roots of the characteristic equation in λ using the determinants of A. We omit the details here and refer the interested reader to one of the many texts on linear algebra and vector spaces.

Eigenvectors and eigenvalues are also called characteristic vectors and characteristic values, respectively. As noted above, they play an important role in many applications since they are often related to parameters of physical systems.

In statistics, the eigenvalues of a covariance matrix are the variances of the variates. There are a number of other instances where eigenvectors are shown to be important toward a better understanding of neural network behaviors. In particular, some neural networks are capable of performing a kind of transformation on the input patterns that summarizes the importance of the individual features or variables in the pattern. The transformation is known as principal components, the subject of the next section.

Principal Component Analysis (PCA)

The use of one or a few numbers to characterize an object or a population of objects is common practice in many fields. An examination grade is used to "summarize" the knowledge a student has gained in a course. The mean and variance are used to summarize the characteristics of a population distribution.

Principal component analysis is a method used to summarize the properties of a set of multivariate data patterns. It is a linear transformation method often used for data analysis (e.g. feature extraction) or data compression. The transform is a variance maximization process that diagonalizes the covariance matrix of the input pattern distribution. Given input patterns from an n-dimensional vector space, we want to find some subset $m < n$ of the n variates that account for as much of the data's variability (variance) as possible. To achieve this, we project the n-dimensional space onto m-dimensional space choosing each component in the direction of maximum variance and such that the components are mutually orthogonal (uncorrelated).

Given p observations (samples) on n variates (the samples are the p rows of the $\mathbf{X}$ matrix),

$$\mathbf{X} = \begin{bmatrix} x_{11} & x_{12} & \cdots & x_{1n} \\ x_{21} & x_{22} & \cdots & x_{2n} \\ \vdots & \vdots & \vdots & \vdots \\ \vdots & \vdots & \vdots & \vdots \\ x_{p1} & x_{p2} & \cdots & x_{pn} \end{bmatrix}$$

we construct a set of n new variables y_j ($j = 1, 2, \ldots, n$) the "principal components" of the x_j which are linear combinations of the x_j. Let $\mathbf{w}_i$ and $\mathbf{y}_i$ be column vectors of dimension n and p respectively. The PCA method can be summarized as follows:

1. Take the first principal component along the direction of maximum variance.

Let

$$\mathbf{y}_1 = \mathbf{X}\mathbf{w}_1 \tag{3.5}$$

where $\mathbf{y}_1$ and $\mathbf{w}_1$ are column vectors.

Note that this quantity must be constrained since the variance can be made larger and larger just by increasing the value of $\mathbf{w}_1$. This can be done by taking all weight vectors to be unit length, that is, by setting

$$\mathbf{w}_1^T\mathbf{w}_1 = \Sigma_i w_{i1}^2 = 1 \tag{3.6}$$

2. Maximize the sum of squares due to $\mathbf{y}_1$, i.e. maximize

$$\mathbf{y}_1^T\mathbf{y}_1 = \mathbf{w}_1^T \mathbf{X}^T\mathbf{X}\mathbf{w}_1 \tag{3.7}$$

Maximization problems of this type with an equality constraint are most easily solved using the method of Lagrange. A new composite function L is formed using both equations (3.5) and (3.6) as follows:

$$L = \mathbf{w}_1^T\mathbf{X}^T\mathbf{X}\mathbf{w}_1 - \lambda_1(\mathbf{w}_1^T\mathbf{w}_1 - 1) \tag{3.8}$$

where λ_1 is a Lagrangian multiplier. The second term will be zero at the values of $\mathbf{w}_1$ which satisfy the constraint (3.6). Thus, at these values, L takes on the form of the original function (3.7). We need to solve for the maximum of L. Thus, we take partial derivatives of L with respect to $\mathbf{w}_1$ and λ_1, set the results equal to zero and solve. We have

$$\frac{\partial L}{\partial \mathbf{w}_1} = 2\mathbf{X}^T\mathbf{X}\mathbf{w}_1 - 2\lambda_1\mathbf{w}_1 = 0$$
$$\mathbf{X}^T\mathbf{X}\mathbf{w}_1 = \lambda_1\mathbf{w}_1$$

From this result and (3.7), we can write

$$\mathbf{y}_1^T\mathbf{y}_1 = \mathbf{w}_1^T\lambda_1\mathbf{w}_1 = \lambda_1 \mathbf{w}_1^T c\mathbf{w}_1 = \lambda_1$$

The solution $\mathbf{y}_1$ is the first principal component with maximum variance λ_1. Also, note that λ_1 is an eigenvalue of $\mathbf{X}^T\mathbf{X}$.

3. To find the second principal component $\mathbf{y}_2$, we use the same procedure as for $\mathbf{y}_1$, but we also take $\mathbf{y}_2$ orthogonal to $\mathbf{y}_1$. Thus, we must maximize

$$\mathbf{y}_2^T\mathbf{y}_2 = \mathbf{w}_2^T\mathbf{X}^T\mathbf{X}\mathbf{w}_2$$

subject to the two constraints

$$\mathbf{w}_2^T\mathbf{w}_2 = 1 \text{ and } \mathbf{w}_1^T\mathbf{w}_2 = 0$$

We have, taking into account the new orthogonality constraint,

$$L = \mathbf{w}_2^T\mathbf{X}^T\mathbf{X}\mathbf{w}_2 - \lambda_2(\mathbf{w}_2^T\mathbf{w}_2 - 1) - \mu\mathbf{w}_1^T\mathbf{w}_2$$

where λ_2 and μ are both Lagrangian multipliers. Proceeding as before, taking the partial derivative of L with respect to $\mathbf{w}_2$, setting the result equal to zero and solving, we find

$$\mu = 2\mathbf{w}_1^T\mathbf{X}^T\mathbf{X}\mathbf{w}_2 = 2 \times 0 = 0 \text{ and } \mathbf{X}^T\mathbf{X}\mathbf{w}_2 = \lambda_2\mathbf{w}_2$$

Now choose λ_2 to be the second largest eigenvalue of $\mathbf{X}^T\mathbf{X}$.

4. Continuing the process, we obtain the p eigenvalues λ_1, λ_2, ..., λ_p and associated orthogonal matrix $\mathbf{W} = [\mathbf{w}_1\mathbf{w}_2 ... \mathbf{w}_p]$ where now the p principal components of $\mathbf{X}$ come from the matrix $\mathbf{Y} = \mathbf{X}\mathbf{C}$ and where

$$\mathbf{Y}^T\mathbf{Y} = \mathbf{W}^T\mathbf{X}^T\mathbf{X}\mathbf{W} = \Lambda = \begin{bmatrix} \lambda_1 & 0 & ... & 0 \\ 0 & \lambda_2 & ... & 0 \\ \vdots & \vdots & & \\ 0 & 0 & ... & \lambda_p \end{bmatrix}$$

Since Λ is diagonal with off-diagonal elements zero, we see that the principal components of the $\mathbf{Y}$s are uncorrelated (orthogonal) by pairs, and the sums of squares are the λ_i. When the rank of $\mathbf{X}$ is $s < p$, then $p - s$ eigenvalues will be zero. In this case, we use the s independent variables to "explain" the variability of the data samples (also true when some eigenvalues are small).

The total variation in $\mathbf{X}$ then, is just: (the summations below are taken over the n sample observations)

$$\Sigma x_1^2 + \Sigma x_2^2 + \ldots + \Sigma x_p^2 = \text{Trace}(\mathbf{X}^T\mathbf{X}) = \text{Tr}(\mathbf{W}^T\mathbf{X}^T\mathbf{X}\mathbf{W})$$
$$= \sum_{j=1}^{p} \lambda_j = \sum_{j=1}^{p} \mathbf{Y}_j^T \mathbf{Y}_j$$

since $\mathbf{W}\mathbf{W}^T = \mathbf{I}$ and $\text{Tr}(\mathbf{W}^T\mathbf{X}^T\mathbf{X}\mathbf{W}) = \text{Tr}(\mathbf{X}^T\mathbf{X}\mathbf{W}\mathbf{W}^T) = \text{Tr}(\mathbf{X}^T\mathbf{X})$.

So $\lambda_j/\Sigma_j\lambda_j$ measures the proportion of contribution made by the jth principal component of $\mathbf{X}$. One can also show that the product moment correlation coefficients ρ_{ij} between $\mathbf{x}_i$ and $\mathbf{y}_j$ satisfy the relation

$$\frac{w_{i1}^2\lambda_1}{\Sigma \mathbf{x}_j^2} + \frac{w_{i2}^2\lambda_2}{\Sigma \mathbf{x}_j^2} + \ldots + \frac{w_{ip}^2\lambda_p}{\Sigma \mathbf{x}_j^2} = \rho_{i1}^2 + \rho_{i2}^2 + \ldots + \rho_{ip}^2 = 1$$

In Chapter 14, an example of the utility of PCA is given in relation to a particular type of neural network learning algorithm.

3.3   Review of Calculus Concepts

It is assumed the reader is familiar with limits and continuity of functions. The limit of a function $f(x)$ as x approaches the value a is denoted by

$$\lim_{x \to a} f(x) = L$$

The limit, if it exists, is equal to L. A function $f(x)$ is said to be continuous at $x = a$ if the function is defined at $x = a$ and

$$\lim_{x \to a} f(x) = f(a)$$

Differentiation

Let $\Delta x = x_1 - x_2$ denote the difference between two points x_1 and x_2. Given a function $y = f(x)$, the derivative of the function, denoted by dy/dx is

$$\frac{dy}{dx} = \lim_{\Delta x \to 0} \frac{f(x + \Delta x) - f(x)}{\Delta x}$$

provided the limit exists. The derivative is the instantaneous rate of change of the function at each point of the independent variable. One can always find a derivative, if it exists, from the above definition. For example, the derivative of the polynomial function $f(x) = -2x^2 + 3x - 10$ is found directly as

$$\frac{f(x + \Delta x) - f(x)}{\Delta x} = \frac{[-2(x + \Delta x)^2 + 3(x + \Delta x) - 10] - (-2x^2 + 3x - 10)}{\Delta x}$$

$$= \frac{-4x\Delta x - 2(\Delta x)^2 + 3\Delta x}{\Delta x} = -4x - 2\Delta x + 3$$

Therefore the derivative of $f(x)$ is just

$$\frac{dy}{dx} = \lim_{\Delta x \to 0} (-4x - 2\Delta x + 3) = -4x + 3$$

A simpler way to find the derivative of $f(x)$ (also denoted as $f'(x)$—f "prime" of x) is to use tables or established rules for different functional forms.

Higher-order derivatives are defined in a similar way. Thus the second derivative is just the derivative of the derivative of a function. Thus, the *second* derivative of the above function $f(x) = -2x^2 + 3x - 10$ is just the derivative of the derivative, $-4x + 3$, or

$$\frac{d^2y}{dx^2} = \lim_{\Delta x \to 0} \frac{[-4(x + \Delta x) + 3] - (-4x + 3)}{\Delta x} = \frac{-4\Delta x}{\Delta x} = -4$$

The second derivative is the instantaneous rate of change of the derivative at each point of the function. Higher-order derivatives are defined in a similar way.

If $y = f(u)$ is a differentiable function and $u = g(x)$ is differentiable, then the derivative of y with respect to x can be found by application of the chain rule,

$$\frac{dy}{dx} = \frac{dy}{du} \cdot \frac{du}{dx}$$

For example, let $y = f(u) = u^3 - 6u$ where $u = g(x) = x^4 + 6x$. Then $dy/dx = (3u^2 - 6)(4x^3 + 6)$.

The above concepts are easily generalized to functions of several variables, where partial derivatives of the function are defined in a similar way, one for each variable, and where all other variables are held fixed (treated as constants). We examine the case for two variables only, since functions of several variables are defined in a similar way. Let $f(x, y)$ be a function of two variables x and y. The partial derivatives of f with respect to x and y are, respectively

$$\frac{\partial f}{\partial x} = \lim_{\Delta x \to 0} \frac{f(x + \Delta x, y) - f(x, y)}{\Delta x} \qquad \frac{\partial f}{\partial y} = \lim_{\Delta x \to 0} \frac{f(x, y + \Delta y) - f(x, y)}{\Delta y}$$

provided the limits exist. Each of these derivatives represents the instantaneous rate of change of the function (dependent variable) with respect to changes in either of the independent variables, separately. For example, let $f(x, y) = 3x^3 + 6xy^4 + 2y$. Then the partial derivative of f, with respect to x, is found by taking the derivative of f and treating y as a constant. The derivative of f, with respect to y, is found in a similar way:

$$\frac{\partial f}{\partial x} = 9x^2 + 6y^4 \qquad\qquad \frac{\partial f}{\partial y} = 24xy^3 + 2$$

One of the most common uses of differential calculus is in optimization problems where the maximum or minimum of a function must be found. In particular, the learning performance of many neural networks is based on a minimum squared error function criterion. Examples involving the minimization of an error functions are given in many chapters of the text.

Integration

Integral calculus is used to find the area between curves and other boundaries. Also, if the derivative of an unknown function is known, integral calculus may provide a way of finding the original function. Given a function f, the methods of the previous section can be used to find the derivative of the function. On the other hand, if one is given a derivative f', it may be desirable to find the original function f. The original function f is called the *antiderivative* of f'. A knowledge of derivatives of different functions allows one to find families of functions that are antiderivatives, but antiderivatives are, in general, not unique since the derivative of a constant is zero. Other constraints are needed to find specific antiderivatives.

Finding antiderivatives is the process of integration, and the family of functions found through this process is called the indefinite integral. The indefinite integral of the function $f(x)$ is written as

$$\int f(x)dx$$

For example, the indefinite integral of the function $f(x) = 2x + 6$ is just $x^2 + 6x + C$, where C is an unknown constant. To verify that $x^2 + 6x + C$ is indeed the integral of $f(x)$ one can simply take the derivative of $x^2 + 6x + C$. If f

is a continuous function, we define the indefinite integral of f as

$$\int f(x)dx = F(x) + C$$

if $F'(x) = f(x)$. In practice, one usually uses a set of rules or tables to find integrals of functions, rules that are, of course, directly related to the derivatives of functions.

The *definite* integral is required for the solution to many real problems. The definite integral provides a method of finding the area under a curve. It may also be interpreted as a limit. In particular, if f is a bounded function on the interval $[a, b]$, the definite integral on the interval $[a, b]$ is defined as

$$\int_a^b f(x)dx = \lim_{n \to \infty} \sum_{i=1}^{n} f(x_i)\Delta x_i = A$$

provided the limit exists. Note that the size of the intervals Δx_i in the subdivision of the interval $[a, b]$ approach zero and the number of intervals n approaches infinity. The values a and b are the lower and upper limits of integration, respectively.

A fundamental theorem of integral calculus is that if F is an antiderivative of a continuous function f over some interval, then for any points $x = a$, $x = b$ with $a \le b$ in the interval,

$$\int_a^b f(x)dx = F(b) - F(a)$$

Note that the unknown constant of integration C cancels out in the above evaluation. For example, to evaluate the definite integral of the polynomial $2x^2 + 4x - 5$ on the interval $[1, 4]$, we have

$$\int_1^4 (2x^2 + 4x - 5)dx = F(4) - F(1)$$
$$= \left[\frac{2x^3}{3} + 4x^2 - 5x \right]_1^4$$

where the notation $]_1^4$ denotes the limits of integration. Thus,

$$F(4) - F(1) = \left[\frac{2(4)^3}{3} + 4(4)^2 - 5(4)\right] - \left[\frac{2(1)^3}{3} + 4(1)^2 - 5(1)\right]$$
$$= 87$$

Like differentiation, there are many rules of integration to assist one in evaluating indefinite or definite integrals. Also, multiple integrals are found by taking multiple antiderivatives over the separate intervals of integration. Likewise, integrals of multivariate functions are defined for each of the variables separately, somewhat like the reverse of partial derivatives. We omit the details here and refer the interested reader to one of the many texts available on differential and integral calculus.

We complete this section with a brief review of one additional topic related to calculus, namely differential equations.

Differential Equations

A differential equation is an equation which contains derivatives or differential terms. Differential equations are used to describe the behavior of dynamic systems including dynamic neural networks. Ordinary differential equations (o.d.e.) involve derivatives of a function of one independent variable, such as time. The *order* of a differential equation is the highest-order derivative appearing in the equation. The *degree* of a differential equation is the power of the highest-order derivative in the equation. To *solve* a differential equation, antiderivatives must be found for all derivative terms in the equation. An example of a system of o.d.e.'s used to model a dynamic neural network are as follows:

$$\frac{dy_j}{dt} = \sum_i w_{ij} x_i + \sum_{k \in S_j} v_{kj} y_k - h(y_j)$$

$$\frac{dw_{ij}}{dt} = \alpha(x_i - w_{ij})$$

The first equation describes the time rate of change of the output y_j of a unit as a function of external inputs x_i and internal inputs y_j weighted by the connection synoptic weights, w_{ij} and v_{kj}, respectively. The second equation defines the learning dynamics of the network where the time rate of change of the weights are a function of the inputs and weights. More details of such systems are given in chapters where specific neural network implementations are described.

3.4 Review of Probability Concepts

A random variable (r.v.) X is a function defined on a sample space, the space of possible outcomes of an experiment. We use capital letters to denote random variables and corresponding lower case letters to denote the values the random variable can assume. A function which determines the probability of each possible outcome of an experiment is called a probability density function (pdf) for continuous variables and probability mass function (pmf) for discrete-valued variables. If X is a continuous random variable, its density function $f(x)$ must satisfy the conditions

1. $f(x) \geq 0$ for all x, and

2. the area under the graph of f is equal to 1.

The first condition implies that probabilities are nonnegative and the second condition insures that events are mutually exclusive and collectively exhaustive. Similar conditions hold for discrete r.v.'s.

The probability that a r.v. X assumes a value in the interval between a and b, where $a < b$, equals the area under the density function between $x = a$ and $x = b$. The probability that X will assume a value between a and b is given by the definite integral of $f(x)$ between $x = a$ and $x = b$ and denoted by $P(a \leq X \leq b)$, that is

$$P(a \leq X \leq b) = \int_a^b f(x)dx$$

The *cumulative* distribution function for the random variable X with density function $f(x)$ is defined as $F(x)$, where

$$F(x) = P(X \leq x) = \int_{-\infty}^x f(t)dt$$

Some parameters of probability distributions that are useful to know when studying the behavior of events or systems governed by chance are the mean, variance, median, mode, range, percentiles and moments. The median is the value of the variate which marks the center of the distribution with half of the probability mass below the median value and half of the mass above the value. The mode is the point (or points) of maximum probability. The range is the interval of the variate over which the probability distribution is non-zero and the percentile points are variate values for which the probability mass equals the percentile value. For example, the median is the 50 percentile point and the quartile is the 25 percentile point. The moments of a distribution (when they exist) completely characterize the distribution. The kth moment ($k = 0, 1, 2, \ldots$) of a probability distribution $f(x)$ is defined by

$$\mu_k = \int_a^b x^k f(x) dx$$

when the moment exists. The first and second moments are the most commonly used moments as they give the central point or mean value and the spread or diversity of the distribution, respectively. The variance σ^2 is defined as the second moment about the mean and the standard deviation σ is just the square root of the variance.

$$\sigma^2 = \int_{-\infty}^{\infty} (x - \mu)^2 \, f(x) dx,$$

where $\mu_1 \equiv \mu$.

Given any function of a random variable X with pdf $f(x)$, say $h(X)$, the mean or expected value of the function is defined as

$$E\left[h(X)\right] = \int_{-\infty}^{\infty} h(x) f(x) dx$$

From this definition, we see that $\mu_k = E[x^k]$.

The most common continuous valued distribution is the normal distribution. The single variate normal distribution has a pdf of the form

$$f(x) = \frac{1}{\sqrt{2\pi}\sigma} e^{-1/2[(x-\mu)/\sigma]^2} \qquad \text{for } -\infty < x < \infty$$

The mean and variance of the normal distribution are μ and σ^2, respectively, and the standard deviation is σ. Other commonly occurring distributions include the binomial, exponential, multinomial, geometric, lognormal, poisson, and uniform to name a few. In the interest of brevity, we omit the details here.

Parameters of distributions, such as the pdf functional form, the mean and variance and other parameters, can be estimated from samples (observed outcomes) taken from the distribution. Such samples are called a statistic. Note that since a function of a random variable is a random variable, any statistic is a random variable. Let x_1, x_2, ..., x_n be a sample of n independent observations taken from the same distribution (independent, identically distributed or for short, iid). The "best" estimator of the population mean is (for many distributions) just the sample mean (we explain below what is meant by best).

$$\bar{x} = \sum_{i=1}^{n} x_i$$

Good estimators will have some of the following properties: (1)An unbiased estimator is one for which the expected value of the estimator equals the parameter being estimated. The sample mean is an unbiased estimator of the population mean, since

$$E[\bar{x}] = E\left[\frac{1}{n}\sum_{i=1}^{n} x_i\right] = \frac{1}{n}\sum_{i=1}^{n} E[x_i] = \frac{1}{n}\sum_{i=1}^{n} \mu = \mu$$

(2) The probability distribution of a good estimator will have minimal dispersion, that is, among all estimators, it should have that smallest or minimum variance. It can be shown that the sample mean does indeed have minimum variance for many distributions.

(3) Finally, as the sample size of a "good" statistic is increased, one would expect that the statistic should approach the true parameter value. In other words, it should converge to the population parameter being estimated. Estimators with this property are known as sufficient statistics.

The concepts described above can all be generalized to include multivariate distributions, distributions of more than one random variable. For such distributions, other parameters can be defined, parameters which describe the relationship between the different variables. Let $f(x, y)$ be the joint pdf of the r.v. X and Y. The univariate distributions of X, $f(x)$, and Y, $f(y)$, are called the marginal distributions. They can be found from the joint distribution by direct integration, that is

$$f(x) = \int_{-\infty}^{\infty} f(x, y)dy, \qquad f(y) = \int_{-\infty}^{\infty} f(x, y)dx$$

One parameter of particular interest for multivariate distributions, is the correlation coefficient ρ. The correlation coefficient measures how one variate changes with changes in the other variate, that is, the dependency one variable has on another.

The correlation between two random variables is defined as the ratio of the product of the two covariances and the product of the square root variances of the two variables,

$$\rho = \frac{\text{cov}(x)\text{cov}(y)}{\sqrt{\text{var}(x)}\ \sqrt{\text{var}(y)}} = \frac{E[(x - \mu_x)(y - \mu_y)]}{\sigma_x \sigma_y}$$

where μ_x and μ_y are the means for the variates X and Y respectively, and σ_x and σ_y the corresponding standard deviations. Note that $-1 \leq \rho \leq 1$. If X and Y are independent, then $\rho = 0$, the two are not correlated. If both variates move directly together, $\rho = 1$. If the two move in opposition to each other, $\rho = -1$. Other probability and statistical concepts will be introduced as required. Next we briefly review information theory, a field that is finding more and more application in neural network theory.

3.5   Review of Information Theory Concepts

Information theory was largely originated by Claude Shannon in the 1940s (Shannon, 1948). He defined a quantitative measure of information based on the amount of uncertainty discovered in newly received information. His original work related to data transmission over communication channels, but has since found wide applicability in many other fields including physics, statistics, engineering, computer science, and psychology. The basic notions behind information theory are as follows. If a given communication from a source to a receiver provides few new facts in the sense of likelihood occurrence, little information is gained. On the other hand, new unlikely facts (unknown, surprising, or perhaps unusual facts) provide much information. This is the basis for Shannon's measure of information he called entropy. It is a measure of the uncertainty contained in a message.

Shannon's measure of information was defined as the amount of prior uncertainty in the outcome of a random experiment when the outcome was observed. In the case of a finite set of events, if the probability of an event X is given by $p(x)$ (we use X to denote a random variable with possible outcomes x), the information contained in that event is defined as $\log(1/p(x))$. Thus, when an event becomes more certain, that is, as $p(x) \rightarrow 1$, the amount of information contained in the event drops to zero. If the likelihood of an event is very small ($p(x) \approx 0$), the information contained in the event is large. For a finite number of events x_i, $i = 1, 2, \ldots, N$, the *average* information or entropy of the events is defined as $H(X)$, where

$$H(X) = - \sum_{j=1}^{N} p(x_i) \log p(x_i) = -E(\log X) \tag{3.9}$$

where E is the expected value. Note that $H(X)$ is maximum when all events are equally unlikely, that is when $x_i = 1/N$ for $i = 1, 2, ..., N$ and minimum when events are known. This is illustrated for the case $N = 2$ ($x_1 = p, x_2 = 1 - p$) where a plot of H is given as a function of p in Figure 3.2. $H(p)$ is maximum at $p = 0.5$ and falls rapidly to zero as p approaches 0 or 1.

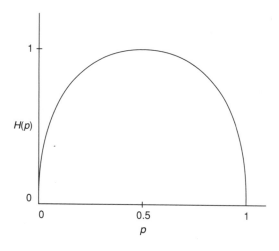

Figure 3.2   Entropy as a Function of the Probability of an Event

In throwing an unbiased six-sided die, the entropy is approximately $H = \log(6) = 2.58$ bits, the information gained when the outcome is observed. Note that we have used log base 2 to get "bits" rather than the natural logarithm (nits).

In what follows, we concentrate on information theoretic concepts for discrete random variables. We consider the continuous case after some basic definitions. The joint entropy of two or more random variables is defined in an analogous way. Thus, the entropy of the jointly distributed random variables X and Y is given by:

$$H(X, Y) = -E(\log[p(X, Y)]) = -\Sigma_x \Sigma_y \, p(x, y)\log[p(x, y)]$$

It can be shown that the joint entropy of a pair of random variables never exceeds the sum of the individual (marginal) entropies, that is, $H(X, Y) \leq H(X) + H(Y)$ with equality when X and Y are independent.

From conditional probability distributions, we can define a conditional entropy. For example, the conditional entropy of Y given X, $H(Y|X)$ is defined as:

$$
\begin{aligned}
H(Y|X) &= -E(\log[P(Y|X)]) = \Sigma_x p(x) H(Y|X = x) \\
&= \Sigma_x p(x) \Sigma_y p(y|x) \log[p(y|x)] \\
&= -\Sigma_x \Sigma_y p(x, y) \log[p(y|x)]
\end{aligned}
\tag{3.10}
$$

where the summations are taken over all possible values of x and y. Equation (3.10) is a measure of the uncertainty remaining about Y after we know X. Clearly, it is less than the uncertainty about Y alone.

Using the relationship between conditional and joint probability distributions, one can show that the joint entropy is the sum of the conditional and marginal entropies,

$$H(X, Y) = H(X) + H(Y|X)$$

From this chain rule, the following relationship can also be established

$$H(X, Y|Z) = H(X|Z) + H(Y|X, Z)$$

The rule can be extended to any number of random variables.

A useful measure of the "distance" between two probability distributions is the relative entropy (also known as the Kullback Leibler distance). Let $p(x)$ and $q(x)$ be probability mass functions for the random variables X and Y. Then the relative entropy is given by

$$D(p\|q) = E\left(\log\left[\frac{p(X)}{q(X)}\right]\right) = \Sigma_x p(x) \log\left[\frac{p(x)}{q(x)}\right]$$

where by definition, $0*\log(0/q) = 0$ and $p*\log(p/0) = \infty$. The relative entropy is always nonnegative and is zero if and only if $p = q$. It is not a true metric, however, since it is not symmetric and does not satisfy the triangle inequality. Even so, it is a useful measure of "distance" between two distributions.

Another information theoretic measure which has a clear physical interpretation is the *mutual information* between two random variables X and Y. The mutual information is a measure of the amount of information one random variable contains about another random variable. Let $p(x, y)$ be a joint probability mass function and $p(x)$ and $p(y)$ the marginal probability mass functions of the random variables X and Y. Then the mutual information of X and Y is defined as

$$I(X; Y) = E\left(\log\frac{p(X, Y)}{p(X)p(Y)}\right) = \Sigma_x\Sigma_y p(x, y)\log\frac{p(x, y)}{p(x)p(y)}$$

$I(X; Y)$ is a symmetrical measure in X and Y since the following relationships hold

$$\begin{aligned}I(X; Y) &= H(X) - H(X|Y) = H(X) + H(Y) - H(X, Y)\\ &= H(Y) - H(Y|X)\\ &= I(Y; X)\end{aligned}$$

When the two variates are independent, $H(X, Y) = H(X) + H(Y)$ and hence, $I(X; Y) = 0$. In this case, neither variate provides information about the other. When X and Y are related, $I(X; Y)$ is positive, and when the two are identical $I(X; Y)$ is maximum. One can also establish the following relationship between the relative entropy and the mutual information between two variates

$$I(X; Y) = D(p(x, y)\|p(x)p(y))$$

Many of the above definitions given for discrete r.v.'s are the same for the continuous case, but care must be taken to define entropy for continuous random variables since they can assume an uncountable number of values and hence carry an infinite amount of information. The term *differential entropy* has been associated with entropy for continuous r.v.'s. Let X be a r.v. with cumulative d.f. $F(x) = \Pr(X \le x)$. If $F(x)$ is continuous, the r.v. is said to be continuous. Also let $f(x) = F'(x)$ be the probability density function for X (assuming the derivative is defined) and let the set where $f(x) > 0$ be defined as the *support set* of X. Then the differential entropy $h(X)$ of a continuous r.v. X with pdf $f(x)$ is defined as

$$h(X) = -\int_s f(x) \log f(x)dx$$

where S is the support set of X.

The definitions of the entropy for continuous multivariate r.v. are similar to the discrete case with the integral sign replacing the summation. The same is true for mutual information and relative entropy. For example, if $f(x, y)$ is the joint density of the random variables X and Y, the mutual information is defined as

$$I(X; Y) = \int f(x, y) \log \frac{f(x, y)}{f(x)f(y)} \, dxdy$$

Also, if f and g are density functions of two continuous r.v.'s, the relative entropy $D(f\|g)$ between the densities f and g are defined as

$$D(f\|g) = \int f \log(f/g)$$

where we define $0 \log(0/0) = 0$. Clearly, for $D(f\|g)$ to be finite, the support set of f must be contained within the support set of g.

Although information theory was first developed within the field of communications, many interesting relationships between information theory and other fields such as statistics, statistical mechanics, and (computation) complexity theory have since been proven. Our main interest in the theory is in the study of neural network architectures and their performance when certain constraints are defined in terms of entropy or mutual information on the networks. Examples of such studies are given in Chapters 5, 7 and 9.

3.6   Review of Fuzzy Set Theory and Fuzzy Logic

Fuzzy set theory was proposed in 1965 by Lotfi Zadeh at the University of California, Berkeley, as an attempt to generalize classical set theory. Since then, the theory has been extended to other fields that are based on set theory, including logic. In classical (two-valued) logic such as propositional and predicate logics, sentences take on one of two possible interpretations or meanings, the values true or false. This is in keeping with "crisp" set theory, wherein objects either belong to a set or do not belong to a set. There is no in-between (the excluded middle).

In classical set theory, a *set* is any well-defined collection of objects. We use the usual notation and definitions of sets here. Sets with a finite number of objects (the elements or members of the set) can be listed. For example, the set of small numbers is listed as {1, 2, 3, 4}. Sets with an infinite number of elements can be described without listing ($\Re = \{x|x$ is a real number$\}$, $\aleph = \{x|x$ is a positive integer or zero$\}$, $Z = \{x|x$ is an integer$\}$. If x is an element of the subset A we write $x \in A$ and if x is not an element of A, we write $x \notin A$. Sets can also be defined by their properties: $\{x|P(x)\}$ are elements x satisfying property P. Equal sets A and B are denoted as $A = B$. A is a *subset* of B if every element of A is also an element of B (written as $A \subseteq B$, proper subsets as $A \subset B$ and $A \not\subset B$ when A is not a subset of P).

A useful way to characterize sets is through an indicator or characteristic function. The characteristic function f of subset A, is defined as

$$f_A(x) = \begin{cases} 1 & \text{if } x \in A \\ 0 & \text{if } x \notin A \end{cases}$$

Likewise, characteristic function values can be defined for derivative sets such as the intersection and union of two sets:

$$f_{A \cap B}(x) = f_A(x) f_B(x) \qquad \text{for all } x$$
$$f_{A \cap B} = f_A + f_B - f_A f_B \qquad \text{for all } x$$
$$f_{A \oplus B} = f_A + f_B - 2 f_A f_B \qquad \text{for all } x$$

and so on.

Fuzzy Set Theory

Fuzzy set theory is a generalization of classical set theory. Definitions, theorems, proofs and results of classical set theory, in general, hold for fuzzy set theory. The theory of fuzzy logic is founded on fuzzy set theory in the same way that classical logics are formulated from (two-valued) set theory. But, fuzzy logic representations try to capture the way humans represent and reason with real world knowledge. In real world situations, we deal with a multitude of inexact concepts: generalities (a concept applies to many things), ambiguities, vagueness, chance events, incomplete knowledge and even unbelievable or contradictory information. Representing such concepts with conventional set theory and logics is difficult if not impossible. For example, it becomes very cumbersome in classical logic to try to classify objects described by expressions such as "slightly more beautiful," "not quite as tall as," "much more expensive," "good, but not as useful," and so on.

Fuzzy sets deal with subsets of the universe that have no well-defined boundaries. Members of fuzzy sets can have varying degrees of membership ranging between 0 and 1. Surely in Figure 3.3 Joe's membership in the fuzzy subset "tall people" is near 1. Jim's membership is more correctly nearer 0. But does a 5' 6" person belong to the set of tall people?

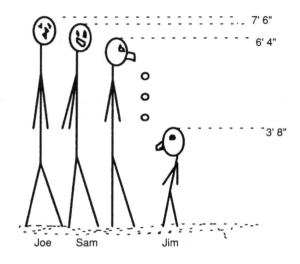

Figure 3.3   The Set of Tall People

Likewise, when is Bill regarded as bald (Figure 3.4)?

We make use of the characteristic function to formally define fuzzy sets as we did for crisp sets. Let X denote the universe of objects under consideration. Then the fuzzy subset A in X is a set of ordered pairs

$$A = \{(x, \mu_A(x))\}, \, x \in X$$

Baldness

When is Bill Bald?

Figure 3.4   The Fuzzy Set of Bald Men

where

$$0 \leq \mu_A(x) \leq 1$$

is the characteristic or membership function that denotes the degree of membership or inclusion of x in A. A value of $\mu = 0$ means that x is not included in A at all and a value of $\mu = 1$ signifies that x is a "full" member of A, corresponding to crisp membership values. Values of μ between 0 and 1 are the relative degrees of set inclusion ranging between complete inclusion and none.

A geometrical way to view a fuzzy set is as a point in the unit cube $\mathbf{I}^n$. Vertices of the cube are nonfuzzy points. Maximal fuzziness then occurs at the midpoint of the unit cube $(0.5, 0.5, \ldots, 0.5)$ (Figure 3.5a).

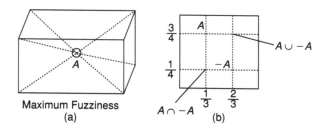

Figure 3.5 "Points as Sets" Geometrical Interpretation of a Fuzzy Set

Referring to Figure 3.5, we can see how intersection and union of the fuzzy set A and its complement set $-A$ are interpreted. For example, in Figure 3.5b if the fuzzy set A is defined as $A = \left(\frac{1}{3}, \frac{3}{4}\right)$, then the complement set is $-A = \left(\frac{2}{3}, \frac{1}{4}\right)$ and intersection and union are then given by $A \cap -A = \left(\frac{1}{3}, \frac{1}{4}\right)$ and $A \cup -A = \left(\frac{2}{3}, \frac{3}{4}\right)$, respectively.

Operations on fuzzy sets such as intersection, union, complementation, and so on are somewhat similar to operations on crisp sets. Some examples are given by the following ("$-$" is used to denote the complement set):

$$A \cup B = B \cup A \qquad\qquad \textbf{Commutative}$$
$$A \cap B = B \cap A$$

$$A \cup (B \cup C) = (A \cup B) \cup C$$
$$A \cap (B \cap C) = (A \cap B) \cap C$$

Associative

$$A \cap (B \cup C) = (A \cap B) \cup (A \cap C)$$
$$A \cup (B \cap C) = (A \cup B) \cap (A \cup C)$$

Distributive

$$A \cup A = A \qquad A \cap A = A$$

Idempotent

$$-(-A) = A \qquad A \cup \emptyset = A$$
$$A \cap \emptyset = \emptyset \qquad A \cap X = A$$
$$A \cup X = X$$

Complement & Other

$$-(A \cup B) = (-A) \cap (-B)$$
$$-(A \cap B) = (-A) \cup (-B)$$

DeMorgan's Laws

We also define the following relationships for fuzzy sets:

$$A = B \text{ iff } \mu_A(x) = \mu_B(x) \qquad \forall x \in X$$
$$A \subseteq B \text{ iff } \mu_A(x) \leq \mu_B(x) \qquad \forall x \in X$$
$$A \cup B: \mu_{A \cup B}(x) \equiv \mu_A(x) \vee \mu_B(x)$$

Note that $\vee$ is the symbol for maximum, so $\mu_{A \cup B}$ is the smallest fuzzy subset having both A and B as subsets.

$$A \cap B: \mu_{A \cap B}(x) \equiv \mu_A(x) \wedge \mu_B(x)$$

In a similar way, $\wedge$ is the symbol for minimum, so $\mu_{A \cap B}$ is the largest fuzzy subset that is a subset of both A and B. Also,

$$-A: \mu_{-A}(x) \equiv 1 - \mu_A(x) \qquad \forall x \in X$$

But, note that in general

$$A \cap (-A) \neq \emptyset \text{ and } A \cup (-A) \neq X$$

since for $\mu_A(x) = c$, with $0 < c < 1$,

$$\mu_{A \cup -A}(x) = \max(c, 1 - c) \neq 1$$
$$\mu_{A \cap -A}(X) = \min(c, 1 - c) \neq 0$$

An example of a fuzzy set is the fuzzy subset A of "small integers." If X is the set of all nonnegative integers, we might define A by

$$\mu_A(x) = \frac{1}{1 + (x/4)^2} \qquad x = 1, 2, \ldots$$

Note that for the above example it was suggested that "we might define ..." since membership function definitions are subjective. They are a matter of personal choice. Of course, one could seek a consensus among a group of people as to how membership functions are defined and use the means of the consensus for the definitions.

As another example, let X be the set of integers in the interval [0, 120] and x interpreted as "age." We might then define the fuzzy subset A as "old" with membership values as depicted in Figure 3.6. Note that the *linguistic* variable AGE can take words as values (VERY YOUNG, YOUNG, ..., OLD, VERY OLD) and these linguistic variables each have fuzzy membership functions as suggested in Figure 3.6.

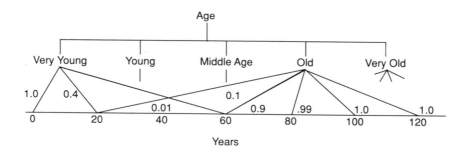

Figure 3.6   The Fuzzy Membership Function for OLD

Some special operations defined for fuzzy sets include the following:

Dilation: $\mathrm{Dil}(A) = [\mu_A(x)]^{1/2} \qquad \forall x \in X$

Concentration: $\mathrm{Con}(A) = [\mu_A(x)]^2 \qquad \forall x \in X$

Normalization: $\mathrm{Norm}(A) = \dfrac{\mu_A(x)}{\max_x\{\mu_A(x)\}}$

Other examples of fuzzy measures include cardinality and entropy. The cardinality M or "size" of a fuzzy set A is defined as

$$M(A) = \sum_{i=1}^{n} \mu_A(x_i)$$

For example, the cardinality of the fuzzy set of Figure 3.5b is just

$$M(A) = \sum_{i=1}^{2} \mu_A(x_i) = \frac{1}{3} + \frac{3}{4} = \frac{13}{12}$$

The entropy of a fuzzy set A is defined as

$$E(A) = \frac{d(A_{near})}{d(A_{far})}$$

where d is Euclidean distance, and A_{near} and A_{far} are line segments from the point A to the nearest and farthest vertex in I^n, respectively. Again, referring to Figure 3.5b the fuzzy entropy E of the fuzzy set A in the figure is just

$$E(A) = \frac{d(A_{near})}{d(A_{far})} = \frac{\frac{1}{3} + \frac{1}{4}}{\frac{2}{3} + \frac{3}{4}} = \frac{7}{17} \; (d \text{ is distance})$$

We have given examples of just a few of the many operations, definitions and theory related to fuzzy sets here. Other definitions and terms are beyond the scope of our treatment here. For this, the reader is referred to one of the many texts available on the subject.

Fuzzy Logic

Predicate logic is a two-valued logic based on traditional set theory. Predicates define classes of objects, and objects that satisfy a given predicate are members of the respective class. Inferences in predicate logic are performed using inferring rules such as *modus ponens*. If P and Q are predicates and $\rightarrow$ is the implication connective (read as IF ... THEN), then modus ponens can be summarized as follows:

$$\begin{array}{ll} P & \text{assumed true} \\ \underline{P \rightarrow Q} & \text{also assumed true} \\ Q & \text{then conclude} \end{array}$$

Similar inferring rules have been defined for fuzzy logic based on fuzzy relations among fuzzy subsets. We omit the formal definitions here. Instead, we illustrate how a fuzzy modus ponens might be interpreted as:

Premiss:	x is little
Implication:	x and y are approximately equal
Conclusion:	y is more or less little

Fuzzy Expert Systems

A popular class of expert systems use "if ... then" rules to represent "chunks" of knowledge. Such systems are known as rule-based systems. Similar expert systems have been implemented with fuzzy "if ... then" rules. These systems are called fuzzy expert systems. They are often able to model commonsense reasoning better than conventional rule-based systems. The basic fuzzy expert system operates in three stages: converting input variable values to fuzzy set values, rule instantiation and converting from fuzzy set values back to "crisp" output variable values. The process is illustrated in Figure 3.7.

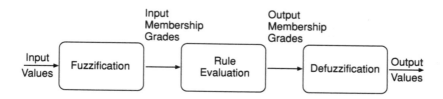

Figure 3.7   Fuzzy Inference in a Fuzzy Rule Expert System

We briefly describe the method of operation of a fuzzy expert system with an example. The application we choose for the example is a fuzzy decision support system for the trading of stocks. The membership functions defined for the *share price* level of the OOB Ltd. Company is illustrated in Figure 3.8 where the triangular shaped fuzzy membership values of negative big (NegBig), medium negative (MedNeg), zero, medium positive (MedPos) and positive big (PosBig) are defined.

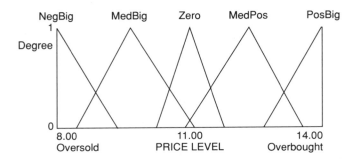

Figure 3.8   Membership Functions for Share Price Level in OOB Ltd.

Fuzzification of price level is accomplished by mapping from price value to membership function value. For example, if the price of OOB shares is \$9.00 the input grades are given by:

LV Label	Grade (Value)
PosBig	0
MedPos	0
Zero	0
MedNeg	0.6
BigNeg	0.2

The mapping is illustrated in Figure 3.9 with the dashed lines.

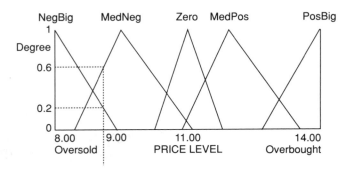

Figure 3.9   The Fuzzification Mapping Process

The other input variable is share position, the number of shares held (long) or owed (short) in inventory by our imaginary trading company OOB Ltd. The membership functions for share position are illustrated in Figure 3.10.

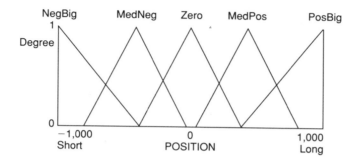

Figure 3.10   Membership Functions for Share Position in OOB Ltd.

The next stage of processing is rule evaluation. The fuzzy rules used here have two conjuncts (if conditions) in the rule premiss corresponding to the two fuzzy input variables and one output variable (action). The rules have the following form:

If *price_level* is MedPos and *share_position* is PosBig
Then *position_change* MedPos

If *price_level* is NegMed and *share_position* is Zero
Then *position_change* is PosBig

A complete decision table for the rules is illustrated in Table 3.1 where the row and column entries are the rule conjuncts and the table value is the corresponding rule action. Note that the designer of this system is somewhat bullish (a fuzzy characterization!).

The final stage of processing is defuzzification, mapping from the "then" part of the rule membership function to variable values—the recommended action of the system.

Table 3.1   Fuzzy Decision Table for Share Trading Decision Support System

	Price Level				
Position	NB	NM	Z	PM	PB
PB	PB	PB	Z	NM	NB
PM	PB	PB	PM	NM	NM
Z	PB	PB	PM	Z	Z
NM	PM	PM	Z	Z	PM
NB	PB	PB	PM	Z	Z

A portion of the complete expert system is illustrated graphically in Figure 3.11 where the two input variables are share price and share position and the output variable is the buy/sell recommendation. Fuzzification takes place in the first stage on the left where the fuzzy values are combined and passed to the rules R3 and R5 in parallel. The action parts of the rules are then combined and defuzzified to give the recommended action to buy or sell shares in the company.

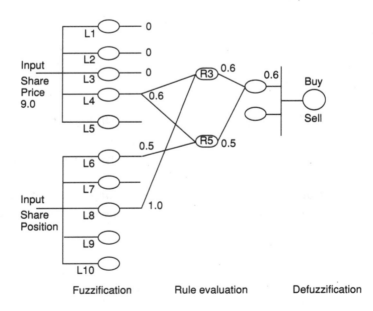

Figure 3.11   A Portion of a Fuzzy Expert System

3.7 Review of Nonlinear Systems Theory and Chaos

The study of nonlinear systems has gained considerable momentum over the past 20 years. This interest stems from a recognition of the fact that the dynamics of many phenomena cannot be accurately described using linear models. Examples of nonlinear systems are ubiquitous. They occur as natural, physical, social, financial and other types of dynamic phenomena found in physics at subatomic levels (Gutzwiller, 1992) to meteorology at macro physical levels in the atmosphere. In fact, many phenomena once thought to be random may actually be due to nonlinear system behavior known as chaos. Indeed, nonlinear behaviors appear to be the rule in many systems of interest rather than the exception, and yet most analytical methods and tools are developed for linear systems.

We include a brief introduction to nonlinear systems concepts and related theory in this section for several reasons. In the first place, important ANN architectures have nonlinear dynamics. Their behaviors cannot be fully appreciated without an understanding of nonlinear dynamical systems theory. Secondly, many ANN applications are related to the prediction of nonlinear systems behavior. For example, ANNs have been shown to be effective as tools in forecasting the future movement of a time series which is known to be driven by nonlinear dynamics. Thus, an understanding of the dynamics of the time series can help one in choosing better ANN models. Finally, ANNs themselves offer a promising approach to better understand, classify and model nonlinear systems. They can be used effectively to estimate system parameters and thereby help to characterize these systems.

The dynamics of nonlinear systems we wish to investigate can be described by the general systems of ordinary differential equations of the form

$$\frac{d\mathbf{x}}{dt} = F(\mathbf{x}) \qquad \mathbf{x} \in \mathbf{R}^n \tag{3.11}$$

where $F : U \to \mathbf{R}^n$ and U is an open subset of $\mathbf{R}^n$, the space of dependent variables referred to as *phase space* or state space. The equations define a vector field on a manifold where the n variable values trace a path in n-dimensional space as the system evolves in time. Integrating equation (3.11), we obtain a solution which is some function $\varphi(t)$ for t in some interval I. The solution φ is called the *orbit* and the set $\{t, \varphi(t) | t \in I\}$ the *trajectory* of φ in phase space. The mapping (the collection of all solutions of (3.11)) is also known as a flow. If time takes on discrete values only, the dynamics are modeled by difference equations of the form

$$\mathbf{x}_{n+1} = G(x_n) \; \mathbf{x} \in \mathbf{R}^n \qquad n = 0, 1, 2, \ldots \tag{3.12}$$

where $\mathbf{x}_n$ is the state of the system at time n. A solution φ_t for a discrete time system is called a map. Maps are the discrete analog of flows with points in the orbit indexed by the integer n.

The choice of representing a system in continuous- or discrete-time is domain, and sometimes, application dependent. When computation time is important, a discrete-time model may be appropriate since the time to iterate maps is typically smaller by a few orders of magnitude than for flows. On the other hand, when accuracy is important, a continuous-time model may be more appropriate. In any case, care must be exercised as models for the two approaches will not in general exhibit the same behaviors (e.g. one may converge to a fixed point and the other oscillate).

Dynamical systems, whether continuous or discrete, can be classified as conservative or dissipative. A system is conservative if volumes in phase space are conserved (volumes remain constant) over time evolution of the flow or map. Such systems cannot have attracting regions in phase space, and hence, there will be no fixed points, no limit cycles nor strange attractors (defined below).

Dissipative systems are characterized by the contraction of volumes in phase space with increasing time. Formally, this means that for systems defined by equations (3.11)

$$\sum_{i=1}^{n} \frac{\partial F_i(\mathbf{x})}{\partial x_i} < 0$$

For dissipative n-dimensional systems, the phase space will time-asymptotically be confined to a subset of smaller dimension than n and one can distinguish between the transient and long-term or permanent behaviors of the systems. For example, in an n-dimensional dissipative system with globally asymptotically stable equilibrium point or limit cycles, the flows will contract to either zero or to one-dimensional final state, respectively. In our study of nonlinear ANN systems, we concentrate on dissipative systems only.

Attractors

To better understand dissipative system behaviors, we need a few definitions. Generally, in what follows, our interest will be more in the qualitative behaviors of nonlinear systems as opposed to quantitative behaviors. Consequently, we do not seek specific solutions or orbits of systems, but rather average flows (maps) for a variety of initial conditions. Attracting sets and attractors play important roles in the understanding of the asymptotic behavior of these systems. Therefore we first look at attractors.

Let φ_t be a flow defined on some set U. A subset $S \subset U$ is *invariant* if $\varphi_t(S) \subset S$ for all $t \geq 0$. A compact set $A \subset U$ is an *attracting set* if:

- A is invariant under φ_t
- A has a shrinking neighborhood, that is, there is an open neighborhood V of A such that for all $x \in V$, $\varphi_t(x) \in V$ for all $t \geq 0$.

Finally, we say a set A is an *attractor* for a flow φ_t if it is an attracting set and also topologically transitive. Topological transitivity implies that for any open sets $U, V \subset A$, $\varphi_t(U) \cap V \neq \varnothing$ for all t. (This is equivalent to a dense orbit on A for φ_t. It implies that A cannot be decomposed into two or more invariant sets.) Informally, we can think of an attractor as a set of points on which orbit points generated by a flow or map accumulate for large t. They include stable asymptotic motion (limit sets), such as sinks, and stable limit cycles. The *basin of attraction* is defined as the set of all initial condition points whose orbits approach and remain near an attractor. In other words, it is the collection of orbits "captured" by an attractor.

Attractors characterize the qualitative behaviors of flows and maps. Systems can have stable or unstable attractors. The unstable attractors can be either hyperbolic or nonhyperbolic in nature. The stable or "tame" attractors are points for which convergence occurs in regular closed paths. There is a trapping region which is a closed simply connected region in phase space such that all orbits outside this region enter it and once inside never leave it. On the other hand, unstable or "strange" attractors are points for which irregular, unpredictable behavior occurs. Points follow widely divergent paths or trajectories that are unpredictable. Altogether, we distinguish between four basic types of attractors: (a) fixed points, (b) periodic orbit or limit cycles, (c) quasiperiodic orbits, and (d) chaotic (strange) attractors.

A fixed point attractor is a point invariant under a mapping (e.g. for the point x_n, $x_{n+1} = x_n$). An invariant curve is just a generalization of a fixed point. Limit cycles are attractors that exhibit regular periodic motion. A trajectory precisely returns to itself in a time T, the period. A period-one orbit is oscillatory behavior at a single frequency. A period-two orbit is oscillatory behavior at two different frequencies, and so on. Periodic solutions can be stable or unstable. Quasiperiodic behaviors are solutions that are formed from the sum of periodic solutions with incommensurate periods (the ratio of the periods is irrational). Chaotic behavior is asymptotic motion that is bounded. It is not an equilibrium point and neither is it periodic nor quasiperiodic. It is "motion" that has a sensitive dependence on initial conditions (SDIC) and apparent random behavior. Chaotic systems are noted for their broad power spectral plots much like random systems plots. And yet, they are completely deterministic. A characteristic of SDIC is that two initial points, even though separated by only an infinitesimal distance, will tend to separate exponentially fast with increasing time, and become totally uncorrelated later in time. This makes it impossible to predict such trajectories, except possibly in the short term. This sensitive dependence on initial conditions is sometimes used as a definition of strange or chaotic attractors.

We illustrate the above concepts with a nonlinear system that has been studied extensively—the logistic or quadratic map. This is an example of low dimensional system that can exhibit very complicated behavior. The map has an extremely simple form, but it can exhibit a variety of behaviors, including periodic and chaotic. The dynamics of this system are given by the one-dimensional iterative equation

$$x_{n+1} = \alpha x_n (1 - x_n) \qquad n = 0, 1, 2, \ldots \tag{3.13}$$

where α is a positive valued control parameter. If we observe the behavior of this system for any fixed value of α, a sequence of numbers $\{x_0, x_1, \ldots, x_n\}$ is generated. The generated sequence will be quite different depending on the value of the parameter α. As α is varied, we will see clear examples of the four types of attractors described above for different interval values of α (after a transitory startup time). For example, for values of $0 < \alpha < 1$, it can be shown that two fixed point attractors exist—one at $x = 0$ and one at $x = 1 - 1/\alpha$. When $\alpha = 1$, a critical bifurcation occurs. Roughly speaking, a bifurcation is a point in the orbit at which the structure of a system suddenly undergoes a qualitative change. At the value $\alpha = 1$, the x_i points suddenly begin to oscillate between two points (a period-2 limit cycle). Increasing α further results in oscillation between four values, then eight, and so on. When the value of $\alpha > 3.56$ the sequence becomes chaotic. The trajectory takes on an apparently random, unpredictable behavior, about a chaotic attractor where a minute difference in initial starting values of two points leads to totally uncorrelated values later in time. The trajectory of the map (motion of the system) as a function of the control parameter α is illustrated in Figure 3.12. The path followed from left to right is referred to as the period doubling route to chaos. This general behavior is exhibited by many dissipative nonlinear dynamical systems irrespective of the number of dimensions. For some values of a parameter, the system will converge asymptotically to one or some number of fixed points. At other parameter values, the system will oscillate at one or several frequencies, and at other values, the system will be chaotic. The apparent random behavior of the trajectory for values of $\alpha > 3.56$ in the logistic map can be regarded as a result of the system oscillating at an infinite number of frequencies.

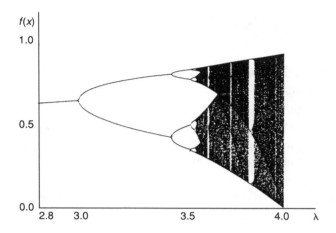

Figure 3.12   Bifurcation Diagram for the Logistic Map

It should be noted that many attractors can coexist in nonlinear systems and such systems can also have repellers or unstable limit sets (sources) the opposite of an attracting set.

Lyapunov Exponents

One of the best ways to quantitatively characterize dynamic nonlinear systems is with Lyapunov exponents. Lyapunov exponents are a measure of the rate at which trajectories diverge or contract in each dimension of phase space. As such, they give a precise definition of SDIC (and hence chaoticity) to systems. If the initial state of a system is slightly perturbed in one of the n dimensions, the exponential rate at which the perturbation increases (or decreases) with time is called the Lyapunov exponent.

Imagine a small spherical volume in phase space. The dynamics of a chaotic system will first distort the evolving spheroid into an ellipsoid shape with some directions being stretched and others contracted. The longest axis of the ellipsoid corresponds to the most unstable direction of the flow and the rate of expansion of this axis is measured by the largest Lyapunov exponent. In time, the volume of the spheroid will be distorted into an extremely complex shape. More precisely, let $r_i(0)$ be an infinitesimal radius of the initial volume and $l_i(t)$ be the length of the ith principal axis of the ellipsoid at time t. Then the ith Lyapunov exponent λ_i is defined as

$$\lambda_i = \lim_{t \to \infty} \frac{1}{t} \log_2\left(\frac{l_i(t)}{r_i(0)}\right)$$

By convention, the Lyapunov exponents are ordered such that $\lambda_1 \geq \lambda_2 \geq \ldots \geq \lambda_k$ $\geq \ldots$. The exponents measure the rate of growth of subspaces in phase space. λ_1 measures how quickly linear distances grow with time. Two points initially separated by an infinitesimal distance ε will, on average, separate at the rate $\varepsilon e^{\lambda_1 t}$. Likewise, $\lambda_1 + \lambda_2$ determines the rate at which two-dimensional areas grow, and so on. If all λ_i are negative, the attractor is a fixed point. So a three-dimensional point attractor system will have three negative Lyapunov exponents and all three-dimensions contract to a fixed point. A simple three-dimensional limit cycle system will have two negative exponents and one zero valued exponent. In case all exponents are nonnegative and zero, the attractor is a limit cycle and the number of zero exponents corresponds to the number of incommensurate frequencies in a quasiperiodic system. When at least one λ_i is positive, the dynamical system is chaotic. Typically, a three-dimensional strange attractor system will have one positive, one negative and one zero valued Lyapunov exponent each. The positive exponent characterizes the system's sensitive dependence to initial conditions and results in rapidly diverging trajectories (the negative exponent causes the diverging points to remain within range of the attractor, however).

Fractal Dimension

A sheet of paper with no thickness is an example of a two-dimensional object. If now the paper is crushed into a ball, it is no longer two-dimensional. On the other hand, it is not really three-dimensional either, but something between two and three dimensions. There are many holes and vacant spaces around the paper. In other words, it is fractional dimensioned. A *fractal* is a fractional dimensioned object as opposed to an integral dimensioned one. Fractional dimension is another important tool by which one can give a quantitative characterization to chaotic attractors. Chaotic attractors typically have fractional dimensions.

Imagine a jagged boundary in a planar region such as a coastline. What is the dimension of this boundary? If the coastline is a smooth curve, we would be inclined to say the dimension is one. If very jagged, we would assign a higher dimension, but surely not two. If not one and not two, can we measure the dimension? Consider the following approach. Take circles of radius r which are large enough to completely cover the coastline. If we successively reduce r, more and more circles of smaller size are needed. In the limit, as $r \to 0$, the number $N(r)$ of circles should be related to the true dimension D.

Let S be a set of points in Euclidean d-dimensional space, and let ε be the radius of hyperspheres in the space with which we wish to cover S. If $N(\varepsilon)$ is the number of such spheres needed to cover S, then the (possibly fractional) dimension D of the set S is given by the limit (assuming its existence):

$$D \equiv \lim_{\varepsilon \to 0} \frac{\log(N(\varepsilon))}{\log(1/\varepsilon)}$$

If S is just a single point one point will cover it, $N(\varepsilon) = 1$ and so $D = 0$. If S is a line sgement of unit length, $N(\varepsilon) = 1/\varepsilon$ and hence $D = 1$. If S is a plane of unit area, $N(\varepsilon) = 1/\varepsilon^2$ and hence $D = 2$, and so on. Thus, we see that for regular geometrical objects, D has the usual integral Euclidean dimension. For other sets, such as the logistic map chaotic attractor defined above, D will be fractional. It can be shown that the dimension in that case is approximately $D = 0.538...$ An interesting example of a three-dimensional nonlinear system with fractional chaotic attractor is given by the three differential equations of Lorentz (1989):

$$\frac{dx}{dt} = \sigma(y(t) - x(t))$$

$$\frac{dy}{dt} = -x(t)z(t) + rx(t) - y(t) \tag{3.14}$$

$$\frac{dz}{dt} = x(t)y(t) - bz(t)$$

The attractor dimension is 2.06. The Lyapunov exponents for the Lorentz attractor are known to be approximately $\lambda_1 = 1.37$, $\lambda_2 = 0.0$, and $\lambda_3 = -22.37$. In Figure 3.13 a plot of the long term orbit for the three degrees of freedom $[x(t), y(t), z(t)]$ illustrates the characteristic Lorentz attractor for parameter values $r = 40.0$, $b = 40$, and $\sigma = 16.0$.

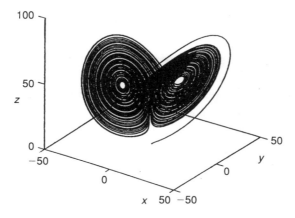

Figure 3.13   Lorentz Attractor in Three-Dimensional Phase Space

The plot of the trajectories given in Figure 3.13 comes from a direct solution to the Lorenz equations (3.14).

We should note that there are other measures (e.g. dimensions) useful in characterizing chaotic systems. They include the correlation dimension, information dimension and Lyapunov dimension. These are all measures of the disorder in a system and are closely related to the fractal dimension defined above. We omit the details here and refer the interested reader to one of the many texts now available on chaotic systems.

Embedding Dimension and Forecasting

At the beginning of this section, it was noted that many phenomena once believed to be random are actually manifestations of chaotic behavior. Since chaos is the product of a deterministically driven system it should be predictable if the nature of the dynamics are known. But how can one discover the dynamics of these complex systems, especially systems with many degrees of freedom? In this concluding section, we address this problem and look at techniques that can be applied specifically in modeling and forecasting chaotic time series.

We are interested in phenomena that are observable as they evolve through time. They are observable through a single scalar variable. For example, market price indices, exchange rates, reservoir levels, bond yields or similar phenomena can all be monitored as a sequence of equally time-spaced variables $y(t)$, $y(t + \tau)$, $y(t + 2\tau)$, ... We believe the time series is the result of a dynamical system driven by a certain number of variables and obeying some unknown dynamical laws. We would like to understand the basic relationships, at least in a qualitative way, to better model the system for predictive purposes. But with only one (or a few) variables available for analysis, how can we hope to discover the hidden relationships? This seems like an impossible task. We don't know the dimension of the system, let alone the important variables. Indeed, the dimension may be large or even infinite.

For a class of simpler systems, linear analysis methods may be sufficient to develop an acceptable model. The use of Fourier power spectra analysis or statistical autoregressive-moving-average (ARMA) methods are well-known and tested. They work well if the dynamics of the system is linear or evolving slowly in state space. These methods fail when the variables have broad spectra as found in nonlinear chaotic systems. Fortunately, some nonlinear methods have been developed to deal with the more onerous problem, at least when attractors of the systems have low dimension. If we are interested in the long term behavior of the system (not the transient behavior), some knowledge of the lower dimensional attractor may be all the information one needs. The modeling process is essentially a reconstruction of state space using the single observed variable.

A theorem due to Takens (1981) and expanded on by Mane (1981) provide a foundation for the reconstruction methods. The theorem is based on geometrical arguments and provides a method of going from a single variable to multi-dimensional state space. The theorem states that for a compact manifold A of dimension m, and for pairs $(\mathbf{F}, g)$ where $\mathbf{F}$ is a smooth vector field and g a smooth function on A, then in general the mapping

$$\Phi_{F,g}(y) : A \rightarrow \mathbf{R}^{2m+1}$$

defined by

$$\Phi_{F,g}(y) = [g(y), g(\phi_1(y)), \ldots g(\phi_m(y))]$$

is an embedding, where ϕ_i is the flow of F. An embedding is the process of mapping from single to multi-dimensional space and selecting the dimension for the space. We wish to find an embedding to learn more about the dynamics of the underlying system. Note that the functions g can be time lagged observations of a series.

What the theorem tells us is that we can reconstruct the original system behavior with state space of dimension m by forming a vector $\mathbf{s}(n)$ of dimension $(2m + 1)$ from a sequence of time lags taken from the observed one-dimensional series. Thus, we can use the lagged observations $y(n)$ to form the vector $\mathbf{s}(n)$, where

$$\mathbf{s}(n) = [y(n), y(n + \tau), \ldots, y(n + 2m\tau)]$$

to represent the dynamics of the original system. The time lag τ must be determined, although Takens and Mane suggest that any time lag will do. However, if τ is chosen too small, the lagged points will be indistinguishable from each other. On the other hand, if τ is too large, there will be no correlation (in a statistical sense) between the points. Therefore some procedure is needed to select an intermediate value of τ.

How do we determine the embedding dimension d_E? The theorem tells us it must be an integer greater than twice the attractor dimension d_A (which need not be an integer). When the dynamics of the system are known, as in the case of the Lorenz attractor described above, we simply choose a dimension $d > 2d_A$. For the Lorenz attractor, a $d_E = 5$ will suffice since it has a fractal dimension of 2.06. When d_A is not known, it must be estimated. It should be noted here that the embedding theorem gives a *sufficient* condition for d_E. Therefore, any d greater than $2d_A$ will suffice. A d_E greater than $2d_A$ will insure that the trajectory orbits are not collapsed and twisted onto themselves for this case. But choosing a d_E that is too large will introduce unnecessary noise and other contamination and hence should also be avoided. Furthermore, the computation required grows exponentially with d_E, another reason for finding a *necessary* value for d_E.

Several methods have been proposed to find estimates for d_A. For example, Abarbanel et al. (1993) describe four methods in their illuminating treatise on the analysis of chaotic data. We briefly describe one of these methods, the method of false nearest neighbors. This method is used to find an estimate for d_N, the smallest dimension necessary to properly unfold the dynamics of the system. Choosing a $d_E = d_N$ then, will give us the best choice of dimension with which to model the system. The dimension d_N is estimated using a procedure that finds the smallest dimension which eliminates all false crossings of the orbits. False crossings arise when the attractor is projected onto too small a dimensional space, thereby collapsing previously separated trajectories onto others. For example, if one visually projects the Lorenz attractor of Figure 13.13 onto two dimensions, one can see how the orbits collapse onto each other to produce false crossings, points where the trajectories touch or are very near each other.

To determine false neighbors that are a result of an insufficient choice of dimension size d, we work with the vector

$$\mathbf{s}(n) = [y(n), \, y(n + \tau), \, \ldots, \, y(n + (d - 1)\tau)]$$

For a given dimension d, this vector will have a nearest neighbor, $\mathbf{s}_{NN}$, where nearness is based on Euclidean distance. If this distance is small for dimension d, but relatively large when computed for dimension $d + 1$, we can assume the smaller neighborly distance is due to the projection from a higher-dimensional attractor down to the lower dimension d. By going to dimension $d + 1$ from d, the two points have been "unprojected" away from each other. They were, in fact, *false* neighbors. Therefore, $d + 1$ is the smallest dimension that permits unrestricted trajectories in phase space near the attractor. The procedure then is simply to begin by finding the distance for $\mathbf{s}_{NN}$ for small dimension d, then comparing that distance with the distance for $d + 1$ and so on until a sharp increase in distance occurs. At some threshold value, the jump in distance will suggest the estimated dimension is d_N.

Let R_d^2 denote the squared Euclidean distance between $\mathbf{s}(n)$ and $\mathbf{s}_{NN}$, then Abarbanel et al. (1993) have suggested a way to decide when nearest neighbors are actually false. If the absolute distance between $s(k + \tau d)$ and $\mathbf{s}_{NN}(k + \tau d)$ divided by R_d exceeds some threshold R_T, the nearest neighbors at time point k is declared false, that is, if

$$\frac{|s(k + \tau d) - \mathbf{s}_{NN}(k + \tau d)|}{R_d(k)} > R_T$$

then the nearest neighbors at time k are false neighbors. In practice, values for R_T should lie in the range $10 \leq R_T \leq 50$.

Although the above criterion may work in some cases, it is actually flawed. In determining a distance threshold with which to determine an embedding dimension, one should bear in mind that closeness is relative since distance scales relative to the dimension d and the size of the attractor. Therefore the threshold should be based not only on R_d, but also on the size of the attractor. If we estimate the attractor size R_A by the mean square variability of the observations,

$$R_A^2 = \frac{1}{N} \sum_{k=1}^{N} (s(k) - \bar{s})^2 \qquad \text{where} \quad \bar{s} = \frac{1}{N} \sum_{k=1}^{N} s(k)$$

then the suggested criteria for false neighbors is modified, such that if

$$\frac{R_{d+1}(k)}{R_A} \geq 2$$

then $s(k)$ and $\mathbf{s}_{NN}$ (both of dimension d) are declared false neighbors. Therefore, a necessary embedding dimension is $d + 1$.

When the above methods were applied to the Lorenz attractor, the number of false neighbors dropped to zero at a value of $d_N = 3$ adding some assurance that the above technique is quite powerful and does work in practice.

An example of the use of the embedding techniques described above is given in Figure 3.14, where a plot of a reconstructed Lorenz attractor for three-dimensional embedding space is illustrated.

The Lorenz attractor constructed from a three-dimensional embedding vector was constructed from the single dimension Lorenz time series as plotted in Figure 3.15.

We have not described how the time lag τ should be determined. It was noted above that although the choice of τ is not critical in the embedding theorem, some criteria should be given for its selection. Here again, various methods could be used including the autocorrelation function, but perhaps the most appropriate measure for nonlinear systems is one that is based on the use of the information theory. In particular, a measure based on mutual information is the nonlinear equivalent of the linear measure, correlation. When the two variates X and Y are completely independent, their joint probability function $P(x, y)$ factors into the two marginal probability functions $P(x)P(y)$.

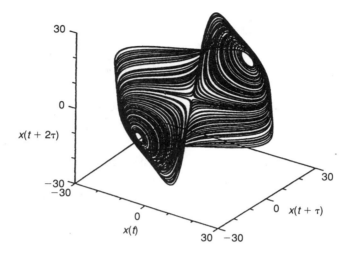

Figure 3.14   The Lorenz Attractor in Three-Dimensional Embedding Space

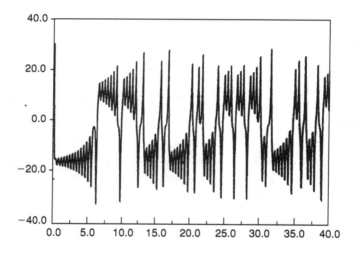

Figure 3.15   A Single Dimensional Plot of the Lorenz Time Series $x(t)$

Therefore, the mutual information between X and Y,

$$I_{XY}(x_i, y_i) = \log_2 \left[\frac{P_{XY}(x_i, y_i)}{P_X(x_i)P_Y(y_i)} \right]$$

will tend to zero as the two become less jointly dependent. When the two variates are highly correlated, the mutual information will be large. The average mutual information between X and Y is the average mutual information taken over all observations x_i, y_i,

$$I_{XY}(n) = \sum_{i=1}^{n} P_{XY}(x_i, y_i) I_{XY}(x_i, y_i)$$

This suggests using the average mutual information as a guide to the selection of τ. In this regard, if estimates of the joint and marginal probability functions for $s(k)$ and $s(k + \tau)$ can be obtained for different values of τ, one can compute the average mutual information $I(\tau)$ between the observations. At some value of τ, where the dependency between $s(k)$ and $s(k + \tau)$ is not too great nor too independent, an appropriate time lag will be found. The choice of lag then will be determined by estimating the joint and marginal probabilities for $s(k)$ at time k and $s(k + \tau)$ at time $k + \tau$ using different values of τ. The probability estimates for $P[s(k)]$, $P[s(k + \tau)]$ and $P[s(k), s(k + \tau)]$ can be obtained from histograms of the corresponding points taken in one and two dimensions, respectively and normalizing the frequency counts. This approach was used by Abarbanel et al. to determine τ for the Lorenz attractor. They chose the first minimum that occurred in a plot of the average mutual information between $s(k)$ and $s(k + \tau)$ as a function of t. A plot of $I(\tau)$ is given in Figure 3.16.

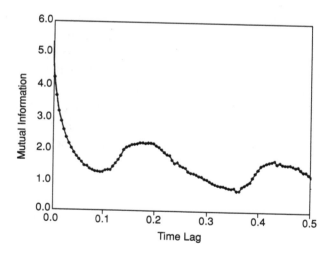

Figure 3.16   Average Mutual Information Between $s(k)$ and $s(k + \tau)$ as a Function of Time Lag

We have only briefly sketched procedures here for carrying out an embedding, but hopefully the general approach should be clear. The methods developed so far are quite powerful and offer some promise in understanding and modeling nonlinear systems dynamics.

We close this section by repeating again that chaotic behavior is deterministic and hence predictable, at least in the short term. Using the methods described in this section, chaotic systems can be characterized by invariants such as Lyapunov exponents and fractal dimensions to establish the intrinsic predictability of the system. These concepts are useful when we look at forecasting time series applications in Chapters 8 and 9.

Summary

In this chapter, we have given a review of several basic mathematical and statistical topics that are closely related to neural network theory and operation. The reviews were designed as a refresher for those who have little occasion to use mathematics and wish to reinforce their understanding of the concepts. Readers who have a good command of the subjects may wish to skim or skip the chapter altogether or make reference to specific topics as and when needed.

The first topics covered basic vector and matrix definitions and operations, including eigenvalues and eigenvectors. Also included in this section were the notions of pseudo-inverse and principal component analysis. This review was followed by two sections. The first introduced differential and integral calculus with a brief look at differential equations. The next section reviewed some basic probability and statistical theory. Following these sections, an introduction to basic definitions in information theory was given, including mutual information and relative entropy. Information theory was followed by an introduction to fuzzy set theory and fuzzy logic, a knowledge representation method that is beginning to have more and more relationship to neural networks. In the final section of the chapter, a brief introduction to nonlinear dynamical theory and the theory of chaos and related topics was covered. This material is useful in understanding the dynamics of recurrent neural networks and application areas such as prediction and time series forecasting.

Part II

Early Neural Networks and Developments

4
Early Neural Network Architectures

In Chapter 1, a simple neural computing unit was introduced and the types of computations they are capable of performing was described. In this chapter we describe some of the earliest architectures introduced. We examine their learning algorithms in detail and look at the computational capabilities and limitations of these simple networks. Much of the work reported on in this chapter was accomplished during the 1950s and 1960s, a period during which the investigation of ANN architectures began in earnest, and a period which just preceded the "cold years" of ANN research following the publication of the Minsky-Papert book on perceptrons and their computational limitations.

4.1 Introduction

Although most of the ANN architectures that were proposed and studied during the 1950s and 1960s were simple, single layer networks, the results obtained were important. Much experience was gained by those working in the field and a good foundation was laid for future researchers. During this period, early research was being carried out by Warren McCulloch and Walter Pitts (1943) on biological neuronal computations at the University of Chicago, by Donald Hebb (1949) on cognition and learning, by Frank Rosenblatt on basic artificial neural computers (1958, 1959), and by Bernard Widrow on adaptive neurons for engineering applications (Widrow, 1959 and Widrow and Hoff, 1960). (A brief history of neural network research is given in Chapter 1.) Of course, a number of other individuals made important contributions during these early years including Wilshaw and associates (1969), Karl Steinbuch (1963) and individuals such as Shun-ichi Amari (1967), James Anderson (1968), Stephen Grossberg (1969), and Teuvo Kohonen

85

(1972). The contributions of these later individuals is reviewed in subsequent chapters.

We begin this chapter with a study of two of the earliest networks. Both are single layer networks, the perceptron and the ADALINE.

4.2   Simple Perceptrons

Perceptrons were first introduced by the psychologist Frank Rosenblatt while at Cornell Aeronautical Laboratories in the mid-1950s. These networks were intended to be computational models of the retina. The input to the perceptron was an array of light sensors arranged in a rectangular grid. The sensors were randomly connected (in a localized sense) to a layer of association units (A-units) which in turn were connected to a layer of response units (R-units). The goal of the system was to activate the appropriate response unit for given input patterns or class of patterns. A simple perceptron is illustrated in Figure 4.1.

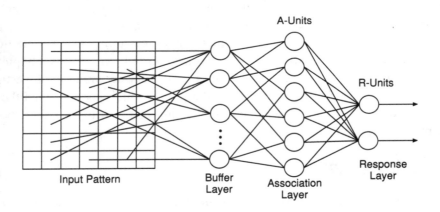

Figure 4.1   A Simple Perceptron Network

The A-units used a linear activation function whose output was passed to the R-units through trainable weights. The output from an R-unit in turn, is zero if the weighted sum inputs are equal or less than zero and equal to the weighted sum (linear function) if the inputs are greater than zero. In other versions of the perceptron, the output is a step function with binary output values (0 or 1) or bipolar values (-1, $+1$). The perceptron training algorithm is a form of supervised learning where the weights are adjusted to reduce errors whenever the network output does not match a known training target output. Rosenblatt proved that this algorithm always converged (found a set of weights) under certain conditions. He also studied a class of self-adaptable or unsupervised learning networks.

A more general multilayer perceptron network is illustrated in Figure 4.2. Many variations of the basic network have been proposed and studied over the years following its introduction by Rosenblatt. Such systems have now become practicable as pattern recognition units with the introduction of new training algorithms described in detail in Chapter 6.

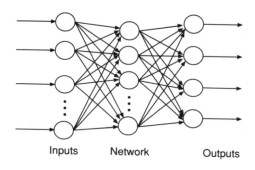

Figure 4.2   A Multilayer Feedforward Perceptron

Basic Perceptron Learning Algorithms

The original perceptron was essentially a single layer, feedforward, threshold logic unit. An equivalent network is illustrated in Figure 4.3.

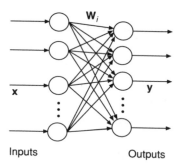

Figure 4.3   Simple Perceptron Network

The inputs, outputs and training patterns are binary valued (0 or 1) and the single layer of adjustable weights are real valued. The weights are on the connections leading to the output layer units. They are represented as a matrix of values **W**. Although there are different versions of the perceptron and corresponding learning rules, the basic rule is to alter the weights only when an error exists between the computed or actual network output and the correct or desired output. In that case, weights on active lines (inputs = 1) are incremented by a small amount when they *should be* 1 but are actually 0 (inactive), and decremented by a small amount when they are 1 (active) but *should be* 0. The amount of increment or decrement may be a fixed value or may be proportional to the product of the error and input activation.

More formally, the fixed incremental learning rule can be stated as follows.

Perceptron Learning Rule:

1. If the output is ONE and should be ONE or if the output is ZERO and should be ZERO, do nothing (no change to weights).

2. If the output is ZERO (inactive) and should be ONE (active), increment the weight values on all active input links.

3. If the output is ONE (active) and should be ZERO (inactive), decrement the weight values on all active input links.

The above algorithm can be expressed more succinctly as follows:

$$\mathbf{W}^{new} = \mathbf{W}^{old} + \Delta\mathbf{W} \tag{4.1}$$

where $\Delta\mathbf{W}$ is the change made to the weight matrix components given by

$$\Delta w_{ij} = \alpha\left(t_j^p - y_j^p\right)x_i^p = \alpha \times \text{error} \times \text{input} \tag{4.2}$$

In equation (4.2), Δw_{ij} is the change made to the weight on the connection from the ith input to the jth output unit, x_i^p is the ith input component for the pth training pattern to the neuron, t_j^p is the desired or target output value for input x_i^p, y_j^p is the actual output computed by the jth neuron when x_i^p is the input and $\alpha > 0$ is a learning rate coefficient. Thus, at the $(k + 1)$th training input, each weight w_{ij} ($i = 1, 2, ..., n, j = 1, 2, ..., m$) is updated as follows:

$$w_{ij}(k + 1) = w_{ij}(k) + \alpha x_i \qquad \text{if the output is 0 and should be 1}$$

$$w_{ij}(k + 1) = w_{ij}(k) - \alpha x_i \qquad \text{if the output is 1 and should be 0}$$
$$w_{ij}(k + 1) = w_{ij}(k) \qquad \text{if the output is correct (no change)}$$

where we have dropped the pattern superscripts p for convenience. Note that the weights are adjusted up or down in value such that the net input to the network will shift toward the value needed to produce a correct output. The rate of the adjustment is determined by the coefficient α. If α is very small, learning will proceed slowly, but stably. If α is large, learning may be fast, but could result in weight assignments that oscillate about the value needed to produce correct outputs for all training patterns.

The outputs y_j of the perceptron are given by the activation function f, where

$$y_j = f(net_j) = \begin{cases} 1 & \text{if } net_j > 0 \\ 0 & \text{otherwise} \end{cases} \qquad (4.3)$$

where net_j is the net input to the neuron, that is

$$net_j = \sum_{i=1}^{n} x_i w_{ij}$$

Some variations that have been made to this simple perceptron model are as follows: (1) the inputs to the network may be real valued, bipolar ($+1$, -1) as well as binary, (2) the outputs may be binary, bipolar or real valued, (3) the output units may have fixed-valued bias inputs (e.g $+1$) with adjustable weights, and (4) the activation functions may have a threshold parameter θ such that the step position is shifted away from the origin, thus

$$net_j = \sum_{i=1}^{n} x_i w_{ij} - \theta$$

The effects of these modifications are considered below. But first, we look at an important theorem related to the perceptron learning algorithm.

Perceptron Convergence Theorem

One of the most important achievements due to Rosenblatt is a convergence theorem for the above learning algorithm. The theorem states that if there is a set of weights that correctly classify the (linearly separable) training patterns, then the learning algorithm will find one such set $\mathbf{W}^*$ in a finite number of iterations. The assumptions here are that at least one such set of weights exist and the number of training patterns is finite. More formally, we have

Perceptron Learning—Convergence Theorem   Given a set of input vectors **x** and desired outputs t, and given that each training pattern is presented with positive probability, then the above procedure is guaranteed to converge (find weights) that give correct outputs if and only if a set of weights **W*** exist for the task.

Because of its importance, we outline a proof of the theorem here. Since the output units are independent, it is sufficient to consider a single output unit only, so now $m = 1$ and the weight matrix **W** can be expressed as an $n \times 1$ matrix or (column) vector **w**. We assume the output activation is binary valued $(0, 1)$, and, without loss of generality, we assume the initial weight vector **w**(0) is set equal to **0** and the threshold θ is also zero. Note that our weight update algorithm is now

$$\mathbf{w}^{\text{new}} = \mathbf{w}^{\text{old}} + \Delta\mathbf{w}$$

where

$$\Delta\mathbf{w} = \alpha(t - y)\mathbf{w}$$

and hence

$$\Delta w_i = \begin{cases} 0 & \text{when } t = y \\ \alpha(t - y)x_i & \text{when } t \neq y \end{cases} \tag{4.4}$$

Since learning takes place only when the output is in error, $t \neq y$, let **w**(k) denote the value of the weight matrix on the kth weight *modification* step and ignore those steps when no error occurs. Thus,

$$w_i(k + 1) = w_i(k) - \alpha(t - y)x_i = w_i(k) - \alpha\varepsilon x_i \tag{4.5}$$

or in matrix notation

$$\mathbf{w}(k + 1) = \mathbf{w}(k) + \alpha(t - y)\mathbf{x} = \mathbf{w}(k) + \alpha\varepsilon\mathbf{x} \tag{4.6}$$

where $\varepsilon = \pm 1$ is the error $(t - y)$. Now if **w*** is a solution weight matrix, there is a number such that

$$\mathbf{w}^T \cdot \mathbf{w}^* > \delta \qquad \text{when } t = 1$$
$$\mathbf{w}^T \cdot \mathbf{w}^* < -\delta \qquad \text{when } t = 0 \tag{4.7}$$

Squaring both sides of (4.6), we have

$$\mathbf{w}^2(k + 1) = \mathbf{w}^2(k) + 2\alpha\varepsilon\,\mathbf{x}^T\cdot\mathbf{w}(k) + \alpha^2\varepsilon^2\mathbf{x}^2 \qquad (4.8)$$

The middle term of the right-hand side of equation (4.8) is never positive since

$$\varepsilon = +1 \qquad \text{when } \mathbf{x}^T\cdot\mathbf{w}(k) < 0$$
$$\varepsilon = -1 \qquad \text{when } \mathbf{x}^T\cdot\mathbf{w}(k) > 0$$

Thus,

$$\mathbf{w}^2(k + 1) \le \mathbf{w}^2(k) + \alpha^2\varepsilon^2\mathbf{x}^2 \le \mathbf{w}^2(k) + \mathbf{m} \qquad (4.9)$$

where $m = \max_{\mathbf{x}}\{\alpha^2\mathbf{x}^2\}$. Also, solving the difference equation (4.6), we have

$$\mathbf{w}(k) = \mathbf{w}(0) + k\alpha\varepsilon\,\mathbf{x} = k\alpha\varepsilon\,\mathbf{x} \qquad (4.10)$$

and hence it follows that $\|\mathbf{w}(k)\|$ is bounded from above by

$$\|\mathbf{w}(k)\| \le (km)^{1/2} \qquad (4.11)$$

On the other hand, $\mathbf{w}(k)$ is bounded from below since from (4.7)

$$
\begin{aligned}
\mathbf{w}^T(k + 1)\cdot\mathbf{w}^* &= \mathbf{w}^T(k)\cdot\mathbf{w}^* + \alpha\varepsilon\,(\mathbf{x}^T\cdot\mathbf{w}^*) \\
&= \mathbf{w}^T(0)\cdot\mathbf{w}^* + k\alpha\varepsilon\,(\mathbf{x}^T\cdot\mathbf{w}^*) \\
&= k\alpha\varepsilon\,(\mathbf{x}^T\cdot\mathbf{w}^*) \ge k\alpha\delta
\end{aligned}
\qquad (4.12)
$$

Hence, using the Cauchy-Schwartz inequality (Chapter 3) and equations (4.11) and (4.12), we have

$$k\alpha\delta \le \mathbf{w}^T(k)\cdot\mathbf{w}^* \le \|\mathbf{w}(k)\|\,\|\mathbf{w}^*\| \le \|\mathbf{w}^*\|(km)^{1/2} \qquad (4.13)$$

The left-hand side of equation (4.13) grows linearly in k and hence, grows faster than the right-hand side of (4.13). Therefore, k cannot grow arbitrarily large. Only a finite number of weight updates can occur, completing the proof.

Following Rosenblatt, other researchers (e.g. Block, 1962; Minsky and Papert, 1969) have given variations on the convergence proof of the perceptron learning procedure given above. Indeed, by now the perceptron is one of the most extensively studied and best understood of all ANN architectures. Several classes of perceptrons were studied extensively by Rosenblatt and a complete book was published on issues related to perceptron capabilities and limitations by Minsky and Pappert (1969). Their treatise was an elegant account of Boolean theory, linear inequalities, and learning theory as they related to perceptrons. But its effect on promoting research was not positive. On the contrary, it effectively killed further work on perceptrons until much later.

It should be clear by now that for many tasks, a set of weights for a problem will *not* exist. In particular, perceptron learning cannot find weights that compute classification tasks that are not linearly separable such as the exclusive OR (XOR) problem as shown in Figure 4.4. This problem requires that the network learn to discriminate between input patterns of even parity (patterns with an even number of one bits, 00 and 11) and odd parity (patterns with an odd number of one bits, 01 and 10). This is an impossible task when the network can only learn to partition regions into two linearly separable spaces. [Recall from Chapter 1, that two sets are linearly separable if they can be separated by a linear surface. Sets in two-dimensional space are linearly separable if all points in the sets can be separated by a straight line (of one dimension) and, in general, sets in *n*-dimensional space are linearly separable if there is a hyperplane of dimension $n - 1$ that separates the sets. It is interesting to note that Minsky and Pappert actually used linearly separability to define perceptrons in their manuscript.] To solve the XOR parity problem requires that the network find a line separating even parity points from odd parity points:

Even Parity			Odd Parity		
0 0	0		0 1	1	
1 1	0		1 0	1	

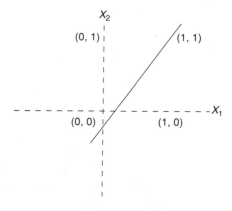

Figure 4.4   Computing the XOR Logic Problem

For linearly separable tasks, the perceptron algorithm will always find a set of weights $\mathbf{w}^*$ to do the job. The separating boundary can be portrayed for the two- and three-dimensional case. For example, given two input patterns x_1, x_2 and a bias input of $+1$,

$$net = \sum_{i=0}^{2} x_i w_i = w_0 + x_1 w_1 + x_2 w_2 \tag{4.14}$$

is the equation for a straight line

$$x_2 = -\frac{w_1}{w_2} x_1 - \frac{w_0}{w_2}$$

with slope $-w_1/w_2$ and intercept $-w_0/w_2$. Patterns that give positive values of *net* (equation (4.14)) lie on one side of the decision line and patterns that give negative values lie on the other side (Figure 4.5). The value of the intercept determines the offset displacement of the line from the origin. When $w_0 = 0$, the line passes through the origin. By an appropriate choice of weights, the line separating the plane can be placed at any orientation anywhere in the plane. This is what the perceptron algorithm does when such a set of weights exist. For an arbitrary number of inputs n, the line becomes a separating hyperplane in n-dimensional space.

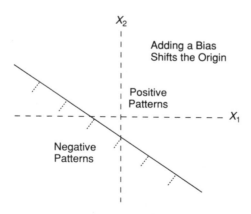

Figure 4.5   Separating Plane Classification Line

It is instructive to see the perceptron learning algorithm in operation. For this, one can quickly program any spreadsheet to implement the algorithm and adjust a set of weights for a specified training set. As an example, we train a perceptron to learn the logical AND and logical OR functions as illustrated in Figures 4.6 and 4.7. We also illustrate how the weight values oscillate indefinitely when trying to train a perceptron to learn the impossible XOR problem (Figure 4.8). There is no progressive improvement in the weight set chosen for this case.

Perceptron Learning Example											
		Bias Input X0 = ±1					Alpha = 0.05				
Input	Input				Net Sum	Target	Actual	Alpha	Weight Values		
X1	X2	1.0*W0	X1*W1	X2*W2	Input	Out	Out	*Error	W0	W1	W2
									0.1	0.1	0.1
0	0	0.10	0.00	0.00	0.10	0	1	−0.05	0.05	0.10	0.10
0	1	0.05	0.00	0.10	0.15	0	1	−0.50	−0.45	0.10	−0.40
1	0	−0.45	0.10	0.00	−0.35	0	0	0.00	−0.45	0.10	−0.40
1	1	−0.45	0.10	−0.40	−0.75	1	0	0.50	0.05	0.60	0.10
0	0	0.05	0.00	0.00	0.05	0	1	−0.50	−0.45	0.60	0.10
0	1	−0.45	0.00	0.10	−0.35	0	0	0.00	−0.45	0.60	0.10
1	0	−0.45	0.60	0.00	0.15	0	1	−0.50	−0.95	0.10	0.10
1	1	−0.95	0.10	0.10	−0.75	1	0	0.50	−0.45	0.60	0.60
0	0	−0.45	0.00	0.00	−0.45	0	0	0.00	−0.45	0.60	0.60
0	1	−0.45	0.00	0.60	0.15	0	1	−0.50	−0.95	0.60	0.10
1	0	−0.95	0.60	0.00	−0.35	0	0	0.00	−0.95	0.60	0.10
1	1	−0.95	0.60	0.10	−0.25	1	0	0.50	−0.45	1.10	0.60
0	0	−0.45	0.00	0.00	−0.45	0	0	0.00	−0.45	1.10	0.60
0	1	−0.45	0.00	0.60	0.15	0	1	−0.50	−0.95	1.10	0.10
1	0	−0.95	1.10	0.00	0.15	0	1	−0.50	−1.45	0.60	0.10
1	1	−1.45	0.60	0.10	−0.75	1	0	0.50	−0.95	1.10	0.60
0	0	−0.95	0.00	0.00	−0.95	0	0	0.00	−0.95	1.10	0.60
0	1	−0.95	0.00	0.60	−0.35	0	0	0.00	−0.95	1.10	0.60
1	0	−0.95	1.10	0.00	0.15	0	1	−0.50	−1.45	0.60	0.60
1	1	−1.45	0.60	0.60	−0.25	1	0	0.50	−0.95	1.10	1.10
0	0	−0.95	0.00	0.00	−0.95	0	0	0.00	−0.95	1.10	1.10
0	1	−0.95	0.00	1.10	0.15	0	1	−0.50	−1.45	1.10	0.60
1	0	−1.45	1.10	0.00	−0.35	0	0	0.00	−1.45	1.10	0.60
1	1	−1.45	1.10	0.60	0.25	1	1	0.00	−1.45	1.10	0.60
0	0	−1.45	0.00	0.00	−1.45	0	0	0.00	−1.45	1.10	0.60
0	1	−1.45	0.00	0.60	−0.85	0	0	0.00	−1.45	1.10	0.60
1	0	−1.45	1.10	0.00	−0.35	0	0	0.00	−1.45	1.10	0.60
1	1	−1.45	1.10	0.60	0.25	1	1	0.00	−1.45	1.10	0.60
0	0	−1.45	0.00	0.00	−1.45	0	0	0.00	−1.45	1.10	0.60
0	1	−1.45	0.00	0.60	−0.84	0	0	0.00	−1.45	1.10	0.60
1	0	−1.45	1.10	0.00	−0.35	0	0	0.00	−1.45	1.10	0.60
1	1	.45	1.10	0.60	0.25	1	1	0.00	−1.45	1.10	0.60

Figure 4.6   Perceptron Learning of the Logical AND Function

Perceptron Learning Example											
		Bias Input X0 = ±1					Alpha = 0.80				
Input	Input				Net Sum	Target	Actual	Alpha	Weight Values		
X1	X2	1.0*W0	X1*W1	X2*W2	Input	Out	Out	*Error	W0	W1	W2
									1	1	1
0	0	1.00	0.00	0.00	1.00	0	1	−0.80	0.20	1.00	1.00
0	1	0.20	0.00	1.00	1.20	1	1	0.00	0.20	1.00	1.00
1	0	0.20	1.00	0.00	1.20	1	1	0.00	0.20	1.00	1.00
1	1	0.20	1.00	1.00	2.20	1	1	0.00	0.20	1.00	1.00
0	0	0.20	0.00	0.00	0.20	0	1	−0.50	−0.30	1.00	1.00
0	1	−0.30	0.00	1.00	0.70	1	1	0.00	−0.30	1.00	1.00
1	0	−0.30	1.00	0.00	0.70	1	1	0.00	−0.30	1.00	1.00
1	1	−0.30	1.00	1.00	1.70	1	1	0.00	−0.30	1.00	1.00
0	0	−0.30	0.00	0.00	−0.30	0	0	0.00	−0.30	1.00	1.00
0	1	−0.30	0.00	1.00	0.70	1	1	0.00	−0.30	1.00	1.00
1	0	−0.30	1.00	0.00	0.70	1	1	0.00	−0.30	1.00	1.00
1	1	−0.30	1.00	1.00	1.70	1	1	0.00	−0.30	1.00	1.00
0	0	−0.30	0.00	0.00	−0.30	0	0	0.00	−0.30	1.00	1.00
0	1	−0.30	0.00	1.00	0.70	1	1	0.00	−0.30	1.00	1.00
1	0	−0.30	1.00	0.00	0.70	1	1	0.00	−0.30	1.00	1.00
1	1	−0.30	1.00	1.00	1.70	1	1	0.00	−0.30	1.00	1.00
0	0	−0.30	0.00	0.00	−0.30	0	0	0.00	−0.30	1.00	1.00
0	1	−0.30	0.00	1.00	0.70	1	1	0.00	−0.30	1.00	1.00
1	0	−0.30	1.00	0.00	0.70	1	1	0.00	−0.30	1.00	1.00
1	1	−0.30	1.00	1.00	1.70	1	1	0.00	−0.30	1.00	1.00
1	0	−0.30	0.00	0.00	−0.30	0	0	0.00	−0.30	1.00	1.00
0	1	−0.30	0.00	1.00	0.70	1	1	0.00	−0.30	1.00	1.00
1	0	−0.30	1.00	0.00	0.70	1	1	0.00	−0.30	1.00	1.00
1	1	−0.30	1.00	1.00	1.70	1	1	0.00	−0.30	1.00	1.00
0	0	−0.30	0.00	0.00	−0.30	0	0	0.00	−0.30	1.00	1.00
0	1	−0.30	0.00	1.00	0.70	1	1	0.00	−0.30	1.00	1.00
1	0	−0.30	1.00	0.00	0.70	1	1	0.00	−0.30	1.00	1.00
1	1	−0.30	1.00	1.00	1.70	1	1	0.00	−0.30	1.00	1.00
0	0	−0.30	0.00	0.00	−0.30	0	0	0.00	−0.30	1.00	1.00
0	1	−0.30	0.00	1.00	0.70	1	1	0.00	−0.30	1.00	1.00
1	0	−0.30	1.00	0.00	0.70	1	1	0.00	−0.30	1.00	1.00
1	1	−0.30	1.00	1.00	1.70	1	1	0.00	−0.30	1.00	1.00

Figure 4.7   Perceptron Learning of the Logical OR Function

Perceptron Learning Example											
		Bias Input X0 = ±1					Alpha	= 0.80			
Input	Input				Net Sum	Target	Actual	Alpha	Weight Values		
X1	X2	1.0*W0	X1*W1	X2*W2	Input	Out	Out	*Error	W0	W1	W2
									0.1	0.1	0.1
0	0	0.10	0.00	0.00	0.10	0	1	-0.20	-0.10	0.10	0.10
0	1	-0.10	0.00	0.10	0.00	1	0	0.50	0.40	0.10	0.60
1	0	0.40	0.10	0.00	0.50	1	1	0.00	0.40	0.10	0.60
1	1	0.40	0.10	0.60	1.10	0	1	-0.50	-0.10	-0.40	0.10
0	0	-0.10	0.00	0.00	-0.10	0	0	0.00	-0.10	-0.40	0.10
0	1	-0.10	0.00	0.10	0.00	1	0	0.50	0.40	-0.40	0.60
1	0	0.40	-0.40	0.00	0.00	1	0	0.50	0.90	0.10	0.60
1	1	0.90	0.10	0.60	1.60	0	1	-0.50	0.40	-0.40	0.10
0	0	0.40	0.00	0.00	0.40	0	1	-0.50	-0.10	-0.40	0.10
0	1	-0.10	0.00	0.10	0.00	1	0	0.50	0.40	-0.40	0.60
1	0	0.40	-0.40	0.00	0.00	1	0	0.50	0.90	0.10	0.60
1	1	0.90	0.10	0.60	1.60	0	1	-0.50	0.40	-0.40	0.10
0	0	0.40	0.00	0.00	0.40	0	1	-0.50	-0.10	-0.40	0.10
0	1	-0.10	0.00	0.10	0.00	1	0	0.50	0.40	-0.40	0.60
1	0	0.40	-0.40	0.00	0.00	1	0	0.50	0.90	0.10	0.60
1	1	0.90	0.10	0.60	1.60	0	1	-0.50	0.40	-0.40	0.10
0	0	0.40	0.00	0.00	0.40	0	1	-0.50	-0.10	-0.40	0.10
0	1	-0.10	0.00	0.10	0.00	1	0	0.50	0.40	-0.40	0.60
1	0	0.40	-0.40	0.00	0.00	1	0	0.50	0.90	0.10	0.60
1	1	0.90	0.10	0.60	1.60	0	1	-0.50	0.40	-0.40	0.10
0	0	0.40	0.00	0.00	0.40	0	1	-0.50	-0.10	-0.40	0.10
0	1	-0.10	0.00	0.10	0.00	1	0	0.50	0.40	-0.40	0.60
1	0	0.40	-0.40	0.00	0.00	1	0	0.50	0.90	0.10	0.60
1	1	0.90	0.10	0.60	1.60	0	1	-0.50	0.40	-0.40	0.10
0	0	0.40	0.00	0.00	0.40	0	1	-0.50	-0.10	-0.40	0.10
0	1	-0.10	0.00	0.10	0.00	1	0	0.50	0.40	-0.40	0.60
1	0	0.40	-0.40	0.00	0.00	1	0	0.50	0.90	0.10	0.60
1	1	0.90	0.10	0.60	1.60	0	1	-0.50	0.40	-0.40	0.10
0	0	0.40	0.00	0.00	0.40	0	1	-0.50	-0.10	-0.40	0.10
0	1	-0.10	0.00	0.10	0.00	1	0	0.50	0.40	-0.40	0.60
1	0	0.40	-0.40	0.00	0.00	1	0	0.50	0.90	0.10	0.60
1	1	0.90	0.10	0.60	1.60	0	1	-0.50	0.40	-0.40	0.10

Figure 4.8   Perceptron Attempt at Learning the Logical XOR Function

The Pocket Learning Algorithm

An important lesson to learn from the Perceptron learning algorithm is that the learning process should be more persistent. When a set of weights produces correct classifications, there should be some adjustment to reward the network as well. As it is, the network is only penalized when errors are produced, a form of learning by negative reinforcement. Clearly, in its present form, the algorithm should never be used for problems that are not linearly separable. Instead of finding a set of weights that are able to satisfy many, but not necessarily all of the training patterns for such problems, the algorithm will tend to wander, selecting weight sets that perform poorly, misclassifying most examples. This behavior can be seen by reviewing the weight selections during the XOR training exercise presented above in Figure 4.8, where even after some training a set of weights are chosen that misclassifies all examples. This type of behavior is what prompted Gallant (1993) to call the Perceptron learning algorithm poorly behaved. The reason for this, of course, is the algorithm does no learning when it performs well. The learning process does not reward good performance. It only penalizes bad performance.

One way to overcome this problem is to modify the algorithm to retain a separate copy of the weight set **w** during training and whenever a newly trained weight set has a longer run of correct classifications than the stored set, the stored set is replaced with the new set together with the length of run of correct classifications. Gallant (1993) calls this modified Perceptron algorithm the "pocket algorithm" since a copy of the best current weights are "held in a pocket" for later use. Another version of this algorithm, the "rachet pocket algorithm," is an improvement over the original algorithm in that both the current run of correct classifications must be longer than the pocket run and the new weights must also correctly classify more examples than the pocket weight set. The pocket algorithm has been shown to produce good weight sets for classification problems with a finite set of training examples. A convergence theorem proved by Gallant shows that the pocket weights become optimal with high probability after a finite number of iterations. Optimal is defined as a weight set that classifies the maximum possible number of examples correctly (with a linearly separable decision boundary). Comparative studies made with three classification problems have shown the pocket with rachet algorithm to be superior to Perceptron algorithm in both classification performance and stability.

Simple perceptrons have been used in various applications including pattern recognition tasks such as speech processing (Rosenblatt, 1962 and Burr, 1988), in expert systems classification tasks (Gallant, 1987), in various prediction problems, and in computer vision (Kollias and Kuppa, 1988). Since Perceptrons can, in general, be used in applications similar to the ADALINE network which is described in the following section, we give no further details of applications here.

4.3 ADALINE Neural Units

The ADALINE (ADAptive LInear NEuron) was conceived in 1959 by Bernard Widrow while at Stanford University and subsequently extended and developed by Widrow and his colleagues. It is a single, threshold logic neuron as depicted in Figure 4.9 with a bipolar output of -1 and $+1$. Inputs to the unit are also usually chosen to be bipolar. There is no restriction to bipolar. They may be binary or real valued as well. Although these units are only capable of classifying linearly separable patterns like the simple perceptron, they have been effectively used in a number of interesting engineering applications.

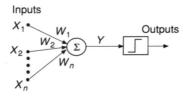

Figure 4.9   An ADALINE Processing Element

The trainable weights associated with each input link are adjusted by an adaptive learning algorithm to provide the desired output for given inputs. A bias weight w_0 is connected to a fixed input of $+1$. It acts as a threshold value for the weighted sum of the inputs. The total weighted sum of the inputs is presented to a quantizer which produces $+1$ if the input is greater than or equal to zero and a -1 if the input is less than zero. Learning rules for the ADALINE neural unit are summarized below.

Widrow-Hoff Learning Algorithms

The learning procedure introduced by Widrow and Hoff (Widrow and Hoff, 1960) is similar to the perceptron learning algorithm. The procedure, which is a form of supervised learning, is also known as the least mean square (LMS) method or the Delta Rule. It can be applied to any single layer feedforward ANN using differentiable activation functions. In the case of the ADALINE neuron, this is just an affine (linear) function, that is, the output is just $y = \mathbf{x}^T\mathbf{w} = \Sigma_i x_i w_i$, where w_i is the weight on the connection between the ith input pattern element and the single output neuron (the linear output from the neuron is sent to a threshold logic unit to obtain the final bipolar output). For a given input training pattern $\mathbf{x}$, the learning rule is given by the iterative formula

$$w_i^{new} = w_i^{old} + \alpha(t - y)x_i \qquad (4.15)$$

where α is a learning coefficient, t is the desired or target output value for the input vector $\mathbf{x}$, and y is the actual value computed by the neuron.

In the following derivation of this rule, we assume the more general case of a network consisting of n inputs to m output neurons. ADALINE learning is then a special case where $m = 1$. Thus, we wish to adjust the weights to reduce the total error E_{tot} over all output units and all training patterns $p = 1, 2, ..., P$, where

$$E_{tot} = \sum_{p=1}^{P} E^p$$

and the error for a single pattern p over all output units is given by the sum of the squared errors

$$E^p = \sum_{j=1}^{m} \left(t_j^p - y_j^p \right)^2$$

The error can be reduced by adjusting the weights in proportion to the negative of the gradient, the direction of most rapid decrease in the error function, E_{tot}, with respect to each weight change. Thus, we want an expression for the weight change Δw_{ij} proportional to the negative gradient of the error, that is

$$\Delta w_{ij} = -\eta \frac{\partial E_{tot}}{\partial w_{ij}} = -\eta \sum_{p=1}^{P} \frac{\partial E^p}{\partial w_{ij}}$$

where η is a positive constant. Taking partial derivatives of each term in the summation gives the following,

$$\frac{\partial E^p}{\partial w_{ij}} = \frac{\partial}{\partial w_{ij}} \left(\sum_{j=1}^{m} \left(t_j^p - \sum_{i=1}^{n} w_{ij} x_1^p \right)^2 \right) = -2 \sum_{j=1}^{m} \left(t_j^p - y_j^p \right) x_i^p \qquad (4.16)$$

For convenience in what follows, we omit the training pattern superscripts p. Hence, when $m = 1$ (we can drop the subscripts j) we have the simple Delta Rule for the ADALINE neuron, given by

$$\Delta w_i = \eta(t - y)x_i = \eta\varepsilon x_i \tag{4.17}$$

where the factor of 2 in (4.17) has been absorbed in the learning coefficient η and ε is the error term $(t - y)$. Note the similarity between the perceptron learning rule (equation (4.2)) and (4.17). Also note that when the inputs are chosen to be binary and $x_i = 0$ in (4.17), no learning occurs. This explains why it is more convenient to work with bipolar input vectors than binary ones. Learning never stops unless the error vanishes when bipolar inputs are used.

A "normalized" form of (4.17) is obtained by dividing the right-hand side by the squared norm of $\mathbf{x}$ to get

$$\Delta w_i = \frac{\eta\varepsilon x_i}{\|\mathbf{x}\|^2} \tag{4.18}$$

In this form, one can show that the error is reduced on the kth update by $-\eta\varepsilon_k$, that is,

$$\begin{aligned}\Delta\varepsilon_k &= \Delta(t_k - y_k) = \Delta(t_k - \mathbf{x}_k^T\mathbf{w}_k) = -\mathbf{x}_k^T\Delta\mathbf{w}_k \\ &= -\eta\varepsilon_k\mathbf{x}_k^T\mathbf{x}_k/\|\mathbf{x}_k\|^2 = -\eta\varepsilon_k\end{aligned}$$

since in vector form $\Delta\mathbf{w}_k = \eta\varepsilon_k\mathbf{x}_k/\|\mathbf{x}_k\|^2$.

The above procedures are, as noted, a form of gradient descent and, for which, convergence in $\mathbf{w}$ is assured since the error surface is a smooth paraboloid with a unique minimum (Kohonen, 1977). A solution weight matrix is one that will compute perfect input/output pattern associations when the training input patterns are linearly independent. When the inputs are not linearly independent, the actual output patterns will differ from the desired output patterns in a minimal least squares sense (as the sum of the squared errors).

Pursuing the above notions where we have linearly independent input patterns, transformations can be applied to the input and output vectors (assuming m output nodes) to obtain a change in basis. We apply transformations to get orthogonal input and output pattern basis vectors. If the resultant joint transformations are also applied to the weight matrix in the update rule, one can isolate the correlation matrix $\mathbf{C}$ for the input patterns (Stone, 1986). In this new form, it is possible to gain additional insights into the Delta Rule. We briefly sketch the process below.

Let the resultant transformation on the input patterns $\mathbf{x}$ be the matrix $\mathbf{P}$ and the transformation on the output $\mathbf{y}$ be $\mathbf{Q}$ to obtain $\mathbf{x}^* = \mathbf{Px}$, $\mathbf{y}^* = \mathbf{Qy}$. We must also apply $\mathbf{Q}$ to the target outputs $\mathbf{t}$ to get $\mathbf{t}^* = \mathbf{Qt}$. Finally, applying the joint transformation to $\mathbf{w}$, we obtain $\mathbf{w}^*\mathbf{x}^* = \mathbf{y}^*$. From this last equation, we can write

$$\mathbf{w}*\mathbf{Px} = \mathbf{Qy} \text{ and hence } \mathbf{Q}^{-1}\mathbf{w}*\mathbf{Px} = \mathbf{y} = \mathbf{wx}$$

Therefore, since $\mathbf{Q}^{-1}\mathbf{w}*\mathbf{P} = \mathbf{w}$, the transformation matrix for $\mathbf{w}$ is just $\mathbf{w}* = \mathbf{QwP}^{-1}$. Applying this transformation to the learning rule (equation (4.17) in vector form) by pre-multiplying by $\mathbf{Q}$ and post-multiplying by $\mathbf{P}^{-1}$ and simplifying, we obtain the transformed equation

$$\Delta\mathbf{w}* = \eta\varepsilon*(\mathbf{x}*)^T\mathbf{C} \tag{4.19}$$

where $\varepsilon* = (\mathbf{t}* - \mathbf{y}*)$. The matrix $\mathbf{C}$ in (4.19) holds correlational information among the original input patterns. The element in the ith row and jth column of $\mathbf{C}$ are the inner product of two patterns $\mathbf{x}_i$ and $\mathbf{x}_j$. In this form, one sees that the output produced for a given input can be interpreted as a weighted average of the target patterns. A step-by-step simulation of learning using the new basis illustrates this relationship well (Stone, 1986).

When the input patterns are random vectors drawn from any stationary distribution, it can be shown that after learning is complete, the expected value of the output computations equals the mean value of the target. Furthermore, if the inputs $\mathbf{x}$ and targets $\mathbf{t}$ are also normally distributed with zero means, it can be shown that the expected value of the weight vector $\mathbf{w}$ (in the limit) satisfies

$$E(\mathbf{y}) = E(\mathbf{t}|\mathbf{x})$$

In other words, for a particular input, the Delta Rule produces an output equal to the average of the targets for that particular input.

ADALINE Applications

These simple processing elements have been used widely in engineering applications, such as for adaptive filtering, echo suppression, pattern recognition and prediction. In adaptive filtering, the input signals are usually sampled analog values obtained from an analog-to-digital converter. The digital inputs x_k are applied to a string of serially connected delay units as illustrated in Figure 4.10 (Widrow and Winter, 1988). Each delay unit delays the signal by one sampling period. A form of ADALINE (an adaptive linear combiner) is connected to the taps between the delay units and the filtered output is a linear combination of the current and past samples. By adjusting the weights, the impulse response of the signal from input to output is controlled. Controlling the impulse response is equivalent to controlling the frequency response (the frequency response is the Fourier transform of the impulse response). For this, the weights are adjusted so the output signal

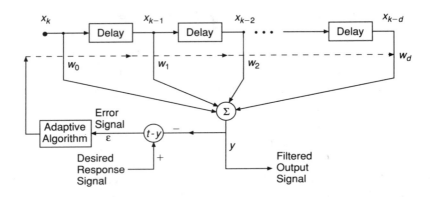

Figure 4.10   An ADALINE as an Adaptive Filter
(Adapted from Widrow and Winter, 1988. © 1988 IEEE. Courtesy of Professor Bernard Widrow.)

gives the best least-squares match over time to the desired response to the input signal.

Adaptive filters of this type can also be used to perform channel equalization to compensate for digital pulse smearing introduced by data communication circuits which have nonlinear frequency response characteristics. In this case the filter is placed directly in the communication channel to receive and equalize the smeared x_k pulses. The output of the equalizer is passed through a quantizer to restore the distorted pulse to its original shape. Without an equalizer, a typical telephone channel can only reproduce transmitted data at about 0.9 error free rates. Once an adaptive filter has been trained to cancel noise, the error rate drops to about 10^{-6} (one error per million pulses transmitted). The ADALINE can be trained to cancel noise using the actual output of the quantizer as the target output since on average the initial outputs are correct 90% of the time. Once the weights have converged, the error rate drops permitting higher transmission rates. In fact, when an equalizer is used with a modem, the permissible transmission rates are four times the rate when no equalizer is used for the same level performance. The added cost of the equalizer is a small price to pay considering the cost of transmission bandwidth.

Another interesting application of adaptive filtering is in signal prediction. In this case the current sample of a correlated analog time series is used as the desired target output and delayed (earlier) time samples become the input pattern. An example of this unit is illustrated in Figure 4.11 for the case where a single delayed sample is the input to the network.

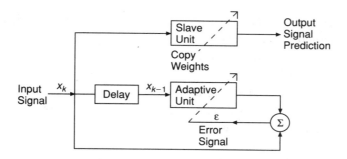

Figure 4.11   An Adaptive Predictor
(Adapted from Widrow and Winter, 1988. © 1988 IEEE. Courtesy of Professor Bernard Widrow.)

The last example of an ADALINE application is for adaptive echo cancellation in long-distance communication circuits. Simultaneous two-way communication on telephone circuits is complicated due to energy coupling between transmitter and receiver at the two ends of the long-distance circuit. The coupling results in a "reflection" of energy that results in a disruptive echo received at the transmission end. Conventional echo suppressors can provide a form of circuit switching between the two ends, but this is not equivalent to true (virtual) two-way communication. The two-way problem can be resolved through the use of adaptive echo suppressors (ADALINE units) at each end of the communication path. This process is illustrated in Figure 4.12.

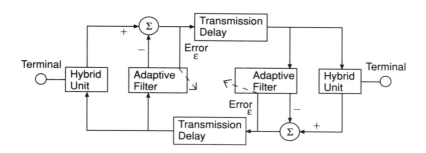

Figure 4.12   Long Distance Circuit with Echo Cancellation
(Adapted from Widrow and Winter, 1988. © 1988 IEEE. Courtesy of Professor Bernard Widrow.)

The hybrid units at each end of the communication path are transformers that are designed to prevent incoming signals from coupling over to the return transmission path. These units are designed to serve the average local telephone circuit. But, due to impedance differences in circuits, the hybrids allow some energy to be coupled to the transmission side resulting in a return echo signal. The adaptive filters compensate for the design mismatch between the hybrid transformers and differing electrical properties of the local circuits. They perform a cancellation of any signal that leaks through from the receiver to transmitter circuit, eliminating much of the echo. The use of these adaptive units are now in widespread use throughout the world.

4.4 MADALINE Networks

By combining a number of ADALINEs into a network, we create a MADALINE (Many ADALINEs) network. MADALINEs can be made up of two or more layers of ADALINEs as shown in Figure 4.13.

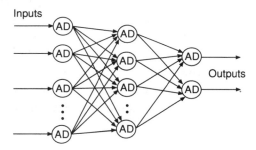

Figure 4.13   Multiple ADALINEs in a Multilayer MADALINE

The use of multiple ADALINEs to form multilayer MADALINEs is one way of overcoming the problem associated with computing mappings that require nonlinear separability. For example, by appropriate choice of weights, the two unit MADALINE of Figure 4.14 can solve the XOR problem referred to in Section 4.2. Each of the input ADALINEs has two pattern inputs and a fixed bias. The linear weighted sum of inputs is computed by each ADALINE and the result passed to a bipolar threshold unit. The two outputs are then passed to a single AND logic unit (bipolar) which produces a $+1$ when both ADALINEs have the same output and a -1 when the two outputs are different as required by the XOR problem. Figure 4.15 shows two separating boundaries which discriminates between even and odd parity for the two unit MADALINE of Figure 4.14. Even parity inputs $(-1, -1)$ and $(+1, +1)$, produce positive outputs, while odd parity inputs, $(-1, +1)$ and

$(+1, -1)$, produce negative outputs. One set of weights which produce the desired result are given in Figure 4.14. Of course, the weights are not unique.

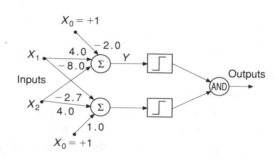

Figure 4.14   Two Unit MADALINE Capable of Solving the XOR Problem

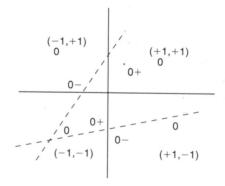

Figure 4.15   XOR Problem Solution Boundaries

The MADALINEs of the 1960s had adjustable weights in the first layer and fixed threshold units for the outputs similar to the one shown in Figure 4.14 (Widrow, 1988). Later, in the 1980s and onward, the MADALINEs had multiple layers with adjustable weights on each layer. The most recent enhancements include the use of continuous nonlinear activation functions and improved learning methods.

Learning methods for MADALINEs are a form of systematic trial and error. The general procedure is described below.

Training Algorithms for MADALINEs

The MADALINE adaptation Rule (MR) is a form of supervised learning. It is based on the notion that weights should be modified to reduce the error for the current training pattern with as little disruption to the representations learned for previous training patterns. Widrow calls this the *minimal disturbance principle.* It works in the following way.

Given an input training pattern, the procedure begins by selecting the neuron in the first layer whose output analog response is nearest zero. The weights for this neuron are changed so as to reverse the output binary response. This change is propagated to the output neurons where a check is made to see if the change reduces the total number of output errors. If so, the change is accepted. If not, the weights are restored to their previous value and the neuron in the first layer with output response next closest to zero is selected for change. This process is continued until all neurons in the first layer have been selected for adaptation. Next, pairs of neurons are selected in the first layer using the same "nearest zero" response selection criteria. The pair is adapted jointly and the output errors are then checked to see if there is a reduction in the total number. If so, the changes are accepted. If not, the weights are returned to their original values. After all pairs have been adapted, triple sets are selected for possible change if needed (in practice selection by pairs is usually adequate). After all neurons in the first layer have been checked, neurons in the second layer are selected and adapted, if necessary, following the same procedure as that used in the first layer for adaptation. This process is repeated until the output layer is reached. Training neurons in the output layer is different. These neurons can be trained using the Delta Rule or other supervised learning method since the errors are known for individual ADALINEs in this layer. Once all ADALINEs in the network have been trained for the first pattern, the second training pattern is chosen for input and the whole process repeated again. The next pattern is then chosen and so on until all patterns have been used for training. By selecting the ADALINE units with analog sums closest to zero, one is choosing a unit that can give the opposite response, and hence have the most effect on the output with the smallest change to the weights (satisfying the principle of minimal disturbance for most effect).

The MR procedure has been extended and refined over time with each new version being labeled differently (e.g. MR, MRII, MRIII). The procedure outlined above is MRII. MRIII is about the same as MRII except it is applied to multilayer networks with sigmoidal activation functions rather than threshold logic functions (Andes et al., 1990). To determine if weights for ADALINEs in any layer should be modified, an input vector **x** and desired output target vector **t** are presented to the network and the sum of the squared output errors determined. To see if the kth unit weights should be updated, its input net_k is perturbed by changing the input by a small amount Δs and observing the change in the output squared error sum

$$\Delta \varepsilon^2 = \Delta(\Sigma \varepsilon_k^2)$$

To update the weights of the selected ADALINE, the gradient of the squared error term with respect to its weight vector needs to be estimated. The estimate is then used in the update rule to reduce the error through weight adjustment. The weight adjustment we seek is based on the method of steepest descent. We first find the gradient of the squared error sum with respect to the ADALINE's weights

$$\nabla_k = \frac{\partial(\varepsilon_k^2)}{\partial w_k} = \frac{\partial(\varepsilon_k^2)}{\partial s_k}\frac{\partial s_k}{\partial w_k} = \frac{\partial(\varepsilon_k^2)}{\partial s_k}x_k \qquad (4.20)$$

Estimating derivatives with differences in the last term of equation (4.20) gives

$$\nabla_k \cong \frac{\Delta(\varepsilon_k^2)}{\Delta s}x_k$$

We now use this in the weight update rule to adjust the weights such that the error is reduced in the direction of the negative of the gradient, as given by

$$w_{k+1} = w_k - \eta\frac{\Delta(\varepsilon_k^2)}{\Delta s}x_k \qquad (4.21)$$

Equivalently, we can use

$$w_{k+1} = w_k + 2\eta\varepsilon_k\left(\frac{\Delta y_k}{\Delta s}\right)x_k \qquad (4.22)$$

which may be used, where

$$\varepsilon_k = (t_k - y_k)$$

is the error at the kth output unit and η a proportionality constant. The equivalency of (4.20) and (4.21) follows by taking the derivative of ε^2 and making appropriate substitutions. When Δs is small, the two are essentially the same and in effect, either can be replaced by a form which uses the ratio of differentials $\partial y_k/\partial s_k$ in place of differences. This gives an update rule of the following form:

$$w_{k+1} = w_k + 2\eta\varepsilon_k f'(s_k)x_k$$

where $f' = f(1 - f)$ is the derivative of a sigmoid function (see Chapter 1 or Chapter 6). It has been pointed out that this update rule is equivalent to the popular backpropagation rule derived in Chapter 6 (Widrow and Lehr, 1992). Both methods use a form of gradient descent to modify the weights and reduce the errors. In some ways however, MRIII is superior to the backpropagation method. For example, when applying backpropagation, the functional form of the neural processing, includng the activation function must be known. This is not the case in MRIII. Therefore it is possible to use MRIII training for networks in which the functional model is not fully known. This will often be the case for analog neural systems. Another important area where MRIII training can be used is in recurrent networks. These networks are difficult to train due to the feedback connections. Recurrent networks are studied in Chapters 5, 9 and 15. Unfortunately, MADALINE learning can require a large amount of computations. The learning can also get trapped in local minima of the error surface just as the backpropagation learning rule is sometimes trapped.

MADALINE networks can, as noted, be used to solve a much broader class of problems than the simple ADALINE units. We briefly describe some applications below.

MADALINE Applications

MADALINE networks are capable of learning to compute any well-behaved function. This fact has been established for the class of multilayer feedforward (MLFF) networks that are described in Chapters 6 and 7. The MLFF networks use nonlinear activation functions such as the sigmoid squashing function. MADALINE networks have the same basic architecture and perform the same transformations on the input vector when using nonlinear activation functions. Consequently, they belong to the same class of mapping networks as the MLFF networks, and hence they too are capable of being used in any application that an MLFF networks is used. In Chapter 8, several applications have been described for which MLFF networks have been employed. Multilayer MADALINEs could also be used in these same applications. Consequently, we limit the applications described here to a single application related to vision.

The application is a type of invariant pattern recognition, recognition of patterns independent of their position and orientation. This is a difficult problem. It requires that a network first learn to recognize different objects, say in some given position within a visual image, and then later be able to recognize the same objects when appearing at other locations or other orientations in the image. That is what is meant by "invariant" pattern recognition. Such a network can require many square arrays (slabs) of ADALINE neurons with special interconnections. The basic architecture as described by Widrow and Winter (1988) is outlined below.

The input layer consists of a square array of photosensitive cells. All the cells are fully connected to ADALINEs organized in a similar square array as illustrated in Figure 4.16. In Figure 4.16 we have used a 4 × 4 array for simplicity to illustrate the concepts. In practice, the size of the array will depend on the resolution required in the image.

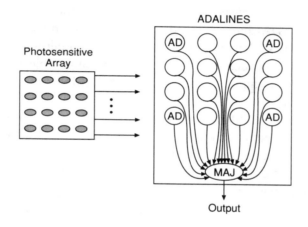

Figure 4.16   Array of Neurons for Up-Down, Left-Right Translation Invariance (Adapted from Widrow and Winter, 1988. © 1988 IEEE. Courtesy of Professor Bernard Widrow.)

The ADALINE in the upper left corner of the array has a square weight matrix W_1 on its input connections. These weights can be set equal to random values. The weights on the ADALINE just to the right of the corner ADALINE are given the same value, but transformed as a group to account for a shift of one pixel to the right. Call this transformation $T_{R1}(W_1)$ for "translate right one pixel." A translate right two pixel transformation is applied to the third ADALINE from the end in the top row. This transformation is denoted as $T_{R2}(W_1)$, and so on for the remaining ADALINEs in the top row. The transformations roll around so the weights of the last unit in the top row are a single transformation shift from the upper left corner unit. The ADALINE directly below the upper left corner ADALINE has its weights transformed to reflect a downward shift of one pixel using the transformation $T_{D1}(W_1)$. The ADALINE below this unit has its weights transformed by $T_{D2}(W_1)$

and so on. The weights on all of the first slab ADALINEs are given in the following matrix

$$
\begin{array}{cccc}
(\mathbf{W}_1) & T_{R1}(\mathbf{W}_1) & T_{R2}(\mathbf{W}_1) & T_{R3}(\mathbf{W}_1) \\
T_{D1}(\mathbf{W}_1) & T_{R1}T_{D1}(\mathbf{W}_1) & T_{R2}T_{D1}(\mathbf{W}_1) & T_{R3}T_{D1}(\mathbf{W}_1) \\
T_{D2}(\mathbf{W}_1) & T_{R1}T_{D2}(\mathbf{W}_1) & T_{R2}T_{D2}(\mathbf{W}_1) & T_{R3}T_{D2}(\mathbf{W}_1) \\
T_{D3}(\mathbf{W}_1) & T_{R1}T_{D3}(\mathbf{W}_1) & T_{R2}T_{D3}(\mathbf{W}_1) & T_{R3}T_{D3}(\mathbf{W}_1)
\end{array}
$$

The output of the ADALINEs are connected to a majority voting threshold logic unit (MAJ) so that a positive output is generated for the slab whenever one half or more of the ADALINEs respond positively to the input pattern. Since the MAJ unit treats all ADALINEs in the slab equally, the output will remain invariant to an input pattern, independently of its location. When an object is translated up-down or left-right in the input, the roles of the ADALINEs change, but the slab output remains the same.

A second slab of 16 ADALINEs is organized using the same translations as the first slab but with a different randomly set weight matrix $\mathbf{W}_2$ for the "key" values. This slab will, in general, respond to patterns differently from the first slab, but still be invariant to translations in the input pattern. Additional slabs of ADALINEs organized the same as the first two, but with different key weight matrices are also connected to the input array, and the outputs from all the slabs are connected to an adaptive MADALINE network as illustrated in Figure 4.17. The adaptive MADALINE network serves as a descrambler. It can be trained to give the appropriate response for different patterns using one of the MR training algorithms described above. The network as described can easily be manufactured since the slab translations are all the same. Only the output descrambler network requires training. The operation of the resultant network in hardware would be very fast and effective for robust invariant pattern recognition tasks.

The above ideas can be extended to invariant rotational pattern recognition through the use of a number of rotational transformations $T_{Ri}(\mathbf{W}_1)$ on the key weight matrix $\mathbf{W}_1$. Invariance to scale changes in the patterns can also be developed through similar transformations in the weight matrices. We omit the details here and refer the interested reader to the article by Widrow and Winter (1988).

We conclude this chapter by noting that analog MADALINE networks have been developed in VLSI hardware chips and are currently being used in various military applications, including missile guidance and detonation by the U.S. Naval Air Warfare Center, China Lake, California (Widrow et al., 1994).

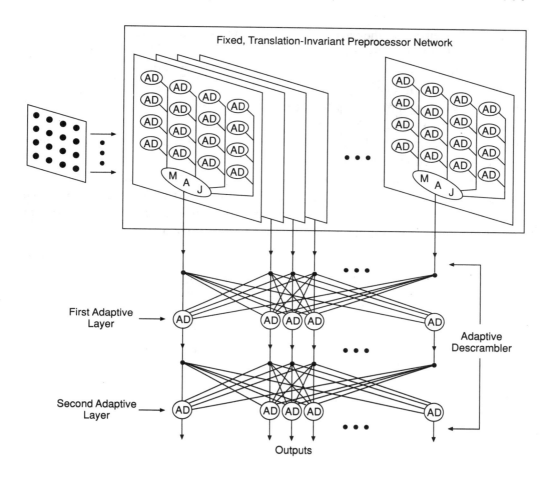

Figure 4.17   A Translation Invariant System with Adaptive Descrambler Network
(Adapted from Widrow and Winter, 1988. © 1988 IEEE. Courtesy of Professor Bernard Widrow.)

Summary

In this chapter we have introduced two classes of the earliest ANN architectures, the Perceptron and ADALINE families of neural networks. We have described two of the earliest attempts at adaptive learning algorithms, the simple Perceptron learning rule and the Widrow-Hoff or Delta learning rule. We showed that in both cases the rules would find a set of weights to perform a given set of tasks under certain conditions. Convergence of the weights for Perceptrons required that a set of weights existed. Of course the same is true of the Delta Rule which essentially requires that the training set be separable. The Delta rule will always converge to a minima, however. In addition to these single layer networks, we described a multilayer extension to the basic ADALINE network called MADALINE networks. The MADALINE networks are composed of two or more ADALINE units arranged in one or more feedforward layers. The added layers extend the computation power of these networks in that they can learn to solve nonlinearly separable classification problems. Training procedures for MADALINE networks were also given. These procedures are known as MRI, MRII, and MRIII. The procedures are a form of exhaustive trial and error by systematically modifying weight or input signal values on the ADALINE units one at a time and observing the output errors. If the errors are reduced as a result of the change, the change is accepted. Otherwise, no change in weight values are made. MRIII training is applied to MADALINE networks that use nonlinear activation functions. This form of training is equivalent to the popular backpropagation training algorithm described in Chapter 6.

5
Associative Memory Networks

Associative memory networks are simple one- or two-layer networks that store patterns for subsequent retrieval. They include the class of networks known as content addressable memories or memory devices that permit the retrieval of data from pattern keys that are based on attributes of the stored data. Associative memories were the subject of active research during the 1970s and 1980s. Although limited in application, they form an important part of the foundations of neural network architectures. In this chapter, the basic properties of associative memories are presented and several different types of memory networks are studied.

5.1   Introduction

One of the simplest but important forms of learning in humans is rote learning or memorization—storing facts or patterns in memory with little or no inferring involved. We perform this type of learning when we memorize multiplication tables. We learn by *associating* and storing in memory a pair of numbers together with their product. Recall of an associated product number is then achieved using the pair of numbers (multiplier and multiplicand) acting as retrieval keys.

Another useful form of learning is the storage and recall of data by content or degree of similarity between the input pattern and stored patterns. This is sometimes referred to as content addressable memory where the stored pattern that most closely resembles some attributes of the input pattern is retrieved. Here, "resemblance" would be defined by some measure of association such as similarity or distance between the two patterns or their attributes. For example, we recall a complete melody when hearing only a few notes or a familiar place when encountering one that is similar in some aspects.

Neural networks can also act as associative memories where some P different patterns are stored for subsequent recall. When a pattern, the input key, is presented to a loaded (prestored) network, the pattern associated with that key is output. These associative networks are simple networks that essentially have a single functional layer as illustrated in Figure 5.1. The n inputs are distributed to each of the output units through m different weight connections. Altogether, the $n \times m$ weight vector stores the associative pairs $\{(\mathbf{x}^p, \mathbf{y}^p)|p = 1, 2, ..., P\}$ in a distributed representational form.

Assuming P pairs of associated patterns have been learned by a network, the objective is simply to retrieve that pattern $\mathbf{y}^p$ which has been associated with $\mathbf{x}^p$, whenever a vector $\mathbf{x}'$ close to $\mathbf{x}^p$ is input to the network, that is whenever

$$d(\mathbf{x}', \mathbf{x}^p) = \min_q \{d(x', \mathbf{x}^q)\} \tag{5.1}$$

holds. Here, $d(\mathbf{x}, \mathbf{y})$ is the Hamming or other distance measure between the vectors $\mathbf{x}$ and $\mathbf{y}$.

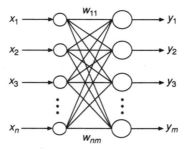

Figure 5.1   A Feedforward Associative Network

As a measure of associative network performance, it is customary to use the capacity, C. The capacity is the maximum number of distinct patterns that can be stored and retrieved with an acceptable error rate no larger than ε. We say that an error has been made whenever (5.1) is not satisfied. Note that the capacity C is given as a function of network size m, the number of functional units. All associative memory networks have severely limited storage capacities and therefore have somewhat limited applicability. Even so, they are important from a theoretical point of view and they do offer the possibility of simple hardware implementations.

Two classes of associative memory can be implemented: autoassociative and heteroassociative. Autoassociative memories recall the same pattern $\mathbf{y}$ as the input key $\mathbf{x}$, that is $\mathbf{x} = \mathbf{y}$. Actually, this type of memory is just the storage of P patterns, and not associated pairs of patterns. In heteroassociative memories however, the recalled pattern is, in general, different from the key, thus $\mathbf{x} \neq \mathbf{y}$. Clearly, in this case, pairs of associated patterns are being stored.

One might question the usefulness of autoassociative memories. Indeed, why recall an already known input pattern? In spite of this seemingly useless task, there are applications for such memories, particularly where a noisy or partially complete pattern is the only available key and the recalled pattern is the original, complete, non-noisy pattern. For example, in vision applications, the input image may contain partially occluded objects or be corrupted with noise or system distortion and the objective is to recall original, complete objects with no loss or distortion. Likewise, in data communications applications, transmitted patterns may be corrupted with channel noise and the objective is one of error correction—to recover the original signals that were transmitted by the source. In both of the above cases, original patterns are recovered from imperfect key patterns through suppression of noise or by pattern completion by the network.

One of the simplest types of associative networks is the linear associator. Such networks are of the feedforward type where the recalled vector $\mathbf{y}$ is computed from the input vector $\mathbf{x}$ in a single feedforward operation. A second type of associative network is the recurrent feedback type which has the output from one or more units connected back to unit inputs. These networks recall the output pattern after a cyclical recursive computation where the output is mixed with the input until the network becomes stable. Recurrent networks have dynamics that differ significantly from static feedforward networks. Three types of recurrent associative networks are described in Sections 5.5, 5.6 and 5.7.

With one exception, we consider only single layer networks with n inputs and m outputs in the remainder of this chapter. (The single exception is the BAM network described in Section 5.6.) For linear associators, the input to the jth unit is given by

$$net_j = \sum_{i=1}^{n} w_{ij}x_j = \mathbf{w}_i \cdot \mathbf{x} \tag{5.2}$$

where $\mathbf{x}$ is the input vector and $\mathbf{w}_i$ is the ith row of the weight matrix $\mathbf{W}$.

One might question whether some advantage can be gained through the use of multiple layers in such networks. Recall from previous chapters that single layer networks such as the perceptron are limited in their computational power to linearly separable classification tasks. Multiple layered networks with nonlinear activation functions such as the MADALINE or multilayer perceptrons, on the other hand, are capable of learning much more complex decision regions. The answer is that for linear associaters no added capacity or power is gained through the use of multiple layers. Clearly, in such networks, multiple linear transformations are equivalent to a single linear transformation. For example, in a two-layer network with input vector $\mathbf{x}$ and weight matrix $\mathbf{U}$, the output from the first layer is $\mathbf{y} = \mathbf{Ux}$. If now the output $\mathbf{y}$ is used as the input vector to a second layer with weight matrix $\mathbf{V}$ and corresponding output $\mathbf{z}$, we have $\mathbf{z} = \mathbf{Vy} = \mathbf{VUx} = \mathbf{Wx}$ where $\mathbf{W}$ is the product matrix $\mathbf{VU}$. This result extends to any number of layers: multiple linear transformations are equivalent to a single linear transformation. Nothing is gained through the use of two or more layers when intermediate layer activations are all linear.

5.2 Learning Algorithms for Associative Memories

Assuming a single layer network with weight matrix $\mathbf{W}$, the next question is how to determine the weight values to achieve effective storage (high capacity C) and accurate retrieval. We consider the three most commonly used approaches. The first method we consider is Hebb's Rule.

Hebb's Learning Rule

Hebb's simple learning rule served as a model for a number of associative memory ANNs. Remember that simple Hebbian learning is based on the notion that the change in synoptic strengths (weights) of a neuron is proportional to the pre- (input) and post- (output) synoptic excitations. In other words, if the input to a group of neurons is $\mathbf{x}$ and the output excitations are $\mathbf{y} = \mathbf{y}(\mathbf{x})$, then the synoptic weight values w_{ij} are given by

$$w_{ij} = \alpha x_i y_j \qquad (5.3)$$

where α is a proportionality or normalizing constant. In matrix notation (5.3) can be written as

$$\mathbf{W} = \alpha \mathbf{y}(\mathbf{x})^T \qquad (5.4)$$

where the vector product on the right-hand side is the outer product. The weight matrix $\mathbf{W}$ in (5.4) stores only a single pattern pair $(\mathbf{x}^p, \mathbf{y}^p)$, the pth pattern, so more correctly, (5.4) should be written as

$$\mathbf{W}^p = \alpha \mathbf{y}^p(\mathbf{x}^p)^T$$

to indicate that the pth pattern pair has been stored. To store multiple patterns, the individual patterns are superimposed by simply adding the individual pattern matrices

$$\mathbf{W} = \sum_{p=1}^{p} \mathbf{W}^p$$

Initially, the weights are all set to zero and the components of the matrix $\mathbf{W}$ are developed using the superimposition relationship

$$w_{ij}^{new} = w_{ij}^{old} + \alpha x_i^p y_j^p$$

for $p = 1, 2, ..., P$.

From (5.3) and (5.4) we see that Hebb's rule is essentially a covariance or correlation relationship between input and output patterns. Therefore, to implement Hebb's rule requires that both input and output patterns be available. Note that when using this rule for network learning, we will want to use the desired or *target* outputs to associate (correlate) with $\mathbf{x}^p$, rather than a computed output $\mathbf{y}^p$ which could differ from the target. Therefore, in what follows, we shall continue to use $\mathbf{x}^p$ to denote the input vector for the pth pattern, $\mathbf{y}^p$ to represent the actual output vector computed by the network given input $\mathbf{x}^p$, and $\mathbf{t}^p$ will denote the target or desired output given input $\mathbf{x}^p$. This rule will be applied to various associative networks in subsequent sections. It has the property that perfect retrieval can be achieved when the input patterns are mutually orthogonal. Less than perfect retrieval will be realized when the input vectors are not orthogonal. The amount of degradation in storage capacity depends on the degree of correlation among the input vectors. Hebb's rule is relatively easy to compute since the individual weights are dependent only on local terms and not on other weights. However, the utility of the rule depends on the degree of correlation between the input patterns as shown below. Also, there is a potential problem with the simple form of Hebbian learning. Referring to equation (5.3), it should be clear if α is a constant, there is nothing to prevent the weights from growing without bound unless some constraints are placed on the input pattern values or on the weight values. This has led to several modifications to Hebb's simple learning rule. The modifications include the addition of a forgetting term, forming products of the x and y signal strengths about their mean values (true covariance values), combining signal strengths with changes in signal strengths, and so on. These variations are reviewed in Tesauro (1986).

Delta Rule Learning

Another possible learning approach for associative memories is based on iterative gradient descent such as performed with the Widrow-Hoff or Delta Rule where weights are adjusted to minimize the squared errors over all patterns (see Section 4.3 for a derivation of the Delta Rule). Using (5.2) for inputs and identity linear activation functions, $f(x) = x$, the jth unit output is just

$$y_j^p = \sum_{i=1}^{n} w_{ij} x_i^p$$

and hence, the total network error over all m output units and all P patterns, is just

$$E_{\text{tot}} = \sum_{p=1}^{P} E^p = \sum_{p=1}^{P} \sum_{j=1}^{m} \left(t_j^p - \sum_{i=1}^{n} w_{ij} x_i^p \right)^2 \tag{5.5}$$

The weights w_{ij} are adjusted to reduce the total error in the direction of the negative gradient. This is given by a solution to the following set of equations

$$\Delta w_{ij} = -\alpha \frac{\partial E_{tot}}{\partial w_{ij}}$$

The solution is the resultant Delta Rule, which in component form is

$$w_{ij}^{\text{new}} = w_{ij}^{\text{old}} + \alpha \left(t_j^p - y_j^p \right) x_i^p$$

or in matrix notation, we have

$$\Delta \mathbf{W} = \alpha \sum_{p=1}^{P} (\mathbf{t}^p - \mathbf{W}\mathbf{x}^p)(\mathbf{x}^p)^T \tag{5.6}$$

The Delta Rule is an effective rule to apply to associative memory learning since it finds a set of weights that insures accurate retrieval when the input patterns form a linearly independent set and the errors are minimized even when the input patterns are not linearly independent. The Delta Rule solution matrix will always be unique.

Pseudo-inverse as Learning

There is still another approach which can be applied to minimize the total error in retrieved patterns. In this case the weight matrix is obtained by direct computation using the pseudo-inverse of the input pattern matrix. The input matrix is the $n \times P$ matrix $\mathbf{X}$ consisting of P columns of pattern vectors $\mathbf{x}^p$, where each vector is n-dimensional. In Chapter 3 the pseudo-inverse of a matrix is derived and it is shown that the pseudo-inverse of $\mathbf{X}$ (denoted as $\tilde{\mathbf{X}}$) always exists, even when $\mathbf{X}$ is a nonsquare matrix. Thus, one can compute directly the pseudo-inverse $\tilde{\mathbf{X}}$ to solve the linear system of equations

$$\mathbf{WX} = \mathbf{T}$$

where $\mathbf{T}$ is the matrix of target vectors associated with the input matrix $\mathbf{X}$. The solution matrix is given by

$$\mathbf{W} = \mathbf{T}\tilde{\mathbf{X}}$$

where (as derived in Section 3.1)

$$\mathbf{W} = \lim_{\lambda \to 0} \left[\mathbf{TX}^T (\mathbf{XX}^T + \lambda \mathbf{1})^{-1} \right] = \mathbf{T}\tilde{\mathbf{X}} \tag{5.7}$$

The solution matrix $\mathbf{W}$, equation (5.7) gives a least squares solution in the sense of retrieval errors the same as the Delta Rule when the input vectors form a linearly independent set. When more than one solution exists, the pseudo-inverse will be the one with the smallest sum of squares. When $\mathbf{X}$ has a normal inverse, $\mathbf{X}^{-1}$, the pseudo-inverse will be identical to $\mathbf{X}^{-1}$. This method is not computationally appealing, however, since to compute each weight all other weights must be used. They are all interdependent.

Associative memories have been studied by several researchers. For a comprehensive description see Anderson et al. (1977) and Kohonen (1984). In the following section, heteroassociative memories and their corresponding learning algorithms are presented. Examples of simple networks using Hebbian learning are presented to demonstrate the basic operation and storage capabilities. In Section 5.4 autoassociative memory networks are described and in subsequent sections, special recurrent network types are considered, including Hopfield networks, Bidirectional Associative Memory (BAM) networks, and the Brain-State-in-a-Box (BSB).

5.3   Feedforward Heteroassociative Memory Networks

Feedforward heteroassociative networks store pairs of patterns $(\mathbf{x}, \mathbf{t})$, where in general, $\mathbf{x} \neq \mathbf{t}$. Let $\mathbf{x}^p$ and $\mathbf{t}^p$ $(p = 1, 2, ..., P)$ denote pattern pairs to be associated where $\mathbf{x}^p$ is n-dimensional and $\mathbf{t}^p$ m-dimensional vectors, respectively (Figure 5.2). The objective is to retrieve pattern $\mathbf{y}^p$ where $\mathbf{y}^p = \mathbf{t}^p$ whenever $\mathbf{x}^p$ is input to the network.

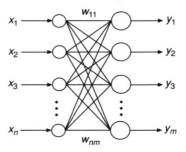

Figure 5.2   Heteroassociative Memory Network

In the spirit of Hebbian learning described above, one can compute directly an outer product or correlation matrix $\mathbf{W}^p$ for the pair of patterns to be associated, $(\mathbf{x}^p, \mathbf{t}^p)$, where

$$\mathbf{W}^p = \mathbf{t}^p(\mathbf{x}^p)^T \tag{5.8}$$

Note that the ijth element of $\mathbf{W}^p$ in (5.8) is just $w_{ij}^p = t_j^p x_i^p$. To retrieve the single pattern $\mathbf{t}^p$ from $\mathbf{W}^p$, given input pattern $\mathbf{x}^p$, we use linear inputs to the network units (equation (5.2) or in matrix notation $\mathbf{W}^p\mathbf{x}^p$) and the identity activation functions for outputs, $f(x) = x$. In this case, retrieval of $\mathbf{t}^p$ can be accomplished directly if the $\mathbf{x}^p$ patterns are normalized, that is if $\|\mathbf{x}^p\|^2$, since then

$$\mathbf{W}^p\mathbf{x}^p = \mathbf{t}^p(\mathbf{x}^p)^T \cdot \mathbf{x}^p = \mathbf{t}^p$$

Of course, we want to store more than a single pattern. We do this by computing the outer product matrix $\mathbf{W}^p$ for each $p = 1, 2, ..., P$. The individual pattern matrices $\mathbf{W}^p$ can then be superimposed to store P patterns in the resultant $m \times n$ matrix $\mathbf{W}$, where

$$\mathbf{W} = \sum_{p=1}^{P} \mathbf{W}^p$$

In component form, this is just

$$w_{ij} = \sum_{p=1}^{P} w_{ij}^p = \sum_{p=1}^{P} t_j^p x_i^p$$

To retrieve the pattern $\mathbf{t}^k$, the associated pattern $\mathbf{x}^k$ is input to the network, thus

$$\mathbf{W}\mathbf{x}^k = \left(\sum_{p=1}^{P} \mathbf{t}^p(\mathbf{x}^p)^T \right) \cdot \mathbf{x}^k = \mathbf{t}^k(\mathbf{x}^k)^T \cdot \mathbf{x}^k + \sum_{p \neq k}^{P} \mathbf{t}^p(\mathbf{x}^p)^T \cdot \mathbf{x}^k \qquad (5.9)$$

Now the first term on the right-hand side of (5.9) is equal to $\mathbf{t}^k$ provided the scalar product $(\mathbf{x}^k)^T \cdot \mathbf{x}^k$ is one. Again, this will be the case if the $\mathbf{x}$ vectors are normalized, $\|\mathbf{x}^p\| = 1$. Furthermore, the second term on the right-hand side of (5.9) is zero provided the $\mathbf{x}$ vectors are mutually orthogonal, that is if $(\mathbf{x}^p)^T \cdot \mathbf{x}^k = 0$ for all $p \neq k$. In other words, the network gives perfect recall if the input patterns are pairwise orthonormal. Of course, the maximum number of patterns that can be stored is $m \leq n$ since the maximum number of mutually orthogonal vectors in an n-dimensional space is n.

Even when the input vectors are not orthogonal, accurate recall is still possible if the $\mathbf{x}$ vectors are normalized and the second term on the right-hand side of (5.9), the "crosstalk term," is small compared to the $\mathbf{t}^k$ term. This will be the case when the input vectors are nearly orthogonal or only slightly correlated with each other. When the input vectors are correlated, the crosstalk term sets limits on the storage capacity and erroneous retrievals may result, such that $\mathbf{y}^k \neq \mathbf{t}^k$. Of course, the other learning methods described in the previous section can also be used to determine the weight vector with resultant improvement in accuracy and/or capacity when the input vectors are not orthogonal.

Next, we consider an example of a simple heteroassociative network to illustrate the above concepts. For this, any one of the learning methods described above can be used (e.g. Hebbian learning). We also use bipolar input and corresponding target patterns. Thus, the bipolar activation function for the jth unit output is given by

$$y_j = \text{sgn}\left(\sum_{i=1}^{n} w_{ij} x_i \right) = \begin{cases} +1 & \text{if } w_{ij}x_i \geq 0 \\ -1 & \text{otherwise} \end{cases} \qquad (5.10)$$

Using input and output dimensions of $n = 4$ and $m = 3$ for our example, assume the following input-to-output associations are to be learned:

$$\mathbf{x}^1 = \begin{bmatrix} +1 \\ -1 \\ -1 \\ -1 \end{bmatrix} \quad \mathbf{x}^2 = \begin{bmatrix} -1 \\ +1 \\ +1 \\ -1 \end{bmatrix} \quad \mathbf{x}^3 = \begin{bmatrix} -1 \\ -1 \\ +1 \\ +1 \end{bmatrix} \quad \mathbf{x}^4 = \begin{bmatrix} -1 \\ -1 \\ -1 \\ +1 \end{bmatrix}$$

$$\mathbf{t}^1 = \begin{bmatrix} +1 \\ -1 \\ -1 \end{bmatrix} \quad \mathbf{t}^2 = \begin{bmatrix} -1 \\ +1 \\ -1 \end{bmatrix} \quad \mathbf{t}^3 = \begin{bmatrix} -1 \\ -1 \\ +1 \end{bmatrix} \quad \mathbf{t}^4 = \begin{bmatrix} +1 \\ -1 \\ +1 \end{bmatrix}$$

The four corresponding weight matrices for the four non-orthogonal $(\mathbf{x}, \mathbf{t})$ associations are easily computed (for simplicity, the abbreviated forms $+ \equiv +1$ and $- \equiv -1$ are used in the following computations).

$$\mathbf{W}^1 = \mathbf{t}^1(\mathbf{x}^1)^\mathbf{T} = \begin{bmatrix} + \\ - \\ - \end{bmatrix}[+ \; - \; - \; -] = \begin{bmatrix} + & - & - & - \\ - & + & + & + \\ - & + & + & + \end{bmatrix}$$

$$\mathbf{W}^2 = \begin{bmatrix} - \\ + \\ - \end{bmatrix}[- \; + \; + \; -] = \begin{bmatrix} + & - & - & + \\ - & + & + & - \\ + & - & - & + \end{bmatrix}$$

$$\mathbf{W}^3 = \begin{bmatrix} - \\ - \\ + \end{bmatrix}[- \; - \; + \; +] = \begin{bmatrix} + & + & - & - \\ + & + & - & - \\ - & - & + & + \end{bmatrix}$$

$$\mathbf{W}^4 = \begin{bmatrix} + \\ - \\ + \end{bmatrix}[- \; - \; - \; +] = \begin{bmatrix} - & - & - & + \\ + & + & + & - \\ - & - & - & + \end{bmatrix}$$

The final weight matrix $\mathbf{W}$ is just the sum of the four pattern matrices:

$$\mathbf{W} = \mathbf{W}^1 + \mathbf{W}^2 + \mathbf{W}^3 + \mathbf{W}^4 = \begin{bmatrix} 2 & -2 & -4 & 0 \\ 0 & 4 & 2 & -2 \\ -2 & -2 & 0 & 4 \end{bmatrix}$$

To retrieve each associated pattern, one can readily compute the following $\mathbf{y}^k$ vectors ($k = 1, 2, 3, 4$) where use has been made of (5.10).

$$\mathbf{W}\mathbf{x}^1 = \begin{bmatrix} 2 & -2 & -4 & 0 \\ 0 & 4 & 2 & -2 \\ -2 & -2 & 0 & 4 \end{bmatrix} \begin{bmatrix} +1 \\ -1 \\ -1 \\ -1 \end{bmatrix} = \begin{bmatrix} +8 \\ -4 \\ -4 \end{bmatrix} \quad \text{Thus, } \mathbf{y}^1 = \mathrm{sgn}\left(\begin{bmatrix} +8 \\ -4 \\ -4 \end{bmatrix} \right) = \begin{bmatrix} +1 \\ -1 \\ -1 \end{bmatrix}$$

and similarly,

$$\mathbf{y}^2 = \begin{bmatrix} -1 \\ +1 \\ -1 \end{bmatrix} \qquad \mathbf{y}^3 = \begin{bmatrix} -1 \\ -1 \\ +1 \end{bmatrix} \qquad \mathbf{y}^4 = \begin{bmatrix} +1 \\ -1 \\ +1 \end{bmatrix}$$

Note that all four patterns retrieved ($\mathbf{y}^1 - \mathbf{y}^4$) are correct. This might be expected since the $\mathbf{x}^i$ vectors are linearly independent even though they are not orthogonal. The reader is urged to construct another example where the input vectors are linearly dependent and compare the performance with the above example.

We close this section by noting that use of bipolar representation is computationally preferable to binary patterns and generally gives better performance.

5.4 Feedforward Autoassociative Memory Networks

Feedforward autoassociative networks are a special case of the heteroassociative networks of the previous section. They store patterns $(\mathbf{x}, \mathbf{t})$, where now $\mathbf{x} = \mathbf{t}$ and $m = n$. For autoassociative memory applications, the objective is to retrieve original patterns $\mathbf{x}^p$ from noisy or incomplete input patterns $\mathbf{x}' = \mathbf{x}^p + \eta$ where η represents some form of distortion or noise.

Since autoassociative networks are special cases of heteroassociative networks, all of the characteristics of heteroassociative networks hold for autoassociative networks. In particular, the networks give perfect recall if the input patterns are pairwise orthonormal and the maximum number of patterns that can be stored is n. Practically, less than n orthogonal patterns should be stored and not the maximum. When n patterns are stored, the networks are unable to generalize. Every state is stable and the network remains where it starts. It fails to generalize and hence, is unable to recover noisy or partially incomplete patterns, thereby failing to meet the operational objective.

As in the case of heteroassociative networks, any of the three learning methods described in Section 5.2 can also be used for autoassociative networks. We consider a simple example of these memories to illustrate their operation. For this, Hebbian learning is used as in the previous section. We also use bipolar input and corresponding target patterns (equation (5.10)). In this example we use the following four input vectors of dimension $n = 5$.

$$\mathbf{x}^1 = \begin{bmatrix} +1 \\ +1 \\ +1 \\ +1 \\ -1 \end{bmatrix} \quad \mathbf{x}^2 = \begin{bmatrix} -1 \\ +1 \\ -1 \\ +1 \\ -1 \end{bmatrix} \quad \mathbf{x}^3 = \begin{bmatrix} +1 \\ +1 \\ -1 \\ -1 \\ +1 \end{bmatrix} \quad \mathbf{x}^4 = \begin{bmatrix} +1 \\ +1 \\ +1 \\ -1 \\ -1 \end{bmatrix}$$

The weight matrix for pattern $\mathbf{x}^1$ is readily computed as the outer product (for simplicity, the abbreviated forms $+ \equiv +1$ and $- \equiv -1$ are used interchangeably in the following).

$$\mathbf{W}^1 = \mathbf{t}^1(\mathbf{x}^1)^{\mathbf{T}} = \begin{bmatrix} +1 \\ +1 \\ +1 \\ +1 \\ -1 \end{bmatrix} [+1\ +1\ +1\ -1] = \begin{bmatrix} + & + & + & + & - \\ + & + & + & + & - \\ + & + & + & + & - \\ + & + & + & + & - \\ - & - & - & - & + \end{bmatrix}$$

The remaining weight matrices are also easily computed. They are

$$\mathbf{W}^2 = \begin{bmatrix} + & - & + & - & + \\ - & + & - & + & - \\ + & - & + & - & + \\ - & + & - & + & - \\ + & - & + & - & + \end{bmatrix} \quad \mathbf{W}^3 = \begin{bmatrix} + & + & - & - & + \\ + & + & - & - & + \\ - & - & + & + & - \\ - & - & + & + & - \\ + & + & - & - & + \end{bmatrix} \quad \mathbf{W}^4 = \begin{bmatrix} + & + & + & - & - \\ + & + & + & - & - \\ + & + & + & - & - \\ - & - & - & + & + \\ - & - & - & + & + \end{bmatrix}$$

The final 5×5 network weight matrix $\mathbf{W}$, which is the sum of the four corresponding matrices for the four $(\mathbf{x} = \mathbf{t})$ associations, is just

$$\mathbf{W} = \mathbf{W}^1 + \mathbf{W}^2 + \mathbf{W}^3 + \mathbf{W}^4 = \begin{bmatrix} 4 & 2 & 2 & -2 & 0 \\ 2 & 4 & 0 & 0 & -2 \\ 2 & 0 & 4 & 0 & -2 \\ -2 & 0 & 0 & 4 & -2 \\ 0 & -2 & -2 & -2 & 4 \end{bmatrix}$$

To retrieve each of the stored patterns, one first computes the inputs $\mathbf{W}\mathbf{x}^k$ ($k = 1$, 2, 3, 4). For example, to retrieve $\mathbf{x}^4$ we find

$$\mathbf{Wx}^4 = \begin{bmatrix} 4 & 2 & 2 & -2 & 0 \\ 2 & 4 & 0 & 0 & -2 \\ 2 & 0 & 4 & 0 & -2 \\ -2 & 0 & 0 & 4 & -2 \\ 0 & -2 & -2 & -2 & 4 \end{bmatrix}\begin{bmatrix} + \\ + \\ + \\ - \\ - \end{bmatrix} = \begin{bmatrix} 6 \\ 8 \\ 8 \\ -4 \\ -6 \end{bmatrix} \quad \text{Thus, } \mathbf{x}^4 = \text{sgn}\left(\begin{bmatrix} 6 \\ 8 \\ 8 \\ -4 \\ -6 \end{bmatrix}\right) = \begin{bmatrix} + \\ + \\ + \\ - \\ - \end{bmatrix}$$

The other $\mathbf{x}^k$ vectors are retrievable from similar computations. A more interesting attempt, however, is a noisy input version of $\mathbf{x}^4$—by perturbing $\mathbf{x}^4$ by one bit (the third bit) to give

$$\mathbf{x}^* = \begin{bmatrix} +1 \\ +1 \\ -1 \\ -1 \\ -1 \end{bmatrix}$$

as input. Note that this is also a noisy $\mathbf{x}^3$ with a single bit perturbed. We have for the retrieval computation

$$\mathbf{Wx}^* = \begin{bmatrix} 4 & 2 & 2 & -2 & 0 \\ 2 & 4 & 0 & 0 & -2 \\ 2 & 0 & 4 & 0 & -2 \\ -2 & 0 & 0 & 4 & -2 \\ 0 & -2 & -2 & -2 & 4 \end{bmatrix}\begin{bmatrix} + \\ + \\ - \\ - \\ - \end{bmatrix} = \begin{bmatrix} 6 \\ 8 \\ 0 \\ -4 \\ -2 \end{bmatrix} \quad \text{Thus, } \mathbf{y}^1 = \text{sgn}\left(\begin{bmatrix} 6 \\ 8 \\ 0 \\ -4 \\ -2 \end{bmatrix}\right) = \begin{bmatrix} + \\ + \\ + \\ - \\ - \end{bmatrix}$$

This completes our study of feedforward associative networks. In the following three sections we examine networks with dynamics that differ significantly from these static networks. They are recursive networks that have feedback connections which result in repeated computations on the input and computed output patterns. We begin with a description of Hopfield networks.

5.5 Hopfield Networks

Hopfield networks are single layer recurrent networks with symmetric weight matrices in which the diagonal elements are all zero. (The diagonal elements need not be zero, but we assume that is the case since the performance is improved when taken to be zero.) Thus, for a Hopfield network with weight matrix $\mathbf{W}$, $w_{ij} = w_{ji}$ and $w_{ii} = 0$ for all $i, j = 1, 2, ..., n$. An example of a Hopfield network is given in Figure 5.3. Note that the input and output connection structure resembles a crossbar switch arrangement from which the name crossbar associative networks is

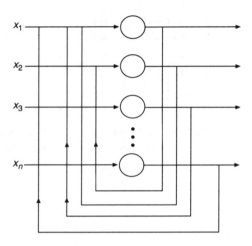

Figure 5.3   Example of a Hopfield Network

sometimes used. Because of their simplicity, one might wonder how such a network can produce an output different from the input. This comes about through the recursive operation of the network as described below.

Hopfield networks store some number P of prototype patterns called fixed-point attractors. The locations of the attractors are determined by the weight matrix $\mathbf{W}$. The stored patterns may be specified by computing them directly such as with Hebbian learning or they may be learned through some gradient descent update scheme such as the Delta Rule.

Once a network has learned P prototype patterns $\mathbf{x}^1$, $\mathbf{x}^2$, ..., $\mathbf{x}^P$, they may be used for associative recall. To recall a pattern $\mathbf{x}^k$, the network operates recursively by feeding the output signals of the network back to the inputs repeatedly at each update time point t until the network finally stabilizes. Starting at some initial arbitrary state, an input signal $\mathbf{x}(0)$ is "clamped" onto the input connections at time 0, and the outputs are then computed by the units. For discrete-time systems, the outputs are determined by the difference equations

$$x_i(t + 1) = \text{sgn}\left(\sum_{j=1}^{n} w_{ij} x_j(t) - \theta \right) \tag{5.11}$$

for $i = 1, 2, ..., n$, where the threshold is a positive constant or zero and where we use the bipolar activation functional form, $x_i \in \{-1, +1\}$ with

$$\text{sgn}(x) = \begin{cases} +1 & \text{if } x > 0 \\ -1 & \text{if } x < 0 \end{cases} \tag{5.12}$$

and by convention

$$x_i(t + 1) = x_i(t) \text{ if } x = 0.$$

Starting with a vector **x** as input, the outputs are computed according to (5.12) and fed back to add to the inputs through some updating scheme. New outputs are then computed and fed back to add to the inputs in the next time increment. This process is repeated recursively until the network stabilizes on a fixed-point corresponding to a learned pattern. The updating scheme may be synchronous, asynchronous, or a combination of the two.

In synchronous updating, the outputs $x_i(t + 1)$, $i = 1, 2, ..., n$ (equation (5.12)) are computed as a group simultaneously before the outputs are fed back to the inputs. In asynchronous updating, the $x_i(t + 1)$ are computed sequentially in some order or according to some probability distribution with the outputs fed back to the inputs following each update computation. For example, the units may be updated in the order of their index number. When combined synchronous-asynchronous operation is used, subgroups or batches of units are updated synchronously and then each group is updated using some asynchronous selection scheme.

During recall, a general Hopfield network can ultimately reach one of two states: (1) a cycle, in which for some sufficiently large t and fixed period $T > 1$, $\mathbf{x}(t + T) = \mathbf{x}(t)$ or (2) a fixed point defined by $\mathbf{x}(t + 1) = \mathbf{x}(t)$ for sufficiently large t.

To function as an associative memory, the network should converge to some fixed point $\mathbf{x}^j$ that is close to the input vector $\mathbf{x}(0)$ after some finite number of iterations. This will always be the case for a symmetric weight matrix **W**.

Energy Function Characterization

One of the interesting aspects of Hopfield networks is the characterization of the state of the network with an energy function. Because the weight matrix in Hopfield networks are symmetric it is possible to define an energy function E, where

$$E = -\frac{1}{2} \sum_{i=1}^{n} \sum_{j=1}^{n} w_{ij} x_j x_j \tag{5.13}$$

This function is similar to the energy function that characterizes magnetic materials in physics using a simple Ising "spin" model where the atoms of the material can assume one of two possible orientations + or − (up or down). In the spin model, the weights correspond to the magnetic field influence between two neighboring atoms. This physical analogy can be used to prove various properties of Hopfield types of networks since there is an isomorphism (a one-to-one relationship) between the spin model and the networks.

Hopfield was able to show that as the ANN system evolves according to its dynamics, the energy must eventually reach a stable state since the defining energy function E cannot increase after each update (Hopfield, 1982). It must decrease or at least remain the same. Because there are a finite number of states, the network must eventually converge to a local minimum. The energy minima correspond to fixed-point attractors, the stored patterns. The state of the system at convergence determines the output pattern. The state the system actually settles to depends on the initial state of the network and the weight matrix $\mathbf{W}$. For fixed $\mathbf{W}$, all initial states within a certain distance from an attracting point form a so-called "basin of attraction" as illustrated in Figure 5.4. From any initial state determined by the input pattern, the system evolves by moving down the surface of the energy function until a local minimum is reached.

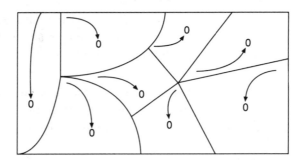

Figure 5.4   Fixed-Point Attractors and Basins of Attraction

To see that the energy function (5.13) never increases, let $\Delta E = E^* - E$ be the change in energy from E to E^* after an arbitrary unit is updated. Suppose the kth unit is updated. If the unit does not change state, the energy remains the same, $\Delta E = 0$. On the other hand, let unit k change state such that the new output is $x_k^* = -x_k$. Therefore, all unchanged terms in ΔE cancel (equation (5.14)). Removing these terms, ΔE can be written as

$$\Delta E = -\frac{1}{2}\sum_{j\neq k} w_{kj} x_k^* x_j + \frac{1}{2}\sum_{j\neq k} w_{kj} x_k x_j$$
$$= -\frac{1}{2} x_k^* \sum_{j\neq k} w_{kj} x_j + \frac{1}{2} x_k \sum_{j\neq k} w_{kj} x_j \qquad (5.14)$$
$$= x_k \sum_{j\neq k} w_{kj} x_j$$

where the last term follows from the fact that $-x_k^* = -x_k$. Note that the last term in (5.14) is always negative, since by assumption the summation term and x_k are of opposite sign (recall that a change of state to E^* was assumed, and

$$x_k^* = \text{sgn}\left(\sum_j w_{kj} x_j\right) = -x_k$$

with $w_{ii} = 0$). Thus, ΔE can only decrease or remain constant at each update. Eventually the system must reach a locally minimal energy state since E is trivially bounded from below, since for all $\mathbf{x}$

$$E = -\frac{1}{2}\sum_{i=1}^{n}\sum_{j=1}^{n} w_{ij} x_i x_j \geq -\sum_{i=1}^{n}\sum_{j=1}^{n} |w_{ij}|$$

and the w_{ij} are all bounded. As already noted, the local energy minima correspond to the stored patterns.

The above discussion applies to the discrete Hopfield network. The network has been generalized to operate in continuous time and produce continuous valued outputs. We briefly review the operation of continuous Hopfield networks next.

Continuous Hopfield Networks

The continuous version of the Hopfield network is a direct generalization of the discrete network through the use of analog or continuous valued activation functions in place of the hard-limiting bipolar (or binary) functions. Typically, sigmoid or hyperbolic tangent ($\tanh(x)$) activation functions are used. The dynamics of the network are modeled in continuous time. For this, nonlinear sets of differential equations describe the behavior of the network. The general equations have been given by Cohen and Grossberg (1983) and Hopfield (1984) as

$$\tau_i \frac{dx_i}{dt} = -x_i + f\left(\sum_{j=1}^{n} w_{ij} x_j\right) \qquad i = 1, 2, \ldots, n \qquad (5.15)$$

where τ_i is a time constant and $f(x)$ the nonlinear activation function

$$f(x) = \frac{1}{1 + \exp(-x)}$$

The dynamics of a system defined by equations (5.15), will in general, exhibit three types of behavior: convergence to a fixed point, oscillatory or chaotic (see Chapters 3 and 9). But, because of symmetry in the weights, the Hopfield network is assured of convergence to a fixed point. Convergence is assured by the Cohen-Grossberg theorem which is stated in the following section. At a fixed point, the system is in equilibrium, and hence, the activations do not change, so

$$\frac{dx_i}{dt} = 0 \qquad \text{for all } i$$

The outputs of the units are then fixed at

$$x_i = f\left(\sum_{j=1}^{n} w_{ij} x_j\right) \qquad i = 1, 2, \ldots, n \tag{5.16}$$

where the x_i are real-valued quantities in the range of 0 to 1.

An equivalent formulation of the system dynamics can be given in terms of the derivative of the net inputs to each unit rather than the outputs. The net inputs to each unit are given by

$$net_i = \sum_{j=1}^{n} w_{ij} x_j \qquad i = 1, 2, \ldots, n$$

The system of differential equations in this case are similar to (5.15) with net_i replacing x_i. They are given by

$$\tau_i \frac{dnet_i}{dt} = -net_i + \sum_{j=1}^{n} w_{ij} f(net_j) \qquad i = 1, 2, \ldots, n$$

At convergence, these equations have the same form of solution as (5.16), namely,

$$net_i = \sum_{j=1}^{n} w_{ij} f(net_j) \qquad i = 1, 2, \ldots, n$$

The Lyapunov energy function argument given above is for discrete nonlinear dynamical systems. A proof of convergence for more general continuous systems is generally much more difficult. Hopfield (1984) has given the following energy function for the continuous case

$$E = -\frac{1}{2} \sum_{i=1}^{n} \sum_{j=1}^{n} w_{ij} x_i x_j + \sum_{i=1}^{n} \int_{0}^{x_i} f^{-1}(x) dx \qquad (5.17)$$

It can be shown that E decreases, and hence converges, as in the discrete case. By differentiating equation (5.17) with respect to time and making appropriate substitutions, it can be shown that $dE/dt \leq 0$. We omit the details here since the approach is similar to the derivation for the discrete case taking into account appropriate substitutions.

The continuous version of the Hopfield network has been used primarily in optimization applications such as the traveling salesman problem, scheduling and function optimization. Other applications include image processing (Bilbro et al., 1988), and control (Tsutsumi et al., 1988). When creating a network to solve an optimization problem, the weight and bias values for the network are used to express the constraints of the problem. Finding a good set of constraint equations for such network solutions is the key to successful solution. Typically, the network solution will not be optimal, only near optimal, but useful for many situations.

A partial answer to the problem of convergence in nonlinear systems with feedback is given in a general theorem which relates to the global stability of a large class of dynamical systems. The theorem was given by Cohen and Grossberg in 1983. It applies to many dynamic neural network architectures and it has been generalized even more to broaden the range of applicability by Kosko (Kosko, 1988b; Kosko, 1988c). We make reference to the theorem in the text whenever questions of stability need addressing. But, because of its complexity and length, the theorem is stated below without proof. The interested reader should refer to the original article by Cohen and Grossberg for a detailed treatment of the proof.

Cohen-Grossberg Theorem

The Cohen-Grossberg theorem proves that the trajectories of a class of nonlinear dynamical systems converge. It states that any nonlinear dynamical system of the general form given by

$$\frac{dx_i}{dt} = f_i(x_i)\left[g_i(x_i) + \sum_{j=1}^{n} w_{ij}h_j(x_j)\right] \tag{5.18}$$

for $i = 1, 2, ..., n$, for which

- the matrix $\mathbf{W} = (w_{ij})$ is symmetric with nonnegative constant elements

- the function $f_i(x)$ is continuous for all $x \geq 0$

- the function $g_i(x)$ is continuous for all $x > 0$

- the function $f_i(x) > 0$ for all $x > 0$; the function $h_i(x) \geq 0$ for all x

- the function $h_i(x)$ is differentiable and monotone nondecreasing for $x \geq 0$

- for all $i = 1, 2, ..., n$, $\lim\sup_{x \to \infty}[g_i(x) - w_{ii}h_i(x)] < 0$

- and either $\lim_{x \to 0+} g_i(x) = \infty$

  or $\lim_{x \to 0+} g_i(x) = \infty$.

  and $\int_0^\varepsilon \frac{dx}{f_i(x)} = \infty$ for some $\varepsilon > 0$

Then all admissible trajectories approach the largest invariant set M contained in the set E, where

$$E = \left\{\mathbf{y} \in \mathbf{R}^n : \frac{dV(\mathbf{y})}{dt} = 0, \mathbf{y} \geq 0\right\}$$

and where

$$\frac{dV}{dt} = -\sum_{i=1}^{n} f_i h'_i\left[g_i - \sum_{k=1}^{n} w_{ik}h_k\right]^2$$

A corollary to the proof is that if each function h_i is strictly increasing, the set E consists of *all* the equilibrium points of the system of equations given by (5.18).

The proof of the Cohen-Grossberg theorem requires that the system of equations given by (5.18), defines a global Lyapunov function and satisfies certain other conditions (e.g. the LaSalle invariance principle and conditions of Sard's theorem).

To use the theorem, one must be able to express the system dynamics in the same form as equations (5.18) and show that all conditions of the theorem are satisfied.

Next, we look at a different type of recurrent associative memory network, the BSB network.

5.6 Brain State-in-a-Box

James Anderson and associates (Anderson et al., 1977) introduced a recurrent ANN autoassociative network that has been called the Brain State-in-a-Box (BSB) because the state of the system is "trapped" within the square box-like hyper-region bounded by unit vertices $\{+1, -1\}$. The network has a single layer of n units as illustrated in Figure 5.5. It is similar in structure and operation to discrete Hopfield networks except that no constraints are placed on the weight matrix. In particular, units may have self-feedback connections, $w_{ii} \neq 0$, and some weight connections may be omitted, that is, $w_{ij} = 0$ for some i, j.

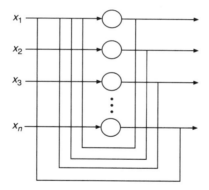

Figure 5.5 Brain State-in-a-Box Network

Either Hebbian or gradient descent (Delta Rule) learning may be used to adjust the weights in a BSB network. When simple Hebbian learning is used, the weight values are prevented from growing without bound by letting the activation values of the units "saturate" at $+1$ or -1 when they try to grow beyond these values. This is accomplished with the following unit activation values

$$x_j(t + 1) = \begin{cases} +1 & \text{if } net_j(t) > +1 \\ x_j & \text{if } |net_j(t)| \leq 1 \\ -1 & \text{if } net_j(t) < -1 \end{cases} \qquad (5.19)$$

where $x_j(t)$ is the output of unit j at time t and $net_j(t)$ is the input to unit j at time t with

$$net_j(t) = x_j(t) + \alpha \sum_{i=1}^{n} w_{ij}x_i(t) \qquad (5.20)$$

Initially, the state of the network lies anywhere within the (bipolar) unit hypercube. As the system evolves according to its dynamics, the state of the system recursively moves toward one of the vertices where it becomes trapped. The vertices correspond to the attractors of the nonlinear dynamical system, the stored patterns.

When Hebbian learning is used to train the network, the weights are initially set to small random numbers $w_{ij} \ll 1$ and a vector pattern **x** is presented to the network. Unit activations are then computed according to (5.19) and the outputs are propagated to all units through feedback connections where the process is repeated until the network stabilizes. Once the network has stabilized, the weights are updated according to the Hebb rule

$$w_{ij}^{new} = w_{ij}^{old} + \alpha x_i x_j$$

where x_i and x_j are the final output activations of units i and j (+1 or −1), respectively. In other words, the weights are storing the vertices visited for each pattern presented. Note that equation (5.20) implies that each unit j has two self-feedback links, one with a weight connection value of +1 and the other, an adjustable weight. Bias inputs with adjustable weights are sometimes used as well in some versions of BSB networks.

When the Delta Rule is used to train the network, the weights are adjusted according to

$$w_{ij}^{new} = w_{ij}^{old} + \alpha(t_i - x_i)x_j$$

where t_i is the target output for unit i, x_i is the actual output of unit i and x_j is the output of unit j that is fed back as input to unit i through the weight connection w_{ij}. The weight updates are performed after the network has stabilized.

To retrieve a stored pattern, an input vector **x** is presented to the network and the jth unit iteratively computes an output according to equations (5.19) and (5.20) until the outputs cease to change.

As in the case of Hopfield networks, an energy function can be defined for BSB networks and hence, the stability of these networks is assured. Proof of stability follows from an argument similar to that given for discrete Hopfield networks or from the Cohen-Grossberg theorem (described in Section 5.5). The energy minima correspond to the hypercube vertices, the fixed-point attractors. As in the case of Hopfield networks, the Lyapunov energy function can only remain the same or decrease after the units have been updated. The network state becomes stable when all units cease to change.

Next, we look at a two-layer recurrent associative network, the bidirectional or BAM network.

5.7 Bidirectional Associative Memory

Bart Kosko introduced Bidirectional Associative Memory (BAM) networks in 1987. These are two-layer, recurrent, heteroassociative networks that have some similarities to both the Hopfield and ART (see Chapter 15) networks except that both layers act as input and output units. Patterns may be input from either set of external connections as illustrated in Figure 5.6. Both sets of external connections also provide outputs. The input **x** vectors are n-dimensional and the input **y** vectors are m-dimensional. The connections between the units are bidirectional (signals flow in either direction) from which the network derives its name. The $m \times n$ weight matrix **W** stores the associated pairs of patterns. Thus, the weight w_{ij} on the connection between unit i from the **x** pattern side to unit j on the **y** pattern side is shared for signals flowing in either direction. Both bivalent (bipolar, binary) and real-valued versions of the BAM have been studied and both synchronous and asynchronous operations are possible.

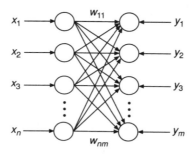

Figure 5.6   Bidirectional Associative Memory

Adaptive learning (learning during operation) and nonadaptive (off-line learning) BAMs have both been studied. Hebbian learning is easily implemented in BAM networks, where the weight matrix is computed directly as the sum of P pattern matrices where each is computed as the outer product matrix from the **x**-**y** pattern pairs, that is

$$\mathbf{W} = \sum_{p=1}^{P} \mathbf{W}^p$$

with

$$\mathbf{W}^p = \mathbf{x}^p(\mathbf{y}^p)^T$$

or in component form

$$w_{ij} = \sum_{p=1}^{P} w_{ij}^p = \sum_{p=1}^{P} x_i^p y_j^p$$

To retrieve a pattern, an input vector is presented to either the left (**x**-input) or right (**y**-input) side of the BAM and the values propagated to the opposite layer where the net input for the ith unit is computed (for example, for **x** input) as

$$net_i = \sum_{j=1}^{n} w_{ij} x_j = \mathbf{w}_i \cdot \mathbf{x}$$

where $\mathbf{w}_i$ is the ith row of the weight matrix $\mathbf{W}$. The opposite side (y-side) of the BAM then computes output activations and the results are propagated back to the opposite side through the transpose matrix $\mathbf{W}^T$. The process is repeated iteratively until the network stabilizes. For bipolar activation functions, the outputs computed at time $t + 1$ by units on the "**y**" side are given by

$$y_j(t + 1) = \text{sgn}\left(\sum_{i=1}^{n} w_{ij} x_i(t)\right) = \begin{cases} +1 & \text{if } w_{ij} x_i(t) > 0 \\ y_j & \text{if } w_{ij} x_i(t) = 0 \\ -1 & \text{if } w_{ij} x_i(t) < 0 \end{cases}$$

Note that the jth unit retains the same value when the net input is equal to zero. The same type of activation functions are computed for the "**x**" side of the network using the net inputs from the **y** side.

Threshold values different from zero may also be used, thereby permitting a range of values for which the network does not change value. For example, a threshold value of $\theta > 0$ results in an activation function defined by

$$
y_j(t + 1) = \begin{cases} +1 & \text{if } w_{ij}x_i(t) > \theta \\ y_j & \text{if } |w_{ij}x_i(t)| < \theta \\ -1 & \text{if } w_{ij}x_i(t) < -\theta \end{cases}
$$

As noted above, binary and continuous (e.g. sigmoid) activation functions are also used in BAM networks. For discrete activation functions, it has been shown that bipolar outputs offer better performance on average than binary outputs (Kosko, 1987). This is due to a reduction in the noise or crosstalk term (equation (5.9)) when bipolar activations are used as opposed to binary activations. An analysis of the recall equation (equation (5.9)), can also be used to show that the maximum number of pattern pairs that can be accurately stored and retrieved is given by $C < \min(n, m)$. As expected, BAMs can store no more patterns than the maximum number of linearly independent rows (columns) in **W**.

As in the case of Hopfield and BSB networks, an energy function can be defined for BAM networks and hence bidirectional stability of the networks is assured. Proof of this stability follows from an extension of the Cohen-Grossberg theorem due to Kosko (1987). (The Cohen-Grossberg theorem is described in Section 5.4.) In the discrete case, an argument similar to the one used for Hopfield networks (Section 5.4) can be used to show that the BAM energy function is bounded from below and can never increase. The energy minima the network converges to correspond to the attractors (the stored patterns) and the specific attractor the network converges to depends on the basin of attraction the input pattern lies in (see Chapter 3 for a description of nonlinear dynamic systems). The Lyapunov energy function for a BAM is formulated as an average of the energy for each direction of propagation (left-to-right and right-to-left). It can only remain the same or decrease after either **x** or **y** unit activations have been updated. The system becomes stable when all units cease to change state. Both discrete and continuous BAM networks have been shown to be bidirectionally stable. In the continuous case, the activation functions need only be monotone increasing (e.g. sigmoidal) for the network to converge. Of course, if too many patterns are stored in any type of BAM, accurate retrieval is no longer possible.

As an illustration of BAM operation, we give an example similar to one provided in Kosko (1987). Two pairs of nonorthogonal patterns are to be stored. They are given by the bipolar vectors

$$(\mathbf{x}^1)^T = [1 \ -1 \ 1 \ -1 \ 1 \ -1] \qquad\qquad (\mathbf{y}^1)^T = [1 \ 1 \ -1 \ -1]$$
$$(\mathbf{x}^2)^T = [1 \ 1 \ 1 \ -1 \ -1 \ -1] \qquad\qquad (\mathbf{y}^2)^T = [1 \ -1 \ 1 \ -1]$$

Using Hebbian learning, the pattern correlation matrices for the two pairs are computed as (for brevity we use $+ \equiv +1$, and $- = -1$ when convenient)

$$\mathbf{W}^1 = \mathbf{x}^1(\mathbf{y}^1)^{\mathbf{T}} = \begin{bmatrix} + & + & - & - \\ - & - & + & + \\ + & + & - & - \\ - & - & + & + \\ + & + & - & - \\ - & - & + & + \end{bmatrix} \qquad \mathbf{W}^2 = \mathbf{x}^2(\mathbf{y}^2)^{\mathbf{T}} = \begin{bmatrix} + & - & + & - \\ + & - & + & - \\ + & - & + & - \\ - & + & - & + \\ - & + & - & + \\ - & + & - & + \end{bmatrix}$$

and

$$\mathbf{W} = \mathbf{W}^1 + \mathbf{W}^2 = \begin{bmatrix} 2 & 0 & 0 & -2 \\ 0 & -2 & 2 & 0 \\ 2 & 0 & 0 & -2 \\ -2 & 0 & 0 & 2 \\ 0 & 2 & -2 & 0 \\ -2 & 0 & 0 & 2 \end{bmatrix}$$

Computing with $\mathbf{x}^1$ input (from left to right) we obtain output $\mathbf{y}^1$

$$\mathbf{x}^1\mathbf{W} = [\ + \ - \ + \ - \ + \ - \ ]\begin{bmatrix} 2 & 0 & 0 & -2 \\ 0 & -2 & 2 & 0 \\ 2 & 0 & 0 & -2 \\ -2 & 0 & 0 & 2 \\ 0 & 2 & -2 & 0 \\ -2 & 0 & 0 & 2 \end{bmatrix} = \begin{bmatrix} 8 \\ 4 \\ -4 \\ -8 \end{bmatrix} \Rightarrow \begin{bmatrix} 1 \\ 1 \\ -1 \\ -1 \end{bmatrix}$$

Computing with the $\mathbf{y}^1$ output as input (from right to left) we obtain $\mathbf{x}^1$ back as expected and with immediate convergence.

$$(\mathbf{y}^1)^T\mathbf{W}^T = \mathbf{W}\mathbf{y}^1 = \begin{bmatrix} 2 & 0 & 0 & -2 \\ 0 & -2 & 2 & 0 \\ 2 & 0 & 0 & -2 \\ -2 & 0 & 0 & 2 \\ 0 & 2 & -2 & 0 \\ -2 & 0 & 0 & 2 \end{bmatrix}\begin{bmatrix} 1 \\ 1 \\ -1 \\ -1 \end{bmatrix} = \begin{bmatrix} 4 \\ -4 \\ 4 \\ -4 \\ 4 \\ -4 \end{bmatrix} \Rightarrow \begin{bmatrix} 1 \\ -1 \\ 1 \\ -1 \\ 1 \\ -1 \end{bmatrix} = \mathbf{x}^1$$

Using a noisy x^2 input this time, say $x*$, where

$$(x*)^T = [1 \ 1 \ 1 \ -1 \ -1 \ -1]$$

(the second bit of x^2 is flipped to get $x*$). We wish to see if the original x^2 is retrieved when the above computations are repeated:

$$x*W = [- \ + \ + \ - \ - \ -]\begin{bmatrix} 2 & 0 & 0 & -2 \\ 0 & -2 & 2 & 0 \\ 2 & 0 & 0 & -2 \\ -2 & 0 & 0 & 2 \\ 0 & 2 & -2 & 0 \\ -2 & 0 & 0 & 2 \end{bmatrix} = \begin{bmatrix} 4 \\ -4 \\ 4 \\ -4 \end{bmatrix} \Rightarrow \begin{bmatrix} 1 \\ -1 \\ 1 \\ -1 \end{bmatrix} = y* = y^2$$

and

$$(y*)^T W^T = Wy* = \begin{bmatrix} 2 & 0 & 0 & -2 \\ 0 & -2 & 2 & 0 \\ 2 & 0 & 0 & -2 \\ -2 & 0 & 0 & 2 \\ 0 & 2 & -2 & 0 \\ -2 & 0 & 0 & 2 \end{bmatrix} \begin{bmatrix} + \\ - \\ + \\ - \end{bmatrix} = \begin{bmatrix} 4 \\ 4 \\ 4 \\ -4 \\ -4 \\ -4 \end{bmatrix} \Rightarrow \begin{bmatrix} 1 \\ 1 \\ 1 \\ -1 \\ -1 \\ -1 \end{bmatrix} = x^2$$

for accurate recall of the pattern pair. The reader is urged to try even noisier input patterns and observe what patterns are actually retrieved. In some cases, noisy inputs retrieve the complement of the stored pattern.

Like most associative memory ANNs, BAM networks have found limited applications. Even so, they have been used in a few vision processing and control applications (Kosko, 1988; Bavarian, 1988).

Summary

In this chapter, we introduced simple one- and two-layer associative memories. These ANN memories can be classified as autoassociative or heteroassociative and as feedforward or feedback recurrent networks. Autoassociative networks store individual patterns for later recall. They are useful when only noisy or partially incomplete input patterns are available and the original undistorted pattern must be recalled. Heteroassociative memory networks store pairs of patterns, where in general, the two patterns differ in value and dimension.

Feedforward memory networks retrieve patterns with a single forward processing operation, whereas recurrent networks mix the computed outputs with the inputs and iteratively recompute outputs until the network relaxes and stabilizes. The dynamics of these networks are much more complex than the static networks. In general, they can exhibit three types of behavior: convergence to a fixed point, oscillatory or chaotic. Symmetry of the weight matrix in networks such as the Hopfield network guarantee convergence to a fixed point. The class of Hopfield networks can be used as associative memories as well as for the solution of optimization problems such as the traveling salesman problem. Both a discrete and continuous versions of the Hopfield network were described and an energy function which characterized the network was given. The energy function is also known as a Lyapunov function. These functions play an important role in characterizing the dynamics of nonlinear networks.

The networks examined in this chapter were feedforward linear associators, both autoassociative and heteroassociative and three recurrent associators, the Hopfield (both discrete and continuous valued), the BSB and the BAM networks.

Part III

Multilayer Feedforward Neural Networks and Backpropagation

6
Multilayer Feedforward Neural Networks and Backpropagation

In this chapter, we describe one of the more popular ANN architectures, the multilayer feedforward (MLFF) network with backpropagation (BP) learning. This type of network is also sometimes called the Multilayer Perceptron because of its similarity to perceptron networks with more than one layer. We begin with a description of the MLFF network architecture and the BP learning process. We derive the generalized delta (backpropagation) learning rule and see how it is implemented in practice. We examine variations on the learning process to improve its efficiency and ways to avoid some of the potential problems that can arise during training. We consider optimal (or good) parameter settings for different network applications. Finally, we examine alternative training methods that offer some promise over the standard BP method. In the following two chapters, we look at the capabilities and limitations of MLFF networks in more detail and describe a number of typical applications of which MLFF have proven to be successful.

6.1 Introduction

Suppose we wish to train a network to approximate some arbitrary mapping $g' : x \rightarrow z$ where $\mathbf{x}$ and $\mathbf{z}$ are random vectors in $\mathbf{R}^n$ and $\mathbf{R}^m$ respectively with joint probability distribution $\psi(\mathbf{x}, \mathbf{z})$. We have available for training the network a training set which consists of P pairs of patterns $\{\mathbf{x}^p, \mathbf{t}^p | p = 1, 2, ..., P\}$, where the input patterns $\mathbf{x}^p$ have some unknown probability distribution $\rho(\mathbf{x})$, and the $\mathbf{t}^p$ are the desired or known target vector values for the corresponding input vectors $\mathbf{x}^p$. Given input $\mathbf{x}^p$, the actual computed output from the network is $\mathbf{z}^p$, where $\mathbf{z} = \mathbf{g}(\mathbf{x})$. We recall that networks with only an input and output layer (such as the simple perceptron or ADALINE) lack the ability to compute complex arbitrary functions such as those bounding nonlinearly separable regions. This is one of the most serious limitations of basic networks without internal layers. Furthermore, we know that multilayer linear systems are equivalent to a single-layer linear system, and hence, they too lack the ability to form general complex mappings. What is required to estimate more complex pattern mappings is an architecture that supports the formation of intermediate representations, representations that are, in general, nonlinear and hence, can transform arbitrary regions from one pattern space to another.

In this chapter we shall investigate feedforward networks having at least one internal layer of neurons, where each neuron is capable of computing a nonlinear activation function. We call such networks multilayer feedforward networks. We shall see that such networks can be trained to compute arbitrary nonlinear functions.

The Multilayer Feedforward Network

A general MLFF network is illustrated in Figure 6.1. This is a feedforward, fully-connected hierarchical network consisting of an input layer, one or more middle or hidden layers and an output layer. The internal layers are called "hidden" because they only receive internal inputs (inputs from other processing units) and produce internal outputs (outputs to other processing units). Consequently, they are "hidden" from the outside world. Real-valued n-dimensional input feature vectors $\mathbf{x}$ are presented in a fan-out arrangement to each of the first hidden layer units through weights w_{ji}. Hidden layer unit j receives input i through the synoptic weight w_{ij}, $i = 1, 2, ..., n$, and $j = 1, 2, ..., h$. Unit j computes a function of the input signal $\mathbf{x}$ and the weights w_{ij}, and passes its output forward to all of the units in the next successive layer. Like the first hidden layer, the second hidden layer units are fully connected to the previous layer through synoptic weights. These units also compute a function of their inputs and their synoptic weights and pass their output on to the next layer. This process is repeated until the final computation is produced by the output units.

Many variations of this basic MLFF network have been proposed and studied over the years following the introduction of the perceptron by Rosenblatt. Such systems have now become practicable as pattern recognition units with the introduction of the BP training algorithm described below. MLFF networks have gained their popularity because they are capable of performing arbitrary mappings $\mathbf{g} : \mathbf{R}^n \rightarrow \mathbf{R}^m$ where $\mathbf{g}(\mathbf{x}) = \mathbf{z}$. Such mappings are possible if a sufficient number of hidden units are provided and if the network can be trained, that is if a set of weights that perform the desired mapping can be found.

Inputs   Outputs

Hidden Units

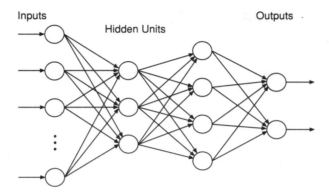

Figure 6.1   A General Multilayer Feedforward Network

We saw in Chapter 4 that the Widrow-Hoff LMS or delta learning rule is similar to the perceptron learning algorithm except that it is defined for linear activation functions. Indeed, because we used a differentiable activation function, we were able to define a differentiable error (or cost) function from which a gradient descent learning method could be developed. That rule, which has the form

$$\Delta w_{ij} = \eta \delta_j x_{ij} \tag{6.1}$$

we recall, is optimal in the sense that it will always find a set of weights which minimize the mean squared error (for a set of linearly independent pattern vectors). Unfortunately, neither the perceptron learning algorithm nor the Widrow-Hoff delta rule can be applied to networks with hidden layers. These methods fail to specify how to adjust the hidden-layer weights. This is known as the "credit assignment" problem since these methods are unable to give credit or assign blame to hidden layer weights for errors that occur in the output layer. The backpropagation learning method, a generalization of the delta rule, does specify how to adjust the weights in hidden layers. It therefore permits the construction of feedforward, multilayer networks which can learn to compute much more complex mappings $\mathbf{g}$ from $\mathbf{R}^n$ to $\mathbf{R}^m$. We examine this generalized delta rule learning procedure next in the context of the MLFF network.

6.2   The Generalized Delta Rule or Backpropagation Learning

The backpropagation learning method was discovered independently by several researchers for different reasons. Werbos (1974) seems to have been one of the earliest to propose its use in his Harvard University doctoral dissertation "Beyond Regression: New Tools for Prediction and Analysis in the Behavioral Sciences." Parker (1985) later rediscovered it in his MIT technical report on "Learning Logic." Even so, credit is usually given to Rumelhart and other members of the Parallel Distributed Processing (PDP) group (Rumelhart et al., 1985) for popularizing it and developing it into a workable procedure. They published a two volume set of manuscripts describing various neural network architectures, including a comprehensive treatment of the generalized delta rule training procedure, BP and related ANN topics.

The backpropagation learning method can be applied to any multilayer network that uses differentiable activation functions and supervised training. Like the delta rule, it is an optimization procedure based on gradient descent that adjusts weights to reduce the system error or cost function. The name backpropagation arises from the method in which corrections are made to the weights. During the learning phase, input patterns are presented to the network in some sequence. Each training pattern is propagated forward layer by layer until an output pattern is computed. The computed output is then compared to a desired or target output and an error value is determined. The errors are used as inputs to feedback connections from which adjustments are made to the synaptic weights layer by layer in a backward direction. Figure 6.2 illustrates an MLFF network modified for backpropagation training. The backward linkages are used only for the learning phase, whereas the forward connections are used for both the learning and the operational phases.

Using BP, the hidden layer weights are adjusted using the errors from the subsequent layer. Thus, the errors computed at the output layer are used to adjust the weights between the last hidden layer and the output layer. Likewise, an error value computed from the last hidden layer outputs is used to adjust the weights in the next to the last hidden layer and so on until the weight connections to the first hidden layer are adjusted. In this way, errors are propagated backwards layer by layer with corrections being made to the corresponding layer weights in an iterative manner. The process is repeated a number of times for each pattern in the training set until the total output error converges to a minimum or until some limit is reached in the number of training iterations completed.

To simplify the derivation of BP, we begin with an MLFF network having a

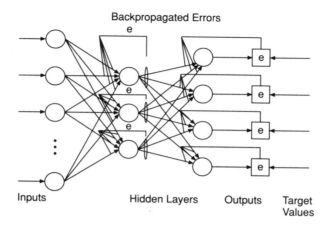

Figure 6.2   An MLFF Network Modified for Backpropagation

single hidden layer. These results are later generalized to an arbitrary number of hidden layers. Thus, our initial system has an input layer that is fully connected to the hidden layer and each unit in the hidden layer is fully connected to the output layer units. We also adopt the following notation for the network parameters. Weight connections between input layer unit i and hidden layer unit j are denoted by v_{ji}, $i = 1, 2, ..., n$, $j = 1, 2, ..., h$ while weight connections between hidden-layer unit j and output unit k are designated as w_{kj}, $k = 1, 2, ..., m$ (Figure 6.3). The n-dimensional input training pattern p is denoted as $\mathbf{x}^p$, $p = 1, 2, ..., P$, and the output of the hidden layer unit j for input pattern $\mathbf{x}^p$ is denoted as y_j^p, $j = 1, 2, ..., h$. Likewise, the output from unit k of the output layer for input pattern $\mathbf{x}^p$ is z_k^p, while the desired or target output is denoted as t_k^p, $k = 1, 2, ..., m$. Unless stated otherwise, we also use the same nonlinear activation function f for each of the hidden and output layer units. Also, when there is no chance of confusion, we sometimes drop the pattern superscript p in what follows to simplify our notation.

Define the following terms:

$$H_j = \sum_i v_{ij} x_i \qquad\qquad j = 1, 2, ..., h \qquad\qquad (6.2)$$

$$I_k = \sum_j w_{kj} y_j \qquad\qquad k = 1, 2, ..., m \qquad\qquad (6.3)$$

H_j is the combined or net input to hidden-layer unit j, while I_k is the net input to unit k of the output-layer. Outputs computed by unit j of the hidden-layer and unit

k of the output-layer are given by

$$y_j = f(H_j) \qquad\qquad j = 1, 2, ..., h \qquad\qquad (6.4)$$

$$z_k = f(I_k) \qquad\qquad k = 1, 2, ..., m \qquad\qquad (6.5)$$

respectively, where f is an arbitrary, bounded, differentiable function. Thus, we have for output unit k the following response to an input pattern $\mathbf{x}$

$$
\begin{aligned}
z_k = f(I_k) = f\left(\sum_j w_{kj} y_j\right) &= f\left(\sum_j w_{kj} f(H_j)\right) \\
&= f\left(\sum_j w_{kj} f\left(\sum_i v_{ji} x_i\right)\right)
\end{aligned}
\qquad (6.6)
$$

These outputs are illustrated in Figure 6.3.

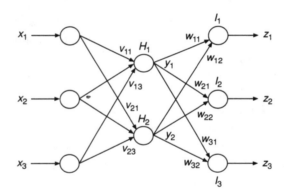

Figure 6.3   MLFF Network Connections and Variables

Clearly, for nonlinear f, z_k is a nonlinear function of the input pattern $\mathbf{x}$ and the system parameters $\mathbf{W} = (\mathbf{v}, \mathbf{w})$, i.e. $\mathbf{z} = \mathbf{g}(f, \mathbf{x}, \mathbf{W})$ where $\mathbf{g}$ is an m-dimensional vector function.

In developing a learning algorithm for this network, we want a method that specifies how to reduce the total system error for all patterns through an adjustment of the weights. We define the mean system error E_{tot} as the average of the output errors over all training pattern errors E^p, $p = 1, 2, ..., P$:

$$E_{tot} = \frac{1}{P} \sum_{p=1}^{P} E^p \tag{6.7}$$

The number of training patterns P in the training set will depend on the application and on the source of the training set. Clearly, P may be finite or not. Of course, in practice, we are limited to a training set of finite size P, which hopefully, is a representative sample from the population distribution, $\rho(\mathbf{x})$. More correctly, for large P, we should define the mean squared error as the limit of this sum, assuming it exists, i.e.

$$E_{tot} = \lim_{P \to \infty} \frac{1}{P} \sum_{p=1}^{P} E^p \tag{6.8}$$

Obviously, the system error will be reduced if the error for each training pattern, E^p, is reduced for any size P. Thus, as in the case of the delta rule, we will develop a weight correction procedure that adjusts the weights in proportion to a reduction in the error relative to changes in the weights. We will change the weights on each successive pattern presentation such that the pattern errors are iteratively reduced from their previous values. This can be accomplished if the weights are adjusted in proportion to the negative of the error gradient. Thus, at step $s + 1$ of the training process, the weight adjustment should be proportional to the derivative of the error measure E^p, computed on iteration s. This can be written as

$$\Delta \mathbf{W}(s + 1) = -\eta \partial E^p / \partial \mathbf{W}(s) \tag{6.9}$$

where η is a constant learning coefficient, and

$$\partial E^p / \partial \mathbf{W} = [\partial E^p / \partial v_{11}, \partial E^p / \partial v_{12}, ..., \partial E^p / \partial w_{11}, ..., \partial E^p / \partial w_{hm}] \tag{6.10}$$

The gradient of the total system error is then given by

$$\frac{\partial E_{tot}}{\partial \mathbf{W}} = \frac{1}{P} \sum_{p=1}^{P} \frac{\partial E^p}{\partial \mathbf{W}} \tag{6.11}$$

The error function E^p, can be defined in different ways, for example, as the mean square error, the absolute error, etc. For the initial development of BP, we will use the mean square error since it is one of the more commonly used measures. It penalizes large deviations more than small ones and it provides us with a differentiable, decreasing function of the difference between the computed and desired outputs. The squared error for input pattern p is defined as

$$E^p = \frac{1}{2} \sum_{k=1}^{m} \left(t_k^p - z_k^p \right)^2 \tag{6.12}$$

where the factor $\frac{1}{2}$ has been included for mathematical convenience.

In finding an expression for the weight adjustment (6.9), we must take the partial derivative of the E^p, with respect to weights v_{ji} and w_{kj}. This requires that the chain rule be utilized since we want our adjustment procedure expressed in terms of the system parameters: the inputs, the computed outputs and the weights. Weight adjustments can then be made in accordance with

$$w_{kj}(s + 1) = w_{kj}(s) + \Delta w_{kj} = -\eta \frac{\partial E^p}{\partial w_{kj}(s)} \tag{6.13}$$

In taking the derivitive of a given E^p, with respect to w_{kj}, we take derivatives with respect to expressions that are functionally dependent on the weights, namely I_k and H_j. (Note that we drop the pattern superscript p in what follows to simplify the notation, i.e. we let $E^p = E$.) Thus, to evaluate the individual terms such as

$$\frac{\partial E}{\partial w_{kj}}$$

in expression (6.13), we use the known relations

$$E = \frac{1}{2} \sum_{k=1}^{m} \left(t_k^p - z_k^p \right)^2 \qquad I_k = \Sigma_j w_{kj} y_j \text{ and } z_k = f(I_k) \tag{6.14}$$

Focusing first on the weight updates for the output units, we can use the actual errors to find the update rule. We have

$$\frac{\partial E}{\partial w_{kj}} = \frac{\partial E}{\partial I_k} \frac{\partial I_k}{\partial w_{kj}} = \frac{\partial E}{\partial I_k} \left(\frac{\partial}{w_{kj}} \Sigma_j y_j w_{kj} \right) \tag{6.15}$$

The term in parentheses in equation (6.15) can be evaluated directly. Thus,

$$\frac{\partial}{w_{kj}} \Sigma_j y_j w_{kj} = y_k$$

Now, using the chain rule again, we can write

$$\frac{\partial E}{\partial I_k} = \frac{\partial E}{\partial z_k}\frac{\partial z_k}{\partial I_k} = -(t_k - z_k)f'(I_k) \qquad (6.16)$$

since from equations (6.14) we have for output unit k

$$\frac{\partial E}{\partial z_k} = -(t_k - z_k) \quad \text{and} \quad \frac{\partial z_k}{\partial I_k} = f'(I_k)$$

If we now define

$$\delta_k = (t_k - z_k)f'(I_k) \qquad (6.17)$$

we can write the update rule for the output units in the same form as the Widrow-Hoff delta rule, that is

$$\Delta w_{kj} = -\eta\frac{\partial E}{\partial w_{kj}} = \eta\delta_k y_j \qquad (6.18)$$

This rule applies to all the hidden to output unit weights for a single pattern presentation.

Turning now to the hidden layer weights v_{ji}, we see that in this case, we do not have target values from which to compute errors. Instead, we must somehow use the errors from the output units to adjust the input to hidden layer weights. For this, we can use the chain rule repeatedly to relate the output errors to these weights. Note that these weights (equation (6.6)) are more deeply embedded in the error function. We want an expression for

$$\Delta v_{ji} = -\eta\frac{\partial E}{\partial v_{ji}} = -\eta\frac{\partial E}{\partial H_j}\frac{\partial H_j}{\partial v_{ji}} \qquad (6.19)$$

Note that the last partial derivative in this expression can be evaluated directly from equation (6.2), that is,

$$\frac{\partial H_j}{\partial v_{ji}} = \sum_i\frac{\partial}{\partial v_{ji}}(v_{ji}x_i) = x_i$$

To solve for the first partial derivative term in (6.19), we use the chain rule to obtain

$$\frac{\partial E}{\partial H_j} = \frac{\partial E}{\partial y_j}\frac{\partial y_j}{\partial H_j} = \frac{\partial E}{\partial y_j}f'(H_j) \qquad (6.20)$$

Differentiating $\partial E / \partial y_j$ directly now we obtain (from equations (6.12) and (6.6))

$$\frac{\partial E}{\partial y_j} = \frac{1}{2} \sum_k \frac{\partial (t_k - f(\sum_j w_{kj} y_j))^2}{\partial y_j}$$

$$= -\sum_k (t_k - z_k) f'(I_k) w_{kj}$$

Combining the above operations, we can now write the update rule for the hidden layer units as

$$\Delta v_{ji} = \eta \delta_j x_i = \eta x_i f'(H_j) \sum_k \delta_k w_{kj} \qquad (6.21)$$

where

$$\delta_j = f'(H_j) \sum_k \delta_k w_{kj} \qquad (6.22)$$

and, as noted above,

$$\delta_k = (t_k - z_k) f'(I_k)$$

To summarize, we repeat the two update rules for output and hidden layer units, respectively:

Output units:

$$\Delta w_{kj} = \eta \delta_k y_j = \eta (t_k - z_k) f'(I_k) y_j \qquad (6.23)$$

where

$$\delta_k = (t_k - z_k) f'(I_k)$$

Hidden units:

$$\Delta v_{ji} = \eta \delta_j x_i = \eta x_i f'(H_j) \sum_k \delta_k w_{kj} \qquad (6.24)$$

where

$$\delta_j = f'(H_j) \sum_k \delta_k w_{kj}$$

Prior to application of the BP learning process, the weight matrices for all the layers are usually initialized by setting the weights to small random, real-valued numbers. The input training pattern vectors $\mathbf{x}^p$, $p = 1, 2, ..., P$ are then presented to the network one at a time and a corresponding output pattern $\mathbf{z}^p$ is computed. This computed output pattern is compared to the desired or target output pattern $\mathbf{t}^p$ and the pattern errors $(t_k^p - z_k^p)$, $k = 1, 2, ..., m$, are determined. These errors are then propagated backwards for the weight adjustment computations as described above (equations (6.23) and (6.24)).

It is worth examining the BP equations more closely to understand the learning process better. Consider the final layer computations. In the forward computation pass, signals y_j from all the hidden layer nodes are multiplied by the corresponding weights w_{kj} connecting to output-layer unit k. Unit k sums these values and computes its output activation value z_k. The error $(t_k^p - z_k^p)$ is then computed and used in (6.17) in the backpropagation process to adjust each of the weights w_{kj} connected to unit k. This is performed for each unit $k = 1, 2, ..., m$, in the output-layer in accordance with

$$w_{kj}^{\text{new}} = w_{kj}^{\text{old}} + \Delta w_{kj} = w_{kj}^{\text{old}} + \eta y_j (t_k - z_k) f'(I_k) \tag{6.25}$$

For the input to hidden layer weights v_{ji}, we do not have target values to use in computing the errors directly. Instead, for this case, we must use the output errors and distribute them in some way to adjust the weights connecting input nodes i to hidden layer nodes j. For this, we use the δ_j values as the errors for each of the hidden units j as in

$$v_{ji}^{\text{new}} = v_{ji}^{\text{old}} + \Delta v_{ji} = v_{ji}^{\text{old}} + \eta x_i f'(H_j) \Sigma_k \delta_k w_{kj} \tag{6.26}$$

Of course, the delta terms δ_k and δ_j in the above equations differ. They are defined by (6.23) and (6.24). Figure 6.4 illustrates the adjustment process for the two layers.

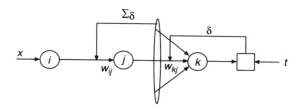

Figure 6.4   Backpropagation Weight Adjustment Process

Off-Line or Batch Process Training

Rather than adjust the weights after each pattern presentation, it is possible to accumulate the errors E^p over the whole training set $\{\mathbf{x}^p, \mathbf{t}^p | p = 1, 2, ..., P\}$, and then make the adjustments. This is known as batch or off-line updating where the update is performed for a complete epoch, that is, a complete pass through the training set. Errors for each pattern presentation are stored during the pass through the training set. After an epoch of training, $E_{tot} = \Sigma_p E^p$ is computed and each weight is then adjusted according to the accumulated errors, that is, $\Sigma_p w_{kj}$ and $\Sigma_p v_{ji}$ as required by the BP update procedure (equation (6.11)). This process is repeated until training is completed. Adjusting the weights after each pattern is presented rather than after each epoch is the more commonly used method, however for some applications batch training may be more efficient. To perform off-line training requires that the whole training set be available prior to the start of the learning process. This requirement cannot always be met for some applications such as in real-time applications (process control) or adaptive signal equalization (Widrow and Stearns, 1985).

The form of the BP update rule can be generalized for any number of layers. It has the following general form:

$$\Delta w_{ji} = \eta \Sigma_p \delta_{out} H_{in} \tag{6.27}$$

where the subscripts *in* and *out* refer to the net input and output signals associated with a given unit, and i and j refer to the connections from unit i to unit j. The form of δ will vary depending on the type of layer for which it applies. In the case of an output-layer unit it has the form given by equation (6.17). For all hidden-layer units it has the form given by equation (6.22). To verify this result, one must apply the chain rule repeatedly for the multi-hidden-layer case. For example, if a network has Q layers, the update rule for the qth layer weights is just

$$\Delta w_{ji}^q = \eta \delta_i^q O_j^{q-1} \tag{6.28}$$

where O_j^{q-1} is the output of the jth unit from layer $q - 1$ and δ^q has the general form

$$\delta_i^q = f'\left(H_i^{q-1}\right)\Sigma_j \delta_j^{q+1} w_{ji}^q \tag{6.29}$$

a product of the derivative of the output of the unit whose weights are being updated and the weighted sum of the output deltas associated with the unit. The deltas are easy to compute when propagating the errors in a successive backward, layer-by-layer manner.

Because of its importance, we summarize the BP learning algorithm below for MLFF with any number of layers Q, where each layer is numbered $q = 1, 2, ..., Q$. We also let H_i^q and O_i^q be the inputs and outputs of the ith unit in the qth layer, respectively, and w_{ji}^q the weight connecting the ith unit in layer $q - 1$ to the jth unit in layer q.

Backpropagation Algorithm

1. Initialize all weights $\mathbf{W}$ to small random values within the range $[-\lambda, \lambda]$.

2. Randomly select a pair of training patterns $\{\mathbf{x}^p, \mathbf{t}^p\}$ (input, target) and compute in a feedforward direction the output values for each unit j of each layer q, thus

$$O_j^q = f\left(\Sigma_i O_i^{q-1} w_{ji}^q\right)$$

Note that the inputs to layer one are indexed with the superscript 0, and hence,

$$O_j^0 = x_j$$

3. Use the values O_j^Q computed by the final layer units and the corresponding target values t_j^p to compute the delta quantities

$$\delta_j^Q = \left(O_j^Q - t_j^p\right)f'\left(H_j^Q\right)$$

for all j using pattern p.

4. Compute the deltas for each of the preceding layers by backpropagating the errors using

$$\delta_j^{q-1} = f'\left(H_j^{q-1}\right)\Sigma_i \delta_i^q w_{ji}^q$$

for all j in each of the layers $q = Q, Q - 1, ..., 2$.

5. Update all weights w_{ji} using

$$w_{ji}^{new} = w_{ji}^{old} + \Delta w_{ji}^q$$

for each layer q, where

$$\Delta w_{ji}^q = \eta \, \delta_i^q \, O_j^{q-1}$$

6. Return to step 2 and repeat for each pattern p until the total error has reached an acceptable level.

Although the above procedure outlines the basic steps needed to train an MLFF network, many questions remain before a specific network can be used effectively in a given application. One should seek answers to the following questions before proceeding with an application.

- What functions (mappings) are MLFF networks capable of computing?

- How many layers should be used and how many units per layer are optimal for the mappings required in a given application?

- What input coding scheme should be employed for the input feature patterns?

- Should they be normalized in some way?

- What is the storage capacity of a given network?

- Is a fully connected feedforward architecture best for the application or should one consider alternative connection schemes such as partially connected networks with three-dimensional layers or sparsely connected networks?

- Should the use of hybrid networks be considered, that is, mixing layers of MLFF networks with BP and other network layer types (Kohonen, RCE, ART, Hamming)?

- What are the best learning procedures to follow?

- What constitutes a good training set?

- How large should the test and evaluation pattern sets be for a given application?

- How can a training set be developed?

- Should training patterns be selected randomly or systematically during training?

- Should noise be added to the training patterns?

- Should weight adjustment be performed after each pattern or after each epoch?

- How can local minima in the error function be detected and avoided?

- How can the learning process be accelerated?

- How should the weights be initialized?

- What activation functions are best for a given application?

- How can a network be taught to generalize?

- What is meant by generalization?

- What performance characteristics (e.g. accuracy, robustness, ability to generalize) are desired for an application?

- How can they be tested and measured?

- How well do behaviors of small networks scale up to large networks?

We address each of the above questions in this chapter and the following two. But first, we consider some update rules for specific activation functions and some commonly used benchmark problems.

6.3   BP Activation Functions

The backpropagation training process requires that the activation functions be bounded, differentiable functions. One of the most commonly used functions satisfying these requirements is the sigmoid function (also known as the logistic function). This function is defined over $\mathbf{R}$ and is bounded between zero and one. It is an S shaped monotonic increasing function that has the general form

$$f(x) = \frac{1}{1 + e^{-\beta x}} \qquad (6.30)$$

where β is a constant that determines the steepness of the S shaped curve. A plot of the function for different values of β is illustrated in Figure 6.5a. The derivative of the function is

$$f'(x) = \beta f(x)(1 - f(x)) \qquad (6.31)$$

It is illustrated in Figure 6.5b. Note that the derivative is maximum at $x = 0$ and has a value of 0.25β at that point. As x moves away from zero, the derivative approaches zero.

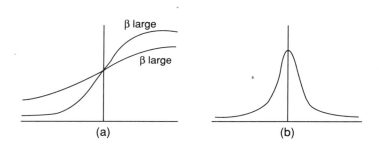

Figure 6.5   Plot of (a) the Sigmoid Function and (b) its Derivative

The BP update rules when using the sigmoid function will have deltas substituted in equations (6.23) and (6.24) given by

$$\delta_k = O_k(1 - O_k)(t_k - O_k) \qquad (6.32)$$

$$\delta_j = O_j(1 - O_j)\Sigma_k w_{kj}\delta_k \qquad (6.33)$$

respectively. This follows directly from (6.31) with $\beta = 1$.

Another commonly used function is the hyperbolic tangent. This function has a shape similar to the sigmoid function. It is also monotonic increasing, but ranges from -1 to $+1$ rather than 0 to 1. It has the following symmetric form

$$f(x) = \frac{e^x - e^{-x}}{e^x + e^{-x}} \qquad (6.34)$$

Substituting βx for x in this equation gives a parameter which can be used to adjust the steepness of the S shaped curve as in the case of the sigmoid function.

The derivative of the hyperbolic function also takes a simple form, given by

$$f'(x) = \beta\left(1 - \left(f(x)\right)^2\right) \tag{6.35}$$

where the coefficient β has been included. A plot of this function and its derivative is portrayed in Figure 6.6.

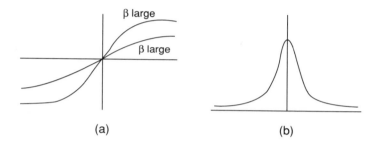

Figure 6.6   Plot of (a) the Hyperbolic Tangent Function and (b) its Derivative

The BP update rules for this function will have deltas substituted in equations (6.23) and (6.24) given by

$$\delta_k = \left(1 - O_k^2\right)(t_k - O_k) \tag{6.36}$$

$$\delta_j = \left(1 - O_j^2\right)\Sigma_k w_{kj}\delta_k \tag{6.37}$$

respectively.

Other activation functions that might be used effectively in MLFF networks include log functions (e.g. entropy functions), trigonometric functions (sine and cosine), and radial basis functions (Gaussian). These functions are introduced in later sections when appropriate.

6.4   Benchmark Problems for MLFF Network Performance Testing

In this section, we describe some of the more commonly used benchmark problems for MLFF networks. These problems are typical of the problems used by researchers to test various performance characteristics of MLFF networks and to verify theoretical results through simulation experiments. We make frequent reference to the problems when presenting examples of theory and empirical results in the remainder of this and subsequent chapters.

Commonly Used Benchmarking Problems

XOR or Parity. These networks are trained to produce an output of one (zero) when the binary input has an odd (even) number of one bits. For the general parity problem, there are n binary inputs and one binary output. For the simple XOR, $n = 2$. The number of hidden layers and number of units varies, but typically, only one hidden layer is used.

Encoder/Decoder. These fully connected networks typically have input and output layers of n units and a hidden layer with m units, where $0 < m \leq n$. The network is presented with n distinct binary input patterns, each with only one different bit position on (one). The other $n - 1$ bits are off (zero). The network is trained to produce an output binary pattern which is identical to the input pattern. This forces the hidden units to encode the patterns. For example, with $n = 16$ and $m = 4$, the network must provide an equivalent binary $\log_2 n$ encoding in the hidden layer. When m is small compared to n (e.g. $m = \log_2 n$), the task is more difficult to learn than when m is near n. This is sometimes referred to as tight encoding.

Complement Encoder. These networks are trained to learn the complement of the Encoder/Decoder problem. Thus the n input and duplicate output patterns are all on (one) except for a single unit which is off (zero). As in the Encoder/Decoder case, the hidden-layer units must learn to encode the input patterns.

Majority Vote. Majority vote networks are trained to output a one when more than half of the binary inputs are on (one). Otherwise, the network outputs a zero. These networks typically have an odd number n of inputs and a single output. The number of hidden units will vary, but typically will be less than the number of inputs.

Random Associations. These networks are trained using pairs of randomly selected patterns, one for input and an independent pattern for output. This is one of the most difficult mapping problems to learn since, in general, there are no clusters of patterns that share similar features. The mappings can be relaxed some by randomly drawing the patterns from pregrouped or clustered sets of patterns.

Character Recognition. A popular type of benchmark tests for networks is that used for character recognition. The number of inputs and outputs will vary depending on the set of characters used for recognition and the choice of features selected for input. In the simplest case, a few printed characters are chosen such as the ten integers (0, ..., 9), with one or more different font types. In the most difficult case cursory handwritten character recognition is attempted. For these tests, the inputs may be individual pixels (say 16 × 16) or a limited number of other specially selected features. The output units usually correspond to the individual characters. The number of hidden layers and units will vary depending on the application, but typically, no more than two hidden layers are required

Chunking. In this problem the network must learn to recognize the number of "chunks" of like bits (zeros or ones), that is, groups of contiguous bits in a string of binary numbers. The string may be considered as circular so that the rightmost bit in the string is treated as being adjacent to the leftmost bit. For example, the network may be trained to recognize when a circular bit string contains more than two such chunks. In that case the string 11000001111011 should produce a negative output (two chunks only) whereas the string 00111100100011 should produce a positive output. The network should be able to learn to recognize other numbers of chunks as well.

Number of Input Bits. For this problem, the network must learn to count the number of one (zero) bits in a binary input string. If no ones (zeros) are present in the number, the net should have only a single output high. If a single one bit is present on the input string, two outputs should be high, and so on. For n inputs, the network requires $n + 1$ outputs. A variation of this problem is to require that the network learn to translate binary numbers into "thermometer" value outputs.

The problems presented above are by no means an exhaustive set, but they are the most commonly occurring ones in the literature.

6.5   Error Surfaces and Convergence Properties

BP training is based on the gradient descent computations derived above. This process iteratively searches for a set of weights $\mathbf{W}^*$ that minimize the error function E over all training pattern pairs, that is,

$$E(\mathbf{W}^*) = \min_{\mathbf{W}} \left\{ \sum_{p=1}^{P} E^p(\mathbf{W}, \mathbf{x}^p) \right\}$$

This is a classic type of optimization problem. For such problems, an objective (or cost) function is usually defined to be maximized (minimized) with respect to a set of parameters. In this case, the network parameters that optimize (minimize) the error function E over the pattern set $\{\mathbf{x}^p, \mathbf{t}^p | p = 1, 2, ..., P\}$, are the synaptic weight values $\mathbf{W}^*$.

In conventional BP, minimization is with respect to the mean-square-error (MSE) cost function E. The use of MSE is not essential (nor even desirable) for BP learning. We could just as well have defined it to be one of a number of other acceptable functions that measure the approximation error of the network, and hence decrease as the difference between the target and computed outputs decrease. For example, we could use the absolute error, the maximum (supremum) error, mean error, median error, entropy, or other such function. The choice of error measure will depend on the way in which we wish to assess the performance, and hence, how we should train the network. For a BP type of learning method, we do require that the error measure chosen should be differentiable and tend to zero as the collective differences between the target and computed patterns ($\mathbf{t}^p - \mathbf{z}^p$) decrease over the entire training set, however.

The MSE measure given by

$$E_{tot} = \frac{1}{P} \sum_{p=1}^{P} E^p \quad \text{where } E^p = \frac{1}{2} \sum_{k=1}^{m} \left(t_k^p - z_k^p \right)^2 \tag{6.38}$$

is by far the most popular error function. This function is often chosen because of its statistical properties and because it is better understood than other measures. It is a non-negative, differentiable function that penalizes large errors more than small ones. Its popularity stems from its similarity to other statistical measures such as the least squares criteria in curve-fitting (e.g. in regression analysis). It is also similar to the sample correlation which tends to one as the difference between the target and computed output patterns decreases. Assuming then that equation (6.38) is our chosen measure for the error, how can the network be trained most effectively to find a global minimum? This question has been the focus of much interest over the past few years with emphasis given to improvements to the BP training process as it relates to the shape of the error surface.

The Error Surface

MLFF networks with nonlinear activation functions have an MSE error surface E above the total Q-dimensional weight space $\mathbf{R}^Q$ which is not, in general, a smooth parabolic surface as in the single-layer, linear activation function case. In general, the error surface is complex and believed to have many local and global minima (McInerny et al., 1989) as illustrated for the two-dimensional weight-space case in Figure 6.7. The multiplicity of minima arises in part from the symmetry of the weights and nodes in the network. At any given error value E, including minima regions, there are many permutations of weights which give rise to the same value of E. Minima also occur as a result of cancellation effects among weights with opposite sign as well as the summation of many nonlinear components over the pattern space. As a consequence, BP is never assured of finding a global minimum as in the single-layer, delta-rule case. The error surfaces for such networks are far more irregular than the smooth parabolic bowl-shape surface for the delta-rule. They contain ravines with steep sides, plateaus, shallow long valleys, local minima and other irregular geometries. Searching for a global minimum on such surfaces is trickier, and can be intolerably slow. Indeed, the search can and often does fail through stagnation or entrapment in a flat valley or local minimum.

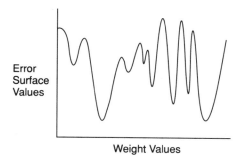

Error
Surface
Values

Weight Values

Figure 6.7   Typical Error Surface for MLFF Networks with Nonlinear Activation Functions

In the general MLFF network case, the error surfaces will have many local minima. One exception to this rule is the class of MLFF networks which satisfy the conditions of Kolmogorov's theorem (Yu, 1991). These networks have an infinite number of minima all of which are global. But even for these networks it is possible for the learning process to get stuck, for example on flat or near flat regions of the error surface.

At the start of the training process, gradient descent search begins at a location with error value E determined by the initial weight assignment $\mathbf{W}(0)$ and the training pattern pair $(\mathbf{x}^p, \mathbf{t}^p)$, where

$$E = \frac{1}{P} \sum_{p=1}^{P} E^p = \frac{1}{2P} \sum_{p,k} \left(t_k^p - f_k(\mathbf{W}(0), \mathbf{x}^p) \right)^2 \tag{6.39}$$

During training, the gradient descent computations incrementally determine how the weights should be modified at each new location to move most rapidly in the direction opposite the direction of steepest ascent (i.e. steepest descent). After the incremental adjustment to the weights has been made, the location is shifted to a different E-value location on the error-weight surface. This process is repeated for each training pattern p (or each epoch $\{\mathbf{x}^p, \mathbf{t}^p | p = 1, 2, ..., P\}$), progressively shifting the location to lower error levels until a threshold error value is reached or until a limit on the total number of training cycles is reached.

In moving down the error-weight surface, the path followed is generally not the ideal path. It depends on the surface shape and the learning coefficient η as described below. There are extensive flat areas and troughs where the weights must be changed many times to realize a perceptive drop in error. At locations with steep slopes, larger steps can result in oscillatory movements across the slopes. Such anomalies make it difficult for gradient descent to choose the right direction to move, thereby making progress slow and uncertain. Indeed, because the error surface is the summation of quadratic terms which describe elliptic rather than circular contours, gradient descent will not usually point directly in the direction of a minimum (Jacobs, 1988). This is illustrated in Figure 6.8 for a two-dimensional surface. Since the error surface is steeper along the w_2 dimension than along the w_1 dimension, the derivative of w_2 is greater than the derivative of w_1, resulting in a combined vector that is shifted more in the direction of the w_2 derivative. Consequently, the combined vector does not point toward the true minimum value.

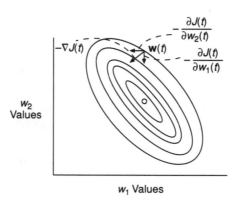

Figure 6.8   Direction of Descent for Two-Dimensional Case

6.6 Improving the Rate of Convergence

We saw that the search process depends on the shape of the error surface as well as the learning procedure and the training set. In this section, we examine factors related to the later topics, namely the learning procedure and the training set. We are interested in finding procedures which improve the learning rate of convergence.

Weight Initialization

Recall that at the start of the training process, initial values are chosen for the weights. The choice of values selected obviously affects the rate of convergence. A choice of initial values $\mathbf{W}(0)$ near $\mathbf{W}^*$ can result in rapid convergence. On the other hand, a poorly chosen assignment can result in tens of thousands of iterations before convergence or even failure to converge. For example, initially setting all weights to the same value will result in failure since all hidden units connected to output units will receive identical error update values (since the backpropagated error is proportional to the weights). Because weight adjustments depend on the backpropagated error signals, all adjustments made to the weights will be the same and the system will remain stuck at an equilibrium point that keeps the weights from changing. Clearly, many other choices of initial weights can also cause the learning process to get stuck in a flat region on the error-weight surface.

It has been shown that setting the weights to small (but not too small) random values, say between -1 and $+1$, is an effective way to avoid shallow troughs and possible entrapment at the start of the training process. If large weights are initially chosen, the activation functions f can become saturated. When this occurs, the derivative of f in the hidden-layer update term

$$v_{ji}^{\text{new}} = v_{ji}^{\text{old}} + \Delta v_{ji} = v_{ji}^{\text{old}} + \eta x_i f'(H_j) \Sigma_k \delta_k w_{kj}$$

is near zero. This is because the derivative of the sigmoid is $f'(x) = f(x)(1 - f(x))$ where $f(x)$ is the output of any sigmoid unit. This quantity is maximum at $x = 0$, $(f'(0) = 0.25)$ and approaches zero as $f(x)$ moves toward 0.0 or 1.0. Therefore, at these points, only small adjustments are made to the weights. As a consequence, downhill progress is slowed. This is illustrated in Figure 6.9. One way to avoid this is to use an error measure that grows larger as $f(x)$ moves toward 0 or 1. Another simple way is to add a constant b to the derivative term so it never falls below this value. Experiments (Fahlman, 1988) have shown that using a value of $b = 0.1$ have resulted in significant improvements in the convergence rate over standard BP methods.

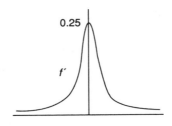

Figure 6.9   The Weight Adjustments are Proportional to the Derivative of the Activation Function f'

In other simulation experiments (Hirose et al., 1991), it was shown that convergence may never be realized for some networks when the initialized weights are poorly chosen. From experiments conducted with two-layer MLFF networks on the XOR and 16×16 pixel character recognition problems (see Section 6.4 for a description of these problems), the number of hidden units was varied to study convergence properties of the networks. It was found that when the weights were initially assigned random numbers that were too small or too large, the networks often failed to converge. On the other hand, when the assignments were confined to values within the range of $[-0.5, 0.5]$ or $[-1.0, 1.0]$ convergence was almost always achieved. Figure 6.10 illustrates some of the results obtained for the XOR problem using conventional BP. Note that when the initial weights are very small (e.g. in $[-0.05, 0.05]$), convergence was never achieved. In these cases the computations became trapped in local minima.

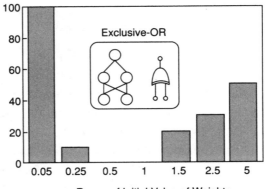

Figure 6.10   Ratio of Nonconvergent Runs for Different Initial Weights
(Adapted from Hirose et al., 1991. Courtesy of the authors.)

Estimating Initial Values

Rather than assigning random values to initialize the weights, it may be possible to estimate values that are near a minimum solution and use these as the initial assignments $\mathbf{W}(0)$ (Chen and Nutter, 1991). To see how this may be achieved, we introduce the following notation:

$\mathbf{X}$: the $P \times n$ matrix of input training patterns (each row vector is a training pattern in $\mathbf{R}^n$)

$\mathbf{T}$: the $P \times m$ target output pattern matrix (each row vector is an output pattern in $\mathbf{R}^m$)

$\mathbf{H}$: the $P \times h$ matrix of hidden unit outputs for P training patterns

f : an invertible vector function (each component of the column vector function has an inverse f^{-1})

$\mathbf{V}$: the $n \times h$ hidden layer weight matrix

$\mathbf{W}$: the $h \times m$ output layer weight matrix

Note that in the case of the sigmoid function,

$$f(x) = [1 + \exp(-x)]^{-1}$$

the inverse of f is just

$$f^{-1}(x) = -\ln(1/x - 1) \tag{6.40}$$

for each component f of $\mathbf{f}$. We also have the following relationships:

$$f(\mathbf{X}\,\mathbf{V}) = \mathbf{H} \tag{6.41}$$

$$f(\mathbf{H}\,\mathbf{W}) = \mathbf{T} \tag{6.42}$$

To estimate the network solution weight values, we begin by initializing the weights $\mathbf{V}$ to small random values in $[-\lambda, \lambda]$ and computing the value of $\mathbf{H}$ from (6.41). We then use the relation

$$f^{-1}(\mathbf{T}) = \mathbf{H}\,\mathbf{W} \tag{6.43}$$

to find an estimate for the weights $\mathbf{W}$. There are three cases to consider depending on the relative ranks r of the matrices $\mathbf{H}$ and $\mathbf{H}\,f^{-1}(\mathbf{T})$. In the case where

$$r(\mathbf{H}) = r(\mathbf{H}f^{-1}(\mathbf{T})) = h \tag{6.44}$$

a unique solution exists and is given by

$$\mathbf{W} = \mathbf{H}^{-1}f^{-1}(\mathbf{T}) \tag{6.45}$$

In the case where

$$r(\mathbf{H}) = r(\mathbf{H}f^{-1}(\mathbf{T})) < h \tag{6.46}$$

there are an infinite number of solutions. In this case, there are no analytical methods to determine the optimal solution, so a minimum-norm solution can be used as given by

$$\mathbf{W} = \mathbf{H}^t(\mathbf{H}\mathbf{H}^t)^{-1}f^{-1}(\mathbf{T}) \tag{6.47}$$

where $\mathbf{H}^t$ denotes the transpose of $\mathbf{H}$ and $\mathbf{H}^t(\mathbf{H}\mathbf{H}^t)^{-1}$ is the pseudo-inverse of $\mathbf{H}$. Finally, if

$$r(\mathbf{H}) < r(\mathbf{H}f^{-1}(\mathbf{T})) \tag{6.48}$$

there is no exact solution, so one can either ignore $n-m$ of the training patterns to make (6.48) a uniquely determined case or find a least-squared error solution such that $E(\mathbf{W})$ is a minimum. In the latter case, the pseudo-inverse can be used again to find $\mathbf{W}$ through the relation

$$\mathbf{W} = (\mathbf{H}^t\mathbf{H})^{-1}\mathbf{H}^tf^{-1}(\mathbf{T}) \tag{6.49}$$

BP can then be applied directly to adjust the weights $\mathbf{V}$ and $\mathbf{W}$. Alternatively, one can use the estimates of $\mathbf{W}$ obtained above to perform a "backward" estimation of $\mathbf{V}$ in a manner comparable to finding estimates of $\mathbf{W}$ in the forward estimation procedure. By iteratively applying the forward-backward estimations one can then obtain a recurrent estimate of both $\mathbf{V}$ and $\mathbf{W}$. We omit the details of the iterative procedure. Experiments performed on six small MLFF network types suggest that a savings of about 50% in computation time can be realized over conventional random initialization techniques using this approach.

Another weight initialization method that shows even more promise in learning-time savings (for MLFF networks used as classifiers) is to set the input to hidden-layer weights v_{ij} to normalized prototype pattern values P_j (i.e. class reference vectors) and the hidden to output-layer weights w_{jk} equal to 1 if the P_j

prototype vector represents the kth class and 0 otherwise (Denoeux et al., 1991). Prototypes are learning set patterns that are good class representatives. For example, they may be cluster centroids, vector quantized code patterns or mean value type vectors determined by well-known clustering techniques. For this, the prototype training vectors should be normalized to have length equal to unity.

Other weight initialization methods have been proposed (Kim and Ra, 1991; Haario, H. and P. Jokinen, 1991), for example, if the weights w_i, rather than the feature vectors, are normalized to

$$u_i = \frac{w_i}{\left(\sum\limits_{j=1}^{n} w_i^2\right)^{1/2}}$$

it can be shown that for **u** to converge, we should have

$$0 < \frac{n}{\left(\sum\limits_{j=1}^{n} w_i^2\right)^{1/2}} < 1$$

and hence, if magnitudes of the initial values are assumed to be approximately the same, the initial weight values $w_i(0)$ should satisfy

$$|w_i(0)| > (n/N)^{1/2} \quad \text{for } i = 1, 2, ..., N$$

We omit the analysis which leads up to the above bound, and note only that impressive savings in learning time over conventional BP (with momentum term) were realized in the XOR and three-parity problems.

Introduction of Random Noise

Local minima traps can often be avoided with the introduction of random noise during the search process. Introducing random noise is another way of shifting the location of the error function thereby permitting the descent process to escape from local minima and continue on its downward search for a global minimum. Randomization can be achieved by direct addition of small random perturbations to the weights when convergence is stalled, directly adding some noise to the patterns, by selecting each pattern presented at random or through some other stochastic process such as simulated annealing (described in Chapter 10). The introduction of noise during the learning process can also improve the network's ability to generalize as shown below. Noise can also cause problems. For example, it is possible to miss a good local minima if the noise significantly changes the position on the error surface during descent.

Effects of the Learning Rate Coefficient

The learning rate coefficient η in the generalized delta-rule determines the size of the weight adjustments made at each iteration and hence influences the rate of convergence. The value of η is important since large variations in learning rate can result with different choices of η. A poor choice can result in failure to converge. It is also known that η should not be constant throughout the learning process for best results. This is because error surfaces that have broad flat shapes near minima require larger coefficient values for rapid convergence, while steep narrow shapes near minima require small values of η to avoid overshooting of the solution. If the chosen value of η is too large for the error surface, the search path will oscillate about the ideal path and converge more slowly than a direct descent. It may even diverge. On the other hand, if the chosen value of η is too small, the descent will progress in very small steps significantly increasing the total time to convergence. Figure 6.11 illustrates typical convergence paths for different values of η used in learning random associations. Of course, the error surfaces for nonlinear MLFF networks are typically not smooth parabolas as depicted in the figure.

From the examples of Figure 6.11, it can be seen that a value of $\eta = 0.9$ appears to be optimal, however, the best choice of η is problem dependent and may require some trial and error before a good choice is found. In fact, for best results, different values of η should be used for each weight during the training process since no single value is optimal for all dimensions. This was illustrated in Figure 6.8 where it was noted that, in general, the error derivatives for each weight will differ unless the error surface is perfectly circular in shape. Furthermore, if each weight has an η_i value, it should be allowed to vary with time. This can be accomplished by continually monitoring the change in error during training and adjusting the value of each η_i to better fit the local region of descent. For example,

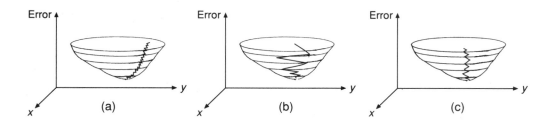

Figure 6.11   Convergence Paths for Different Learning Coefficient Values
(a) $\eta = 0.2$, (b) $\eta = 0.9$, and (c) $\eta = 1.5$

if for a fixed η_i value, several weight adjustments have each decreased the error then that η_i should probably be increased since the current value is too conservative for the local surface shape.

On the other hand, if no increase resulted with an adjustment, it is likely that the process overshot a minimum and hence η_i should be reduced. Some authors, (e.g. Jacobs, 1988) have suggested the use of adaptive coefficients where the value of η_i is a function of the error derivatives on successive updates. It is adjusted prior to each weight update during the training process. Such methods have been shown to converge more rapidly than with the use of a constant parameter, but at the cost of extra computation. Simulations (Tollenaere, 1990; Hirose et al., 1991) have demonstrated how the value of η can influence learning rate on MLFF networks when used to learn I/O pattern association tasks. Figure 6.12 illustrates the rates of convergence for different choices of η in an autoassociative learning task (Figure 6.12a) using a 10-10-10 size network, and a random pattern association problem using a 10-5-2 size network (Figure 6.12b).

It can be seen that an increase in η results in an exponential decrease in learning rate up to some point and that an optimal, but different, value of η occurs, in general, for all runs. The figure also illustrates how the optimal step size can vary with the problem task and how the distribution of learning times (vertical bars) varies as a function of step size.

Adding a Momentum Term

Another possible way to improve the rate of convergence is by adding some inertia or momentum to the gradient expression. This can be accomplished by adding a fraction of the previous weight change to the current weight change. The addition of such a term can help smooth out the descent path by preventing extreme changes in the gradient due to local anomalies. It can act as an averaging effect which smooths the trajectory of the gradient as it moves downhill. A commonly used update rule introduced by Rumelhart et al. (1986) includes such a momentum term. The update equation they used is defined by

$$\Delta w_j(t + 1) = -\eta \frac{\partial E}{\partial w_j(t)} + \alpha \Delta w_j(t) \tag{6.50}$$

where α is the momentum coefficient. The value of α should be positive and less than 1. Typical values lie in the range $[0.5, 0.9]$, but for some problems (see Fahlman, 1988) a value of $\alpha = 0.0$ was shown to be best. It should be noted that equation (6.50) is a difference equation, and hence, that the momentum term is effectively an exponentially weighted sum of a weight's current and past partial

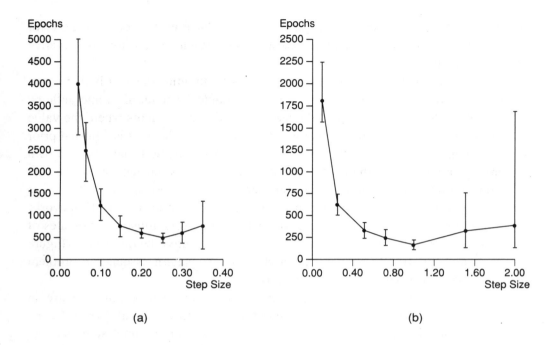

Figure 6.12   Learning Rate as a Function of Learning Parameter Step Size for (a) an
Autoassociative Learning Problem and (b) a Random Association Problem
(From Tollenaere, 1990. Courtesy of Professor Tom Tollenaere.)

derivatives. This term encourages movement in the same direction on successive steps. Therefore, it tends to suppress any oscillations that result from changes in the slope of the error surface.

To be most effective, the momentum constant should be adjusted dynamically as well as the learning constant. But because the two terms are not independent, the two values should be chosen and modified as a pair. For many standard problems, the learning coefficient η should start out large and gradually decrease as the error approaches a minimum. Conversely, the momentum coefficient α should start out small and gradually increase as the error approaches a solution. In this way, a direction for descent will be found and rapid progress made at the start of the search with a slowdown occurring near the end to reduce the possibility of overshoot. But again, it should be emphasized that the values of both parameters are problem dependent and to generalize too freely in this regard can be misleading.

Numerous experiments have been conducted by researchers to determine the effects of the momentum term on speed of convergence and stability of the learning procedures (Fahlman, 1988; Jacobs, 1988; Minai and Williams, 1990; Tollenaere, 1990; Sato, 1991). In general, dynamic adjustment of both parameters can accelerate convergence as noted above. But values of either η or α that are too large can lead to instability in the update process. Simulations performed by Tollenaere, 1990 illustrate the interdependency of the two coefficients. This interdependency is illustrated in Figure 6.13 where families of η vs. epoch curves are plotted for different choices of α. The two plots (Figures 6.13a and b) are for two different autoassociation problems which used randomly generated N-dimensional input and output patterns for training.

To study the effects of the momentum coefficient alone, experiments were conducted (Sato, 1991) in which both η and the initial weights were fixed in advance. Two simple problems (4-to-2 encoder and 4-bit parity) were used for the simulations in which α was varied in steps of 0.1 from 0.0 to 0.9 and in steps of 0.01 from 0.9 to 0.99. The results are summarized in Figure 6.14 from which the following relationships were derived (valid when the number of epochs is large).

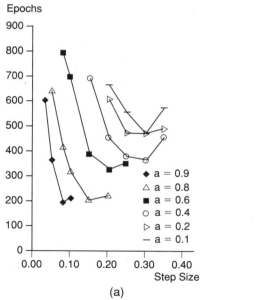
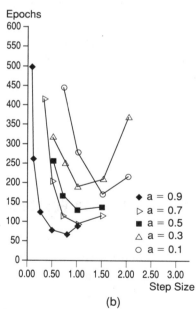

Figure 6.13   Effects of Momentum Term on Convergence
(From Tollenaere 1990. Courtesy of Professor Tom Tollenaere.)

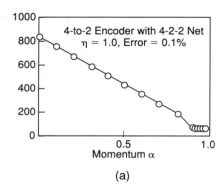

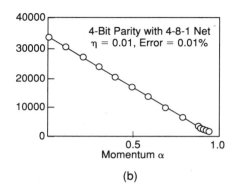

Figure 6.14   Relationship Between Momentum Coefficient α and Number of Learning Epochs to Convergence (From Sato, 1991. Courtesy of Professor A. Sato.)

$$N = 8.28 \times 10^2 \propto (1 - \alpha) \text{ for the encoder problem}$$

$$N = 3.47 \times 10^4 \propto (1 - \alpha) \text{ for the parity problem}$$

where N is the number of learning epochs to convergence. Under certain simplifying assumptions, it can also be shown that when α is small, $N \propto (1 - \alpha)/\eta$ which is in agreement with the above results from the simulation experiments. This suggests that α behaves as an integrator rather than a low pass filter as claimed by other experimenters.

When α is large, the relationship does not apply well as the momentum term then exceeds the Δw trajectory in weight space. This can either accelerate or slow down learning depending on the energy-weight surface.

Effects of Activation Functions on Convergence

From the neural network literature, one can see that the most commonly used activation functions for MLFF networks is the sigmoid function given by (6.30).

Although this function has some biological plausibility and some desirable computational properties, it introduces some serious problems with regard to convergence. In the first place, the error surface induced through the use of sigmoid activation functions is believed to have numerous anomalies (described above) that tend to retard or even prohibit convergence. Secondly, when the PE output values approach 0 or 1 (a common target goal during training) the factors $z_k(1 - z_k)$ in the PB update algorithm (equation (6.32)) make the error signals very small. Consequently, even output units with large errors will not produce strong update adjustments, thereby slowing the convergence. This same phenomenon can occur when the synoptic weights of a PE become large forcing the PE into saturation. Finally, the asymmetry of the standard sigmoid function has been shown to be inferior to the symmetrical (hyperbolic tangent) sigmoid function (Folgeman Soulie, 1991) with regard to convergence. With these limitations, it is a curious fact that the sigmoid is as popular as it appears to be.

Of course, convergence and computation costs are not the only considerations when choosing activation functions. Equally important are the mapping and generalization capabilities which are also dependent on choice of activation function. These subjects are reserved for the following chapter.

Effects of Error Function on Convergence

It was noted above that the MSE error function was not necessarily the best choice of measure of performance or cost for MLFF networks. Indeed, the error surface for the MSE has many irregularities that make convergence difficult. Some possible substitutes for MSE that appear promising are logarithmic based functions of the error $(z_k - t_k)$. Two such functions that have been proposed are described below.

The first example, introduced by Matsuoka and Yi (1991) confirm that the error surface of a log error function similar to the information theoretic entropy has fewer local minima than MSE. This log function is defined as

$$L_1(\mathbf{W}) = \Sigma_p \left(t_k^p \ln\left(\frac{t_k^p}{z_k^p}\right) + (1 - t_k^p)\ln\left(\frac{1 - t_k^p}{1 - z_k^p}\right) \right) \qquad (6.51)$$

where values of t_k^p and z_k^p are restricted to [0, 1] and we assume that $0*\ln 0 = 0$. When this cost function is used with BP, the error propagated backward from output unit k is just $(z_k^p - t_k^p)$ as compared to $z_k^p(1 - z_k^p)(z_k^p - t_k^p)$ for MSE. The error propagated backward from non-output units is the same as that for MSE. Thus, as pointed out below, learning tends to be somewhat faster with the use of $L_1(\mathbf{W})$ than with $E(\mathbf{W})$ and the computation time is no greater. A comparison of learning times for the 4-bit parity problem using both functions and BP training is illustrated in Figure 6.15. Similar results were also obtained for other test problems (Matsuoka and Yi, 1991). Note that for the MSE case (Figure 6.15a), learning appears to be trapped in local minima for four out of the five cases tested, whereas all of the runs using log error functions converged (Figure 6.15b). Thus, we see that in spite of its general popularity, the use of MSE as an error measure is questionable.

The second logarithmic function we describe has the form (van Ooyen and Nienhuis, 1992)

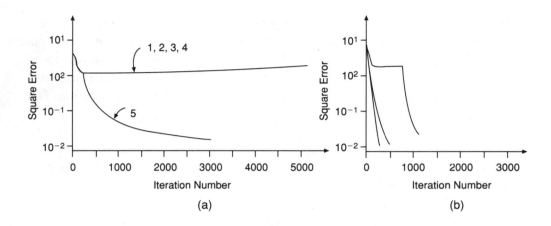

Figure 6.15   Parity Problem Learning Rates for (a) Standard MSE and
(b) Logarithmic Error Function
(Courtesy of K. Matsuoka and J. Yi)

$$L_2(\mathbf{W}) = - \sum_{p,k} \left[t_k^p \ln z_k^p + (1 - t_k^p)\ln(1 - z_k^p) \right] \qquad (6.52)$$

where recall that $0 < z_k^p < 1$.

Note that this function also has a form similar to the information theoretic entropy. Also, we see that for this case

$$\frac{\partial L_2}{\partial z_j} = \frac{z_j - t_j}{z_j(1 - z_j)}$$

and

$$\frac{\partial L_2}{\partial w_{ji}} = (z_j - t_j)$$

Thus, for L_2, the error propagated back from each output is directly proportional to the difference between the target and actual output.

Simulation comparisons of L_2 with standard MSE showed that the convergence rate was improved somewhat. Furthermore, the improvement was more pronounced for difficult problems where a 2-to-1 speedup was realized. Figure 6.16 shows results of multiple simulations for the Number of Bits "Counting" problem. In these experiments, optimal learning parameters were used for both error functions in the comparisons.

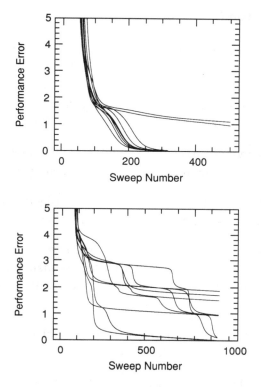

Figure 6.16   Comparison of Log vs Squared Error Performance
(From van Ooyen and Nienhuis, 1992. Courtesy of the authors.)

An analysis of the distance between the target and actual outputs after P epochs or sweeps through the training set gives the following approximation

$$|\mathbf{z} - \mathbf{t}| \approx \frac{1}{P^q}$$

For the standard BP algorithm $q = \frac{1}{2}$ and for L_2, $q = 1$, proving that the final convergence is faster for L_2 than for BP.

Other Learning Methods

Many attempts have been made to increase the learning rate for BP. A number of modifications and variations made to the basic BP method have already been described above. In this section we describe a few of the more important procedures that differ somewhat from the basic gradient descent methods covered above. These methods typically belong to one of the following types:

- Conjugate Gradient (based on second derivative methods of minimization through the use of noninterfering, that is, conjugate directions).

- Newton's Method (based on modeling the function using the first three terms of the Taylor series expansion about the current point $\mathbf{w}_k$).

- Secant methods (based on iterative approximations of the Hessian, the matrix of second derivatives, that is, approximating $\partial^2 E(w)/\partial w^2$ using the slope of the secant line through the values of the first derivative in two nearby points).

- Heuristic methods (methods based on general rules of thumb regarding convergence as in the Delta-Bar-Delta Method described below).

The first method we describe has been named Quickprop. It is a type of Secant method developed by Fahlman (1988).

Quickprop

The Quickprop procedure is effectively a second order method that (sometimes incorrectly) assumes that the shape of the error surface with respect to each weight is parabolic upward. It requires that copies of the error derivative $\partial E/\partial w(t - 1)$ for each weight and the difference between the current and previous values of the weights be retained from the previous training epoch. The Quickprop update computation is given by

$$\Delta w(t) = \frac{s(t)}{s(t - 1) - s(t)} \Delta w(t - 1) \tag{6.53}$$

where $s(t)$ and $s(t - 1)$ are the current and previous values of $\partial E/\partial w$, respectively. Experiments on different problems have shown that Quickprop results are typically better by a factor of 4 over other modified versions of backpropagation. Furthermore, the algorithm seems to scale up well to larger problems of the same type.

Delta-Bar-Delta

Delta-Bar-Delta is a method that implements four basic heuristics regarding gradient descent. It was developed by Jacobs (1988). The method consists of a weight update rule and learning update rule. The weight update rule is applied to each weight $w(t)$ at iteration t through the relationship given by

$$w(t + 1) = w(t) - \eta(t + 1)\frac{\partial E(t)}{\partial w(t)}$$

where $\eta(t)$ is the learning rate for weight w at update iteration t.

The learning rate update rule for a given weight w is defined as:

$$\Delta\eta(t) = \begin{cases} \kappa & \text{if } \overline{\delta}(t - 1)\delta(t) > 0 \\ -\phi\eta(t) & \text{if } \overline{\delta}(t - 1)\delta(t) < 0 \\ 0 & \text{otherwise} \end{cases} \tag{6.54}$$

where

$$\delta(t) = \frac{\partial E(t)}{\partial w(t)}$$

the partial derivative of the error with respect to w at time t, and

$$\overline{\delta}(t) = (1 - \theta)\delta(t) + \theta\overline{\delta}(t - 1) \tag{6.55}$$

and where κ and ϕ are constants used to increment or decrement the learning rate respectively, and $0 < \theta < 1$ is an exponential "smoothing" base constant for the time t.

This rule increases the learning rates linearly and decreases them exponentially. In this way, the learning rates are prevented from becoming too large too fast. It also ensures that the weights are always positive and they decrease rapidly.

As noted earlier, the Delta-Bar-Delta rule implements four heuristics that will normally improve the rate of convergence. The heuristics implemented are as follows:

1. Every parameter (weight) has its own individual learning rate.

2. Every learning rate is allowed to vary over time to adjust to changes in the error surface.

3. When the error derivative for a weight has the same sign for several consecutive update steps, the learning rate for that weight should be increased. This is because the error surface likely has a small curvature at such points and will continue to slope at the same rate for some distance. Therefore, the step size should be increased to speed up the downhill movement.

4. When the sign of the derivative of a weight alternates for several consecutive steps, the learning rate for that parameter should be decreased. This is because the error surface has a high curvature at the current point and the slope may quickly change sign. Thus, to prevent oscillation, the value of the step should be adjusted downward.

Other Second Order Methods

Second order methods are known to converge much more rapidly than methods based on first order. Unfortunately, these methods require calculation of the Hessian matrix, a process that is both complex and costly. A number of approximations that simplify the computations compared to the Hessian and to Newton's method have been introduced and proven to be somewhat effective. Battiti (1992) gives a review of such methods and Bishop (1992) provides complete calculations for the Hessian of a single hidden-layer MLFF. Finally, it should be noted that other, noncalculus based methods have also been investigated with some degree of success, including directed probabilistic search and Genetic Algorithm methods. The convergence rate of learning can also be improved by removing unnecessary or redundant weights and units. We describe some of these approaches in the following chapter.

Summary

In this chapter, we have introduced the generalized delta rule or error backpropagation learning algorithm. This is a local update rule that can be applied to any feedforward network architecture. Through the use of BP, it is possible to build and train multilayer networks that map patterns in n-dimensional space to m-dimensional space. We have derived the BP algorithm for a single hidden-layer network and then generalized this result to networks with any number of hidden layers. We saw that when training a network we would like a procedure that is assured of converging to a global minimum and in such a way that good performance is achieved with as few iterations over the training set as possible. Unfortunately, two of the serious weaknesses of BP training are the risk of being trapped in a nonglobal region and the slow rate of convergence. This becomes a serious problem for large networks. There are no foolproof methods which completely avoid convergence traps, and training for many problems can consume enormous amounts of computer time iterating thousands of times over the training set.

We examined the effects of weight initialization and the effects that different parameters have on the rate of convergence for BP. We introduced alternative error measures that exhibited faster rates of convergence and described several modifications to BP that improve convergence significantly. We saw that even though there are no known theoretical solutions to many of the problems related to rapid convergence, experience has shown that some simple techniques can often be used to overcome them as described in this and the following chapter where we also give a number of implementation guidelines.

7

Capabilities and Limitations of Multilayer Feedforward Networks

This chapter is a continuation of the preceding chapter where we developed the BP training algorithm. We also investigated various methods of avoiding convergence problems due to local anomalies and, in general, ways to improve the rate of convergence. In doing so, we addressed a few of the questions posed at the end of Section 6.2 related to the implementation of MLFF networks. In this chapter, we continue to address some of the other questions listed at the end of Section 6.2. Here, we look at questions related to MLFF capabilities and limitations. In particular, we are interested in their mapping and generalization capabilities, both from a theoretical and empirical point of view. Finally, we bring together the results of this and the preceding chapter in the form of a set of implementation guidelines that are useful in building MLFF networks for specific applications.

In the following chapter, we conclude our study of MLFF networks with BP learning by describing a number of typical applications. These applications illustrate the breadth of applicability for which these popular networks can be effectively employed. We also provide implementation details, thereby linking the guidelines of this chapter to specific applications where appropriate.

7.1   Introduction

The ultimate test of performance for any MLFF network is not just a small MSE. It is the network's ability to accurately and consistently produce an output z that agrees with a target value t. A small MSE indicates that a set of parameter values have been found that produce small errors over the training set. This is not a sufficient condition for continued high performance. A network with a small MSE may have learned the training set well but have failed to construct a good estimator

g' of the underlying mapping g. Before a mapping network can construct a good estimator from training examples, some basic conditions must be fulfilled. They are:

1. Both the fixed parameters (connections and activation functions) and variable parameters (adjustable thresholds and weights) must be rich and varied enough to permit the construction of a function g' that matches g with a high degree of accuracy. The architecture must possess the basic building blocks with which to build such an estimator.

2. The training set must contain enough information to reveal the structure of the underlying mappings. This implies that the training set must be sufficiently accurate and large enough to fully represent the underlying structure.

3. Given the requisite building blocks with which to build the estimator and a suitable training set, the learning algorithm must be powerful enough to extract information about the underlying mapping and find a set of adjustable parameter values that produce a good estimator g', and at a reasonable cost. The learning algorithm must be powerful enough to both draw out the underlying mapping from a limited set of examples and create a good estimator from the available building blocks.

There are two closely related problems here: approximation accuracy and learnability. From our knowledge of Fourier and power series, one would expect that an ANN with a large number of hidden nodes and the use of appropriate activation functions should be able to approximate a broad class of functions. But can a network of moderate size actually learn to approximate such functions well? These questions have been studied extensively over the past few years and some interesting results have now been obtained. We pursue these issues in the following four sections and culminate our findings with a set of implementation guidelines.

7.2 Mapping Capabilities of MLFF Networks

We have stated above that one of the most important issues related to MLFF network performance is their ability to compute arbitrary functions. The question is this—Given any decision function $\mathbf{g}$ which maps real-valued vector patterns from n-dimensional space to real-valued patterns in m-dimensional space, $\mathbf{g} : \mathbf{R}^n \rightarrow \mathbf{R}^m$, is it possible to implement an MLFF network that performs the required mapping or at least approximates it to some desired accuracy? The function $\mathbf{g}$ is, in general, unknown. In practice it must be estimated with a learning rule which produces a sequence of mappings $\{\mathbf{g}^p\}$ from a probability space using a finite set of observations $\{\mathbf{x}^p, t^p | p = 1, 2, ..., P\}$. If it is possible to estimate $\mathbf{g}$ well, how many hidden layers and how many nodes are needed and what activation functions must be used? What restrictions must be placed on the class of mapping functions $\mathbf{g}$ (e.g. continuous, monotone, finite number of discontinuities)?

One of the earliest results related to the mapping capability of parallel computers (e.g. ANNs) was published by Kolmogorov (1957) with his solution to the 13th problem of Hilbert. Hilbert's problem (or conjecture) related to finding an expression for the roots of a general algebraic equation of higher degree using sums and compositions of a single-variable function. Hilbert conjectured that some continuous functions of three variables cannot be represented using such superpositions even with functions of two variables. Kolmogorov's result, as first pointed out by Hecht-Nielsen (1987), established the fact that a two-layer feedforward network can be constructed to perform any continuous mapping $\mathbf{g}$ from the n-dimensional cube $[0, 1]^n$ to $\mathbf{R}^m$. Such a network with n-input and m-output units requires a hidden layer with at most $2n + 1$ units.

Kolmogorov's theorem states that any continuous function g (this can be generalized to m-dimensional vector functions $\mathbf{g}$) defined on a closed n-dimensional cube, (for example $[0, 1]^n$) can be represented in the following form

$$g(x_1, x_2, ..., x_n) = \sum_{j=1}^{2n+1} \psi_j \left(\sum_{i=1}^{n} \phi_{ij}(x_i) \right) \tag{7.1}$$

where ψ_j and ϕ_{ij} are continuous functions of one variable, and the ϕ_{ij} are increasing functions that are fixed for a given n. The functions ψ_j depend on the specific function g. The dependence of the ψ_j on g as a parameter limits the utility of the theorem since different unknown functions ψ_j are required for each continuous function g chosen to be represented.

Kolmogorov's superposition theorem is an existence theorem only. It provides no direct clues as to the form of functions that must be used to approximate a given mapping and its relevance to neural networks has been questioned (Girosi and Poggio, 1989). It does, however, give us the assurance that MLFF networks can, at least in theory, approximate any continuous mapping. Furthermore, it has now been shown (Kurkova, 1991) that staircase-like sigmoidal functions can, in fact, be used to actually construct the approximations to any continuous function g thereby establishing the relevance of the theorem.

Following Kolmogorov, a number of extended results have now been obtained (le Cun, 1987; Lapedes and Farber, 1988). For example, it has been shown that good approximations to an unknown function g can be obtained using MLFF networks having two hidden layers that use monotone squashing functions. A monotone squashing function $g(x)$ is defined as a non-decreasing function such that

$$\lim_{x \to -\infty} g(x) = 0 \qquad \text{and} \qquad \lim_{x \to \infty} g(x) = 1$$

The most familiar class of specialized squashing functions are, of course, the sigmoid (logistic) and hyperbolic tangent functions defined in Section 6.3.

A number of related results have been obtained related to mapping capability (Gallant and White, 1988; Hornik, Stinchcombe, and White, 1989; Hecht-Nielsen, 1989). It has shown that an MLFF network using arbitrary squashing functions (not necessarily continuous) are capable of approximating almost any function of interest (e.g. measurable functions) to any desired degree of accuracy. Similar results were obtained for continuous functions $\mathbf{g} : \mathbf{R}^n \to \mathbf{R}$ independently (Cybenko, 1988). Also, Kreinovich (1991) has shown that it is possible to implement a neural network capable of approximating any continuous mapping $\mathbf{g} : [-x, x]^n \to \mathbf{R}^m$ to any desired accuracy provided the units can compute polynomials, that is, provided they can perform addition and multiplication operations (such operations are easily implemented with hardware). It has also been demonstrated that the so-called class of rapidly decreasing functions can be approximated by a finite sum of integrals of step or sigmoid functions (a function $f(x)$ defined on $\mathbf{R}^n$ is rapidly decreasing if

$$\lim_{|x \to \infty|} \left| x_1^{k_1} x_1^{k_2} \cdots x_n^{k_n} f(x) \right|$$

for any constants k_i (Ito, 1991)).

Carrying the approximation results still further, (Hornik et al., 1990) we can now say that MLFF networks with one or more hidden layers of PEs with appropriately smooth activation functions are capable of arbitrarily accurate approximation to an arbitrary function and its derivatives. Being able to approximate the derivatives as well as the function may be important in some applications such as robotic learning of smooth movements (Jordan, 1989).

Other results have been obtained on the approximation ability of MLFF networks and on the number of hidden units needed to achieve a desired accuracy when certain simplifying restrictions are placed on the MLFF networks (Wei and Ou, 1991; Tamura, 1991; Shigeo et al., 1991).

Finally, some results suggest that the architecture of the MLFF network is more important than the choice of activation function in representing many functions (Hornik, 1991). If sufficiently many hidden units are available, activation functions need only be bounded and non-constant to approximate any function that is in *Lp* (*p*th power integrable) and that any continuous function defined on a compact set can be approximated with activation functions that are continuous, bounded and non-constant.

Radial-Basis Activation Functions

A number of researchers have investigated the use of radial-basis-functions (RBF) as activation functions (Broomhead and Lowe, 1988; Hartman et al., 1990; Park and Sandberg, 1991; Sandberg, 1991). For example, it has been shown that RBF can be used as universal function approximators in networks with a single hidden layer. In RBF networks, the hidden-layer units, called the kernel, each have a centroid $\mathbf{c}_i$ and smoothing factor σ_i. These nodes compute the distance between the input $\mathbf{x}_i$ and the centroid $\mathbf{c}_i$ rather than the vector product of the weights and inputs. The node outputs are a nonlinear, radially symmetric function of the distance. Thus, the output is strongest when the $\mathbf{x}_i$ are nearest the $\mathbf{c}_i$. RBFs are mapping functions $\mathbf{g}$, where $\mathbf{g} : \mathbf{R}^n \rightarrow \mathbf{R}$ has the general form

$$g(\mathbf{x}) = \sum_{i=1}^{M} w_i K[(x_i - c_i)/\sigma_i] \qquad (7.2)$$

where the function K is a radially symmetric kernal function computed by the kernel units. A commonly used RBF is the Gaussian exponential function

$$f(\mathbf{x}) = \alpha e^{-\Sigma i[(xi - ci)/\sigma i]^2} \qquad (7.3)$$

with centroid $\mathbf{c}_i$ and constants α and σ_i. It has been shown that the class of *p*th power integrable functions L_p can be approximated arbitrarily well with RBF networks having a single hidden layer. Empirical tests seem to verify this claim. Simulations carried out by Geva and Sitte, 1991, indicate that general Gaussian activation functions are superior to sigmoid functions in estimating a broad class of functions. The Gaussian functions used in the tests have the general form

$$z = g(\mathbf{x}) \sum_{j=1}^{h} w_j e^{-\|\mathbf{T}_j(\mathbf{x}_i - \mathbf{c}_i)\|^2} \qquad (7.4)$$

where $\mathbf{T}_j$ is a matrix of correlation terms and $\mathbf{c}_j$ is a vector of kernal unit centroid terms. Such functions are, in general "ellipsoid" bell-shaped functions with centers located at c_j, and their principal axis aligned in different directions depending on the matrix $\mathbf{T}$. With the flexibility afforded by such functions, RBF networks are able to model many different functional shapes. Each of the superposed component Gaussians will be appropriately scaled, signed and oriented to fit the required shape.

To train networks using RBF functions requires a modified form of gradient descent training. The network is first initialized by setting the centroids c_i equal to some of the training patterns x_i so the network gives a good approximation to the function $\mathbf{g}$ at these points. The transformation matrices $\mathbf{T}_j$ are simply initialized to multiples of the identity matrix. This gives the Gaussians sharp symmetric peaks with little overlap. As training progresses, the Gaussians are shifted, rotated, and scaled to fill in the training space and the network parameters are modified accordingly. The standard error function E is used as a measure of performance and the partial derivatives

$$\frac{\partial E}{\partial w_{ji}}, \ \frac{\partial E}{\partial c_{ji}}, \ \frac{\partial E}{\partial T_{ji}}$$

are computed and BP applied to adjust the network parameters until a global (or acceptable local) minimum is found. Individual learning rates are computed for each weight to determine the best weight adjustments. The amount of each adjustment is proportional to the magnitude of the individual partial derivatives.

Figure 7.1 illustrates the results of simulations (Geva and Sitte, 1991) in which comparisons are made between a standard MLFF network with sigmoid activation functions and an RBF network with Gaussian activation functions in learning to map a complex function. The increased accuracy of the RBF network over the standard sigmoid MLFF is clearly evident, at least for this application. It has also been found that the use of Gaussian activation functions can result in networks that learn accurately, quickly and form a compact representation using small numbers of units (Platt, 1991).

Clearly, there is much interest in establishing what MLFF networks are capable of computing. The results obtained to date are very important. They show what mappings are theoretically possible. Unfortunately, their practical value is still limited. They do not give us much guidance on the number of hidden layers and the number of nodes needed for a given application or on the best choice of activation functions to use when the number of units are limited. Neither do they tell us how well such networks can generalize nor even if it is possible to train such networks. Much more work is needed before these questions are answered. We pursue these questions further in Section 7.5 in the context of empirical simulation results.

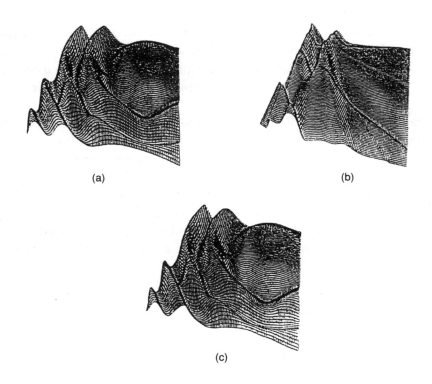

(a)

(b)

(c)

Figure 7.1   Function Approximation: (a) the Given Error Surface to be Approximated,
(b) an MLFF Approximation Using Sigmoid Activation Functions, and
(c) an RBF Network Approximation
(Courtesy of Professors S. Geva and J. Sitte)

We conclude this section with some examples of MLFF mapping experiments using different input patterns and network configurations. Tables 7.1 and 7.2 illustrate the mapping capabilities of some typical MLFF networks. Table 7.1 (Lippman, 1987) shows the general types of regions that can be learned by different MLFF network architectures, while Table 7.2 (Lui, 1989) shows the results of a number of simulation experiments using different network configurations.

In summary, we can now say that MLFF networks with at least one hidden layer using nonlinear activation functions such as the sigmoid, polynomial, arbitrary squashing functions, RBF, or just bounded, non-constant functions are capable of computing any reasonable mapping $\mathbf{g} : \mathbf{R}^n \to \mathbf{R}^m$ to any desired accuracy. The mapping is approximated by the superposition of a number of functional "bumps" and "crevices" which are computed by the hidden-layer nodes and combined by the output nodes. In practice, the mappings will be restricted to a closed compact set (e.g. $[-\mathbf{a}, \mathbf{a}]$) in $\mathbf{R}^n$.

Decision regions that can be formed by single and MLFF networks

Decision regions are denoted by shaded regions A and B

Structure	Types of Decision Regions	Exclusive OR Problem	Classes with Meshed Regions	Most General Region Shapes
Single-Layer	Half Plane Bounded by Hyperplane			
Two-Layer	Convex Open or Closed Regions			
Three-Layer	Arbitrary (Complexity Limited by Number of Nodes)			

Table 7.1   Examples of MLFF Network Mapping Capabilities
(From Lippman, 1987. © 1987 IEEE. Courtesy of Professor R. Lippman.)

Structures	Patterns 1	2	3	4	5
1	9				
2	9	394	4299		
3	19	247	407		
4	16	179	301	155	
5	15	200	224	140	
6	29		285	323	
7	16	184	362	225	
8	16	151	339	289	
9	23		396	174	
10	20	457	299	418	
11	14	169	321	237	
12	16	230	316	246	1897
13	22	248	280		
14	52	1045	455		
15	53	1869	413	406	
16	44	955	337	1170	

Table 7.2   Examples of MLFF Network Mappings for Different Configurations
(Courtesy of Dr. Ho Chung Lui)

We cannot say which class of activation functions are "best" for a given approximation. (Perhaps a mixture of functions is best in the sense that fewer nodes are required for a given mapping and accuracy.) Neither can we say exactly how many hidden layer nodes are required for such a mapping, nor even if it is possible to train such a network. But we have the theoretical assurance that MLFF networks with a finite number of hidden nodes are capable of such approximations. Other theoretical results as well as empirical tests with many MLFF applications now provide us with some guidance on the choice of activation functions to use, on the number of hidden nodes needed for a given application and good testing procedures. These topics are described in more detail in the following sections and in the implementation guidelines.

7.3 Learnability and Generalization

We have seen in theory that MLFF networks can compute estimates of arbitrary functions to arbitrary accuracies, but can they actually *learn* the parameter values needed to perform the mappings? If so, at what cost in network complexity (e.g. size) and computing time? These are questions of network learnability and generalization. We examine these two closely related concepts in this section.

As described in Chapter 1, generalization is the process of describing the whole from some of the parts, reasoning from the specific to the general case, or defining a class of objects from a knowledge of one or more instances. ANNs generalize when they compute or recall full patterns from partial or noisy input patterns, when they recognize or classify objects not previously trained on, or when they predict new outcomes from past behaviors. The ability to classify objects not previously trained on is a form of interpolation between trained patterns. The ability to predict from past behaviors is a form of extrapolation. Both of these types of mappings are a form of generalization.

Network learnability relates to the ability of a learning algorithm to find a set of parameter values (weights) which give the accuracy needed for a good mapping approximation. This is equivalent to a requirement that the network find weights that produce good generalizations. Learnability is another issue of theoretical as well as practical importance. Given a network architecture and learning algorithm, we would like some degree of assurance that the network is, in fact, able to learn a certain concept well, and hence, to accurately map any randomly chosen patterns from the environment. We would also like to know at what cost or penalty such learning comes, particularly for large networks. The answer to these questions lie in learnability theory.

As suggested above, learnability is the ability of an algorithm to realize a set of network parameters that are able to generalize well. Such realization depends on the network architecture, the learning algorithm, the training set and the training process. To be able to generalize, a network must be able to formulate an input-output function that closely agrees with the target concept. In practice, the network must do this with a limited size training set. Generalization is possible only if the training set contains enough information relative to the concept class being learned and if the learning algorithm is capable of extracting the information and formulating the desired function within a reasonable time for the given network architecture. Although they are closely related, generalization depends more on information content, whereas learnability relates more to network and computation-time complexities. A separate, but related issue is the ability of the network to approximate any arbitrary function to any accuracy (Section 7.2) for any realizable set of parameter values.

We measure how well a network has learned by its ability to correctly classify arbitrary patterns drawn from a fixed, but unknown and arbitrary probability distribution (test patterns the network has not seen before). We expect that a good learning algorithm will have a high probability of achieving a low classification error rate. Intuitively, we can describe generalization in the following way. Let U be a universe of concepts (mappings or sets) and $D = \{\mathbf{x}^p, \mathbf{t}^p : p = 1, 2, ..., P\}$ a given training set. Also, suppose $G_1, G_2, ...$ are sets in $\mathbf{R}^{n \times m}$. Then a generalization of D is any G_i such that $G_i \supset D$ and $D \cap G_i = D$. In other words, generalizations of D are supersets of D. Clearly there are many such generalization sets (Figure 7.2). The objective of any learning algorithm is to find those G_i which minimize the probability of erring on a novel or randomly selected sample.

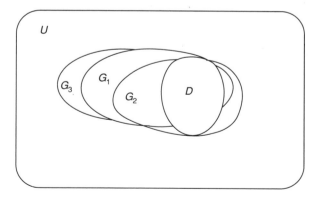

Figure 7.2   The G_i are Generalizations of the Training Set D

We should be careful not to confuse *generalization* error with MSE. Generalization error, which we denote by E_g, is the probability of missclassification of a novel pattern, that is, a pattern not used in the training set, whereas MSE is the cumulative error over all patterns *in* the training set. Consequently, minimum E_g will, in general, differ from minimum MSE. In many ANNs including MLFF networks, it is possible to overtrain the network such that poor generalization results. The network becomes "specialized" and learns the training set too well. The MSE continues to decrease with additional training, but E_g may actually increase. As a consequence, the network is unable to recognize target-class patterns that were not included in the training set.

Excessive or overtraining can occur when a limited training set has been used repeatedly too many times in the training process or even when a very large training set is used extensively. In attempting to more accurately learn the individual pattern mappings, the class boundaries become warped to more closely fit the individual training patterns. As a consequence, the nonsmooth boundaries exclude some patterns in the class that were not in the training set. This same phenomenon occurs in polynomial function fitting when the number of data points and degree of polynomial are not chosen well. A polynomial of degree n can be made to fit n data points exactly, but it may be at the expense of fitting a smooth, low-curvature graph that follows the trend of most of the points rather than the points themselves (Figure 7.3).

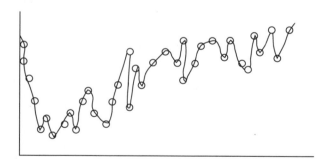

Figure 7.3   Overfitting the Training Examples

To achieve good generalization, training should be terminated before the network starts memorizing the training set. Figure 7.4 illustrates how the performance of an MLFF network can degrade with overtraining. The MSE will continue to decrease with training, but the performance of the network in

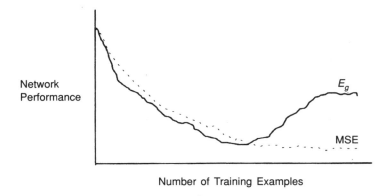

Figure 7.4   Generalization Performance as a Function of Training Iterations

recognizing unseen patterns will degrade after some point in the training process, that is, generalization error tends to increase. Other techniques can also be used to help prevent overtraining. These techniques are summarized in Section 7.5.

Formal models of learning have now been proposed and extensive research is being conducted in this area (Valiant, 1984; Denker et al., 1987; Blumer et al., 1989; Baum and Hessler, 1989; Judd, 1987; Gallant, 1990; Abu-Mostafa, 1989; Schwartz et al., 1990). We give a more rigorous definition of these notions through one of the formal learnability models which we present below.

Learnability

We define a formal model for learnability and measure generalization performance in the following way. Let ρ be a fixed (but unknown) probability distribution on $\mathbf{R}^n$, the environment, and let $\mathbf{C}$ be a class of subsets in $\mathbf{R}^n$, a concept class. For example, the environment might be a set of visual images and the concept class $\mathbf{C}$ a set of male faces. We are interested in learning a target concept $\mathbf{C}_t$, where $\mathbf{C}_t \subseteq \mathbf{C}$ (e.g. a particular male face). A training sample set for $\mathbf{C}_t$ is a finite set P of sample points $\{\mathbf{x}^p | p = 1, 2, ..., P\}$ in $\mathbf{R}^n$, each labeled 1 if the point is in $\mathbf{C}_t$ (a positive example) and 0 if it is not in $\mathbf{C}_t$ (a negative example). A learning algorithm $A(\mathbf{x})$ for $\mathbf{C}$ is a function that, if given a large enough randomly drawn sample set from any target class $\mathbf{C}_t$, finds a region in $\mathbf{R}^n$, called a hypothesis set $\mathbf{H}$ that is, with high probability, a good approximation to the target concept. These notions are illustrated in Figure 7.5, where the hypothesis and target concepts only partially coincide.

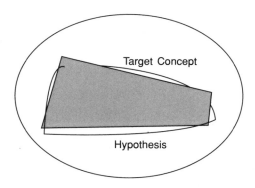

Figure 7.5   Learning an Approximation to a Target Concept

Our definition of learnability is based on a generalization of the so-called PAC model. PAC or Probably Approximately Correct learning is a formal model for learning from training examples (Valiant, 1984; Blumer et al., 1989). Let $A(\mathbf{x})$ be a learning algorithm, that is,

$$A(\mathbf{x}) : [\mathbf{x} \in \mathbf{R}^n] \rightarrow [\mathbf{H} \in \mathbf{C}] \tag{7.5}$$

A concept class is *learnable* if there exists a learning algorithm $A(\mathbf{x})$ such that for any $\varepsilon > 0$ and $\delta < 1$, there exists a finite sample size P, such that for any concept $\mathbf{C}_t \subseteq \mathbf{C}$ and for any probability distribution on $\mathbf{R}^n$, $A(\mathbf{x})$ produces a hypothesis $\mathbf{H}$ that with probability at least $1 - \delta$ has error at most ε.

When we treat a concept class as a class of functions, we ask that our network learn an approximation g' (hypothesis) of the target mapping g (target concept $\mathbf{C}_t$) from a finite set P of training examples $\mathbf{x}$ drawn from a fixed probability distribution $\rho(\mathbf{x})$.

Our measure of how well g' approximates g is just the probability of error for samples drawn from the same distribution of inputs as those used in training the network. Thus, we require that the symmetric error E_g of g' in approximating g satisfy the following inequality

$$E_g = \sum_{x:g'(x) \neq g(x)} P(\mathbf{x}) \leq \varepsilon \tag{7.6}$$

for some $\varepsilon > 0$.

To allow for the fact that examples **x** used to train the network may not represent g well because of noise or other factors, we require that the probability of erring be bounded by some acceptable probability level. Thus, we say that **C** is learnable if there is a learning algorithm A such that for any $\delta < 1$ and $\varepsilon > 0$, we have

$$P(E_g \le \varepsilon) \ge (1 - \delta) \tag{7.7}$$

We see that ε determines *how well* g is approximated whereas δ determines the *confidence* in the approximation.

The smallest sample size $P*$ which satisfies this relation *uniformly* over all $\mathbf{C}_t \in \mathbf{C}$ is called the sample complexity. The concept class

$$\mathbf{C} = \{\mathbf{C}_t\}$$

is *polynomially learnable* if the sample complexity and time complexity of A can be expressed as polynomial functions in $1/\varepsilon$, $1/\delta$, and the parameter t (t indexes the concepts in **C**).

The utility of this model will depend on how difficult it is to achieve good generalization (small values of ε and δ) in practical cases and how well the results scale up to large networks. Given an arbitrary network with weights **W**, one would like to know if, in fact, it is possible to find a general purpose algorithm that is guaranteed to learn any given task in reasonable (e.g. polynomial) time. The answer to this question is negative (Judd, 1987). It has been proven that for this more general case, one cannot hope to find such an algorithm. Thus, we should not attempt to build large networks that can reliably learn even simple supervised learning tasks since we have an intractable problem to solve! How then do we reconcile practice with theory? We circumvent this difficulty by constraining the more general problem to one that is tractable. For this, the constraints can take various forms including the class of nets used, restrictions on the class of tasks to be performed, or by constraining other aspects of the problem. Alternatively, we could allow the learning algorithm to do more than just weight adjustment, for example, if allowed to create new synapses and PEs the problem then becomes tractable (Blum, 1989).

When properly constrained, one can show that certain classes of networks do satisfy the PAC model with a computational complexity that grows only polynomially in network size (N) and accuracy in the bounding parameters (ε, δ). An example of such an MLFF network is the class of bounded, randomized, distributed (BRD) learning algorithms (Gallant, 1990). Learning in these single hidden-layer networks is accomplished with a predetermined number of trials by (1) randomly assigning integer valued weights with values in $[-k, k]$ to each of the hidden layer cells and then (2) applying perceptron learning to the output layer cells using a fixed set of training examples. Given δ, ε, a fixed probability distribution $\rho(\mathbf{x})$ from which training examples are drawn and a target function g, the BRD algorithm will, with probability at least $(1 - \delta)$ produce an approximation g' that differs from g by at most ε. The BRD algorithm is an example of realizable PAC learnability.

The Vapnik-Chervonenkis Dimension

A number of other useful results regarding learnability have now been proven. For example, results which establish worst-case upper and lower bounds on the number of training samples needed for a class of network architectures to achieve good generalization have been established. Many of these results are based on the combinatorial concept known as the Vapnik-Chervonenkis dimension (VC-dimension), a measure of a network's mapping ability with respect to a set of training examples (Vapnik and Chervonenkis, 1971).

The VC-dimension of a set of functions can be defined as follows. Let $\mathbf{C}$ be a concept class (e.g. a class of functions $\{f_i\}$) which are associated with a given network architecture, and let D be a set of P training examples, $D = \{\mathbf{x}^p | p = 1, 2, ..., P\}$, in $\mathbf{R}^n$. (For simplicity we assume the f_i are binary-valued functions $f_i : \mathbf{R}^n \to \{0, 1\}$.) Points in D are labeled as either positive examples of a target concept (1) or negative examples (0). If there is one f_i in $\mathbf{C}$, say f^*, that correctly maps (classifies) all $\mathbf{x}^p$ as either positive or negative examples, then we say the training set D is *shattered* by $\mathbf{C}$. The VC-dimension d of a set of functions, if finite, is the maximum number of training examples for which a function in the concept class can be found that shatters D.

If arbitrarily large subsets are shattered by $\mathbf{C}$, the VC-dimension is infinite. A class $\mathbf{C}$ with only one concept has a VC-dimension of 0. Furthermore, since $\mathbf{C}$ cannot induce more functions than it has, $d \leq |\mathbf{C}|$ where $| \ |$ denotes cardinality. One of the main facts about d that helps characterize $\mathbf{C}$ with regard to generalization is that when d is finite, it is either 2^P for all P or bounded by $P^d + 1$ for constant d. In the latter polynomial case, generalization is assured. A network with a large VC-dimension has a large capacity to store training examples and its capacity to represent a wider variety of functions increases. More training examples are also needed to train the network accurately. On the other hand, if the VC-dimension is too large, the network will not generalize well.

The VC-dimension d for a full network can often be determined by adding the VC-dimensions d_i of the individual network PEs, each with a corresponding mapping class f_i. These results can then be used to determine the sample size versus full network size needed for generalization. Necessary and sufficient conditions for valid generalization can be expressed in terms of bounds on the sample size P expressed in terms of the total number of network weights W and nodes N.

Given a network with a number of weights W, N nodes, and a generalization error bound of $\varepsilon > 0$, the number of training examples P needed for valid generalization can be bounded from below by the following expression (Baum and Haussler, 1989)

$$P \geq O\left(\frac{W}{\varepsilon} \log_2 \frac{N}{\varepsilon} \right) \tag{7.8}$$

Conversely, it can be shown that an MLFF with one hidden layer cannot learn to generalize well when fewer than approximately W/ε random training examples are used, that is when

$$P \geq \Omega\left(\frac{W}{\varepsilon} \right) \tag{7.9}$$

The above results are true of any learning algorithm used with linear threshold networks. It is likely the results also hold for some nonlinear transfer functions such as the sigmoid. Between these two bounds, not much more can be stated for worst-case sample size analysis. For the practitioner however, the last bound can serve as a rule-of-thumb guide. For example, if one wants an accuracy level of at least 90%, corresponding to $\varepsilon = 0.1$, then one should use $10W$ training examples, that is about ten times as many training examples as there are weights in the network.

Similar bounds can be expressed in terms of the VC-dimension d of a network. One such worst case bound is with high probability that the error E_g is bounded by

$$E_g \leq \varepsilon \leq O\left(\frac{d}{P} \ln \frac{P}{d} \right) \tag{7.10}$$

We illustrate the above notions with an example (Blumer et al., 1989). Assume we wish to learn the concept of "average build" defined for men as those having weights between 140 and 190 pounds and heights between 5' 4" and 5' 11". We select random samples of men from a large database that gives height, weight, and classification (average build or not). Based on the sample alone, we want to form a concept rule that approximates the true concept, independently of the underlying probability distribution. To formalize this problem, let $\mathbf{C}$ be the set of all axis-parallel rectangles in the two-dimensional plane $\mathbf{R}^2$ and ρ any probability distribution on $\mathbf{R}^2$. To learn a concept $c \in \mathbf{C}$, we use the following algorithm to form an estimate of c, the hypothesis h.

Record the minimum and maximum x and y coordinate values for all positive examples of average build men. Denote these values by l', r', b', and t' (left, right, bottom, top), respectively. After recording these extreme values for an appropriate number of samples, we predict the concept to be $h = [l', r'] \times [b', t']$. If no positive examples are drawn, we let $h = \varnothing$.

It can be shown that this learning algorithm will learn the given concept in k samples with a symmetric error between c and h being less than ε with probability at least $1 - \delta$, where the sample complexity is at most $k = 4/\varepsilon \ln(4/\delta)$. Furthermore, this quantity is independent of the probability distribution ρ. The result can easily be generalized to $n > 2$ dimensional rectangles. In that case, the bound is given by $k = 2n/\varepsilon \ln(2n/\delta)$ on the sample complexity.

7.4   Stochastic Approach to Generalization

The bounds given in the previous section are worst-case generalization error bounds, and the theory is very general in the sense that it holds for arbitrary learning algorithms, for arbitrary functions being learned and for any sample probability distribution. Such theories are useful, but give little insight into actual performance for a specific network. For many networks, this may not be representative of the actual generalization error that can be realized. This leads one to question just how relevant the results are in terms of a network's average or expected performance. It may be, for example, that many of the real world problems are easier to learn and have lower expected errors than those suggested by the worst-case bounds.

Statistical learning theories provide an alternative view of generalization performance. These theories are based on an analysis of the statistical properties of an ensemble of networks in the performance of a specific task (Schwartz et al., 1990; Tishby et al., 1989; Levin et al., 1989; Amari et al., 1992).

For the statistical approach, we assume a class of networks with a fixed architecture, that is, we restrict the networks to have a fixed number of layers, and fixed number of PEs per layer. The weight values $\mathbf{W}$ assumed for a given network then determines the specific member of the class and, hence, the input-output mapping function $g_{\mathbf{W}}(\mathbf{x})$ realized by that member of the class. Different weight values that can be assumed by the class of networks gives rise to an ensemble of networks defined over weight space $\{\mathbf{W}\}$. We are interested in the mean value or average generalization performance of networks for different values of $\mathbf{W}$ in implementing the target function $g_T(\mathbf{x})$. For perfect performance we should have $g_{\mathbf{W}}(\mathbf{x}) = g_T(\mathbf{x})$, but this is not generally achievable.

Generalization performance is defined as the probability a network trained on k examples will correctly classify a randomly chosen example drawn from the same distribution as the training set. Alternatively, we define the generalization *error* as the probability the network misclassifies a randomly chosen example after training on k examples. We wish to find expressions (or approximations) for these measures in terms of the number of training examples k.

Let $P_0(g)$ denote the probability that a randomly chosen network in configuration space will implement the target function $g_T(\mathbf{x})$. In other words, $P_0(g)$ is the probability that the chosen network correctly classifies a randomly selected pattern $\mathbf{x}$ from the process distribution $\pi(\mathbf{x})$. We want an expression for the probability distribution $P_0(g)$. Suppose $\rho(\mathbf{W})$ is a prior density function defined on weight space $\{\mathbf{W}\}$. Then an effective total volume Z_0 of configuration space is given by

$$Z_0 = \int \rho(\mathbf{W})d\mathbf{W} \tag{7.11}$$

We also want the effective volume $Z(g)$ of configuration space for which a network implements a particular target function g_T. For this, we define a masking or index function $I_{\mathbf{W}}(g)$ that defines the region in $\mathbf{R}^n$ where $g_{\mathbf{W}}(\mathbf{x}) = g_T(\mathbf{x})$, that is,

$$\mathbf{I}_g(\mathbf{W}) = \begin{cases} 1 & \text{if } g_{\mathbf{w}} = 0 \\ 0 & \text{if } g_{\mathbf{w}} \neq 0 \end{cases} \tag{7.12}$$

Hence, the volume $Z(g)$ can be expressed as

$$Z(g) = \int \rho(\mathbf{W})\mathbf{I}_g d\mathbf{W} \tag{7.13}$$

$P_0(g)$, the probability that a randomly chosen network will implement $g_T(\mathbf{x})$, is therefore given by the fraction of weight space that implements $g_T(\mathbf{x})$. This is just the ratio of the two volumes, $Z(g)$ and Z_0

$$P_0(g) = \frac{Z(g)}{Z_0} \tag{7.14}$$

During the training process, the volume of configuration space is reduced. The target function is approximated closer and closer by eliminating all functions g' that are inconsistent with the training patterns $(\mathbf{x}^p, t^p)$. This results in a contraction of the set of functions $g \in G_k$ the network implements after training on k samples, so that for an initial class of functions G_0, we have

$$G_k \subseteq G_{k-1} \subseteq \ldots \subseteq G_0$$

Assuming that learning is successful, the weight vector $\mathbf{W}$ will lie in a region of weight space that contains the training examples, and hence, every $g \in G_k$ will correctly classify all training examples. The corresponding volume of configuration space remaining after successfully learning the kth training sample is therefore reduced to

$$Z_k = \int \rho(\mathbf{W})d\mathbf{W} \sum_{g \in G_k} \mathbf{I}_g(\mathbf{W}) \tag{7.15}$$

Note that the summation in the integrand is over all $g \in G_k$ which correctly classify the training set. The corresponding probability on the space of functions after training on k samples is then just

$$P_k(g) = \frac{Z(g)}{Z_k} \tag{7.16}$$

$P_k(g)$ can be interpreted as the probability that g has not been eliminated by the training process and is still a member of G_k. In other words, $P_k(g)$ is the probability of "survival" for the function g on one additional example having survived $k - 1$ examples. This recursive relationship allows us to write $P_k(g)$ in the form

$$P_k(g) = \frac{P_{k-1}(g)\, p(g)}{\sum_{\{g'\}} P_{k-1}(g')\, p(g')} \tag{7.17}$$

where the denominator is needed for proper normalization and $p(g)$ is the probability that g will correctly classify the kth example randomly drawn from $\pi(\mathbf{x})$. $p(g)$ can be regarded as the generalization ability of the trained network and $E_g = 1 - p(g)$ the generalization error. Note that we have assumed here that $p(g)$ is independent of k, where k is a small subset of the total number of training examples, a reasonable assumption for many problems.

We will return to expression (7.17) below. Before doing so, it is instructive to examine the above development in terms of information-theoretic concepts. Recall that for a given architecture, the information-theoretic entropy of the prior distribution $P_0(g)$ is just

$$S_0 = -\sum_{\{g\}} P_0(g) \log P_0(g) \tag{7.18}$$

where log is base 2 and the summation is taken over all functions g that can be implemented by the given architecture. Note that S_0 is a measure of the functional diversity that the given architecture can implement. It is maximum when the number of functions g is large and the $P_0(g)$ are all equally likely, that is, when $P_0(g)$ is uniformly distributed.

The entropy of the posterior distribution S_k is given by

$$S_k = -\sum_{\{g\}} P_k(g) \log P_k(g) \tag{7.19}$$

Clearly, $S_k < S_{k-1} < \ldots < S_0$ since $G_k \subseteq G_{k-1}$ is a reduction in the number of functions realizable by the network. The decrease in entropy for the kth training sample, that is $(S_{k-1} - S_k)$, is a measure of the efficiency of learning on the kth sample, and the total entropy decrease $(S_0 - S_k)$ is the total information gained from the training set. The quantity

$$\eta = \frac{S_0 - S_k}{k}$$

is the average efficiency of the learning algorithm. Normally, $\eta < 1/k$ since there is usually some redundancy in the training data. S_k, the residual entropy, is a measure of the functional diversity of the ensemble of trained networks. A value of $S_k = 0$ corresponds to the case where no ambiguity remains about the function to be implemented, i.e. $g_{\mathbf{W}}(\mathbf{x}) = g_T(\mathbf{x})$ for all $\mathbf{x}$. A value of $S_k = 0$ is not, in general, realizable. And a value $S_k > 0$ is a measure of the inability of the network to generalize.

Figure 7.6 illustrates the general behavior of the entropy S_k as a function of the number of training examples k. Note that the decrease in entropy is exponential with a rapid fall off initially and decreasing rate as training progresses. This shows that initially training is very effective in eliminating functions g that are inconsistent with the training examples, and as the set of functions G_k grows smaller, the rate of entropy decrease drops off. Thus, we see that if S_k can be computed or estimated, it can serve as an important indicator in monitoring the learning process of a network.

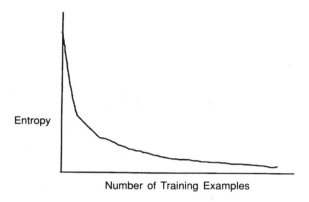

Figure 7.6   Entropy Decrease as a Function of Training

We have been interested in an ensemble of networks. Considering such an ensemble now, we can write the generalization distribution $\rho_k(p)$ over all functions g as

$$\rho_k(p) = \sum_{\{g\}} P_k(g)\delta[p - p(g)] \tag{7.20}$$

where $\delta(x)$ is the Dirac delta function. The quantity $\rho_k(p)dp$ is therefore the probability of producing networks with generalization ability in the range $(p, p + dp)$ after training on k examples, and hence

$$H_k = \int_0^1 p\,\rho_k(p)dp = \sum_{\{g\}} P_k(g)p(g) \tag{7.21}$$

is the network's average generalization ability. H_k can also be regarded as the probability that a randomly selected network trained on k samples will correctly classify an arbitrarily chosen novel example $\mathbf{x}_{k+1}$.

From equations (7.20) and (7.21) we can also write $\rho_k(p)$ in a recursive form as

$$\rho_k(p) = \frac{p\rho_{k-1}(p)}{\int_0^1 p'\rho_{k-1}(p')dp'} \tag{7.22}$$

Iterative application of (7.22) reduces to the equivalent form

$$\rho_k(p) = \frac{p^k \rho_0(p)}{\int_0^1 p'^k \rho_0(p') dp'} \tag{7.23}$$

Note that in this form the density $\rho_k(p)$ is fully determined by the initial distribution $\rho_0(p)$. Thus, $\rho_k(p)$ can be computed if we know $\rho_0(p)$ or can otherwise estimate it.

From (7.22) and (7.23) the average generalization ability H_k can now be written as

$$H_k = \frac{\int_0^1 p^{k+1} \rho_0(p) dp}{\int_0^1 p^k \rho_0(p) dp} \tag{7.24}$$

which is just the ratio of the $(k + 1)$st and kth moments of $\rho_0(p)$.

In general, the form of $\rho_0(p)$ will be unknown. By imposing some constraints on the problem useful estimates can sometimes be obtained, however. For example, if we can assume $\rho_0(p) \approx (1 - p)^d$ as $p \to 1$, then for some $d \geq 0$, $H_k \approx 1 - (d + 1)/k$ or $-\log H_k \approx (d + 1)/k$ (Levin et al., 1989). This shows a possible connection of d to the VC-dimension (cf. equation (7.10)).

Similar results have also been obtained by Amari et al. (1992). For example, it can be shown that for MLFF networks with a single output PE having a signum activation function, the average generalization error $\langle e(k) \rangle$ ($\langle \; \rangle$ denotes average) is given by

$$\langle e(k) \rangle = 1 - \left\langle \frac{Z_{k+1}}{Z_k} \right\rangle \tag{7.25}$$

And, hence, if the approximation

$$\left\langle \frac{Z_{k+1}}{Z_k} \right\rangle = \frac{\langle Z_{k+1} \rangle}{\langle Z_k \rangle} \tag{7.26}$$

holds, $\langle e(k) \rangle$ has the asymptotic form $|W|/k$ where $|W|$ is the number of weights in the network. This result was derived using a saddle-point type of approximation and some moderate regularity conditions.

Nonlinear Regression: Consistency, Bias and Variance

At this point, it is worth recalling that MLFF networks implement a form of nonlinear, nonparametric statistical inference. They learn arbitrary decision boundaries from a set of training examples with no *a priori* assumptions regarding sample distribution or boundary structure. They learn a statistic, an estimator, from samples and represent that statistic as a condensed set of synaptic weight values. We know now that MLFF are capable of making arbitrarily accurate approximations to arbitrary mappings (Section 7.2). But is it possible to actually devise a learning procedure that can learn an arbitrarily accurate approximation to an arbitrary mapping? The answer to this question (which was posed at the beginning of Section 7.3) is positive, at least in an asymptotic sense. MLFF are known to be able to implement consistent estimators of the underlying mapping g from which the training sample is drawn (White, 1989; White, 1990; Geman et al., 1992).

Stochastic consistency is a desirable property of any estimator. Consistency ensures that the approximation error exceeding any specified level tends to zero as the size of the sample set grows large. Estimators that are not consistent will, in general, fail to approximate well. They will always make errors in classification or other mapping tasks. Let $\{g^n\}$ be a (stochastic) sequence of functional estimators (an iterative learning rule for an MLFF). We say that such a sequence is consistent for g if the probability that g^n exceeds any given level of approximation error relative to g tends to zero as n tends to infinity, that is, for any $\varepsilon > 0$

$$\lim_{x \to \infty} P(|g^n - g| > \varepsilon) = 0$$

Thus, learnability is identified with a class of mappings and the existence of a consistent learning rule for that class. Formulating a consistent estimator for nonlinear nonparametric problems is a formidable task. In doing so we are trying to find an optimal set of distribution parameters in an infinite parameter space. This is indeed a difficult search problem. Nevertheless, consistency has been established for MLFF with BP learning.

The consistency results obtained for MLFF networks hold for a wide variety of activation functions, including squashing functions. Furthermore, in the proof of consistency, the network complexity is controlled in such a way that the number of hidden units h grows at a lower rate than the number of training examples p (e.g. at most $h = o(p^{1/4})$). The proofs are achieved through the use of the "method of sieves" (Grenander, 1981; Geman and Whang, 1982; White, 1989) which is a way of finding consistent estimators for infinite nonparametric problem spaces. We omit the details as they are somewhat involved and lengthy.

We turn now to examine other statistical properties of MLFF as estimators. In particular, we are interested in examining the bias and variance aspects. Good estimators should be unbiased and minimum variance as well as consistent.

The BP algorithm with MSE minimization is known to be an effective way to estimate the regression of y on $\mathbf{x}$, $E[y|\mathbf{x}]$ where $E[y|\mathbf{x}]$ is the conditional expectation of y given input $\mathbf{x}$. Regression is a method of fitting a curve or surface in n-dimensional space to a finite sample of two or more variates. That $E[y|\mathbf{x}]$ is an effective estimator can be seen from the following inequality, since for any function $g(\mathbf{x})$ and any (fixed) input $\mathbf{x}$ we have

$$
\begin{aligned}
E&\left[(y - g(x))^2 | \mathbf{x}\right] \\
&= E\left[\left((y - E[y|\mathbf{x}]) + (E[y|\mathbf{x}] - g(x))\right)^2 | \mathbf{x}\right] \\
&= E\left[(y - E[y|\mathbf{x}])^2 + \left(E[y|\mathbf{x}] - g(x)\right)^2\right] \\
&\quad + 2E\left[(y - E[y|\mathbf{x}])|\mathbf{x}\right]\left(E[y|\mathbf{x}] - g(x)\right) \\
&= E\left[(y - E[y|\mathbf{x}])^2 | \mathbf{x}\right] + \left(E[y|\mathbf{x}] - g(x)\right)^2 \\
&\quad + 2\left(E[y|\mathbf{x}] - E[y|\mathbf{x}]\right)\left(E[y|\mathbf{x}] - g(x)\right) \\
&= E\left[(y - E[y|\mathbf{x}])^2 | \mathbf{x}\right] + \left(E[y|\mathbf{x}] - g(x)\right)^2 + 0 \\
&\geq E\left[(y - E[y|\mathbf{x}])^2 | \mathbf{x}\right]
\end{aligned}
\tag{7.27}
$$

This demonstrates that among all functions g of $\mathbf{x}$, the regression

$$
E\left[(y - E[y|\mathbf{x}])^2 | \mathbf{x}\right]
$$

is the best predictor of y given $\mathbf{x}$ in the least MSE sense. It finds a fit of the target data ensemble with smaller MSE than any other function $g(\mathbf{x})$.

During the learning process, an MLFF network constructs an estimate of the mapping g from the learning data set $D = \{(\mathbf{x}_1, y_1), (\mathbf{x}_2, y_2), ..., (\mathbf{x}_P, y_P)\}$. To emphasize the dependence of g on D, we write this function as $g(\mathbf{x}; D)$. Now, the regression problem is essentially one of generalization. It is to construct a $g(\mathbf{x}; D)$ that approximates y well given future observations of $\mathbf{x}$. As before, we use the MSE as a measure of the effectiveness of our learning process in predicting y, that is

$$
\begin{aligned}
E&\left[(y - g(\mathbf{x}; D))^2 | \mathbf{x}; D\right] \\
&= E\left[(y - E[y|\mathbf{x}])^2 | \mathbf{x}; D\right] + \left(g(\mathbf{x}; D) - E[y|\mathbf{x}]\right)^2
\end{aligned}
\tag{7.28}
$$

From the right-hand side of equation (7.28), we see that

$$
E\left[(y - E[y|\mathbf{x}])^2 | \mathbf{x}; D\right]
$$

does not depend on the estimator g or the data D. It is just the variance of y given $\mathbf{x}$. The second term in equation (7.28)

$$\left(g(\mathbf{x}; D) - E[y|\mathbf{x}]\right)^2$$

is the squared error distance of g from the regression function. It measures the effectiveness of g as a predictor of y. Consider now the expected value of this expression. We have (Geman et al., 1992)

$$
\begin{aligned}
E\Big[&\left(g(\mathbf{x}; D) - E[y|\mathbf{x}]\right)^2\Big] \\
&= E\Big[\left((g(\mathbf{x}; D) - E[g(\mathbf{x}; D)]) + (E[g(\mathbf{x}; D)] - E[y|\mathbf{x}])\right)^2\Big] \\
&= E\Big[\left(g(\mathbf{x}; D) - E[g(\mathbf{x}; D)]\right)^2\Big] + (E[g(\mathbf{x}; D)] - E[y|\mathbf{x}])^2 \\
&\quad + 2E\Big[E[g(\mathbf{x}; D)] - E[g(\mathbf{x}; D)]\Big](E[g(\mathbf{x}; D)] - E[y|\mathbf{x}]) \\
&= (E[g(\mathbf{x}; D)] - E[y|\mathbf{x}])^2 \qquad\qquad\qquad\text{``bias''} \\
&\quad + E\Big[\left(g(\mathbf{x}; D) - E[g(\mathbf{x}; D)]\right)^2\Big] \qquad\text{``variance''}
\end{aligned}
$$

where the cross product term is zero (expectation is a linear operator).

We see from the above equation that the squared error decomposes into two terms: a bias term and a variance term. An illustration of this decomposition for MSE is given in Figure 7.7. The significance of this is as follows: When $g(\mathbf{x}; D)$ differs from $E[y|\mathbf{x}]$, the bias component will tend to be large and g is said to be a biased estimator of $E[y|\mathbf{x}]$. But even if g is an unbiased estimator, it is still possible

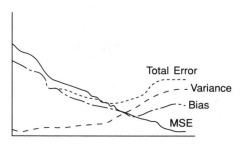

Figure 7.7   MSE Decomposes into Bias and Variance Components

to have a large MSE when g is sensitive to the data and the variance is large. In any event, the size of the MSE is governed by the size of the bias and variance components and there is a trade-off between the two. A large value of either can contribute to poor performance. Of course it is usually possible to change the levels to favor either bias or variance through a choice of smoothing parameters as illustrated in Figure 7.8.

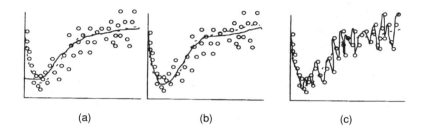

(a)   (b)   (c)

Figure 7.8   Trade-off Between Bias and Variance. (a) Smoothing Parameter Chosen to
Control Variance (b) Smoothing Parameter Chosen to Control Bias
(c) A Compromise Value of Smoothing Parameter
(Adapted from Geman et al., 1992. Courtesy of the authors.)

We can summarize the above observations as follows: Consistency guarantees superior performance of non-parametric MLFF models. It is an essential property of any estimator. Of course, in practice, one can rarely achieve asymptotic performance levels. Too many training examples would be required. Therefore, to reduce the MSE and achieve the performance levels needed for some problems, we must also build a harmless form of bias into the network design or through other problem constraints such as with the input features and representations. This will help to reduce the variance and, in general, improve the network performance. How one builds harmless bias into a network mapping is still much of an art. It can require much ingenuity and patience, but a good place to start is with a clever choice of representation.

7.5   Empirical Tests of MLFF Network Mappings

The previous three sections focused on the theoretical aspects of MLFF networks, their limitations and capabilities. The results presented there are important steps in building a solid foundation for networks, but the theory is far from complete. We still lack sufficient guidance when implementing MLFF networks. For more insight on implementation details, it is useful to review the available empirical knowledge which by now is becoming extensive. Many practical applications have now been successfully implemented (Chapter 8 covers MLFF applications), and a number of simulation tests have been performed by researchers to determine mapping and generalization capabilities (Sietsma and Dow, 1991; Chow et al., 1991; Hirose et al., 1991; Wang and Hsu, 1991; Yeung, 1991; Tollenaere, 1990; Fahlman, 1988; Murase et al., 1991). These results are helpful, but a word of caution is in order. Published test results are often difficult to evaluate and compare since there are no commonly accepted standards for conducting the experiments and reporting of the results. Researchers tend to carry out experiments in different ways and often fail to report important details related to the experiments. They use different criteria for measuring learning times, classification accuracies, and treatment of failures. Different problems are also used for their benchmark tests. Some problems, such as the XOR or parity computation are popular for historical reasons, but poor as tests of features such as generalization which are especially important in real world applications. But even though published experiments are not always conclusive, they do help in our general understanding of networks and they provide us with some general guidance when selecting network parameters for a given application.

Choosing the Number of Layers and Number of Units

Since BP training can be very costly and overtraining is undesirable, we would like to be able to estimate the minimum number of training examples needed for a given network architecture and desired level of performance. A brute force approach is by trial and error. With this approach, one chooses an architecture based on experience, and takes successively larger training sets and tests the performance of the network after each training session. This process is continued as long as the performance increases. It is stopped once the performance begins to decrease. This trial and error process can be expanded to determine the "optimal" number of hidden layers and PEs per layer. Of course, the computation time required grows exponentially with the number of free parameters allowed in the problem, and hence, can require large amounts of computation time.

The above ideas have been used in experiments with BP trained networks to find the optimum number of hidden units (Hirose et al., 1991). For example, an algorithm can be used to dynamically change the number of hidden units until a minimal number was found for which convergence occurs. The method begins with the assignment of a small number of hidden units and initiation of conventional BP training. During training, the error is checked after every 100 weight adjustments. If the decrease in error is greater than one percent of its previous value, training continues for another 100 weight adjustments. If the decrease is not greater than one percent, it is assumed that a local minimum has been found and a new hidden unit is added with its weights set to zero. Adding a new unit changes the weight-error surface so retraining must be done until the network eventually converges or until another hidden unit is added. This process is repeated until convergence (total MSE of less than 0.01) occurs. If convergence occurs before a cutoff of 10,000 adjustments, a unit is removed and training continues. The removal of units is repeated in this way until convergence can no longer be achieved at which time a final unit must be added, the minimum number of units that is needed for convergence. For some applications, a speedup of two to three times over conventional BP learning was realized with the method. Furthermore, the method finds the minimum number of hidden units needed to achieve a small error value. Of course, this may or may not be the best number of units for good generalization. Other tests will be required to make that determination.

Experience confirms theory regarding the ability of a network to generalize. This ability is a function of the number of hidden layers, the number of units in the hidden layers, as well as the training set and the training regime. To test generalization ability, networks have been modified through the removal (pruning) of inessential internal nodes and the insertion of new required layers of pre-trained nodes when pruning resulted in inseparability. In general, it was found that if a network has too few hidden units, it cannot learn the training set well. On the other hand, networks with too many hidden units tend to memorize the training set and cannot generalize well. Therefore, it is best in many applications to use the minimum size hidden layer for the required task. And, the removal of useless redundant units will have no serious ill effects on a network's ability to generalize.

For more complex mappings, two hidden layers may give better generalization (and error) performance than a single layer. This is because the units in one layer tend to interact globally with each other, making it difficult to improve an approximation at one point without worsening it elsewhere. With an additional hidden layer, units in the first hidden layer can partition the input space into small regions and compute functions within those regions, while units in the second layer can combine those outputs and compute the desired functions within the regions and output zero elsewhere giving rise to a more accurate mapping and better generalization.

Effects of Noise on Generalization

Experience suggests that networks generalize well when trained with noise distorted training patterns (Sietsma and Dow, 1991). Furthermore, training with random noise can dramatically improve a network's ability to correctly classify noisy inputs. For example, when compared to full-sized "clean-trained" networks with a failure rate of 17 to 24% on a complex classification task, the same noise-trained network's failure rate was reduced to less than 0.5%. The use of fewer PEs in the hidden layers generally leads to better generalization for networks trained with clean, noise-free patterns only. However, for noise-trained networks, more hidden units are recruited for effective use by the network. Also, removal of unused units in the noise-trained case has less effect on performance than on clean-trained units. Experiments also suggests that narrow, four and five-layer networks generalize far worse than their corresponding two and three-layer "parent" networks.

Noise can be introduced during the training process by adding small random numbers to each training example. Either a uniform or normal distribution with zero mean value can be used. A form of "noise" can also be introduced by randomly selecting members from the training set during the training process.

In summary, one can say that one or two hidden-layer networks tend to generalize better than shallow networks with more than two hidden layers. The amount of training and the order of pattern presentation have a strong influence on the network performance. Overtraining can lead to poor generalization so it should be avoided. For most applications, pattern presentation should be randomly sequenced. Overtraining can usually be avoided by adhering to the following rules:

- Selecting the proper number of hidden-layer PEs for the network.

- Choosing a sufficiently large training set when possible.

- Selecting and presenting the patterns randomly during the training process (thereby introducing a form of noise).

- Stopping the training process before "excessive" training occurs.

- Introducing noise directly into the training patterns.

- Using a combination of the above methods.

Pruning a Network

Pruning a network is the process of removing unnecessary PEs and connections (weights). It is often desirable to prune a network before deploying it for operation to reduce the I/O processing time. Pruning can often be performed without any noticeable effect to the performance of a network. It can be performed by examining the outputs of units across all training set inputs and eliminating noncontributory units and weights. Noncontributory units are those units that have near constant output over the training set or outputs that are nearly identical to (identically opposite to) other units.

Procedures for pruning include the following:

1. When unit i has output $a \pm d$ over the whole training set with a and d constant and d a small value, then, for each unit j in the next layer connected to unit i, substitute for the bias input of unit j, w_{bias}, the new bias weight $w'_{bias} = w_{bias} + aw_{ji}$ and remove unit i. The resultant network is essentially unchanged.

2. When units p and q have almost the same output over the training set, one (say p) can be removed. At each unit j in the next layer that p is connected to replace weights w_{iq} to unit q with $w'_{iq} = w_{iq} + w'_{ip}$. The resultant network is essentially unchanged.

3. When unit p produces a near opposite output of unit q, remove p and replace weights w_{jq} and bias, w_{bias}, to unit q with $w'_{jq} = w_{jq} - w_{jp}$ and $w'_{bias} = w_{bias} + w_{jp}$.

4. Finally, set all weights with relatively small values equal to zero. For example, weight values that are less than 10% of the average absolute magnitude of the other weights can often be eliminated with little or no effect on the network's performance.

Other methods of adding and pruning units have been developed. Typically, the methods use techniques based on time-varying gains factors which depend on the error E and derivative of E with respect to the weights in deciding whether units should be added or removed. These methods have also been shown to converge faster than standard BP, but tend to be more difficult to implement.

Implementation Guidelines

We complete this chapter by providing a summary of general guidelines that can be used as an aid in implementing an MLFF network for a given application. The guidelines follow from the objectives and results presented in the above sections. They are largely heuristic in nature and are by no means foolproof. When building a network for an application, it still may be necessary to experiment to determine some of the parameters. We emphasize again that the suggestions below are intended as *guidelines*, and not as a prescription for network design.

Network Architecture
Use a minimal size network. The number of layers and number of nodes per layer can usually be determined with little or no experimentation from a detailed

consideration of the application. A single hidden layer will be sufficient for most applications. A second hidden layer may provide improved performance when the mapping $f(x) = y$ is particularly complex or irregular. The need for more than two hidden layers is highly unlikely. Only unusual applications are likely to require more than two hidden layers. When in doubt, one can begin with one hidden layer and experiment using the methods of adding or pruning layers, units and weights as outlined above to arrive at the best compromise. In general, one should keep the net as simple as possible (as few layers and units as needed). This will help to insure that the training time is kept within reasonable bounds and other complications are minimized.

Determine the number of input/output PEs from the application. The numbers of PEs for the input and output layers are, of course, application dependent. The numbers will depend on the I/O mapping required. The number of output nodes will usually correspond to the number of different categories or classifications needed or to the dimensions of the output vector space as required for a given mapping. It could also depend on the size of the output code space, or other factors. The number of output nodes chosen should be large enough to avoid any ambiguity in the output responses, but no larger than necessary. The number will usually be apparent from the application specifications. For example, in full English character recognition applications, the number of output nodes will be more than 37: 26 for the letters of the alphabet, ten for the integers, and one or more for space and other special characters. In a time series forecasting application, only one node is required if a single future time value (e.g. price) is being predicted.

The number of input PEs required for the application may not be as easy to determine since these nodes will usually correspond to object features, the independent vector variables. The best choice of features and the representation (encoding) of those values can make the difference between success and failure of the network. This will require a good knowledge of the task domain. Only "relevant" features should be chosen and the coding scheme should be unambiguous. By relevant, we mean essential attributes or features which best characterize objects in the domain and help "group together" objects within the same class and discriminate well among objects belonging to different classes. For some problems the choice will be evident, for others, a careful analysis and preprocessing of the data may be required in addition to some experimentation and a considerable amount of ingenuity.

Determine the number of hidden units. Once the number of input and output units have been established, the number of hidden units can be determined. As we have learned, determining the number of hidden layers and units per layer is more complex than that for either input or output units. The solution is closely influenced by other factors: the complexity of the mapping, the number of patterns in the training set, learnability, and generalization. The number of hidden layers needed will not likely exceed two, and for many applications one will be sufficient as described in Section 7.2. A single hidden layer can be chosen initially unless the mapping is known to be complex, in which case two hidden layers should be chosen. In making a choice between one or two hidden layers a knowledge of the problem domain will help, but experimentation may still be needed. Likewise, the number of PEs needed per layer will also require some experimentation. The numbers should be large enough to permit the network to learn the desired mapping well, but not so large that it memorizes the training set, and is therefore unable to generalize well over the complete range of mappings. To limit the implementation costs (e.g. number of computations or hardware components), the network should be as small as possible provided its performance is consistent with the application requirements.

The "optimal" number of units per layer can be determined by some experimentation. For this, one of the methods described above can be used to synthesize a network of the appropriate size. It is best to start with an estimate of the minimum number and then refine the network by adding and pruning units (and/or weights), or otherwise tuning the network during the training process as described above. Of course, experience is probably the best guide when deciding on the appropriate number of PEs to start with for a given application. But, when experience is lacking, one can use the rule-of-thumb (Widrow, 1987) that the number h of PEs in the first hidden layer should be about

$$h = \frac{P}{10(m + n)}$$

where P is the number of training examples and n and m are the number inputs and outputs, respectively. More generally, one can use the relationship

$$h = \frac{P\varepsilon}{(m + n)}$$

as a guide where ε is the error (fraction of future misclassifications) one is willing to tolerate. This estimate is based on the bounds given for the minimum number of training examples needed for good generalization (Section 7.5), and is in agreement with the rule-of-thumb estimate given above (Baum and Haussler, 1989). In practice, the bound may not work well for some small to moderately sized networks so experimentation will be needed.

When two hidden layers are used, the number of PEs will be less than the number used in the first hidden layer, say about one half as many. But experimentation is still recommended to determine the best number for a given application.

Completing the network. Having established the initial network structure, it remains to choose appropriate activation and error (cost) functions for the mapping task. Some general guidelines that follow from the material presented above are as follows.

The choice of activation function is application dependent. For many straight forward applications a sigmoid function is adequate. But if a sigmoid function is used, it should be a symmetrical form as experience has shown that the rate of learning is increased when symmetrical functions are used (Section 6.3). Therefore, either the tanh can be used or else the symmetric function

$$f(x) = [1 + \exp(-\beta x)]^{-1} - 1/2$$

When using sigmoid functions, it is also advisable to add a small constant (e.g. 0.2) to the derivative term of the error backpropagation equation (equation (6.31)) to force some learning when a PE is working near saturation as described in Section 6.5.

For more complex mappings the use of other activation functions may be advisable. For example, in time series prediction applications a mixture of functions such as sine, tanh and/or radial basis functions may give better performance over the use of a single sigmoid form of function. Indeed, convergence may be possible only with the use of such functions. The final choice will undoubtedly require some intuition as well as some experimentation.

The choice of cost function can also be important for better convergence as well as better performance. For many applications, the standard squared error cost function, the MSE, will be adequate. But for large or otherwise unusually complex applications a log form such as L_1 or L_2 (Section 6.5) may be better.

Once the basic network architecture has been established, the details of the training process and training regime can be determined. Training should not begin until the weights have been set to appropriate initial values. Unless one can easily estimate the set of weight values corresponding to a global minimum, the weights should be initialized by setting them to small random numbers, say numbers in the interval $[-0.2, 0.2]$. For training, one of the quick convergence methods such as Quickprop or Delta-Bar-Delta should be considered. If one of these methods is not easily implemented, the standard backprop formulae can be used. For this case it is best to vary the learning and momentum coefficients during the training process. It is usually best to start with larger values of η (say 0.9) and smaller values of momentum coefficient α (say 0.1) at the start and vary them as learning progresses. During the learning process, η should be decreased and α increased as described in Section 6.5.

The training set should be divided into three groups of samples: a set for training the network, a set for use in testing the performance of the trained network, and a set to be used for final validation of the network. The training and test sets should be of approximately equal size if sufficient numbers of samples are available. Otherwise, the training set should be given preference. The three sets should be treated as mutually exclusive sets and used only for their intended purpose. For better generalization, it is also advisable to introduce some form of noise into the training samples. This can be done by adding small random perturbations directly to the training samples or by simply presenting the samples in a random order during the training process. During training, it is helpful to observe the behavior of the MSE as well as the weight values to monitor the progress of the error toward convergence. A graphical display of the MSE and a histogram display of the weight values can provide useful information during the training process. If the weights all continue to remain small as training progresses, the process may be trapped in a local minima.

Since the MSE will never actually reach zero, it is best to decide in advance a tolerable MSE value for which training can be stopped. To insure good generalization, it may also be necessary to test the network for the best stopping point as described in Section 7.3.

Until now little mention has been made of the preparation of input data prior to training. This should not be overlooked as it is an important part of both the training and operational process. Data seldom comes in a form that is suitable for input without some preprocessing such as normalization. This topic is discussed in more detail in the following chapter as it relates to specific applications.

Once the network has been trained to acceptable levels of performance, it is good practice to "optimize" the network by pruning noncontributory, redundant PEs and weights as outlined earlier. This will help to insure that unnecessary computations are avoided during operation of the network.

Summary

In this chapter, we have examined the capabilities and limitations of MLFF networks as adaptable systems for the estimation of nonlinear mappings. We saw that MLFF networks are capable, in theory at least, of approximating arbitrary functions to arbitrary accuracies provided enough hidden-layer PEs are available. We also saw that such networks are good estimators of nonlinear nonparametric regressions and are capable of learning the desired mappings if a sufficient number of training examples are available. MLFF networks with BP learning have been shown to be consistent estimators when the number of parameters are allowed to increase with the sample (training set) size. Consistency is an essential property of any stochastic estimator.

We have presented two approaches toward a theory of learnability and generalization. One approach is based on bounds which follow from the VC-dimension of networks. For this worst-case approach, upper and lower bounds were given for the number of training examples needed for good generalization. These bounds give some guidance on the number of weights, and hence, the number of hidden-layer PEs needed for tolerable levels of generalization error. The second approach is stochastic based, in which average performance is studied over an ensemble of networks in weight space. An expression for the average generalization ability of a network was derived as the ratio of the $(k + 1)$th and kth moments of an initial generalization distribution. It was shown that the average error can be approximated by $|W|/P$ where $|W|$ is the number of weights in the network and P the number of training examples.

In addition to the theoretical results, a summary of some important empirical tests related to MLFF mapping and generalization abilities were presented. These results, together with the theoretical advances given earlier, served as the basis for a set of implementation guidelines which were presented at the end of the chapter.

8
Applications of Multilayer Feedforward Networks with BP

In this chapter, we describe some typical applications of MLFF networks. Because of the broad popularity of these networks, a complete chapter has been devoted to applications. We should emphasize, however, that the applications described are a small sample only. Although representative, they are in no way an exhaustive list. MLFF networks have proven to be effective mapping tools for a wide variety of problems, and consequently, they have been used extensively by practitioners in almost every application domain one can name. One only needs to examine conference proceedings to see they are filled with papers on user applications ranging from agriculture to zoology. Typically, papers on applications found in the journals and other periodicals contain claims of large cost savings, improvements in accuracy and computation speed, and other benefits gained through their use. These issues are discussed individually with the particular application described below.

8.1 Introduction

The general types of applications that MLFF networks have been successfully employed in are numerous. They have been used successfully in all of the application categories described in Chapter 1. They have been successfully used in many domains, including engineering, law, computer science, process control, statistics, medicine, manufacturing, transportation, finance, telecommunications, and more. They can compete with other architectures for most application areas with the possible exception of categories that are dependent on a form of unsupervised learning. The wide popularity of the MLFF networks for such diverse applications, of course, stems from their mapping ability. If a good set of training

215

data is available for some application, it is likely that a single or at most a two hidden-layer MLFF network can learn to master the desired tasks. Although their performance has proven to be as good as other networks and other non-network techniques in the solution of diverse problems, they can be difficult to train. And, whether their performance can hold when scaled up to large networks remains to be seen. But, in general, when in doubt about a network architecture to use for a given application, MLFF nets with backpropagation should always be considered. This assumes an appropriate training set is available, of course.

In the following sections, representative ANN solutions have been described for four broad categories of applications: classification and diagnosis, control and optimization, prediction and forecasting, and pattern recognition. In each of these application areas, we present at least two representative applications.

8.2   Classification and Diagnosis Applications

Classification and diagnosis problems are ubiquitous. They occur in many problem domains. An electronic or mechanical system that develops operational problems will have developed one or more faults that needs diagnosing for identification and repair. Manufactured products must be inspected for quality and either accepted or rejected, a form of classification task, and so on. The variety of applications are endless. In this section, we describe two classification applications: the classification of cells in the diagnosis of bladder cancer and fault isolation and identification in electronic telephone switching systems.

Classifying Cells for Cancer Diagnosis

The structure and other characteristics of cells observed from urine samples of patients can provide an accurate indication of bladder cancer. A simple two category classification scheme of "Well" and "Not Well" is sufficient for the cell diagnosis task when well chosen, discriminant features are used. Several approaches to the classification problem have been proposed, including the use of Selective Mapping Tree Classifiers, MLFF networks and others (Moallemi, 1991). Of the methods reported, only the ANN approach has achieved levels of classification accuracy acceptable for clinical use. For example, the tree classifier system accuracy was on the order of 23% with other non-ANN methods reporting even poorer performance levels. Accuracies achieved using a simple two-layer MLFF network were on the order of 96%, a significant improvement over the other approaches.

In performing the diagnosis, 43 microscopic images containing 597 objects were used to train and test the network. The images were first examined visually and cells were classified by experts. Of the total objects, 77 were classified as Well and 520 as Not Well. For the experiments, about one half of the objects were selected randomly for training and the balance for testing. Several descriptive features were selected for cell descriptors. These included: (1) the cell area which ranged between 100 and 400 pixels for Well cells (larger for Not Well cells), (2) cell circularity, a measure of how well the cell approximated a circle defined as the ratio of the cell's area to the area of a rectangular box containing the cell ($\pi/4$ for a true circle), (3) area of the cell nucleus, (4) circularity of the nucleus and (5) the ratio of the entire cell area to the nucleus. These features were used as input to the neural network which had five input nodes, two hidden layers, each with ten nodes, and a single output node. A cell was interpreted as Well if the output node value was greater than or equal to 0.5 and Not Well otherwise.

Each microscopic image consisted of 256×240 pixels with 256 gray levels. Preprocessing of the images was performed as follows: The gray-level images were first partitioned into 16 segments of 32×120 pixels to account for different lighting backgrounds and shading conditions. The segments were then digitized and binarized after determining threshold levels from a histogram computation and analysis of the segments. The threshold intensity level was chosen to separate the cytologic objects from the background and thereby permit object segmentation. Segmentation was performed using a blob coloring algorithm which assigns homogenous neighboring pixels 0/1 values (Ballard and Brown, 1982). The five-object descriptors defined above are then computed and fed to the neural network as an input pattern vector.

After training the network, tests were conducted on the data set and an accuracy of 93.4% was reported in accepting Well cells and 97.0% in detecting Not Well cells. This gave an average error rate of 3.5%, an acceptable level for clinical use. The time spent for the diagnoses was also quite acceptable. Preprocessing time for each image required 2.6 seconds and classification 0.4 seconds for a total diagnostic time of 3.0 seconds. This compares with other methods which took on the order of 32 seconds per image. Overall, the neural network approach outperformed the other approaches by a significant margin.

Fault Identification in Telephone Switching Systems

Modern computer-based electronic telephone switching systems (ESS) are designed to be very reliable. Faults rarely occur in these systems. As a consequence, maintenance engineers have little opportunity to gain experience in troubleshooting equipment faults. When a fault does occur, troubleshooting is carried out in an exhaustive, unit elimination process by systematically swapping fault-free standby units for suspected faulty units until the faulty unit is eventually isolated. Even more difficult to diagnose are intermittent faults, faults which may occur at intermittent times and for unpredictable durations. The fault may disappear before the troubleshooting process is complete. As a consequence, intermittent fault identification can be very time-consuming and costly. To assist engineers in identifying such faults, MLFF networks were trained to help locate and identify a variety of faults using data created by a dummy fault generator (Sone, 1993).

The fault generator simulates a failed ESS component by blocking the proper functioning of the component in a fault-free ESS. The symptoms of the dummy fault in the ESS are then available for use in diagnosing the system through some 32 different signal monitoring points. The signals, together with the true fault provide the training data for the MLFF networks as illustrated in Figure 8.1.

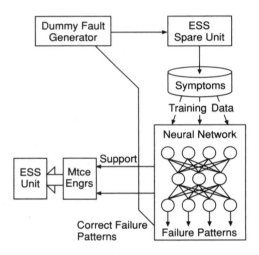

Figure 8.1   Generating Training Data for Fault Identification in an ESS
(Courtesy of Lawrence Erlbaum Associates, Inc. and T. Sone)

Actually, each of the monitored signals must be monitored over some period of time for effective troubleshooting. To accomplish this, a technique used for general time series analysis and prediction is used. Input to the diagnostic ANN is taken from a "time delay window" consisting of several consecutive equally spaced time points from the series and used as a single input pattern. The next input pattern is taken from the same signal with the window shifted one vector pattern sample later in time. The next sample is shifted two pattern vectors later in time, and so on until the end of the time series is reached. This time delay window sampling scheme is illustrated in Figure 8.2.

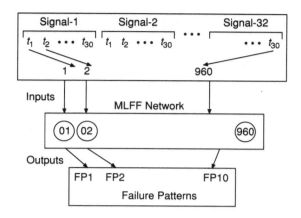

Figure 8.2   Input Signal Patterns Taken from Sliding Time Series Windows

The complete training set is made up from a sequence of the window patterns (the symptoms) and the true target pattern, the known fault for the symptoms. Note that when time series data is sampled in real-time, time delay units like those used for the application of ADALINE networks to adaptive noise reduction on communication circuits must be used (see Chapter 4). In this application the time series data has been prerecorded, so successive time points can be taken directly from a database containing the input pattern data.

In the present application, a time delay window consisting of 30 equally spaced time points are used for each signal input. Thus, there are a total of $30 \times 32 = 960$ "static" signal values that make up a complete input pattern vector. In practice, it has been shown that for many neural network problems, the performance of several small ANNs each working on a (subdivided) portion of a large problem are more effective than a single large ANN in solving the overall problem. Furthermore, the training time is significantly reduced when the problem is subdivided and given to several smaller networks. This is a form of problem solving strategy known as "divide and conquer" that was verified to hold for the ESS fault identification task. Consequently, the final system was made up of five distributed MLFF networks for the diagnosis and a conventional rule-based expert system which integrated the neural networks outputs together with heuristic expert knowledge. Four of the ANNs were reduced in size to have 320 input nodes and a single network with 960 input nodes acted as an overall symptom evaluator. The complete hybrid system is illustrated in Figure 8.3.

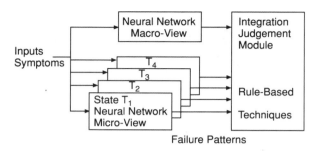

Distributed MLFF Network System

Figure 8.3   The Complete Hybrid Fault Diagnosis System

The four distributed ANNs each have 320 input nodes, 600 hidden-layer nodes and ten output nodes with a total of 198,000 connections. The single large monitoring network has 960 input nodes, 510 hidden-layer nodes and ten output nodes with a total of 495,000 connections.

By subdividing the problem into four network subproblems as illustrated in Figure 8.3, the performance of the system was significantly improved over the use of a single large network alone. For example, the system realized a score of about 89% correct fault identification on non-training data using the four smaller networks as compared to a score of 64% correct identifications using a single large network, an improvement of some 25%.

8.3   Control and Optimization Applications

Control and optimization problems are some of the more difficult applications for ANNs to master. The mapping functions that must be learned are generally very complex in nature and problem constraints that must be satisfied are often conflicting. Even so, the application of MLFF networks to such problems has been moderately successful. In this section, we describe three important applications of MLFF networks in the solution of control and optimization problems. The first application is still an active area of research. It relates to the control of an autonomously driven (driverless) vehicle. The second application is in the production of steel, an area that has great potential for cost reduction. The final topic discussed, covers a number of timely applications, the optimal control of consumer products.

Autonomously Driven Land Vehicle

Carnegie-Mellon University has converted a commercial van into a laboratory vehicle (Navlab I) in 1986 to act as a test bed for autonomous driving experiments (Thorpe et al., 1991; Kanade et al., 1994). One of the control systems, the ALVINN (Autonomous Land Vehicle in a Neural Network) is neural net based. The van is equipped with several video cameras, a scanning laser range finder, global positioning system, inertial navigation system and sonar sensors. It also carries several computers onboard.

The ALVINN automatic road following control system uses a fully connected three layer BP network with color vision inputs from a video camera. The input image is reduced resolution with input retina of 30 × 32 (also 45 × 48) pixels. The hidden layer has nine units and the output layer 45 units. The network learns different sets of weights to follow different types of roads. The basic network architecture is illustrated in Figure 8.4.

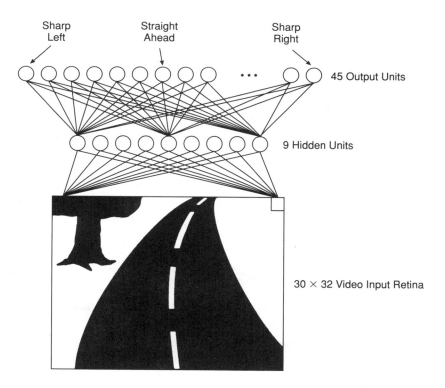

Figure 8.4   Multilayer Network Control Unit for NavLab
(From Kanade et al., 1994. © 1994 ACM. Courtesy of the authors.)

During operation, the image is preprocessed to enhance road contrast and the result is fed directly to the network input. The network computes the steering angle directly with no reasoning about road location. The output nodes provide commands to steer the vehicle with varying degrees of angular turning; (45 different angle positions) sharp-left, varying degrees of left, straight ahead, varying degrees of right and far-right. During operation, the output is updated 15 times per second to provide real-time control of the vehicle while traveling at speeds of up to 55 mph or more.

To train the network, a unique "on-the-fly" procedure is used. Images are input and processed while someone drives the vehicle down a section of road or highway to be followed. Thus, the training set consists of "snapshots" of the highway images (input vector) and the angular position of the steering mechanism (target vector). Actually, each image is reused in several positions during training. The image is transformed through lateral translations to provide several positions shifted to simulate erroneous correspondences between road and steering angle. The appropriate commands to correct the error are also determined. These modified images and steering angles are all provided as part of the training set. This type of training gives a "view" of the road more consistent with ideal human driving. The system also uses three-dimensional images from laser range finders to detect obstacles along the roadways (trees, cars, mailboxes, rocks).

The ALVINN project has met with good success where the vehicle has traveled at speeds of 55 mph for distances of 90 miles or more. It has also been tested successfully on various road types (dirt, paved, single and double-lane) and under various weather conditions.

ALVINN is not the only successful ANN control system for autonomous vehicle driving. The Advanced Research Projects Agency (ARPA) have also built autonomous vehicles (ALV) as well as European and Japanese organizations. The potential for (commercial and military) driverless vehicle applications is great indeed and warrants considerable attention.

Intelligent Controller for Steel-Making

In the steel-making process, scrap metal is placed into a furnace and electric arc heaters are used to melt the raw scrap metal. The cost of operating such furnaces is great due to the immense quantity of electric energy consumed during the melting process. Maintenance costs are also high because of the extreme operating environment and high cost of plant equipment. Therefore, efficient control of the whole process is critical. A change in operating efficiency of only a few percent can result in large operating cost differences.

In making steel, when a new batch of "heat" is started, some 100 tons of scrap metal is loaded into a furnace chamber which measures 15 to 30 feet in diameter. Three large graphite electrodes are then lowered toward the pile of scrap by servo motors. The cylindrical electrodes measure 12 to 24 inches in diameter and 20 feet in length and each can weigh as much as several tons. The sheer size and consumption of multi-megawatt power of these units results in an impressive display of sparks and a deafening explosion when the electrodes are first struck. For cost-effective operation, the position of the three electrodes must be carefully coordinated and controlled throughout the melting process. Conventional control systems are not ideal. They use independent controllers for each electrode and use a fixed impedance set point to position the electrodes. To be more efficient, control should be dynamic and closely regulate the three phase current in the electrodes throughout the hour long melting process.

An intelligent arc furnace ANN controller invented by Bill Staib (1993) of Neural Applications Corporation has been developed to control the positioning of the electrodes in the furnace as described above. These systems, which have already been installed in a number of steel-making plants, have been shown to be cost effective over traditional control systems, with improvements of some 5 to 8% in the reduction of electric power consumption and a 20% reduction in plant wear-out. The overall cost savings realized from these operating efficiencies are reportedly worth millions of dollars per year.

The ANN controller architecture for the furnace is an MLFF network using a variant of BP training. Input to the network includes the furnace state conditions (currents, voltages and furnace sounds from a microphone) and the outputs are control signals for the three phases. The system is illustrated in Figure 8.5.

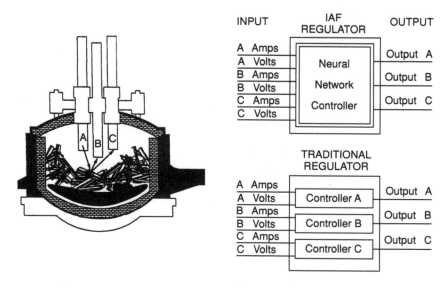

Figure 8.5   Furnace Acquisition and Control System (Courtesy of Bill Staib)

The training process for the network controller consists of two stages. In the first stage, an MLFF network is taught to emulate the behavior of an operational furnace. Both the network and the furnace are presented with the same input regulator, $R(t)$ and state signals $S(t)$ at times t and $t - 1$. Signals representing the output state of the furnace is then compared to the emulated state output $s(t)$ computed by the network at time $t + 1$. The difference between the emulated network output and the actual furnace output then serves as the error signal needed to train the network. This training stage is illustrated in Figure 8.6.

Once the emulator network has been trained to model the operation of a specific real furnace, it is used to train a second MLFF network to serve as a cost-effective regulator controller for the first network. In this case, the *desired* state of the furnace is compared to the emulator network output state and the error difference between the two is used to train the controller network. The second training stage is illustrated in Figure 8.7.

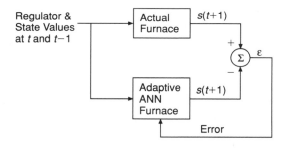

Figure 8.6   Training a Network to Emulate a Furnace

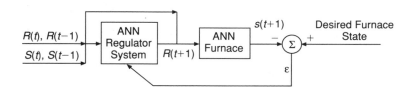

Figure 8.7   Training a Network to Control a Furnace Using a Network Trained to Emulate a Furnace

The process of training a network to emulate the dynamics of a complicated system and then using the emulator network to train another network to act as a controller for the process is a powerful concept. It can lead to a number of interesting applications as described by Widrow et al. (1994). This process is called model identification in control systems. The emulator is an identifier. Applications of this type are described in the following chapter (Section 9.6) in conjunction with control systems.

In summary, one can conclude that the use of intelligent network controllers for steel-making has resulted in large cost savings for many companies in the steel industry. Further refinements in this application of ANNs for control of complicated systems can be expected in future.

Control Optimization in Consumer Products

Japanese consumer products companies were among the earliest to adapt fuzzy logic technology into their products beginning in 1990 (see Chapter 3 for a review of fuzzy logic). Further improvements were subsequently made to a number of these products using neural network technology. For example, Japanese products that incorporate neural network controllers that have already been put on the market include air conditioners, electric fans, electric and kerosene heaters, induction cookers, microwave ovens, refrigerators, vacuum cleaners, clothes dryers, washing machines, photocopying machines, word processors as well as others. ANNs have been used both independently and in conjunction with fuzzy logic controllers to improve the performance of a product. They have also been used in the design of optimal fuzzy membership functions for fuzzy controlled systems.

Mitsubishi Electric company developed a refrigerator which is controlled by both a neural network and fuzzy logic controller. Control is household customized, taking into account the daily usage pattern of the family. Each day is divided into 12 time blocks and the frequency of door openings in each block is counted. From this data, an eight-day moving average is computed to smooth out daily variance. Using this and other status data as input, a neural network decides when to defrost, when to precool prior to heavy usage, when to deodorize, and when to use low-noise drive (Asakawa and Takagi, 1994). By fixing defrost time in the period of infrequent openings and precooling just prior to frequent door openings, more efficient cooling is achieved. Temperature variations of the food is reduced to about 2.2 °C. A fuzzy reasoning component also uses the door opening frequency data and a sensor to detect the amount of frost to exercise overall control of the refrigerator.

After the introduction of fuzzy controller technology into consumer products, Japanese companies sought further improvements by incorporating more sensor data to make control smoother, more sensitive and more accurate. This increased the overall complexity of the systems in proportion to the increase in the input space dimension. To counter this problem, neural networks were introduced to handle the larger sensor variable set. In one system, a neural network was also used to correct the output of a fuzzy controller which was originally designed for a different set of inputs. This eliminated the need for a complete system redesign, resulting in substantial savings in both time and expense. A case in point is the washing machine introduced by Hitachi. The first model incorporated a fuzzy system as illustrated by the upper block in Figure 8.8.

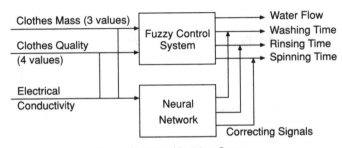

Fuzzy Washing Machine System

Figure 8.8   Neural Network Correcting the Output of a Fuzzy Controller

Later, an improved model was introduced with additional sensors to measure the transparency of the water. To accommodate the additional inputs without a complete redesign, a correcting neural network was added (the lower block in Figure 8.8). The additional inputs were fed only to the network which enhanced the washer control and corrected the fuzzy reasoning component output.

Many other Japanese products combine the salient features of ANNs with fuzzy reasoning systems. As a final example, Toshiba developed a microwave-oven-toaster which estimates the number of items being cooked and the oven temperature. The network then decides the optimum cooking time using fuzzy reasoning. The cooking time depends on the number of items in the cooker and their initial temperature. This is sensed and estimated by the neural network which regulates the flow of cooking gas. The output of the network is passed to a fuzzy reasoning component which determines the cooking time and power.

8.4   Forecasting and Prediction Applications

Prediction is a task every organization must learn to do. A consumer products company will want to know the growth in sales for a new product they plan to introduce. Meteorologists need to predict the weather. Banks want to predict the creditworthiness of companies as a basis for granting loans. Airport management groups want to know the growth in passenger arrivals at busy airports, and electric power companies want to know customer demand for power in the future, and so on. ANNs have been shown to be successful as predictive tools in a variety of ways—predicting that some event will or will not occur, predicting the time at which an event will occur, or predicting the level of some event outcome. To predict with an acceptable level of accuracy, an ANN must be trained with a sizable number of examples of past patterns together with known future outcome values. The training set will generally come from historical data that has been collected over a given time period. The ANN must then learn to generalize and extrapolate from new patterns to predict future outcomes.

In this section, we describe five interesting types of predictive applications using MLFF networks: forecasting financial and chaotic time series, forecasting sport outcomes, prediction of incipient faults in helicopter drive trains and assessing the creditworthiness of loan applicants. We begin with an application in financial time series forecasting.

Forecasting Financial Time Series

In Chapter 3, the theory of nonlinear systems was reviewed and procedures were given to model and predict chaotic time series. Time series, like other "systems" can be manifestations of deterministic or probabilistic behavior, or a mixture of both. MLFF networks have been shown to be capable of learning to model and predict both types of phenomena. When the underlying dynamics are stochastic, the network learns to model nonlinear nonparametric regression. When the system's dynamics are deterministic, the network learns to model the system's equations of motion. When the dynamics are a mixture of both, the network learns to model the mixed dynamics. How well the network can learn depends on the degree of correlation between the sequence of input patterns and quality and quantity of data available.

The problem of forecasting time series can be stated as follows: Given a number of values (observations) of a time dependent variable x_t ($t = 1, 2, \dots$), we wish to accurately predict the value of the variable at some future time $t + h$. For simplicity, we assume the time series is stationary, that is, the underlying probability distribution or dynamics driving the system remains constant over time. To be able to forecast the series using a MLFF network, an appropriate training scheme must be devised. The most common method is to use the MLFF as a time delay neural network (TDNN). We assume some historical time series data is available to train the network. Using this data, a sequence of $k \geq 2$ consecutive discrete time values of the series are used for input to the network. Usually the series values are equally spaced in time (hourly, daily, weekly, monthly). For input, the k values $x_{t-k} \, x_{t-k+1} \cdots x_{t-1}$ are used with a single target or desired value of x_t (or x_{t+h}). The input time delay "window" is then shifted one or more time points later in the series and a second training vector is formed using the values $x_{t-k+1} \, x_{t-k+2} \cdots x_t$ with target value x_{t+1}. The window and target values are shifted later in time again for the next point and so on. This training set is used over some chosen time interval repeatedly to adjust the weights through some form of backpropagation or other training method until the prediction error is sufficiently small. Once the network has learned to predict with small error on the training set, the next step is to test it on a sequence of time points not used for the training. If the accuracy of forecasting is within tolerable levels on the test set, the network can be used to forecast real future events. The training and testing samples are illustrated in Figure 8.9.

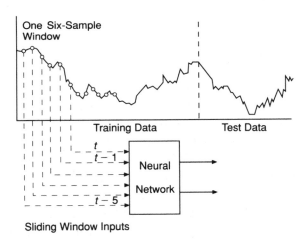

Figure 8.9   Training and Testing a TDNN Multilayer Network

Several questions need to be answered before attempting to forecast with an MLFF. How many training samples are required? How many input data points should be used, that is, what window size is best? What prediction horizon should be chosen (how far into the future to predict), how should the test and training data be divided, what network configuration should be used (number of hidden layers, number of nodes per layer, type of activation functions, type of output nodes) and so on. Perhaps the most difficult question of all to answer is *what* to predict. For example, if the series is the Standard and Poor (S&P) 500 stock index, should the index value be forecast or should the direction of the series be forecast? The above questions are not easily answered. A knowledge of the dynamics driving the system to be forecast can provide some suggestions on a good network architecture and network parameters. Therefore, if the user has tools to carry out statistical and chaotic data analyses (see Section 3.6), it may be possible to characterize the "system" and provide some insight into the best choice of network parameters. In any case, one should set realistic objectives on what is achievable and then experiment with different architectures and training data. The general guidelines given in Chapters 6 and 7 for the construction of MLFF networks should also be followed, if applicable, but usually, some experimentation will still be necessary. Besides the time series itself, other data or indicators may also be useful to improve the accuracy of forecasting. For example, the author has found that the use of moving averages, trading volume, momentum, and other relevant data can sometimes improve forecasting accuracy significantly (Patterson et al., 1993). Preprocessing the raw data can also be critically important.

Forecasting Individual Stock Returns

Many financial institutions are now using ANNs in a big way for foreign exchange (Forex) trading, for stock selection and for portfolio management. Some organizations have developed sophisticated systems that require periodic training of hundreds or even thousands of ANNs to predict stock market index movements as well as individual stock price behaviors. Financial institutions try to model broad markets such as the Dow Jones Industrial Average or Standard and Poor 500 indices, a form of *macromodeling*. Others concentrate on the returns of specific companies. They perform *micromodeling* to predict returns on individually selected stocks.

LBS Capital Management, a mutual fund management company based in Florida, has chosen to do the latter. They manage over $600 million by tracking and predicting the returns on some 3,000 U.S. and foreign-based companies (Barr and Mani, 1994; Lewinson, 1994; and Schmerkin, 1992). To predict the returns, LBS trains some 3,000 MLFF networks using backpropagation every weekend using a battery of PCs and workstations. Inputs to the networks are both fundamental factors (per share income, price to earnings ratio, annual growth rate) and technical factors (closing price, volume, momentum). When the projected return on a security shows up as an outlier, that is, with its percent of return being in a high or low percentile range relative to other securities, the stock is selected for possible acquisition (long) or sale (short). These are the securities that potentially have greater likelihood for either appreciation or depreciation and hence offer more opportunity for higher returns.

All of the networks trained at LBS Capital Management are MLFF nets using BP gradient descent training. Although the company has experimented with different architectures and investment objectives, their greatest successes have come from micromodeling with MLFF networks. For example, they claim neural networks have been used to generate rules for their OMNI expert system. This system has reportedly made recommendations leading to a compound annual return of 26.8% over the six-year period 1987 to 1992 as compared to a 14.04% return using a buy and hold policy on the S&P 500. They have also claimed to be among the top performers for several times running in stock selections from the S&P 400 Mid Cap.

Forecasting Chaotic Time Series

Lapedes and Farber (1988) were among the earliest to use ANNs to forecast chaotic time series (see Section 3.6). They used a two hidden-layer MLFF network trained with BP for their tests. Sigmoidal activation functions were used in the hidden layers and a linear output unit was used to predict the value of the chaotic time series (using floating point, real-valued numbers). The differential equation for the series is the Glass-Mackey delay equation:

$$\frac{dx}{dt} = \frac{ax(t - \tau)}{1 + x^{10}(t - \tau)} - bx(t) \tag{8.1}$$

The values of the constants used in the equation were $a = 0.2$, $b = 0.1$ and a delay of τ in the range of 30. The series generated by this equation is chaotic with a fractal attractor dimension that increases with τ. For example, with $\tau = 17$ the dimension of the attractor is 2.1 and for $\tau = 30$ the dimension is 3.5, and the system exhibits more chaotic behavior. Solving equation (8.1) (that is integrating (8.1) using the Runga-Kutta method) produces a plot of x as a function of time (Figure 8.10). Note that the series appears to be almost random and unpredictable.

To train the network, a training set of 500 samples was taken from the series. A time delay window of the type illustrated in Figure 8.9 was used for each input in the training set with the target value chosen for different prediction horizons, P (e.g., $P = 6$, $P = 12$ and so on). The size of the sample window was chosen to be $n = 4$, a value consistent with the embedding dimension suggested by Taken's theorem (described in Section 3.6). The value of the time delay between successive points was chosen to be $T = 6$. To test the accuracy of predictions, an additional 500 points beyond the last training point was used for testing.

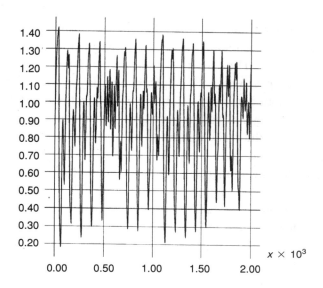

Figure 8.10   The Glass-Mackey Series with a Delay Parameter Value of $\tau = 30$

The results of the forecasting experiments described above were very positive. It was shown that the MLFF network could predict with significantly better accuracy than conventional methods. As expected, the predictive accuracy dropped off with the prediction horizon P. In the same paper, Lapedes and Farber (1988), also demonstrate through a heuristic argument that no more than two hidden layers are needed to accurately approximate any of a large class of mapping functions $f: \mathbf{R}^n \to \mathbf{R}^m$.

Since the publication of their results, numerous forecasting experiments have been reported using various chaotic time series and different ANN architectures. Comparisons of forecasting accuracies for the chaotic series and other series such as stock and bond indices, foreign exchange currency rates and others have been made. For example, Patterson et al. (1993), compared the performance of MLFF networks with recurrent networks and radial basis function networks in forecasting two chaotic and two financial time series. Other comparative results have been reported where MLFF networks play the role of a benchmark network.

Forecasting Sports and Stock Event Outcomes

Financial forecasting need not be restricted to foreign exchange rates nor to stock market predictions. Another interesting challenge at forecasting for monetary gain or personal satisfaction is to predict the outcome of certain sport events. One such effort was reported by Chang et al. (1993), who attempted to predict the future performance of the Los Angeles Lakers basketball team, given their performance for the 1991–92 season. They used a single hidden-layer MLFF network with 25 input nodes, including a bias node, eight hidden-layer nodes, including bias and two output nodes. Input data used for the sport application included such factors as home winning percentage, divisional winning percentage, average win/loss streak, opponent's position in the league, injuries suffered by each team, day and time of game, game point spread and so on.

Training data for the application initially consisted of four games that occurred prior to the first test prediction game of April 13, 1992. For each subsequent game, an additional seven previous games were added to the training set. A total of 17 games was used for training and testing during the spring, 1992 schedule.

The results as reported in predicting wins and point spreads for five games during the season were: two wins correct, three wrong and for predicted spread four, were correct and one wrong.

As part of the same study, attempts were made to predict the price movement of two popular computer stocks: Microsoft and Apple Computer. For this study, an MLFF network with a two-dimensional input of $K \times N$ neurons were used, where $K = 8$ is the number of financial input variables (market and monetary indices) and N is the number of days of data. N was allowed to vary between one and five. The eight financial indices used were: risk assessment which, was just the number of days required to hold a stock (e.g. two days over a weekend), stock price, stock volume, Dow Jones Industrial Average index, Standard and Poor 500 index, Nikkei index, 90-day Treasury bill interest rate and the aggregate strength of the U.S. dollar in the world market. The number of hidden-layer nodes was chosen to be four times the number of input nodes. A single output node was used to predict the next day's stock price. The training set was made up of data for the quarter November 4, 1991 to January 31, 1992 for each of the eight input variables. Input data was scaled to range between 0 and 1. The network was trained until error values were on the order of 5×10^{-6}, predictions were then made for six weeks of closing prices.

The best results were achieved for inputs of three days followed closely by a five-day input. A percentage error as low as 5.8 was reportedly achieved for an entire week of daily predictions. The results, as reported, are indeed promising (if sustainable) for modeling individual company stock price movements.

Sensor Data Fusion and Fault Prediction

Sensor data fusion is the process of combining multisource sensor data for purposes of detection, correlation, identification, prediction and situation assessment. Many fusion techniques have been devised, particularly over the past twenty years, and the number of potential applications is growing at a rapid pace. Current methods use techniques such as statistical hypothesis testing, Bayesian and other probabilistic combining techniques (e.g. Dempster-Shafer evidential reasoning), fuzzy logic, figure of merit, conventional expert systems and neural networks. Typical applications of ANNs to sensor fusion are many. They include military command, control, communication and intelligence (C^3I), incipient fault detection of complex electromechanical systems, robotics, process monitoring and control and so on. Studies have shown that for many fusion applications, neural networks perform as well as or better than conventional methods.

One area of great promise for ANN applications is in the prediction of impending faults (incipient fault detection) that may result in costly repairs or even the loss of life. For example, a helicopter's main gearbox will have a mechanical failure on average every 300,000 hours of operation. Fatigue or "hard fault" failures such as the failure of gears, shafts and other key components of the drive train can have catastrophic results. If such faults can be accurately predicted in advance, the vehicle can be safely landed and repaired thereby avoiding more major repairs and serious injury to the crews. Laboratory tests at Boeing have shown that the detection of fatigue cracks in the initial stages are possible when only 10% of the area of a part is fractured. Thus, real-time detection and impending fault detection is possible through vibration signature analysis.

Many conventional monitoring systems are unacceptable since they are more prone to failure than the systems they are monitoring. For example, when complex computers are used to monitor a helicopter's main gearbox, the computer failure rate is every 3,000 hours, some 100 times more frequent than the gearbox it is monitoring. Therefore, more reliable, robust systems are needed. Solid state ANNs appear to meet this requirement. They are reliable, have reduced complexity and high computation speed. They can do real-time diagnostics onboard a craft by fusing data from several sources: the powertrain, drivetrain, structure, rotor system, and oil systems. It would appear then that if low cost diagnostic ANN chips can be mass produced, the commercial potential for their application is enormous. They could be used cost-effectively for the maintenance of any land, air or sea vehicle requiring costly maintenance work. A number of military and government agencies have now recognized the potential for this type of diagnosis. They call the approach health and usage monitoring (HUM) technology, and have initiated programs for their implementation. For example the U.K. and Norway will require all helicopters flying over the North Sea to have HUM technology on board by 1995 (Rock et al., 1993).

HUM Technology

The goal of the helicopter HUM programs is to develop real-time airborne, vibration signature analysis methods to reliably diagnose impending transmission fatigue failures thereby providing time for safe landings before a fault occurs. A typical HUM system is illustrated in Figure 8.11.

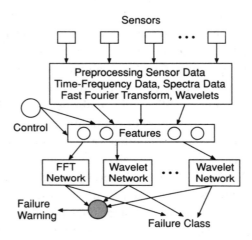

Figure 8.11   Diagram of a Real-Time Health and Usage Monitoring System

The system consists of multiple sensors (accelerometers, strain gauges, acoustic sensors), a signal preprocessor, one or more MLFF predictive networks and various output devices. The number of preprocessed input features to the networks typically range between 10 and 20. These inputs may be subdivided and distributed to several feature extractor networks before being fused (combined) by a predictive classifier network or combined and diagnosed by a single large network. The former type of architecture is illustrated in Figure 8.12 (Brotherton and Pollard, 1992). Orincon used this architecture in a series of promising tests. The outputs from the first layer networks were merged into the second layer network for fusion processing. This type of hierarchical processing allows long signal integration times which give the output network time to learn which inputs are dropouts or false alarms and can be ignored.

When training the network, the Orincon group learned that only 20 rotations of a propeller shaft were needed to generate enough data to accurately differentiate among the different transmission states.

Although experience with HUM systems utilizing ANNs for sensor fusion and

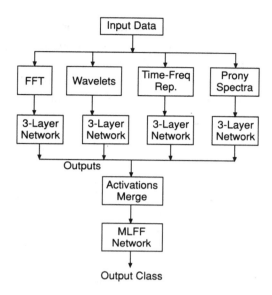

Figure 8.12   Hierarchical System for Feature Extraction, Fusion and Classification

incipient fault prediction is still limited, initial tests are very promising and the potential for wide applicability of these systems seems encouraging. It is likely ANN chips will become a required component for many types of air, land and sea vehicles in future.

Predicting Creditworthiness for Loan Applications

One of the most successful applications of predictive models using neural networks was implemented by Chase Manhatten Bank. The system is a hybrid, statistical-based network that assesses the creditworthiness of public corporations seeking business loans. Chase loans out some $300 million annually to qualifying companies. Since this can be a significant source of profit (or loss), the ability to accurately forecast the creditworthiness of potential customers is essential.

The overall system known as Creditview performs three-year forecasts that assign a risk classification of *good*, *criticized*, or *charged-off*. The system also provides a detailed listing of items that significantly contribute to the forecast. A conventional expert system interprets the items and produces various comparison reports for senior loan officers. A front-end system to the neural network known as ADAM receives historical input data from a financial database, together with good and bad obligor data. This data serves as part of the training set. ADAM also receives input on industry norms, financial data for the normalization of specific industry categories. ADAM generates candidate variables that may indicate the future financial condition of a company. This is compiled as profile data in the form of logical feature vectors which forms the basis for a neural network model of the company in question. The neural network, known as the public company model (PCLM) Forecaster then produces a rating for the company. The combined system is illustrated in Figure 8.13.

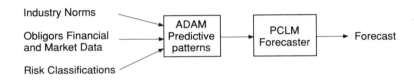

Figure 8.13   Chase Manhatten Bank's Hybrid Neural Network Credit Rater

The PCLM accepts six years of past financial data for the company being rated. It uses the expressions produced by ADAM to predict the financial health of the company three years into the future. The predictions give the likelihood of a company being rated as good, criticized or charged-off. In addition, the PCLM identifies the strengths and weaknesses in the financial structure of the obligor. Extensive reports giving comparative risk estimates and a text explanation of the analysis is provided to the user. Morose (1990, 1993) reports that Chase has tested the system extensively and uncovered a number of troublesome loans. The system was put in operation around 1990 and is being extended and enhanced to include private corporation evaluations as well.

8.5   Pattern Recognition Applications

Pattern recognition includes such applications as speech and character recognition for various languages, visual image recognition and classification, and various types of signal and chart analysis including electrocardiograms, electroencefelographs, electrocardiographs, and various graph analysis for process alarm monitoring. Pattern recognition applications are generally difficult to master. They are closely related to cognitive tasks performed by humans almost effortlessly.

In this section we describe three applications of pattern recognition: handwritten character recognition, early detection of epileptic attacks and text-to-speech conversion.

Handwritten Character Recognition

The automatic recognition of handwritten characters is an area that has received much attention over the past decade. Indeed, because of its difficulty, it has become a benchmark problem for different approaches. This effort is certainly justified as there are numerous industrial and business applications where automated recognition will result in substantial cost savings. Various approaches to the problem have been studied including conventional pattern recognition methods as well as neural network solutions. A high degree of success has been realized in both approaches, and a few commercial ANN systems are now currently in use (Schwartz, 1992). With these successes, it is likely that low cost commercial solid state systems will soon be available on the market.

MLFF networks are perhaps the most widely used ANN architecture for the recognition problem, the differences in approach are mainly in the type of image preprocessing used and refinements to the network architecture. Our description given below is mainly based on the results achieved by researchers at AT&T Bell Labs, as presented by le Cun (1987), and le Cun et al. (1990).

In the recognition of handwritten characters, a common grid size used by researchers is a 16×16 pixel array with 16 or more gray levels per pixel as illustrated in Figure 8.12. Several stages of preprocessing are usually required. First, it is necessary to segment each character, that is to isolate and extract the character from the text if necessary. Next, the image is usually thresholded and binarized, so individual pixels are set to either zero or one. Finally, some normalization is needed to standardize the size of the characters. The normalized image size is usually taken to be $16 \times 16 = 256$ pixels. Thus, when the preprocessed normalized character image is used as the input, the network will have 256 nodes in the input layer.

The structure of one AT&T network that has realized good classification performance is illustrated in Figure 8.14.

Figure 8.14   Typical Segmented Characters for Recognition

In this four-layer network, the first two hidden layers perform feature extraction while the final two layers act as digit classifiers. The total number of network parameters (weights) is reduced by constraining the network to assume a form of weight sharing, a scheme whereby nodes receive inputs from different parts of the input plane, but use the same weight values. The first hidden layer consists of 12 planes or feature maps of 64 nodes each partially connected. Each plane corresponds to a different feature detector. Units within a given plane have different local receptive fields, but share the same weight values. The second hidden layer is similarly structured with 12 planes of 16 nodes each partially connected. The two final layers are fully connected with 30 and 10 nodes respectively.

The above type of selective connectivity has been used by Fukushima in his Neocognitron network (see Chapter 12) to achieve shift invariant pattern recognition. Keeler et al. (1991) and Lee (1991) also use local receptive fields (connections from different spatial locations) and weight sharing in MLFF networks for handwritten character recognition applications. The architecture used by Keeler et al. is able to perform simultaneous segmentation and recognition requiring little image preprocessing.

A number of databases are available for training and testing ANNs. One source in particular is the U.S. Postal service database consisting of 9000 handwritten zip code digits (OAT Handwritten Zip Code Database, 1987). A sample of this database is presented in Figure 8.15.

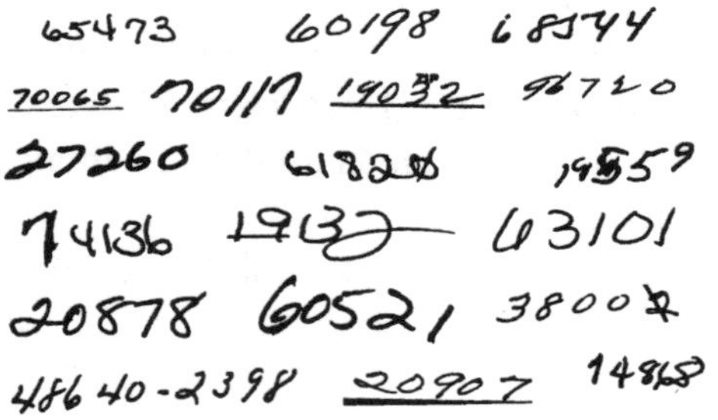

Figure 8.15   Examples of Zip Codes from the U.S. Postal Service Database

It is customary to randomly partition the data source into two sets: a training set containing about 80% of the database and a set of about 20% for testing. The performance of the trained network is then based on the numbers of correct classifications and misclassifications, taking into account the number of rejections allowed over both the training and test set data. Typical performance figures reported are in the range of 0.14% misclassifications for the training set and 5.0% misclassifications for the test set when an error rate of 1.0% is used. The 1% error rate is achieved when a 12.1% rejection rate is allowed.

Although a high degree of success has been realized in the recognition of some handwritten characters (3 to 4% errors on unrejected characters), accurate recognition of general, unconstrained cursive handwriting remains largely unsolved. Recent experiments in recognizing scanned images of a page of cursive handwriting with no constraints resulted in letter recognition accuracies ranging from 61% to 81% (Yanikoglu and Sandon, 1993). The one hidden layer MLFF network used in the experiments had 1,000 input nodes corresponding to a preprocessed image of 20 $\times$ 50 gray scale pixels. The network had 70 hidden-layer nodes and 26 output nodes, one for each lowercase letter of the alphabet. The hidden-layer nodes were connected to subimages of the segmented letters with a 10 $\times$ 10 input receptive field. They were fully connected to the output nodes.

In one set of experiments, the network was trained using 28 alphabets of 26 handprinted letters each written by 28 different writers. The test set consisted of seven other alphabets written by seven other writers. In this case, the recognition rate was 75% on the test set after the network was trained to recognize all of the training alphabets. In other experiments, recognition accuracies were both above and below this level with an average accuracy of about 61%. Part of the success realized in these experiments were due to the image preprocessing steps which used new methods to segment words into letters and slant and size normalization of the segmented letters.

A comprehensive description of the state-of-the-art for handwritten character recognition is given in the Special Issue on Optical Character Recognition (Pavlidis and Mori, 1992).

Detection of Epileptic Attacks

Early detection of an impending attack in epileptic patients makes it possible to start early reactions and treatment. The preictal period is not easily detected however, since the temporal data varies greatly from patient to patient and the course of the attack is also a source of variability. Because of the strong patient dependency, conventional statistical and AI methods have not been very effective in early detection. With patient specific data available on prior attacks, the use of ANN technology is possible since training data sets can be constructed.

Patient data is collected by implanting EEG electrodes subdurally in a patient and recording the analog brain wave signals over a period of time prior to an attack. A number of 100–200 Hz signals from different locations are recorded graphically for analysis by an electrophysiologist and also digitized and stored for subsequent use in training MLFF networks. The physiologist can analyze and edit the data using a graphical screen editor, eliminating artifacts and other irrelevant data. Further preprocessing of the data has also been found to be effective in reducing the size of the data set. Sliding windows over the time series data are used to selectively sample sections of pattern data points. This data is used in the computation of averages, variances, histograms and other summary statistics. The data from different channels is then divided among several MLFF networks for independent training and the outputs from these networks are then used for input to a final prediction network. By combining the outputs of several independent networks into a vector for input to a final network, researchers were able to improve the response-quality of the early detection system (Hamilton and Hufnagel, 1992). The detection system is illustrated in Figure 8.16.

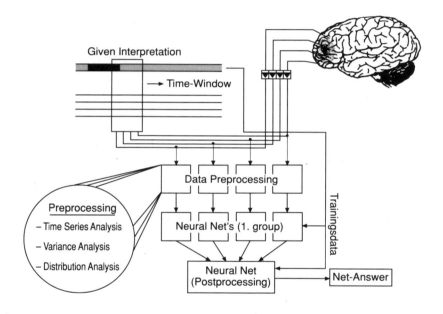

Figure 8.16   System for Early Detection of Epileptic Attacks
(Courtesy of Hamilton and Hufnagel)

The success of the system was found to be heavily dependent on the quality of the human data interpretations, and particularly on the preprocessing methods applied to the source data. The use of ANNs for early detection has led to more efficient analysis and resulted in more precise and more stable detection. This work has helped to pave the way for the development of a real-time automatic detection system which is now deemed feasible.

Automatic Identification of Individuals

Automatic methods of validating the identity of individuals has broad application in the areas of security and crime prevention. The daily routines of individuals in many facets of work are controlled through a verification of the individual's identity for authorized access to facilities and information. Common verification techniques generally rely on the use of secret passwords or the use of personal identity cards, both of which are subject to compromise. Therefore, reliable methods for automated identification are important.

In this subsection, we describe a method of user recognition based on the fusion of speech and image data from ten subjects as reported by Colombi et al. (1993). The approach is based on the use of training data collected over a period of ten days. For each subject, both utterances and facial image data were collected. The speech data were rich phonetic sentences, together with subject and imposter name recordings. The image data for the ten subjects consisted of more than 2,000 gray scale images, where each image was 32×32 pixels of 256 gray scale levels. Equal numbers of target and nontarget images were collected in the training database. Multiple day data was used for training to improve recognition performance by compensating for daily changes in an individual's appearance and speech patterns. Multiple day training resulted in better generalization and the ability to accommodate distortions.

The facial image data was used to train a single hidden-layer MLFF network with 1,024 input nodes, ten hidden-layer nodes and two output nodes. The two outputs correspond to "Me/Not Me" responses. The neural network was trained on the training data samples until 100% accuracy was achieved.

Although successful speech recognition systems have been built using ANN technology, the speech data for these experiments were processed using non-ANN techniques. The techniques were based on conventional methods known as Linear Predictive Coding and cepstral and auditory neural model representations (Colombi et al., 1993). Verification in this case was also based on a form of "Me/Not Me" (codebook) scheme. After independent training of speech and image verification, the two outputs are fused using a weighted probability scheme to obtain final verification of subject identities. The overall recognition system is illustrated in Figure 8.17.

The facial verification experiments were conducted using two different MLFF networks for two types of input features. The normalized raw pixel data as described above and principal component (PC) coefficients (also known as the Karhunen-Loeve Transform) derived from the facial image (see Chapter 3 for a description of principal components). The network using the PC coefficients for inputs consisted of ten input nodes, 20 hidden-layer nodes and two output nodes.

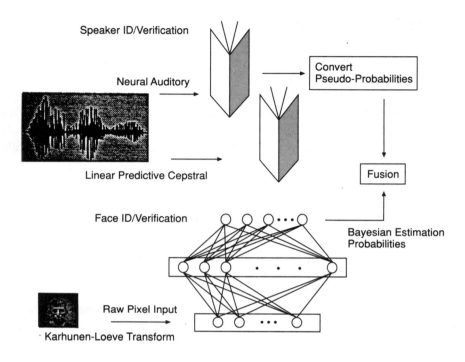

Figure 8.17   Fusion of Facial Image and Speech Data
(Courtesy of J. Colombi, D. Krepp, S. Rogers, D. Ruck and M. Oxley)

Somewhat better performance was actually achieved with the PC inputs over the raw pixel input approach. The performance difference was greatest for short term training. When a one to two days training with nine to ten days testing period was used, the PC input method was twice as accurate (47.2% *vs* 90.6% recognition accuracy). For longer term training, the PC input method was still somewhat better. For example, when seven, eight and nine days training with three, two and one test days were used respectively, the PC coefficient input performance was better by some 10% (86.0% *vs* 98.3%, 89.5% *vs* 99.0%, and 90.0% *vs* 100.0% respectively).

In a second set of experiments, ten output nodes were used in both MLFF networks, one node to identify each subject. The network with the 1,024 normalized raw pixel data inputs used a hidden layer with 20 nodes while the network with the ten PC coefficients for inputs had a hidden layer with 40 nodes. Both networks were trained until 100% accuracy was achieved on the training data. Test data accuracies were somewhat poorer. When one through nine days training with tenth day testing was performed, the raw input network achieved an accuracy of 58.9% as compared to an 87.8% accuracy for the PC input network.

Although high identification accuracies were achieved from each input source independently (speech and facial imagery) for the multiple day training data, additional confidence was gained from the fusion of the two sets of features. Fusion of the two sources was based on a linear combination of the speech output computed as a pseudo-probability and post-probabilities computed directly by the neural network. The highest accuracies (100% true accept, 0% false accept) were achieved for multiple-day training using the PC as inputs to the neural networks. The best results used a training composition of 50% target and 50% nontarget individuals over the multiple days. One important conclusion learned from the experiments was that a training period of less than six separate days dramatically reduced the accuracy of the network's verification. This is likely due to the shift and scale sensitivity of the networks.

Summary

In this chapter, we have described typical applications of MLFF networks to illustrate the versatility of these most popular networks. The applications described were from four broad classes: classification and diagnostics, control and optimization, forecasting and prediction, and pattern recognition. The applications presented included the classification of cells for cancer diagnosis, fault identification in telephone switching systems, autonomously driven land vehicle, intelligent controller for steel-making, control optimization in consumer products, forecasting economic and chaotic time series, predicting the creditworthiness of companies for loan payback, handwritten character recognition, detection of epileptic attacks and the automatic identification of individuals. These applications are representative of the kinds of tasks MLFF networks are being trained to perform. Because of their ability to adapt and learn complex mappings, MLFF networks can be used successfully in a great many applications. Of course, a good training set is essential. Because of their high success rate, MLFF networks are often used as a benchmark architecture with which to compare other network types. Consequently, applications of MLFF networks will appear in other chapters as well when their performance is being compared to that of other architectures.

Part IV

Dynamic Recurrent and Stochastic Neural Networks

9
Dynamic Recurrent Networks

In this chapter, we examine a special class of dynamic networks, including general recurrent neural networks (RNN). The recurrent networks of this chapter differ from the Hopfield types described in Chapter 4 in that they may have the equivalent of multiple layers, asymmetric weight matrices, and self-feedback. It is also possible to utilize backpropagation supervised learning algorithms to train these networks. We begin the chapter with a general description of recurrent networks and their dynamics. We then consider the class of recurrent backpropagation networks, including some special cases. We also look at some special RNN architectures and their computational capabilities. Finally, we conclude the chapter with some typical applications for RNNs.

9.1 Introduction

The feedforward networks described in the previous chapters can be generalized to operate in a recurrent manner by connecting the output of one or more PEs to the inputs of one or more PEs in the same or preceding layers. These generalized architectures may have lateral connections among units of the same layer including self-feedback connections as well. Incorporating feedback connections into an MLFF network results in significant changes in the operation and learning processes of the networks as compared to their static counterparts. But, as we shall see, the added complexity of these networks is not without some rewards. They have increased computational power over the conventional MLFF networks.

Unlike static feedforward networks, recurrent networks exhibit dynamic behavior. They can perform mappings that are functions of time and/or space or converge to one of a number of limit points. As a result, they are capable of performing more complex computations than static feedforward networks. For example, they are capable of learning temporal pattern sequences, that is, sequences of patterns that are context or time dependent. This desirable trait is also characteristic of biological systems that learn various types of sequences such as phoneme or character sequences that occur in a language, step dependent plans or sequential problem solving methods. For some applications that RNNs are good at performing, the corresponding MLFF networks required for the same application may need an arbitrarily large number of hidden-layer nodes in order to realize the same performance levels.

General RNN architectures may have lateral connections within a given layer as well as connections that feedback signals from subsequent layers, including the output layer. In fact, we no longer need to think of the network as having multiple layers at all. Instead, we simply view these networks as a number of interconnected processing units, where any unit i may be connected to any other unit j, including the case $i = j$. Any of the units may be taken as an output unit, while some designated units will receive inputs, possibly including bias inputs. If the network has a total of n units and m of them receive external inputs, then a single weight matrix $\mathbf{W}$ of dimension $n \times (n + m)$ can be used to specify the complete synaptic weight parameters of the network. Units with cyclical connections receive feedback signals, that is, signals that are at least partially dependent on earlier computations by the same unit. The recurrence of signals being fed back for recomputation explains the name of these networks. And, the feedback signals for such networks are responsible for the dynamic behavior of the RNN systems.

We saw in Chapter 5 that neural networks such as the Hopfield network, have physical analogies which can sometimes be useful in describing them and understanding their behaviors. In this regard, the behavior of RNNs can be better understood with a knowledge of nonlinear dynamic phenomena, such as turbulent fluid flows or nonlinear control systems. Such systems also have coupled interdependencies and feedback paths. Their behaviors or dynamics are governed by sets of coupled nonlinear differential equations. Likewise, the dynamics of RNNs can be completely described by sets of first order nonlinear differential equations of the form

$$\frac{dx_i}{dt} = G_i(\mathbf{w}, \mathbf{I}, \mathbf{x}(t)) \qquad i = 1, 2, ..., n$$

where $\mathbf{x}$ is the state vector, $\mathbf{w}$ the matrix of synaptic connection strengths, $\mathbf{I}$ the external input vector and G_i is a nonlinear differentiable function. In the discrete time model case, the dynamics are governed by sets of nonlinear difference equations of the form

$$x_i(t + 1) = G_i(\mathbf{w}, \mathbf{I}, \mathbf{x}(t)) \qquad i = 1, 2, ..., n$$

where $x_i(t)$ is the output of the ith unit at time t.

For systems with feedback, questions of stability become important. The parameters $\mathbf{I}$ and $\mathbf{w}$ and the initial conditions or starting point $\mathbf{x}(0)$ of an RNN determine its behavior. The behavior can evolve in one of four ways: convergence to a stable attractor point, settle to cyclical oscillations (periodic), tend toward quasiperiodic behavior (oscillations at multiple frequencies) or exhibit a form of chaotic wandering behavior (described in Chapter 3). We will be concerned primarily with the stable convergence case where the network converges to a single attractor point or performs some desired mapping on the input vector. We state some conditions later that are sufficient to insure this stable behavior.

An example of a general recurrent network is illustrated in Figure 9.1 where the network has three external inputs, three outputs and a number of internal connections among the units including some self-feedback links. To see how the network operates, we assume a discrete time model.

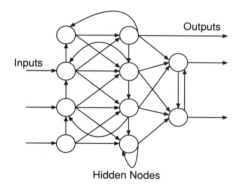

Figure 9.1   A General Recurrent Neural Network

Thus, suppose the RNN depicted in Figure 9.1 has been operational for some time. At time $t > 0$, an input pattern $\mathbf{x}$ is presented to the input units of the network. These units compute activations $f_i(\mathbf{x}, \mathbf{W})$ and transfer the values on to units they are connected to at time $t + 1$. Other units, including non-input units also compute output activations and pass them on to the units they are connected to at time $t + 1$. The process is repeated at each successive time point $t + i$ ($i = 1, 2, ...$). During each cycle, feedback signals combine with feedforward signals to produce net inputs to each unit. The output from units are activation values that may converge (stabilize to a fixed point), oscillate (repeat the same set of different values over time), or produce a form of chaotic wandering, depending on the input vector **x** values and the network parameters. The actual dynamics of the continuous time convergent RNN model are similar to the dynamics of the continuous time Hopfield networks (Chapter 5). They are described in the following section.

It was claimed above that RNNs are generalizations of feedforward networks. To show that they are in fact generalizations, one can always derive an equivalent MLFF for any RNN (Minsky and Papert, 1969). They are equivalent in that the two networks exhibit the same behavior. This can be accomplished through an unfolding-in-time process, where each time step t of the RNN corresponds to an additional layer of the MLFF. An example of the MLFF equivalent of a simple two-unit fully connected RNN is illustrated in Figure 9.2 (Rumelhart et al., 1986). The MLFF equivalent network (9.2b) of the fully connected two-unit RNN (9.2a) has identical weights for all layers (the weights are the same as those of the two unit RNN), but distinct PE outputs on each of its successive layers. Such a network can be taught to solve the nonlinear XOR problem, an impossible task for any MLFF network with only two PEs. Clearly, a form of error backpropagation can be used to train such networks.

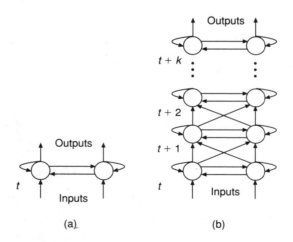

Figure 9.2   (a) A Simple Fully Connected Recurrent Network, and (b) the Equivalent Unfolded-in-Time Equivalent Multilayer Feedforward Network

RNNs have been used in a number of interesting applications including associative memories, spatiotemporal pattern classification (e.g. speech recognition), control, optimization, forecasting and the generation of pattern sequences. As we will see in Section 9.4, they are capable of learning lengthy time or context dependent sequences, a feat that feedforward MLFF are incapable of performing well. For example, they have been shown to perform computational tasks equivalent to finite state automata (Elman, 1990) as well as more general Turing Machines (Williams and Zipser, 1989).

In the following section, we investigate the dynamics of general RNNs. Next, we examine some useful training algorithms for these networks. In subsequent sections, we consider special types of RNN architectures and look at some specific applications in more detail.

9.2   The Dynamics of General Recurrent Networks

Like many other nonlinear dynamical systems, the behavior of general RNNs are still very much a topic of research. Even so, a number of studies have been completed using different architectures and successful learning algorithms have been developed. Generally, RNNs have been used to perform two basic types of computations. One type of task is in learning to perform general mappings $\mathbf{f} : \mathbf{R}^n \to \mathbf{R}^m$ that are also time dependent, that is, $\mathbf{y}(t) = \mathbf{f}(\mathbf{x}(t))$. In practice, the mapping $\mathbf{x} \to \mathbf{y}$ will be performed for a number of discrete time points in the interval $[t_0, t_k]$. Thus, if the initial state of the system is $\mathbf{y}(t_0)$, the set of temporal patterns $\{\mathbf{y}(t_0), \mathbf{x}(t_0), \mathbf{x}(t_1), ..., \mathbf{x}(t_{k-1})\}$ will be mapped to the set $\{\mathbf{y}(t_1), \mathbf{y}(t_2), ..., \mathbf{y}(t_k)\}$. These mappings are one-to-one onto and are useful for applications such as control, classification, or forecasting where generalization is required. They can also be used to perform many-to-one mappings where small changes in the input values produce no change in the output. This mode of computation is useful for applications such as associative memory recall or error correction.[1]

The behavior of RNNs have been described by Pineda (1988, 1989) and studied by several other researchers, including Almeda (1987), Pineda (1987), Rumelhart et al. (1986), Williams and Zipser (1989), Williams and Peng (1990), Zipser (1989), Pearlmutter (1988), among others.

We first saw an example of an RNN in Chapter 5 with the Hopfield type of networks. The Hopfield network, recall, is a special type of RNN with a symmetric weight matrix $\mathbf{W}$ and no self-feedback links ($w_{ij} = w_{ji}$, $w_{ii} = 0$). The dynamics of

---

[1] They have also been used to model oscillatory and chaotic system behaviors, but we will not consider such behaviors in this chapter.

the continuous-time Hopfield networks are governed by coupled, nonlinear differential equations (equations (5.15)) which are repeated here for convenience:

$$\tau_i \frac{dz_i(t)}{dt} = -z_i(t) + \sum_{j=1}^{n} w_{ij} y_j + I_i \quad i = 1, 2, \ldots, n \qquad (9.1)$$

$$y_i(t) = f[z_i(t)]$$

where the τ_i are relaxation times, z_i are the internal states of unit i, y_i is the output state (activation value) of unit i, w_{ij} is the strength of the weight connection from unit j to unit i and I_i are external inputs, including biases, to unit i. A flow diagram for this system is portrayed in Figure 9.3. In the diagram, the block containing Γ^{-1} accounts for the time coefficient which is required to satisfy equation (9.1). Diagrams such as this clearly illustrate the effect of the feedback connections (also how easily an analog simulation model of the network can be built). Recall that a symmetric weight matrix in the Hopfield model is a sufficient condition to guarantee stable asymptotic behavior (convergence to a stable fixed point).

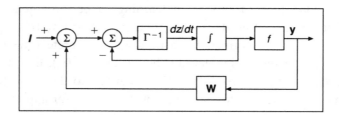

Figure 9.3   Continuous Time Hopfield Network Flow Diagram

We have repeated the equations and given the flow diagram of Figure 9.3 for the Hopfield network here in order that the dynamics of this network may be compared with that of the general RNN dynamics which we look at next.

Continuous RNN Dynamics

The dynamics of the general continuous time RNN model are similar to the dynamics of Hopfield networks. In general, they are governed by the coupled nonlinear differential equations of the form

$$\tau_i \frac{dx_i(t)}{dt} = -x_i(t) + g_i\left(\sum_{j=1}^n w_{ij}x_j + I_i\right) \quad i = 1, 2, \ldots, n \qquad (9.2)$$

where the τ_i are relaxation time coefficients, $x_i(t)$ the state of the ith unit at time t, w_{ij} the strength of the connection from unit j to unit i, I_i an external input to unit i and g_i the nonlinear activation functions. Note that equation (9.2) is related to (9.1) through a simple linear transformation $\mathbf{z}(t) = \mathbf{wx}(t) + \mathbf{I}$ where $\mathbf{z}(t)$ is the state vector of the Hopfield network, $\mathbf{w}$ the (invertible) weight matrix, $\mathbf{x}(t)$ the state vector of the general RNN and $\mathbf{I}$ the input vector. A flow diagram for the general RNN (Figure 9.4) illustrates the differences between these networks and Hopfield networks. In particular, one should compare the location of the activation functions g and f and the two feedback links in the two models.

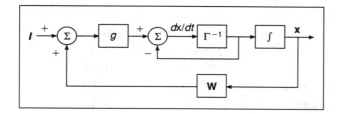

Figure 9.4   Continuous Time General Recurrent Network Flow Diagram

We denote the initial state of the system by $\mathbf{x}^0$ and the asymptotic steady (final) state by $\mathbf{x}^t$. The time independent point attractors are solutions of the steady state equations (i.e. at $dx/dt = 0$):

$$x_i^f = g_i\left(\sum_{j=1}^n w_{ij}\, x_i^f + I_i\right) \quad i = 1, 2, \ldots, n \qquad (9.3)$$

Systems with the dynamics of equation (9.2) are characterized by three important properties. First, they possess many degrees of freedom. The degrees of freedom correspond to the number of activation levels and time derivatives of the levels that make up the phase space of the system. Secondly, their dynamics are nonlinear. A consequence of the nonlinear activation functions g_i which are essential for the general mapping capabilities performed by these networks. And thirdly, they are dissipative. The phase space volume converges onto a manifold of lower dimensionality. These characteristics give such systems unusual behaviors as well as important computational abilities as pointed out earlier.

In reviewing the general recurrent model, one can distinguish between three classes of network dynamics depending on the values of the weight matrix **w**. For the case where **w** is a lower triangular matrix, the network is just a standard feedforward network (MLFF) without feedback links studied in the previous chapters. In this case, the network performs a continuous mapping of input to output. When **w** is symmetric with zero diagonal, the network is, as already noted, a dynamic recurrent network of the Hopfield type. Such systems possess a Liapunov (energy) function and are therefore, guaranteed to converge to one of a number of fixed point attractors. When **w** is a general asymmetric matrix, the network is a dynamic RNN and convergence is not always assured unless some restrictions are placed on the weight matrix. For this general RNN case, the system will evolve in one of the ways noted above depending on system parameters and on the initial state, that is, they may converge to one of a finite number of stable states (fixed point attractors like Hopfield networks), exhibit some form of oscillatory behavior, or go into a form of chaotic wandering behavior (oscillating at an infinite number of frequencies). The resultant behavior for a specific network will depend on the network connections, the parameter values and the initial state. It has been shown however, that stable behavior can be assured if the magnitude of the weights are limited (Atiya, 1988). For example, if g' is the derivative of g, a nonlinear differentiable activation function ($g' = dg(x)/dx$) and w_{ij} is the weight connecting unit j to unit i, then the system is assured of convergence to a unique point attractor provided the following relation is satisfied:

$$\sum_i \sum_j w_{ij}^2 < \frac{1}{(\max_i |g_i'|)^2} \qquad (9.4)$$

In this chapter, our main interest is in the convergent case. For the stable case, two types of operation are possible depending on the method of data input to the network: continuous mappings or convergence to one of many fixed point attractors. The two methods of operation are determined by the type of data input to the network, either by setting the initial state values $\mathbf{x}^0$ or by specifying the external inputs **I** (biases and input patterns). We refer to the two types of operation as fixed-point mapper and continuous mapper (Pineda has called them initial-state input and parametric input, respectively (Pineda, 1988)).

When the initial state $\mathbf{x}^0$ represents the input to the network and the **I** are clamped to some constant value for all relaxations, the RNN computes a mapping M from the initial state $\mathbf{x}^0$ to the final state $\mathbf{x}^t$, $M : \mathbf{x}^0 \rightarrow \mathbf{x}^t$. Initial points $\mathbf{x}^0$ lying within a given "basin of attraction" converge to the fixed point within the given basin as illustrated in Figure 9.5. This is the many-to-one type of mapping

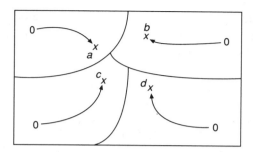

Figure 9.5   Fixed Points a, b, c and d and Their Basin Boundaries

performed by the network. It is useful for associative recall and error correction types of applications where an input pattern may be incomplete or corrupted with noise.

Continuous mapper behavior is realized when the external inputs **I** are treated as an input to the network and the $\mathbf{x}^0$ for all input units are set to constant values. The computation performed in this case is a mapping from the parametric input **I** to the final state $\mathbf{x}^t$, $M : \mathbf{I} \to \mathbf{x}^t$. This one-to-one onto mapping is smooth in that a small change in **I** produces a small change in $\mathbf{x}^t$. The mapping in this case is similar to the mappings performed by MLFF networks. They are useful in performing general mappings where generalization is needed, such as in robotic control, classification, or in forecasting time series data.

Discrete Network Dynamics

The discrete time dynamics of the general RNN can be obtained from equation (9.2) by setting $\tau_i = 1$ and making the substitution

$$\frac{dx}{dt} = \frac{\Delta x}{\Delta t} = \frac{x(t + \Delta t) - x(t)}{(t + \Delta t) - t}$$

and letting $\Delta t \to 1$ to obtain

$$x_i(t + 1) = g\left(\sum_{j=1}^{n} w_{ij} x_j(t) + I_j \right) \tag{9.5}$$

The corresponding system flow diagram for the discrete case is illustrated in Figure 9.6. In the figure, the block with the z^{-1} represents a unit delay which is introduced in the feedback signal.

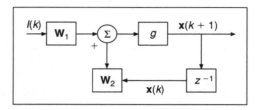

Figure 9.6   Discrete Time Recurrent Network Flow Diagram Model

Note the difference between the continuous and discrete RNN models. In the continuous model, there are two signal feedback paths as opposed to only one in the discrete case and two weight matrices are needed in the discrete model to accurately depict the network behavior. The operational behavior of the two networks will be the same if the time increment chosen is small ($\Delta t \rightarrow 0$) for the discrete time approximation. On the other hand, their behaviors can be significantly different if the simulation time scale chosen is not kept small. For example, given a discrete and continuous network with identical parameters, one network may converge while the other oscillates if the time difference between the two is not chosen small enough.

9.3   Training Recurrent Networks

A number of learning algorithms have been proposed for different RNN architectures. For many of these, simple modifications to the standard backpropagation (BP) algorithm will work. For example, when certain classes of special RNN architectures with only partial feedback links are used, conventional BP with no modification may work. Also, in the case of the network of Figure 9.2, a simple form of "backpropagation through time" can be used. The method requires that errors due to self-feedback connections must also be accumulated and included in the weight adjustment process. Other proposed modifications are not so simple. They require collecting and storing errors over whole trajectories before the gradient descent weight updates are made. In this section, we review a few of the more important proposed methods. In particular, we derive a few generalizations for forms of BP for both the continuous time and discrete time models for RNN learning algorithms.

BP learning can be generalized to train general RNN networks to function either as a continuous mapper or as a fixed-point mapper (Pineda, 1987, 1988, 1989). We derive the algorithm for the continuous mapper here and refer the reader to the references for the latter method.

When a network has stable outputs (fixed points) we can use equation (9.3) to derive an appropriate BP error rule based on gradient descent. For this, we ignore the effects of any propagation time delays in the network dynamics. Proceeding, we need to find a solution to the weight update equation

$$\Delta w_{ij} = -\eta \frac{\partial E}{\partial w_{ij}} = \eta \sum_k E_k \frac{\partial x_k^f}{\partial w_{ij}} \tag{9.6}$$

where, as usual the total error E is a sum of individual node errors squared,

$$E = \frac{1}{2} \sum_{k=1}^{n} E_k^2$$

with

$$E_k = \begin{cases} d_k - x_k^f & \text{if } x_k^f \text{ is an output unit} \\ 0 & \text{otherwise} \end{cases}$$

Dropping the superscript f now for convenience and setting all activation functions $g_i = g$, we find, by differentiating the steady state equation (equation (9.3)),

$$\frac{\partial x_k}{\partial w_{ij}} = g'(H_i) \sum_l \left\{ \frac{\partial x_{kl}}{\partial w_{ij}} x_1 + w_{k1} \frac{\partial x_1}{\partial w_{ij}} \right\}$$

$$= g'(H_i) \left[\delta_{ki} x_j + \sum_l w_{k1} \frac{\partial x_1}{\partial w_{ij}} \right] \tag{9.7}$$

where

$$H_i = \sum_{j=1}^{n} w_{ij} x_j + I_i$$

In equation (9.7), note that the first term in brackets following the summation simplifies to $\delta_{ki} x_j$ because the elements in **w** are assumed to be independent of each other and the δ_{ki}, which are diagonal elements of the identity matrix, can replace the partial derivative terms since they are one if and only if $k = i$ and $l = j$ and zero otherwise. We can also write the left-hand side of equation (9.7) as a sum of products of the identity matrix and the partial derivative of x_l, that is,

$$\frac{\partial x_k}{\partial w_{ij}} = \sum_l \delta_{kl} \frac{\partial x_l}{\partial w_{ij}}$$

Making this substitution and collecting all derivative terms on the right-hand side of equation (9.7), it can be rewritten in the following form

$$\delta_{ki} x_j g'(H_i) = \sum_l L_{kl} \frac{\partial x_l}{\partial w_{ij}} \tag{9.8}$$

where

$$L_{kl} = \delta_{kl} - g'(H_k)w_{kl}$$

Now, let $\mathbf{L}$ denote the matrix with elements L_{kl} and let $\mathbf{L}^{-1}$ be the inverse of $\mathbf{L}$. Multiply both sides of equation (9.8) by $(\mathbf{L}^{-1})_{lk}$, the elements of $\mathbf{L}^{-1}$ and sum over k to get

$$(\mathbf{L}^{-1})_{lk} x_j g'(H_k) = \frac{\partial x_l}{\partial w_{ij}} \tag{9.9}$$

Equation (9.9) is one solution that could be used for the weight update rule (equation (9.6)). Unfortunately, this solution requires a matrix inversion. To avoid this extra computation, one can introduce an *associated* dynamical system by setting

$$y_i = g'(H_i) \sum_r E_r (\mathbf{L}^{-1})_{ri}$$

Solving this equation now for E_r we get

$$E_r = \sum_i L_{ir} \{ y_i / g'(H_i) \}$$

Next, multiply both sides of this equation by $g'(H_r)$, substitute the explicit form for $\mathbf{L}$, and sum over r. One should then obtain the somewhat familiar form of expression

$$0 = -y_r + g'(H_r)\left\{ \sum_i w_{ir}y_i + E_r \right\}$$

Indeed, one should recognize that the solutions to this linear equation are the fixed points of the corresponding differential equation, that is solutions of

$$\frac{dy_r}{dt} = -y_r + g'(H_r)\left\{ \sum_i w_{ir}y_i + E_r \right\} \tag{9.10}$$

To summarize, the complete dynamics of the continuous mapper network are thus given by equations (9.11)–(9.13).

$$\tau_i \frac{dx_i}{dt} = -x_i + g_i\left(\sum_{j=1}^{n} w_{ij}x_j + I_i \right) \qquad i = 1, 2, \ldots, n \tag{9.11}$$

$$\tau_i \frac{dw_{ij}}{dt} = x_j g'(H_i) \sum_r E_r(\mathbf{L}^{-1})_{ri} \tag{9.12}$$

$$\frac{dy_r}{dt} = -y_r + g'(H_r)\left\{ \sum_i w_{ir}y_i + E_r \right\} \tag{9.13}$$

Equations (9.11) can be regarded as the forward propagation operation. During this phase, the network is relaxed using this equation to find the values of the x_i and then the corresponding errors E_i. Equation (9.13) corresponds to the backpropagation signal phase. These equations apply when the network is relaxed in order to find the y_r values. Finally, equation (9.12) is used to perform the weight updates.

With some modifications, the above type of derivation can be used to find a learning algorithm for the fixed-point operational form of RNN. We omit the details of the derivation here and refer the interested reader to the references provided above.

Discrete Time RNN Training

General, unconstrained recurrent networks can also be trained using a form of recursive BP, where we include a time trajectory dimension in the error computations. As in previous cases for BP, we define a performance measure or cost function such as mean square error (MSE) but now over the full trajectory of patterns. We derive the general RNN training algorithms below, but first, we introduce some useful notation. We limit our discussion now to a discrete-time formulation.

Let the m-dimensional vector $\mathbf{x}(t)$ denote the external inputs to the network at time t, and $\mathbf{y}(t)$ denote the n-dimensional outputs (states) of all the network units at time t. When we need to distinguish hidden units from other units, we use $\mathbf{h}(t)$, a q-dimensional vector to denote the state of those units which are neither input nor output units. It will also be useful to introduce the vector $\mathbf{z}(t)$, an $(n + m)$-dimensional vector obtained by concatenating $\mathbf{x}(t)$, and $\mathbf{y}(t)$. We also let O denote the set of indices k for output units in $\mathbf{z}$, and I denote the set of indices k for input units in $\mathbf{z}$. With this notation, we relate $\mathbf{z}$ to $\mathbf{x}$ and $\mathbf{y}$ with the following:

$$z_k(t) = \begin{cases} y_k(t) & \text{for } k \in O \\ x_k(t) & \text{for } k \in 1 \end{cases} \tag{9.14}$$

It should be noted that the components of $\mathbf{z}(t)$ have some duplications. Every input unit appears twice in $\mathbf{z}$: once as an $\mathbf{x}$ component and once as a $\mathbf{y}$ component.

Consider the values $s_k(t)$, the net input to unit k at time t. The value of $s_k(t)$ at time t is computed as a function of both the state of the network and the input to the network at time t:

$$s_k(t) = \sum_{l \in 0 \cup I} w_{k1} z_1(t) \tag{9.15}$$

The output of unit k at time $t + 1$ is then given by

$$y_k(t + 1) = f_k[s_k(t)] \tag{9.16}$$

where f_k is the activation function of unit k. Equations (9.15) and (9.16) give the complete discrete-time dynamics of the system.

Networks can be trained adaptively or nonadaptively. All of the training algorithms described thus far have been of the nonadaptive type. The network was trained over a fixed set of training examples, the weights changed until some stopping criteria was reached at which point the weights were fixed for all subsequent operation. If the environment later changed in some way, it was necessary to retrain the network. In true adaptive training, the network is trained continually, during the training and operational phases. Training never ceases as in the case of many network paradigms. Of course, adaptive training in a changing environment requires that some current training data be available throughout the life of the system.

In Chapter 5, we saw examples of nonadaptive training for the Hopfield and other recurrent networks using precomputed loading of memory instances and variants of Hebbian learning. In Chapters 4 and 6, we saw further examples of nonadaptive training (the standard delta and generalized delta BP rules). We now look at both nonadaptive and adaptive algorithms for RNNs.

As in the case of the MLFF networks, we define a performance measure or cost function for the RNNs. In this case, however, we add a time dimension to the measure. Let $d_k(t)$ be the desired output or target value for unit k at time t. We assume that at least some supervised teacher values $d_k(t)$ are available over the trajectory, although values need not be available at every time increment. To represent this set of values, we use $T(t)$ as the set of indices $k \in O$ for which there are specific target values $d_k(t)$ that the kth unit should compute at time t in response to the input signal $\mathbf{x}(t)$. We let $E_k(t)$ denote the time varying error at the kth unit at time t, where

$$E_k(t) = \begin{cases} d_k(t) - y_k(t) & \text{for } k \in T(t) \\ 0 & \text{otherwise} \end{cases} \tag{9.17}$$

This definition permits target values to be specified for different units at different times if desired. This may be necessary when target values are not available at every discrete time point, for example. For the total error at time t, we set

$$E(t) = \frac{1}{2} \sum_{k \in O} [E_k(t)]^2 \tag{9.18}$$

We are interested in minimizing this error over some time interval (t_0, t_f), that is, we want to minimize $E_{tot}(t_0, t_f)$, where

$$E_{tot}(t_0, t_f) = \sum_{\tau=t_0+1}^{t_f} E(\tau) \tag{9.19}$$

The total adjustment to weight w_{ij} over the entire trajectory then is just

$$\Delta w_{ij} = \sum_{\tau=t_0+1}^{t_f} \Delta w_{ij}(\tau) = -\eta \sum_{\tau=t_0+1}^{t_f} \frac{\partial E(\tau)}{\partial w_{ij}} \tag{9.20}$$

where η is the positive learning rate parameter and the changes to weight w_{ij} are proportional to the gradient:

$$\Delta w_{ij}(t) = -\eta \frac{\partial E(t)}{\partial w_{ij}}$$

Now,

$$-\frac{\partial E(t)}{\partial w_{ij}} = \sum_{l \in O} E_k(t) \frac{\partial y_k(t)}{\partial w_{ij}}$$

But,

$$\frac{\partial y_k(t + 1)}{\partial w_{ij}} = f'_k(s_k(t)) \left[\sum_{l \in O} w_{kl} \frac{\partial y_l(t)}{\partial w_{ij}} + \delta_{ik} z_j(t) \right]$$

where δ_{ik} is the Kronecker delta, that is, $\delta_{ik} = 1$ for $i = k$ and $\delta_{ik} = 0$ otherwise. Also, since the initial state of the network is independent of the weights,

$$\frac{\partial y_k(t_0)}{\partial w_{ij}} = 0 \quad \text{for all } k$$

Setting

$$\frac{\partial y_k(t)}{\partial w_{ij}} = p_{ij}^k(t)$$

we can define the recursive equations

$$p_{ij}^k(t_0) = 0,$$

$$p_{ij}^k(t + 1) = f'_k(s_k(t)) \left[\sum_{l \in O} w_{kl} p_{ij}^k(t) + \delta_{ik} z_j(t) \right]$$

(9.21)

and hence, define corresponding weight updates,

$$\Delta w_{ij}(t) = \eta \sum_{k \in O} E_k(t) p_{ij}^k(t)$$

(9.22)

One can specify different adaptive algorithms for the training process depending on the training set and other factors. For example, one can accumulate the weight changes computed at each point t along the whole trajectory using equation (9.22) and then adjust each weight with the sum (9.20). This requires that the inputs, the network states and the target vectors be saved over the entire trajectory. Summing the errors over the whole trajectory provides true gradient updates for the error function. Also, it is like treating the whole trajectory as an epoch. Alternatively, the weights can be adjusted in real-time at each time step along the trajectory, simplifying the learning process and eliminating the need for epoch boundaries. In this case, however, the learning step must be kept very small to effectively reduce the time scale of the weight updates relative to the network operation. This will result in a better approximation to the true gradient and reduce the effects of any negative feedback due to weight changes made along the trajectory. Clearly, this latter approach requires much more computation than the epoch-trajectory method. We call this latter approach real-time backpropagation learning (RTBP).

For the computation of weight updates, it is convenient to write equation (9.20) as

$$\Delta w_{ij} = \eta \sum_{\tau=t_0+1}^{t_f} \delta_i(\tau) x_j (\tau + 1) \tag{9.23}$$

where

$$\delta_k(\tau) = \begin{cases} f'_k[s_k(\tau)]E_k(\tau) & \text{for } \tau = t_f \\ f'_k[s_k(\tau)]\left[E_k(\tau) + \sum_{l \in O} w_{lk}\delta_l(\tau + 1)\right] & \text{for } t_0 < \tau < t_f \end{cases} \tag{9.24}$$

Thus, to summarize, epochwise BP through time (EBPT) learning can be performed by letting the network run through the entire interval $(t_0, t_f]$, saving the input, network state, and target vectors for each $\tau \in (t_0, t_f]$ and then perform a backward pass starting at the last time step t_f to compute $\delta_k(\tau)$ for all $k \in O$ and all $\tau \in (t_0, t_f]$ (equation (9.24)). Equations (9.23) and (9.20) are then used to update the weights for the whole trajectory (epoch). Computation begins with the last time step and proceeds backwards to earlier time steps through repeated application of the second equation in (9.22). This method can be viewed as normal BP applied to an MLFF wherein target values are given for a number of layers, not just the output-layer. After the computation has been completed back to $t_0 + 1$, the weight changes can be made according to equation (9.20), that is

$$\Delta w_{ij} = \eta \sum_{\tau=t_0+1}^{t_f} \delta_i(\tau) x_j(\tau + 1) = -\eta \frac{\partial E_{tot}(t_0, t_1)}{\partial w_{ij}} \tag{9.25}$$

When the network is updated in real-time at each time t during network operation (RTBP) only the history of inputs and network states need to be saved. Then, for each t, the values

$$\delta_k(\tau) = \begin{cases} f'_k[s_k(\tau)]E_k(\tau) & \text{for } \tau = t \\ f'_k[s_k(\tau)] \sum_{l \in O} w_{lk}\delta_l(\tau + 1) & \text{for } t_0 < \tau < t \end{cases} \qquad (9.26)$$

are computed for all $k \in O$ and $\tau \in (t_0, t]$ beginning at the most recent time step t. The weight changes are then made once the BP computation has been completed back to $t_0 + 1$ using the equation

$$\Delta w_{ij} = \eta \sum_{\tau=t_0+1}^{t} \delta_i(\tau)x_j(\tau - 1) = -\eta \frac{\partial E_{tot}(t_0, t)}{\partial w_{ij}} \qquad (9.27)$$

Note that for RTBP earlier target values need not be saved since only the error $E_k(\tau)$ for $\tau = t$ is needed in the computation of equation (9.26). Unfortunately, this algorithm requires computation time and storage that grows linearly with time as the network runs, so it is not likely to be of much practical use. One can limit the amount of time and storage required, however, by introducing an arbitrary number of time steps h as a window or epoch and forgetting everything earlier than the most recent h steps. This "truncated BP" through time (TBPT) is only an approximation to the true gradient, but may be appropriate when the weights are adjusted while the network runs. For this case, it is necessary to compute at each time step t, the values $\delta_k(\tau)$ for all $k \in O$ and only those times $\tau \in [t - h, t]$ using equation (9.26). After these values have been computed, the weights are then updated using the equation

$$\Delta w_{ij} = \eta \sum_{\tau=t-h+1}^{t} \delta_i(\tau)x_j(\tau - 1) \qquad (9.28)$$

Choosing a small h clearly results in reduced computation and storage requirements, but at the risk of poorer performance. For some applications, however (e.g. applications with slow changing environments), a small value of h may be adequate.

Finally, one can develop an algorithm requiring less computation time than that for TBPT that is a compromise between both EBPT and TBPT. This method could be used for problems in which either of these algorithms might be applied. This is accomplished by selecting a window of size h as before for learning, but now the updates are carried out less frequently. We choose two time values h, and h' say, where $h' \leq h$ and performing the $\delta_k(\tau)$ computations over the longer interval $[t - h, t]$, but rather than performing the backward pass at each time step t, it is performed instead after running h' steps starting at step $t + h'$. This compromised approach requires that the inputs, network states, and target values be saved in the intervening time even though no processing is done during the h' time steps. The equations for the $\delta_k(\tau)$ in this case are given by

$$\delta_k(\tau) = \begin{cases} f'_k[s_k(\tau)]E_k(\tau) & \text{for } \tau = t \\ f'_k[s_k(\tau)]\left[E_k(\tau) + \sum\limits_{l \in O} w_{lk}d_l(\tau + 1)\right] & \text{for } t - h' < \tau < t \\ f'_k[s_k(\tau)]\sum\limits_{l \in O} w_{lk}d_l(\tau + 1) & \text{for } t - h < \tau \leq t - h' \end{cases}$$

Weight updates are then performed using the equation

$$\Delta w_{ij} = \eta \sum\limits_{\tau = t-h+1}^{t} \delta_i(\tau)x_j(\tau - 1)$$

as with TBPT.

Note that when $h' = 1$, this procedure reduces to TBPT and when $h' = h$, the procedure is just EBPT. The choice of values for h and h' are important. If the ratio h/h' is kept small (close to 1), the procedure is more efficient. On the other hand, to better approximate true gradient descent, the difference $h - h'$ should be large. So a trade-off must be made to satisfy these two conflicting constraints. This last procedure we call TBPT(h, h'). It has time and storage complexities in the order of $O(n^2h/h')$ and $O(nh)$ respectively for RNNs with n units and some n^2 weights.

Simulation experiments have shown that the TBPT(h, h') method performs as well as EBPT for several types of problems but with significantly reduced computation times. For example, in learning a task to balance left and right parentheses (the task of "learning to be a Turing machine" reported by Williams and Zipser (1989)), a TBPT(16, 8) network with 12 to 15 units ran 50 times faster than the corresponding EBPT network. Variations on the above learning algorithms have been performed by other researchers in an attempt to shorten the learning time. We omit the details here.

General RNNs will learn to configure themselves to solve a given problem in different ways depending on the training scheme. For example, layer ... the same network will configure as a three-layer network when ...

9.4 Simple Recurrent Network Architectures

Some researchers, including Elman (1991) and Servan-Schreiber et al. (1991), have experimented with a class of networks having only partial feedback which they call simple recurrent networks (SRN). In an SRN, the outputs of the hidden layer are allowed to feedback onto itself through a buffer or "context" layer. These are the only feedback connections in the network and the weights from the hidden layer to the context layer are constant values. All other connections are feedforward with adjustable weights. The architecture for a typical SRN is illustrated in Figure 9.7. Although simple in structure, we will see that these networks are capable of learning to perform powerful tasks.

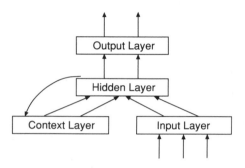

Figure 9.7   A Simple Recurrent Network

In an SRN, signals are processed in two time steps. During the first step at time $t - 1$, signals from the input and context layers, which are fully connected to the hidden layer, are distributed to the hidden-layer units. The pattern of activation outputs from the hidden layer are then computed and passed on to the output layer for processing at time t. At the same time, the hidden-layer outputs are copied back onto a set of context units. Outputs from the context units then combine together with new input signals on the next cycle to feed the hidden units again at time $t + 1$. Thus, the external inputs are being mixed with the previously computed inputs "in context" to give recurrent combinations of transformed inputs to the output layer. The weights on the feedback connections from the hidden to the context layer are fixed, typically as unit valued weights. All other weights in the network are adjustable. The adjustable weights learn to encode sequences of input patterns during the training process. The activation functions are typically nonlinear differentiable functions although the output activation functions may be linear for some applications.

SRNs such as the one depicted in Figure 9.7 have been shown to be capable of performing computations equivalent to a finite automaton. This has been demonstrated well by a series of experiments conducted with an SRN which learns to encode long distance dependencies in character strings generated by a finite-state grammar (FSG), a so-called Reber grammar (Servan-Schreiber et al., 1991). Grammatical character strings are strings which are generated by the FSG transition graph portrayed in Figure 9.8.

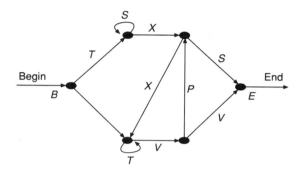

Figure 9.8   A Transition Graph for the Reber Finite State Grammar (Adapted from Servan-Schreiber et al., 1991. Courtesy of the authors.)

Starting at the leftmost node *B* (Begin) of the graph, a (grammatical) string is generated by traversing the graph in the direction of the arrows from node to node and selecting at each transition point (the solid nodes), with equal probability, either one of two possible paths from the node. The link on the path selected determines the next character in the sequence and the next node in the traversal path from left to right. This probabilistic selection process is repeated at each node until the final end node *E* (End) is reached. The "word" or character sequence generated by a complete graph traversal is one of the FSG's valid strings. Because of the two repeat node loops, there are potentially an unlimited number of grammatical strings that can be generated. For example, two valid strings of different lengths are BTSSSXTVPSE and BPVVE.

The experiments were designed to see if an SRN could learn to recognize valid, grammatical character strings, that is, strings generated by the Reber grammar. To carry out the experiments, an SRN consisting of seven input and seven output units (one for each of the seven characters used in the graph including the begin *B* and end *E* links) and three hidden-layer and three context-layer nodes. (Experiments were also carried out with a larger number of hidden-layer and context-layer nodes as well.) The architecture of the SRN used in the experiments is illustrated in Figure 9.9. On each trial, the network is presented at the input with a character belonging to a string and is expected to predict the next character in the string at the output layer.

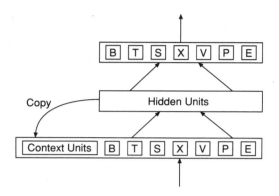

Figure 9.9   The SRN Used to Learn Character Strings from the Reber Grammar
(Adapted from Servan-Schreiber et al., 1991. Courtesy of the authors.)

To train the network, a training set of 60,000 strings were used. The strings were generated randomly using the Reber grammar where each character in a string was chosen by traversing the transition graph and selecting one of two possible successive arcs from each node, each with a probability of 0.5. Each string began with a *B* and ended with *E*. The strings in the training set ranged in size from 5 to 32 characters with an average size of seven characters (excluding the *B* and *E*). During training, each letter was presented to the network as a seven-dimensional binary vector. The characters making up a string were presented sequentially starting with a *B* and ending the string with an *E*. After each letter was presented, the error between the network's prediction and the *actual successor* in the string was computed and backpropagated using the conventional BP training algorithm. The activations in the context layer nodes were reset to zero at the beginning of each character string to eliminate any residual activation values carried over from the previous string. Training was carried out until the computed error value reached a level plateau. This usually occurred after some 2,000 to 10,000 training epochs.

To test the network, two different sets of randomly generated strings were used. One set of 20,000 strings were generated directly from the grammar. The network was considered to give a right answer if it correctly predicted every successor letter in a given string. A prediction was considered correct if the right output node had an activation value greater than 0.3 (corresponding to a probability of about 1/2). If this criterion was not met, presentation of the string was stopped and the string was considered rejected. For this test, the network performed flawlessly. It correctly predicted all character sequences in the 20,000 strings used in the test set.

The second test set consisted of 130,000 randomly generated strings that were mostly ungrammatical. Only 0.2% (260 strings) were grammatical strings. An ungrammatical string consisted of the same set of letters used in the Reber grammar, but was not a valid sequence. Again, the network performed flawlessly, rejecting all ungrammatical strings and accepting only valid strings. Even when extremely long grammatical strings such as

"BTSSSSSSSSSSSSSSSSSSSSSSSXXVPXVPXVPXVPXVPXVPXVPXVPXVPXVP
XVPXTTTTTTTTTTTTTTTTTTTTTTTTTTTVPXVPXVPXVPXVPXVPX"

were presented to the network, it correctly predicted the successor letter and no others. To do so, the network had to learn representations in the hidden layer that were copied back to the context layer which encoded the current position of the input grammar on which the network was trained. A cluster analysis made on the activations of the hidden-layer nodes during testing helped to reveal the hierarchical tree structure that developed in the representations. The activation patterns grouped according to the different nodes in the finite state grammar. Patterns that produced similar predictions grouped together.

More complex experiments were also carried out to test the network's ability to learn dependent character sequences, all with positive results. More complex grammars were also used in some of the tests. The overall conclusions drawn from the experiments is that SRNs can learn to behave as a finite automaton, with the ability to learn FSG and generalize on the patterns learned.

9.5   Other Recurrent Network Architectures

Variations of the simple recurrent networks of the previous section can be defined by adding additional hidden layers and by changing the connectivity of the context layers. For example, a second hidden layer can be added and the output connections can be copied back to the first hidden layer or back to itself as illustrated in Figure 9.10.

Networks of the type shown in Figure 9.10 have been tested extensively in forecasting financial and chaotic time series by Patterson et al. (1993). Hybrid networks using a mix of sigmoid and radial basis activation functions with partial feedback have also been used in forecasting chaotic time series. These and other networks are described in the following section.

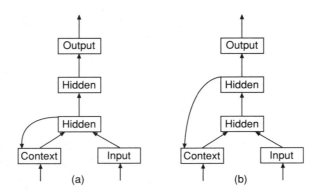

Figure 9.10 Adding a Second Hidden Layer to an SRN (a) Context-Layer Input from First Hidden Layer, (b) Context-Layer Input from Second Hidden Layer

9.6   Applications of Recurrent Networks

Recurrent networks of the type described in this chapter have seen limited application in real business problems. This is understandable, since RNNs are not that well known and their behavior is not that well understood. They are still very much objects of research. Only recently have the numbers of published papers on RNN applications begun to increase in various periodicals. This trend will most likely accelerate particularly since there will be a requirement for more and more real-time applications and other complex applications which require spatio-temporal mappings that need the computing power of coupled nonlinear feedback systems. Even though the number of applications are limited, some impressive results have been obtained in such areas as control, constraint satisfaction, handwritten character recognition, speech recognition, vision, and forecasting. In the remainder of this chapter, we look at some representative applications for which RNNs have been used.

Composition of Polyphonic Melodies

Neural networks have been trained to learn the music of composers in an attempt to have them compose new music, but in a style similar to the composer. One of the most ambitious projects reported by Freisleben (1992) uses an RNN to compose polyphonic melodies, that is, melodies consisting of multiple simultaneous pitch. The RNN was trained with up to six two-voiced melodies for up to 100 time-slices each. Two sets of training data were used: German folk songs and Mozart violin duets. The architecture of the RNN is based on an expanded version of the SRN of Section 9.5, one with more feedback links. It uses two sets of input units, a sequential memory and an exponential memory. The exponential memory is designed to gradually forget its previous values. The input units are fully connected to hidden-layer units which are fully connected to the output units. The output units have feedback connections to the two input memories as illustrated in Figure 9.11. Note that the sequential memory has multiple feedback connections to the leftmost unit and an output from this unit is connected laterally to the neighboring unit sequential memory unit which is connected to its neighbor and so on. The last unit in this memory has no lateral connection. The exponential memory units each have a direct feedback connection from an output unit as well as self-feedback connections. With this connection arrangement, the exponential memory acts as a long-term memory to represent the complete melody, while the sequential memory stores the last few notes only. The output units are laterally connected to implement a winner-takes-all competition. The number of output nodes is determined by the number of different pitches within the pitch range considered in the melodies.

For training, the hidden-layer units have adjustable weights which are modified through backpropagation. Weights on feedback links are fixed. A total of 50 context units (input memories) were used in the network, 25 for each memory. Although not shown in the figure, there are actually multiple networks connected through feedback connections, where each network is trained for each voice. Up to 50 hidden-layer units were used for each voice unit and 25 output units for each voice.

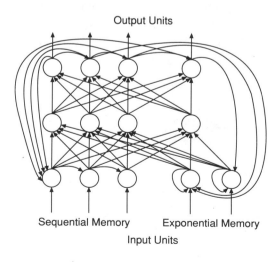

Figure 9.11   Extended Recurrent Network

The network learned the individual melodies perfectly and was able to continue them in "a manner stylistically similar to the original." The compositions are reported to be subjectively quite appealing. An excerpt of a folk song composed by the network is provided by Freisleben (1992).

Control Applications

Control system problems typically require nonlinear time dependent mappings of the input signals. The complete dynamics of these systems are often unknown. Therefore, it would seem that an RNN might be a likely candidate for controller tasks if input/output training data is available for the system. Indeed, the potential applications for RNNs in the area of control appear to be numerous.

The general control problem can be stated as follows: Given a system with unknown dynamics, in order to construct a suitable controller for the system a model is often required. A model is any device that can imitate the behavior of the system. The process of constructing a model when only the relationship between the inputs to the system and the outputs from the system are available is known as an *identification*. The model itself is called an *identifier*. Once a model is available, an inverse model can be constructed to serve as a controller of the real system or plant. This type of problem occurs in many control settings including robotic systems, drive motors for various systems (crane loading and unloading systems), automatic weld control, truck backer upper and so on. Examples of two such systems are described below. The notion of using an adaptive ANN as a model is illustrated in Figure 9.12, where the weights of the ANN, which is receiving the same input signal as the unknown system, are adaptively modified until its output closely matches the output of the system. Once the ANN has learned to model the

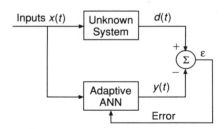

Figure 9.12   Adaptive ANN Learning to Model an Unknown System

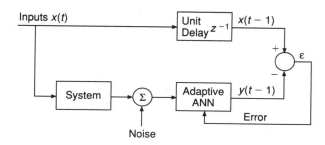

Figure 9.13   Adaptive ANN Controller for a Dynamic System

system, an inverse of the model can be constructed. The inverse model is then capable of acting as a controller for the system. A typical system with its ANN controller is illustrated in Figure 9.13 where a unit time delay has been added to account for the signal delay through the system/controller loop. Noise has also been added in the system loop to depict a more realistic system. Note that the ANN is attempting to drive the system to produce an output which matches the delayed input to produce a zero error. In doing so, it must learn the inverse of the system dynamics.

With these introductory remarks, we are ready to look at a specific RNN application, a gantry crane controller system.

Gantry Crane Controller. A gantry crane is an electromechanical lifting device used in factories to move large parts and assemblies from one location to another. The crane moves from point to point in the overhead structure of the factory and uses a liftable cable assembly to raise the load being moved. A control system for the crane operates the drive motor which produces the horizontal motion of the crane and load. The control mechanism should function in such a way that it can move to a new site specified by position coordinates while the load motion is well damped to prevent erratic or oscillatory movement and still allow for variable load mass and cable lengths. The control unit should maintain a high degree of stability. The system uses position and velocity sensors to monitor the motion and requires a closed loop control path with a large bandwidth to allow for variable load and cable lengths.

The system can be represented as a set of nonlinear differential equations in the variables describing crane position, angle and length of the cable, mass of both the crane and load gravity, damping coefficients and the applied force. The differential equations can be rewritten to obtain time difference expressions in terms of the velocities of the crane and the load at time $t + 1$ as functions of the voltage applied to the motor and velocities at time t and other parameters. The remaining parameters of the system are expected to be realized by a neural network controller. For the gantry crane control problem, an RNN and an MLFF network were trained to perform both system identification and inverse system identification by Fernando et al. (1992). The identification task required that the network learn to emulate the system and the inverse identification task required that the network perform the control function.

A total of 240 data points were generated for training and testing with equal numbers of points used for each task. The data set was generated from the differential equations which describe the system. Random selections of voltage ranging from 0 to 200 were made at each time point and the corresponding velocities were then computed. In addition, sinusoidal voltages were used for the test data to compare the results in more realistic situations.

For system identification, an RNN was used with a single input for voltage and two outputs, one each for the crane and cable velocities. The network also had five hidden nodes. The MLFF network for this task was trained as a time delay network (see Chapter 8). As such, it required more input nodes to capture the temporal aspects of the problem. The MLFF net had five input nodes, one for voltage, and four for the crane and load velocities, two at time t, and two at time $t - 1$. The outputs from the network were the two velocities for time $t + 1$. Four hidden nodes were used. The choice of architectures for both networks was made after much experimentation.

For the inverse identification problem, the same data set of 240 points was used for training and testing. The RNN used for this problem had two input nodes for the crane and load velocities at time t, three hidden-layer nodes and one output node, the motor voltage at time $t - 1$. The MLFF network used for the same task had six input nodes for the two velocities, each at times t, $t - 1$ and $t - 2$. Two nodes were used in the hidden layer and a single output node for the motor control voltage at time $t - 1$.

Both networks learned the identification task well. The error on the training data was slightly smaller for the MLFF network (mean square error of 0.0003 vs 0.0005 for the RNN), but the RNN performance was slightly superior on the test data. However, as noted, the RNN offered other advantages. The RNN does not require *a priori* knowledge of the time structure of the system as opposed to the MLFF network and secondly, the MLFF network requires explicit past data points for training. The RNN does not.

A second area of control applications is in robotics which we briefly consider next.

Manipulator Arm Control. A fertile field for control applications is in robotics. Robotics control tasks can be very challenging since the state space the system must function in can be very large. Even so, ANNs have been shown to be competitive choices for control units in this area because of their adaptive learning capability and ability to generalize. To illustrate the basic notions, we describe a two-joint manipulator arm control problem. The manipulator is illustrated in Figure 9.14.

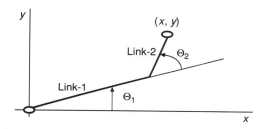

Figure 9.14   Two-Joint Manipulator Arm

To construct a controller for the manipulator, the same approach can be used as in the gantry crane case described above. As in that case, we first need to identify the manipulator and then construct the controller. The manipulator is not easy to identify however, since it is impossible to use all the data in the phase space. There are too many possible training trajectories to anticipate. A short cut method has been devised by Hoshino et al. (1991) to train the network. They use the defining equations of motion which are known. The model equations can give approximate state data which can be used to train the RNN more efficiently. For this, an additional unit they call a K-identifier provides the trajectory data needed. The modified system identifier is illustrated in Figure 9.15. In the figure, $v(t)$ is the control vector at time t, and $s(t)$ is the state vector. $v(t)$ is a function of the state $s(t)$, which in turn, is a function of the link angle values and rates of change in angle values. Backpropagation (BP) is used to train the RNN identifier based on the error difference between the system state at time $t + 1$, $s(t + 1)$, and the output from the K-identifier network at time $t + 1$. The ANN identifier, with output ε, learns the difference as a training signal.

To control the manipulator, the tip should be stopped at the target position t^f within an allowable time period. This is expressed as a performance constraint, a function E of a convex function J which depends on the state, velocity and torque of the arm, where

$$E = \sum_{t=0}^{t^f} J(s(t),\ v(t),\ t)$$

RNNs with one hidden layer were used for the simulations. The identifier network had 20 nodes and the controller network ten. Learning was initiated with the joint angles at zero and successive states at time intervals of 0.02 s. The K-identifier used the equations of motion which were solved (integrated) using a fourth-order Runga-Kutta method. In constructing the controller, only 3,000 iterations were needed when using the K-identifier.

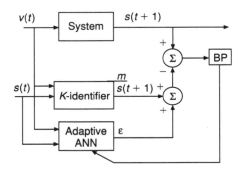

Figure 9.15   The Modified Identifier System for the Manipulator

Forecasting

One of the most promising areas of application is in forecasting time series of various types: physical, natural, social and economic series. Many such series are driven by nonlinear interacting variables that are best modeled by networks that have similar dynamics, dynamics not found in static types of networks. Several applications of successful forecasting experiments using RNNs have been reported in the literature. We briefly describe a few of these results as applied to the forecasting of chaotic and financial time series (see Chapter 8 for more details on forecasting applications).

A time series forecasting competition was organized under the auspices of the Sante Fe Institute starting in the fall of 1991. Entrants in the competition were given the first portion of six data sets: a chaotic laser series, a computer generated series, Swiss franc-U.S. dollar exchange rate series, astrophysical data from a variable white dwarf star, physiological data from a patient with sleep apnea, and

J. S. Bach's last (unfinished) fugue from *Die Kunst der Fuge*. The remaining part of the six series were withheld, the portion the contestants were expected to forecast. Any type of forecasting method was permitted, but contestants were required to fully report on the algorithm used and submit an analysis of the data (degrees of freedom, noise characteristics and nonlinearity of the data). The complete results of the competition were published in a text edited by Weigend and Gershenfeld (1993). Among the methods that performed best were two neural networks, a multilayer feedforward network (MLFF) and an RNN, both trained using error backpropagation.

Patterson et al. (1993) have also presented results of forecasting using variations of the SRN described in Section 9.5 as well as with MLFF and radial basis function networks. The time series used in the forecasts were two well-known chaotic series, the Mackey-Glass and Henon series and two financial series, 132 weekly closing prices of the S & P 500 index and monthly closing prices of the U.S. dollar—German Deutchmark exchange rate from February 1985 to August 1992. The overall performance of the RNN networks was superior to the other networks with short-term prediction accuracies ranging from about 70 to 90%.

Other RNN architectures have been used successfully for financial time series forecasting, including Lee and Park (1992), Sterzing and Schurmann (1993), and Rao and Ramamurti (1993). Liang and Haykin (1993) have used a cascaded RNN to predict chaotic sea clutter data obtained from an instrument quality radar off the east coast of Canada. Mori and Ogasarawa (1993) have used an RNN to forecast short-term load requirements in electric power systems. We omit the details here and instead, turn to a diagnostic application next.

Diagnosis Application

High Impedance Fault Detection in Electric Power Systems. High impedance faults are low current faults that occur in electric utility power systems. These faults are difficult to detect since they are low current faults that do not normally trigger over-current relays or fuses. They may persist for some time without detection and hence pose a safety threat to the public. Furthermore, they can result in a significant energy loss to the power company. As such, electric utility companies have been trying for many years to detect these faults in a timely manner. Algorithmic methods have met with some success, but they lack the ability to adapt to the environment. Fernando et al. (1992) have trained both a MLFF network and a partially recurrent RNN to perform the detection tasks. They used 14 sets of test data provided by the Texas Electric Service Company which contained arching of various intensities, line switch operations, and capacitor bank switching. The analog data was first digitized at a rate of 7,680 Hz. A fast Fourier transform was then performed on each frame of the data. The energies of 128 frequency components were computed and the even harmonics, odd harmonics and in-between harmonics energies were computed for each frame. The energy of the filtered high frequency current in the time domain was also computed. These four quantities served as input to the networks.

For testing, twenty-eight 1,500 sample data segments from seven staged fault data files were selected. The segments included ten normal data, three line switch operations, three capacitor bank operations, and 12 high impedance faults. With their limited data, they were able to achieve 100% success rate in detecting the high impedance faults. They have yet to try the networks on unpredictable environments, however.

Pattern Recognition

Pattern recognition applications for ANNs are numerous. For RNN applications in this area we include a vision type of application and a speech recognition application. We begin with a special type of character recognition task.

Recognition of Lateral Character Strings. One of the most actively studied areas in the application of ANNs is in character recognition. Much progress has been made in this area, including the recognition of handwritten characters (both cursive and block) where recognition accuracies of 95 to 98% have been reported. Here, we describe a novel approach to the recognition of printed characters by scanning a lateral string of characters. This type of problem can occur, for example, in manufacturing operations where parts must be identified by preprinted characters on the parts. Typically, the characters are distorted due to surface irregularities, dirt and poor lighting conditions.

The approach used by Imai (1991) is to scan an image of the character string from left to right using a narrow slit as input to an RNN. The scan takes place in steps of four pixels where the size of the image slit is 6 × 4 pixels. At each position of the scan, the network is trained to recognize whether the image actually belongs to some letter, part of the segmentation step, and what that letter is, the recognition step. There are 30 inputs to the network (24 + 5 + 1) consisting of the slit pixels, the feedback outputs of the recognized characters (five in this set of experiments) and the scanning step signal output. The outputs from the network consist of the five letter categories, and the scan step signal. The number of hidden nodes was determined experimentally to be 120. The weights on the hidden-layer and the output-layer nodes are adjustable. Weights on the feedback connections are fixed. The recognition system is illustrated in Figure 9.16.

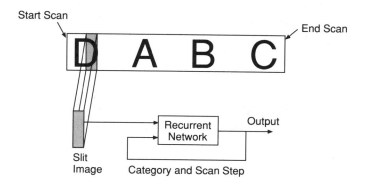

Figure 9.16   Sequential Character Recognition System
(Courtesy of Dr. K. Imai.)

During training, the slit is stepped from left to right as each letter in the sequence to be learned is presented to the network. The correct category and step signal are compared to the network's output and the error used to backpropagate the weight correction quantities. The category and step signals are set to zero at the start of each scan and after each letter has been scanned. Learning was carried out for 4,500 iterations.

Once the network had been trained, the system was tested on a number of character strings. The recognition rate was 100% in these test cases. Further testing was conducted on connected character strings with some additional noise included in the images. 52 images with some 203 characters were used in this test set. The network achieved a recognition rate of 93% on the test data. No letters were recognized as a wrong category, only no response errors were experienced.

The results reported above demonstrate the ability of RNNs to capture temporal information well. Next, we consider a speech recognition application.

Text-Dependent Speaker Verification

Speaker identification is important for many applications including access to secure facilities or information and bank and credit authorizations. In addressing the problem, two models of speaker recognition have been used: speaker identification and speaker verification. From a speech utterance, speaker identification is the process of identifying a speaker from a population of known speakers whereas speaker verification is the process of verifying the claimed identity of an unknown person.

Many methods of identification and verification have been attempted including vector quantization (Chapter 14), hidden markov models and MLFF neural networks. Recently, Wang (1993) conducted experiments with an RNN architecture using a speech database of 480 utterances.

Summary

In this chapter, we studied the behavior of dynamic recurrent networks, networks that have one or more feedback connections where unit outputs activations are recursively computed. We learned that these general nonlinear networks, like other coupled nonlinear systems, can exhibit three types of behavior: convergence to a fixed point, oscillatory, or chaotic. Sufficient conditions for convergent dynamics, the particular case studied in some detail in this chapter, were given.

We learned that RNNs can be trained to act as function mappers or as associative memories. That an RNN has an equivalent multilayer feedforward network architecture, and hence, can, at least in principle, be trained using standard backpropagation (BP) weight adjustment. We also looked at other generalized versions of backpropagation learning including real-time BP.

We examined a class of simple RNN architectures, the SRN which has a single hidden-to-context layer feedback path. These simple networks were trained to mimick a finite automaton and learn arbitrarily long character sequences generated by a finite state grammar, a Reber grammar. Variations on the SRN architecture were also reviewed.

In the concluding section, RNN applications were presented including forecasting chaotic time series, control, and pattern recognition.

10
Boltzmann Machines and Simulated Annealing

From the previous chapter, we saw how networks with feedback connections differ from networks with only feedforward connections (also in Chapter 4). The dynamics of networks with feedback, recurrent networks, are more complicated than networks with static behavior. Their dynamics are governed by sets of coupled nonlinear differential equations. Potentially, they are also more powerful as a computing system since they are capable of modeling spatiotemporal processes as well as time or space independent system behaviors. In this chapter, we continue to investigate the behavior of recurrent networks, but with a new dimension. The networks studied in this chapter are also stochastic networks. The states that can be assumed by the network are governed by a probability distribution. This class of networks was first studied in the 1980s. They have since been used successfully to solve several types of problems including combinatorial optimization, encoding, text-to-speech conversion and image storage and retrieval.

10.1 Introduction

The Boltzmann machine is another type of interesting recurrent network. It has been studied by Hinton and Sejnowski (1983, 1986), Ackley et al. (1985), Hinton (1985), and others. Unlike the networks studied in the previous chapter, the Boltzmann machine is a stochastic network. The states which the network assumes are governed by the Boltzmann distribution, an exponential form of probability distribution which is used to model the states of a physical system at thermal equilibrium. Like the Hopfield network, a Boltzmann machine has a symmetrical weight matrix $\mathbf{W}$ which insures convergence to a stable state. Unlike the Hopfield network, however, the Boltzmann machine may have hidden units, units which are neither input nor output units. As such, there is a credit assignment learning problem found in multilayer feedforward networks in finding weight values for the hidden units when using supervised training. Backpropagation training could, of course, be used to adjust the weights in the hidden units, but we know from Chapter 6 that this algorithm may end in failure. The learning process may become trapped in a local minimum. To overcome this problem, researchers have adapted some notions from condensed matter physics and applied them to create Boltzmann machine networks. A method known as simulated annealing is applied to the network during operation and learning. This process permits the network to escape from local minima and converge to a global equilibrium state.

The Boltzmann machine can be operated in one of three different modes. It can be used as an associative memory in which case a single set of units is used for both input and output like the Hopfield network. It can also be used for general heteroassociative mapping applications similar to multilayer feedforward networks. When used for these applications, the network uses separate input and output units called visible units. The third class of applications are in the solution of optimization problems. When used to solve optimization problems no adaptive learning is required. The weight values are determined *a priori* as part of the solution to the objective or cost function associated with the problem.

We begin with a description of the network architecture and the supervised learning process. The operation of the network for heteroassociative mappings is then presented. The other two modes of operation are then addressed. Following this, we look at variations on the basic Boltzmann machine. The modifications have been studied in an effort to speed up the learning process which can be extensive. These differences are also described. We also present a description of a hybrid form of the Boltzmann machine that incorporates concepts from genetic algorithms. These hybrid stochastic genetic hillclimbers have been used effectively in solving a variety of optimization problems. Finally, we complete the chapter with a section on applications.

10.2 Characteristics of the Boltzmann Machine

The Boltzmann machine is an extension of the Hopfield network in that it may have hidden units as well as input and output units. The hidden units act as stochastic feature detectors enhancing the representational and computational power of the Boltzmann machine over the Hopfield network. The basic architecture is illustrated in Figure 10.1 where a hidden unit is any unit with internal connections only. Non-hidden or "visible" units are either input or output units (or both).

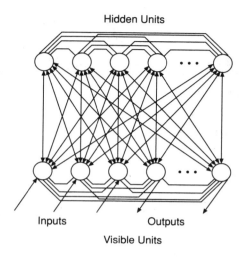

Figure 10.1 A Typical Boltzmann Machine Network

Generally, the units are not fully interconnected so some connection weights are zero, $w_{ij} = 0$. All non-zero connections, however, are symmetric, $w_{ij} = w_{ji}$. The interconnection from unit i to unit j has the same weight value as the connection from j to i which can be viewed as a single bidirectional weight connection between units i and j. Units have no self-feedback connections, so $w_{ii} = 0$. They may have a constant bias term, or equivalently, a threshold parameter term θ in the net stimulus input to each unit. The net input to unit j is given by

$$net_j = \sum_{i \in S_j} w_{ij} y_i - \theta \qquad (10.1)$$

where S_j is the set of units connected to unit j, the w_{ij} are weights connecting unit i to unit j, the y_i are binary output activation functions and θ is a threshold constant term that may be zero. The state y_j of unit j which is binary $(0, 1)$ or bipolar valued $(-1, 1)$, is determined probabilistically as

$$y_i = \begin{cases} +1 & \text{with probability } p(net_j) \\ -1 & \text{with probability } 1 - p(net_j) \end{cases} \qquad (10.2)$$

where the probability $p(x)$ is given by the logistic distribution function

$$p(x) = [1 + e^{-x/T}]^{-1} \qquad (10.3)$$

The parameter T in equation (10.3) is a "temperature" control parameter that is adjusted during the operation of the network. The role of this parameter is described below.

Before considering the complete operation of the network, we examine the supervised learning algorithm.

Boltzmann Machine Learning

As noted above, the learning process in the Boltzmann machine is stochastic. Weight adjustments are made probabilistically using a modified form of Hebbian learning. The learning process is based on a model used in condensed matter physics known as annealing. Therefore, before describing the actual network learning algorithm, we give a brief description of simulated annealing to illustrate the learning process and operation of the network.

Simulated Annealing

The name "simulated annealing" was borrowed from physics, an analogy with the annealing of solid materials in physics. Annealing is a process whereby a solid is placed in a heat bath and the temperature is continually raised until the solid has melted and the particles of the solid are physically disarranged or positioned in a random order. The orientation of the particles are referred to as the "spins." From this high energy level, the heat bath is cooled slowly by lowering the temperature T to allow the particles to align themselves in an orderly crystalline lattice structure. This final structure corresponds to a stable low energy state. The temperatue must be lowered slowly to allow the solid to reach equilibrium after each temperature drop. Otherwise, undesired alignments may occur resulting in defects which get "frozen" into the solid. This can result in a metastable structure rather than the stable low energy structure desired. If the energy E of the solid in state k is denoted by E_k, thermal equilibrium occurs in state k with a probability determined by the Boltzmann distribution defined by

$$Pr(E = E_k) = \frac{1}{Z(T)} e^{-E_k/Tk_\beta} \tag{10.4}$$

where $k_\beta = 1.38 \times 10^{-16}$ ergs/K (kelvin) is Boltzmann's constant and the partition function $Z(T)$ is a normalization factor to make the total probability mass equal unity. Thus,

$$Z(T) = \Sigma_k e^{-E_k/Tk_\beta} \tag{10.5}$$

The summation in equation (10.5) is taken over all possible 2^N states (assuming a binary model with a total of N particles).

In simulating the cooling process, a sequence of states are generated through a Monte Carlo probability selection method. Each state k of the solid corresponds to some alignment position of all the particles. Starting from an initial random alignment state, a small perturbation is applied by making a displacement to a randomly selected particle (In a binary model, the "perturbation" is a change of binary state). If the resultant energy change ΔE due to the displacement is negative (decreasing energy), the new state is accepted. If $\Delta E > 0$, the new state is accepted with a probability given by

$$P = \frac{1}{1 + e^{-\Delta E/Tk\beta}} \tag{10.6}$$

The perturbation process is repeated until eventually the system reaches equilibrium and the state probability distribution is given by (10.4). From equation (10.6), note that when the temperature T is very high and $\Delta E > 0$, an increase in energy may occur with probability near 1/2. On the other hand, when T is near zero, the new state is computed deterministically. The displacement behaves like a discrete 0/1 case. Thus, the annealing process favors a decreasing energy state, but does permit increases in accordance with equation (10.6). At high temperatures, increases in energy are more likely to occur. As the temperature approaches zero, increases in energy become less and less likely. Equation (10.6) is a local decision rule since the change in state depends only on the perturbed particle (unit). It ensures that when thermal equilibrium has been reached, the state of the network obeys the Boltzmann distribution given by the probability ratio relationship

$$\frac{P(\alpha)}{P(\beta)} = e^{-(E(\alpha)-E(\beta))/T}$$

where α and β are given states and $E(\alpha)$ is the energy for state α. Taking the natural logarithm of both sides of this expression shows that the difference in energy level between two states is proportional to the difference in log probabilities of the states.

Simulations similar to the annealing process described above are also carried out for the Boltzmann machine. Since the weight matrix is symmetrical, an energy function can be defined for the network as in the case of the Hopfield network (Chapter 4). For binary states, the network energy E is defined as

$$E = -\frac{1}{2} \sum_{ij} w_{ij} y_i y_j \tag{10.7}$$

This function has a minimum at a stable network state. The network state plays the role of the solid state of the physical system and the energy function is replaced with an objective or cost function. The temperature parameter becomes a control parameter that is reduced step by step to slowly reduce the state probability in accordance with an annealing schedule. With the annealing process in mind, we are ready now to look at the Boltzmann machine learning process.

One form of learning for Boltzmann machines is supervised learning where the training set consists of input patterns $\mathbf{x}^p$ and the corresponding target output patterns $\mathbf{t}^p$, for pattern pairs $\{\mathbf{x}^p, \mathbf{t}^p\}$, $p = 1, 2, ..., P$. As noted above, the network can be trained for either autoassociative or heteroassociative mappings. In the autoassociative case, the target pattern is just the input pattern and the network is used to retrieve stored patterns when noisy or partially complete input patterns are presented to the network. When trained to perform heteroassociative mappings, the target and input patterns are, in general, different.

For the present discussion, we assume the network has a total of N units with n input units, m output units and h hidden units ($N = n + m + h$). When we wish to refer to any visible unit without regard to function, we use z_i to denote the ith visible unit ($i = 1, 2, ..., n + m$). Also, all input and unit activation values are assumed to be bipolar ($-1, +1$) for mathematical convenience. We first describe a sequential training process for heteroassociative mappings. The learning process is somewhat tedious since it involves carrying out several operational steps before weights can be updated. For each training pattern, simulated annealing is first applied until a stable state is reached. This is done while the input and output units are "clamped" to the input and target pattern values. Following each annealing run, the state of the network at equilibrium state is saved. Statistics on the saved network states are eventually collected for use in estimating equilibrium probabilities when all visible units are clamped. The complete process is then repeated when only the input units are clamped and the output units are allowed to change state or run "free." Probabilities for the free running equilibrium state are also estimated from saved states. The weights are then adjusted using gradient descent based on an information-theoretic measure. The whole process is then repeated until the weights converge over the whole training set. The complete procedure is outlined below.

Boltzmann Learning Algorithm

1. Set all weights to small random numbers and set hidden unit activations to some initial random bipolar values. Set the temperature control parameter to a high initial value T_0.

2. For each pair of input-output training patterns $(\mathbf{x}^p, \mathbf{t}^p)$, present the selected patterns to the network visible units. The $\mathbf{x}^p$ pattern is "clamped" to the input and $\mathbf{t}^p$ to the output units while the hidden units are allowed to change state.

3. Select a hidden unit at random, say unit k, and change its state from y_k to y_k'. The changed state results in a change in network energy ΔE_k, where, from equation (10.7) and symmetry of the weights,

$$\Delta E_k = E_k' - E_k = -\left[\sum_i w_{ik} y_i (y_k' - y_k) - w_{kk} y_k y_k' \right] \tag{10.8}$$

where the summation index i runs over all units. Since no self-feedback is allowed,

$$\Delta E_k = \pm 2 \sum_i w_{ik} y_i \tag{10.9}$$

(recall that $y_k' = -y_k$). The $+$ sign holds when unit k is changed from -1 to $+1$ and the $-$ sign holds when the reverse is true. Note that except for a multiplicative constant, this is just the total input to unit k. If $\Delta E_k < 0$, set unit k activation to a one regardless of its previous activation state (the energy decreases). If $\Delta E_k > 0$, set unit k activation to a one with probability

$$P_k = \frac{1}{1 + e^{-\Delta E_k / T}} \tag{10.10}$$

This can be accomplished by drawing a random sample U from a uniform distribution and making the change if $P_k > U$. Otherwise, return unit k to its original state.

4. Repeat step 3 for m unit selections such that on average, all hidden units will have their state changed once (allowing the network to relax according to (10.4)). Increase the iteration number $t = t + 1$.

5. Reduce the temperature according to some annealing schedule. A simple exponential decay rate schedule is

$$T_{t+1} = \beta T_t \tag{10.11}$$

where T_t is the temperature at step t and $0 < \beta < 1$ is the constant cooling rate.

6. Repeat steps 3 through 5 until a final temperature T_{final} is reached. The system is at equilibrium at this point, E is at a minimum.

7. Save the states of all hidden units for the clamped training pattern p in the vector $\mathbf{r}_c^p$ for later use in estimating unit state probabilities.

8. When the above steps have been completed for all training patterns, compute estimates r_{ij}^c of the correlations ρ_{ij}^c for all pairs of units having the same states using the saved statistics $\mathbf{r}_c^p$ ($p = 1, 2, ..., P$), where

$$r_{ij}^c = \frac{1}{P} \sum_{p=1}^{P} \varphi(z_i^p, h_{cj}^p) \qquad i, j = 1, 2, ..., N \quad i \neq j \qquad (10.12)$$

and where

$$\varphi(x, y) = \begin{cases} 1 & \text{if } x = y \\ 0 & \text{otherwise} \end{cases}$$

9. Repeat steps 2 through 8 again, but this time without clamping the output units to the target values. The output units are allowed to run freely. Using the saved vectors $\mathbf{r}_f^p$ to estimate the free running correlations, compute estimates r_{ij}^f of the correlations ρ_{ij}^f using

$$r_{ij}^f = \frac{1}{P} \sum_{p=1}^{P} \varphi(z_i^p, h_{fj}^p) \qquad i, j = 1, 2, ..., N \quad i \neq j \qquad (10.13)$$

10. Update the network weights w_{jj} according to the rule

$$\Delta w_{ij} = \alpha[r_{ij}^c - r_{ij}^f] \qquad i, j = 1, 2, ..., N \quad i \neq j \qquad (10.14)$$

where α is a learning coefficient and r_{ij}^c and r_{ij}^f are the estimated correlations (co-occurrence probabilities) of both units i and j being on for the clamped and unclamped conditions respectively.

11. Repeat the whole process for all i, j and p until the weight changes given by equation (10.14) are zero or sufficiently small.

Discussion

Several points are worthy of notice regarding the above process. In step 2, there may actually be several target patterns related to a single input pattern. For example, this may be the case when there is an uncertain or fuzzy relationship between input and output patterns as in the case of a diagnostic expert system. For this case, the target patterns would each be presented with the input pattern a number of times corresponding to the relative uncertainties of the output patterns.

Step 3 above insures that occasionally the energy will actually increase, thereby permitting the system to escape local minima when moving down the energy landscape. This guarantees convergence in probability to a global minimum, at least asymptotically. Gemen and Gemen (1984) have shown that if the cooling schedule satisfies the relation

$$T_t \geq \frac{T_0}{1 + \log t}$$

for all t, with T_0 sufficiently large, then with probability one, convergence is assured asymptotically. Of course, in practice this will never be achieved, but generally, simulations of the learning process suggest that convergence will occur to acceptable local minima levels.

Two important factors in the annealing process are the cooling schedule and the relaxation process. The initial temperature T_0 should be set high enough such that almost all network states are equally probable ($P_k \cong 1/2$ in equation (10.10)). It should then be reduced slowly. This type of schedule permits the network to perform more global explorations of the energy landscape initially and allow it to escape local minima traps. As annealing progresses, increasing the rate at which the temperature is reduced will then decrease the probability of transitions favoring lower energy states. As T approaches zero, the probability of accepting the lower energy state approaches one. The relaxation operation iteratively finds the equilibrium state at the new temperature using the final state of the network and the previous temperature as a starting point. It is essential that equilibrium be reached during annealing before reducing the temperature. Otherwise, a global minimum may not be found.

It has been shown that when the learning coefficient α is small, the weight update rule (equation (10.14)) is equivalent to gradient descent on the information-theoretic relative entropy measure G (see Chapter 3 for a definition of relative entropy) between the clamped and unclamped (free running) distributions. If P_{ij}^c denotes the joint probability of units i and j being on ($+1$) when the visible units are clamped and P_{ij}^f the joint probability of units i and j being on when only the input units are clamped and the output free running, the weights should be adjusted such that the two distributions are constrained to be "closer" to each other. One way to do this is to adjust the weights to minimize the relative entropy of the two distributions or to reduce the "distance" between them. We can accomplish this by performing gradient descent on the relative entropy by adjusting the weights proportional to the negative gradient of the relative entropy, that is

$$\Delta w_{ij} = -\alpha \frac{\partial G}{\partial w_{ij}} \qquad (10.15)$$

where G is the relative entropy between P^c and P^f defined by

$$G(P^c \| P^f) = \sum_{i,j} P_{ij}^c \log \frac{P_{ij}^c}{P_{ij}^f} \qquad (10.16)$$

where the summation runs over all $i, j = 1, 2, ..., N$. P_{ij}^c represents the *desired* state probabilities for the network while P_{ij}^f represents the *actual* state probabilities of the network. G is positive unless the two distributions are identical at which point G is zero. Therefore, solving equation (10.15) provides a weight update rule that tends to bring the desired and actual state probabilities together. The solution can be found by taking partial derivatives of G with respect to the weights and making appropriate substitutions to obtain the update rule (10.14). When taking partial derivatives in equation (10.15), it should be noted that P_{ij}^c are independent of the weights since the input units are clamped to the input pattern values. The P_{ij}^f are dependent on the weights, however, and the Boltzmann distribution (10.4) must be used to determine the weight values. The solution is found in a straightforward, but tedious number of steps. Consequently, we omit the details here.

Once the weights have been found for a set of training patterns, the network can be used for unknown mapping tasks. In this case, the recall or mapping operation is somewhat simpler than the lengthy learning algorithm. We will address this issue next.

Boltzmann Mapping Algorithm

Given a trained network, it can be used to perform the desired mapping by presenting an input pattern to the input units, annealing the network until it stabilizes and reading the output units. As in the case of learning, the network operation is driven stochastically. The complete heteroassociative mapping operation is summarized as follows:

1. Set all hidden and output unit activations to some initial random values (± 1), and set the temperature control parameter to a high value T_0. Present (clamp) the input pattern $\mathbf{x}$ to the input units. The output and hidden units are allowed to change state.

2. Select an output or hidden unit at random, say unit j, and compute the net input to the unit

$$net_j = \sum_{i \in S_j} w_{ij} y_i \qquad (10.17)$$

3. Regardless of the current state of unit j, set it on ($= +1$) with probability

$$p(net_j) = [1 + e^{-net_j/T}]^{-1} \qquad (10.18)$$

This can be accomplished by drawing a random sample U from a uniform distribution and setting unit j on if $p > U$. Otherwise, return unit j to its original state.

4. Repeat steps 2 and 3 until on average, all output and hidden units will have been selected once. This is regarded as one sample cycle.

5. Repeat step 4 for several cycles until equilibrium has been reached. Reduce the temperature according to the schedule

$$T_{t+1} = \beta T_t$$

where $0 < \beta < 1$, and where

$$T_t = \frac{T_0}{1 + \log t}$$

T_0 is the initial temperature.

6. Repeat steps 2 through 5 until the network stabilizes at a low temperature. The mapped output can be taken from the output units.

The mappings performed using the above algorithm can be used in classification problems where each of k objects are classified into one of C classes. When a feature vector describing the object is presented at the input nodes, the network finds a consensus among the unclamped nodes that gives the category of the input pattern at the output nodes.

Next, we look at the Boltzmann machine when used as an autoassociative network for pattern completion applications.

Boltzmann Machine in Pattern Completion

When the Boltzmann machine is used as an autoassociative memory, partial or noisy input patterns are presented to the network and original stored patterns are retrieved. The process is essentially the same as for heteroassocative mapping except there are no input and output units, only visible units that serve as both input and output. In this case the network architecture will be different. It is similar to the Hopfield network as illustrated in Figure 10.2.

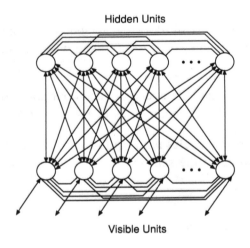

Figure 10.2   Boltzmann Machine Configuration for Pattern Completion

To retrieve a previously stored pattern, the partial pattern is clamped to the input and the network annealed until equilibrium is reached. The units with unknown input pattern components and the hidden-layer units are allowed to run freely during the annealing process. Once equilibrium is reached, the completed output is then taken from the visible units.

In training this type of network, the same training procedure as outlined above for heteroassociative learning holds except that only the input pattern, the pattern to be stored, is clamped to the visible units. The hidden-layer units are allowed to run free. The annealing schedule is followed, and statistics collected on the states of the unclamped units after equilibrium is reached and running the network for several cycles. The same process is then repeated with the input units unclamped (allowed to run freely) and co-occurrence statistics once again collected on the network state. The weights are adjusted according to equation (10.14) until little change occurs. The process is repeated for all training patterns.

Once trained, the network can perform pattern completion from partially complete or noisy input patterns, acting as an autoassociative or content addressable memory.

It has been noted that one of the main drawbacks of the Boltzmann Machine is the excessive amount of computation required for both training and operation. This has prompted much research into methods to speed up the process. The Cauchy Machine, which we consider next, offers some improvement in this direction.

The Cauchy Machine. Boltzmann Machine networks have mapping capabilities comparable to MLFF and radial basis function networks. Furthermore, with simulated annealing, they can avoid the local minima traps that plague MLFF networks. Why then have they not received the same attention as MLFF networks? Clearly, the reason is due to the high computational burden associated with the annealing process. Many computations are required to reach equilibrium at each temperature and the temperature schedule reduces exponentially. This has prompted some researchers such as Szu and Hartley (1987) to look for methods to speed up the annealing process. Through their efforts, some success has been achieved in this respect. The approach they use makes use of the Cauchy probability distribution in place of the Boltzmann distribution. The resultant network is then referred to as a Cauchy Machine.

The Cauchy probability density function is given by

$$f(x; \theta) = \frac{1}{\pi[1 + (x - \theta)^2]}$$

This symmetrical distribution centered at θ has very long tails and an infinite variance (none of the moments exist). Sampling from this distribution results in an increase in the probability of a larger step size during the annealing. With the Cauchy distribution substituted for the Boltzmann distribution, a faster annealing schedule can be used. The temperature reduction schedule is

$$T_t = T_0/(1 + t)$$

Note that this schedule is inversely linear rather than inversely logarithmic, as in the Boltzmann case. The end result is a significant improvement in the cooling process. Even with the speed up, training time can still be very long requiring as much as 100 times as much computation as an equivalent MLFF network trained with backpropagation.

Another approach used to speed up the annealing process is based on another concept borrowed from statistical mechanics called mean field annealing. We outline the details of this approach next.

Mean Field Annealing. As noted above, simulated annealing has not received much popular support due to the high computational training costs involved. This has prompted efforts to find methods which speed up the annealing process. Among the approaches that have realized some success is mean field annealing. Mean field annealing is a method borrowed from statistical mechanics where the probabilistic process of annealing is replaced by a mean value deterministic one. The discrete probabilistic states in simulated annealing are replaced with their average values as computed by the mean field approximation. The net result of this is that equilibrium at a given temperature is achieved one to two orders of magnitude faster than with simulated annealing. Our goal then is to replace the weight update rule given by equation (10.14) with a suitable mean-value rule which eliminates many of the lengthy computations required in finding the co-occurrence probabilities.

Equations (10.12) and (10.13) are estimates of the mean value co-occurrence probabilities $E(y_i y_j)$ for the whole network averaged over the training set in both the clamped and free running states, respectively. These estimates are obtained after saving the equilibrium states of the clamped and free running networks following many intermediate computations. If an estimate of the mean values can be obtained without collecting the state statistics, a possible speed up in learning time could be realized.

Consider a single unit in the network, say unit j. The state of this unit is determined probabilistically by equation (10.2). Therefore, the average or mean value state of the unit is just

$$E(y_j) = (+1)p(net_j) + (-1)(1 - p(net_j))$$
$$= 2p(net_j) - 1 \qquad (10.19)$$

where

$$p(net_j) = \frac{1}{1 + e^{-2net_j/T}}$$

Therefore, from equation (10.19),

$$E(y_i) = \frac{1 - e^{-2net_j/T}}{1 + e^{-2net_j/T}} = \tanh(net_j/T) \tag{10.20}$$

where $\tanh(x)$ is the hyperbolic tangent of x. Also, from (10.17) setting $m_j = E(y_j)$, we have

$$E(net_j) = \sum_i w_{ij} E(y_j) = \sum_i w_{ij} m_j, \quad j = 1, 2, \ldots, n \tag{10.21}$$

These averages are for single isolated units, and hence are of little value when we really need co-occurrence averages, $E(y_i \, y_j)$ over all units $i \neq j$. We could take a naive approach and just use the product of the mean state values to estimate the mean products of state values, that is, we could assume that $E(y_i \, y_j) \cong E(y_i)E(y_j)$. Such a substitution is justified only if the units are independent. Even so, it is a useful substitution as demonstrated by Peterson and Anderson (1987). They have also justified this approximation more formally on the basis of a mean field annealing derivation.

We still must find solutions to the n nonlinear equations (10.20). This can be done by solving the following system of n equations iteratively (Hertz et al., 1991)

$$m_j^{\text{new}} = E(y_j) = \tanh\left(\frac{1}{T} \sum_i w_{ij} m_i^{\text{old}}\right), \quad j = 1, 2, \ldots, n \tag{10.22}$$

Once these solutions have been found, the mean field weight update rule can be used to modify the weights according to

$$\Delta w_{ij} = \alpha \left[M_{ij}^c - M_{ij}^f \right] \qquad i, j = 1, 2, \ldots, N, \, i \neq j$$

where the $M_{ij}^c = m_i^c m_j^c$ and $M_{ij}^f = m_i^f m_j^f$ are the mean field co-occurrence quantities for the clamped and free running states, respectively. This type of approximation is used in statistical mechanics when it becomes impossible to compute mean values for each of a large number of interacting particles. A summary of the learning rule for mean field theory is given below.

Mean Field Theory Learning Algorithm

1. Set all weights to small random numbers and set hidden unit activations to some initial random bipolar values. Set the temperature control parameter to a high initial value T_0.

2. For each pair of input-output training patterns ($\mathbf{x}^p$, $\mathbf{t}^p$), present the selected patterns to the network visible units. The $\mathbf{x}^p$ pattern is "clamped" to the input and $\mathbf{t}^p$ to the output units. For a sequence of decreasing temperatures T_0, T_1, ..., T_{final}, solve the equations (10.22) iteratively to obtain solutions m_j for all non-clamped units. Clamped units are assigned values $m_j = \pm 1$ depending on whether the unit is clamped on or off. At T_{final} compute the mean field co-occurrence probabilities M_{ij}^c, for $i, j = 1, 2, ..., n, i \neq j$.

3. Repeat the steps outlined in step 2 except the output units are allowed to run freely. At T_{final} compute the mean field co-occurrence probabilities M_{ij}^f, for $i, j = 1, 2, ..., n, i \neq j$.

4. Repeat steps 2 and 3 until all training patterns have been presented to the network. Adjust the weights according to the mean field learning rule,

$$\Delta w_{ij} = \alpha \left[M_{ij}^c - M_{ij}^f \right] \qquad i, j = 1, 2, ..., N, i \neq j \qquad (10.23)$$

where α is a learning coefficient and M_{ij}^c and M_{ij}^f are the estimated correlations (co-occurrence probabilities) of both units i and j being on for the clamped and unclamped conditions respectively.

5. Repeat the whole process for all i, j and p until the weight changes given by equation (10.23) are zero or sufficiently small.

When the standard annealing learning rule is replaced with this rule, a speed up of one to two orders of magnitude can be realized with little loss in level of performance. Bilbro et al. (1989) have used mean field annealing methods in the solution of the graph partitioning problem, an NP-hard combinatorial optimization application. Their results show a speed up by a factor of 50 with results that are comparable in performance to standard annealing.

Markov Chain Model

The simulated annealing process can be characterized mathematically as a Markov chain. A Markov chain is a sequence of trials, where the outcome of any trial corresponds to the state or configuration of the system (the network). The characteristic feature of the Markov property is that the new state depends only on the previous state and not on earlier states. These one-step dependencies can be expressed as transition probabilities, $p_{ij}(n)$, the conditional probability of moving to state j on the nth trial given the system is in state i on the $(n - 1)$th trial, that is

$$p_{ij}(n) = Pr\{\mathbf{x}(n) = j | \mathbf{x}(n - 1) = i\}$$

where $Pr\{A | \mathbf{x} = k\}$ denotes conditional probability of event A given that $\mathbf{x} = k$ and $\mathbf{x}(n)$ is a random variable.

There is an extensive theory established for Markov chains and that theory applies to the Boltzmann Machine with simulated annealing. Indeed, this theory was the basis for the proof of convergence to a global energy minimum used by Gemen and Gemen (1984). The theory has also been helpful in understanding the behavior of the annealing process.

10.3 Solving Optimization Problems

Optimization problems are ubiquitous. They occur frequently in many different guises. Companies want to maximize productivity and profits, minimize costs and wastage, minimize risk, maximize growth, and so on. In the application of neural network modeling and problem solving, the objective is to minimize the mapping errors over the population of patterns to be processed or to maximize some information theoretic criteria. Significant advances have been made in the solution of optimization problems over the past few decades. Solution methods have been extended to include linear and goal programming, dynamic programming, heuristic and probabilistic search, constraint programming, genetic algorithms and neural networks. The types of neural networks that have been used successfully in this area are recurrent networks such as the Boltzmann Machine with simulated annealing, and Hopfield networks. Both have been used to solve a number of optimization problems such as the traveling salesman problem, the n-queens problem, graph coloring and max (graph) cut. Typically, these are combinatorial NP-complete problems, problems for which the solution space grows at exponential rates with the problem parameter size. Optimal solutions to these problems may require prohibitive computational costs. Therefore, good, but less than optimal solutions may be an acceptable compromise for many applications.

Since many of the benchmark problems such as graph coloring and max cut are described elsewhere (e.g. Aarts and Korst, 1989), we limit our description here to different types of applications. We begin with an optimization application, an example of the use of simulated annealing in finding the solution to an optimal typewriter keyboard layout.

Typewriter Keyboard Layout

Most typewriter keyboards use the so-called QWERTY key arrangement, where the name comes from the first six keys in the top row of letters. It is known that this keyboard arrangement is not optimal in the sense that: (1) it places an unequal typing load distribution among the hands, favoring the left hand over the right hand even though most people are right-handed, (2) the layout gives weaker fingers a heavier load than the stronger fingers, (3) the home or middle row, is used less than one-third of the time, resulting in increased finger travel time, and (4) the design does not take into account the fact that alternate-hand typing of common letter pairs is faster than same-hand typing. A more optimal keyboard layout would satisfy certain constraints that eliminate the above inefficiencies and result in faster average typing rates. For example, keys should be arranged to take advantage of the statistics of English letters to minimize finger travel times. The frequencies of occurrence of letter pairs (digrams) or even triples (trigrams) should be taken into account in the layout and the typing load should be distributed to give the right hand more work than the left hand. Since the goal is increased typing speed, it would be useful to capture and summarize the above constraints in a single performance measure that can be used to evaluate different keyboard configurations.

In the design of a keyboard, there are more than $26! \cong 4 \times 10^{26}$ combinations of key arrangements to consider if we look at the 26 letters of the alphabet only. Evaluating each is, of course, impractical if not impossible. The search space is too large to do an exhaustive evaluation of each possible layout. This is another example of an NP-complete problem, a combinatorial problem which grows exponentially with the number of keys. On the other hand, as suggested above, we need not insist on the optimal configuration if a good enough solution can be found with less computation.

To be confident that a good solution will be found, we need a method that explores many different parts of the solution space without getting trapped in a local minimum. This is where simulated annealing can provide an approach. Light and Anderson (1993) describe a simulated annealing solution to the typewriter keyboard problem using a simple cost function. The function is based on the relative frequencies of all English letter pairs and travel time between pairs of keyboard keys. If we consider the letters of the English alphabet only, there are some

$$\binom{26}{2} = 325$$

such pairs that must be taken into account when evaluating keyboard layouts. Some letter pairs will, of course, have zero frequencies in English (e.g. *qx* or *zq*).

The cost function used by Light and Anderson (1993) is an approximation to the average travel time between letter pairs for all 325 combinations. The function is just the summation of products of all letter pair frequencies $F_{\alpha\beta}$ and the associated travel times $T_{pos(\alpha)pos(\beta)}$, between letter pairs α and β,

$$\text{cost} = \sum_{\alpha=a}^{z} \sum_{\beta=a}^{z} F_{\alpha\beta} T_{pos(\alpha),pos(\beta)}$$

where the indices α and β both run through all letters of the alphabet. Although this cost function ignores some factors in typing speed, it is a reasonable approximation.

In performing the simulations, keyboard solutions quite different from the QWERTY keyboard were generated. An example of the solutions generated by the annealing process is illustrated in Figure 10.3 where the cost of the annealing solution is compared to the cost of the QWERTY keyboard. The best solution cost is 1,428 compared to the QWERTY cost of 1,542, a reduction of 7.4%. Annealing solutions were found to satisfy some of the other desirable keyboard properties noted above, including the assignment of a heavier workload to the right hand, assigning common letter pairs to alternate hand typing and the assignment of frequent letters (such as *E, T, A, O* and so on) to stronger fingers and less frequent letters being assigned to the weaker fingers. Overall, the optimal solution keyboard resulted in significant time savings for English language diagrams and produced a better workload on the hands.

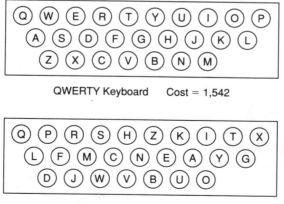

QWERTY Keyboard   Cost = 1,542

Best Solution Keyboard   Cost = 1,428

Figure 10.3   Cost and Layout Comparison of the QWERTY and Best Simulated Annealing Solution Keyboards

Traveling Salesman Problem

The keyboard layout problem described above can be solved with a Boltzmann Machine and simulated annealing if we specify the network parameters (the number of units, connections, and weight values) correctly in relation to the cost function. A simpler approach, however, is to recognize that this problem is isomorphic to the traveling salesman problem (TSP) and can be mapped directly to one of the solution formulations already published. Hopfield and Tank (1985) have given a solution to this problem using a Hopfield network. Since then, many other solutions have been proposed, including Boltzmann Machine solutions. In particular, a solution we describe below is one based on that of Aarts and Korst (1989).

The traveling salesman problem is one of those easy to describe problems that are very costly to solve. The problem is to find a minimum distance tour connecting n cities. A tour is a sequence of n distinct inter-city distances that represent a trip starting from one city and returning to that city after visiting each of the other cities once only. There are $(n - 1)!$ different tours for n cities, a number that grows exponentially with n. To examine all tour distances for values of n larger than even 20 requires a prohibitive amount of computer time. This problem belongs to the class of NP-complete problems (Garey and Johnson, 1979).

Let N be the number of keyboard keys (cities) and $\mathbf{D} = (d_{ij})$ be the matrix of the products of key pair frequencies and travel times (inter-city distances). Also define the indicator variable x_{ip} as

$$x_{ip} = \begin{cases} 0 & \text{if key } i \text{ is pressed at position } P \\ 1 & \text{otherwise} \end{cases}$$

Then we wish to minimize the objective function

$$f(x) = \sum_{i,j,p,q=0}^{N-1} a_{ijpq} x_{ip} x_{jq}$$

subject to the constraints

$$\sum_{i=0}^{N-1} x_{ip} = 1 \qquad p = 0, \ldots, N - 1$$

$$\sum_{p=0}^{N-1} x_{ip} = 1 \qquad i = 0, \ldots, N - 1$$

$$a_{ijpq} = \begin{cases} d_{ij} & \text{if } q = (p + 1) \bmod N \\ 0 & \text{otherwise} \end{cases}$$

For the Boltzmann Machine solution, Aarts and Korst have defined units u_{ip} associated with the x_{ip} and bias, distance and inhibitory connections for the network. Their solution formulation uses a network consisting of $(2N^3 - N^2)$ connections.

In repeated simulations of 10 and 30 city TSP problems, the solutions produced by their networks were close to the smallest known tours. For example, their average tour distance for the 10 and 30 city problems were 2.815 and 5.459 compared to the smallest known distances of 2.675 and 4.299, respectively. The smallest solutions obtained during the simulations were 2.675 and 4.929, respectively.

10.4 Other Applications

The ANNIE project (Applications of Neural Networks for Industry in Europe) was sponsored by European Artificial Intelligence program ESPRIT in November, 1988, to promote the awareness and application of neural networks in Europe. The results of this effort are documented in the Project ANNIE Handbook, Croall and Mason (1991). One application chosen for investigation under this program is the crew scheduling problem. Like many scheduling problems, the objective is to optimally satisfy a given set of tasks using available resources subject to certain constraints (priorities, deadlines, costs). The goal is to minimize a cost function which depends on service time and cost of service. In airline crew scheduling an anonymous crew must be assigned to sequences of flight legs that make up a rotation. Several legs (a route) including flight and transition times constitutes a rotation. Normally, a rotation can last for several days, and hence, is too long to be flown by a single crew. The goal is to minimize the amount of working days subject to various constraints: temporal (a crew must complete one leg before being assigned another, checking in/out times and so on), local (arrival airport of a leg must be the departure airport of succeeding leg) maximum working and rest times, and bounds on the number of legs per day.

Conventional approaches to solve this scheduling problem are based on the set covering or set partitioning formulations. Given a set $S = \{1, 2, ..., m\}$ (the flight legs) and a class of subsets of S labeled $T = \{S_1, S_2, ..., S_n\}$ (the set of all feasible pairings of legs-to-crews), each with an associated cost C_j, the problem is to cover all members of S at minimum cost using members of T. This can be seen as an integer programming problem formulated as follows:

min **CX**

subject to

$$\mathbf{AX} \geq \mathbf{e}, X_j = 0 \text{ or } 1, \text{ for } j \in \{1, 2, ..., n\}$$

where

m is the number of members of S

n is the number of members of T

C is an n-dimensional vector, and C_j is the cost of subset j

X is an n-dimensional vector of 0s and 1s with

$X_j = 1$ if subset j is used in the solution

$= 0$ otherwise

A is an $m \times n$ matrix of 0s and 1s

with $A_{ij} = 1$ if member i of S is included in subset j

$= 0$ otherwise

$\mathbf{e} = (1, ..., 1)$ is an m-dimensional vector.

The solution to this problem is a set of valid crew rotations covering all flight legs in the set of all aircraft rotations.

For a Boltzmann machine solution to the above problem, it is first transformed into a weighted node packing problem (WNP) and then solved with a Boltzmann machine. The WNP problem amounts to finding a set of edges in an undirected graph $G(V, E)$, such that no two edges E share a vertex V and the total weight of the subset is maximal. This problem is mapped to a Boltzmann machine by associating with each unit u_j the corresponding subset S_j, where the state of u_j determines the value of the variable X_j. The weights are set *a priori* to **W**, where

$$\mathbf{W} = (w_{ij}) = \begin{cases} \Theta|S_i| - c_i & \text{if } i = j \\ -\{\max\{\Theta|S_i| - c_i, \Theta|S_j| - c_j\} + \varepsilon\}\delta_{ij} & \text{if } i \neq j \end{cases}$$

where $i = 1, 2, ..., M$, $j = 1, 2, ..., N$ and $|S_i|$ is the cardinality of the subset represented by the unit u_i, c_i is the cost associated with the subset S_i,

$$\Theta = \sum_{i=1}^{N} c_i$$

ε is a positive, very small constant and $\delta_{ij} = 1$ (0) if pairs S_i, S_j are not disjoint (otherwise).

The above problem was solved successfully using a Boltzmann machine, but for small sample problems only. Examples of the solutions are given in Croall and Mason (1991).

Summary

In this chapter, the Boltzmann Machine (BM) network with simulated annealing was described. BM networks are recurrent networks that operate in a stochastic manner. The discrete states the network can assume are determined probabilistically. Starting with some input binary pattern, a trained network should relax to an equilibrium state that produces the desired output pattern. These networks can operate in one of three different modes: as an associative memory, for general heteroassociative mapping (classification) tasks, and in the solution of optimization problems. The most general BM architecture has input, output and hidden units with symmetrical, bidirectional connections between units. Simpler architectures have only visible (input/output) units with hidden units and the simplest type has visible units only (no hidden-layer units).

A form of supervised training is used in conjunction with a simulated annealing process where equilibrium is eventually reached after a sequence of "temperature" reductions. A gradient descent learning rule based on the relative entropy between desired and actual state probabilities is used to adjust the network's weights. The annealing process insures that local minima traps are avoided during the learning process. Autoassociative learning is usually regarded as unsupervised learning, however.

Because the network has symmetric weights, an energy function can be defined for BMs in the same way as for Hopfield networks. At thermal equilibrium, the energy of the system will be at a minimum.

Although BM networks have some advantages over other network architectures such as MLFF networks with BP training, they have not enjoyed the same popularity as the other networks due to the heavy computational burden in training them. Even with variations to speed up training such as that provided with the Cauchy Machine and mean field annealing, the computational load is still great compared to BP. Perhaps further research will result in acceptable learning rates.

BM networks have been used to solve combinatorial optimization problems, as well as general mapping tasks. To illustrate their capabilities, a few typical examples have been described including two different optimization tasks.

Part V

Other Neural Network Architectures

11
Self-Growing Network Architectures

This is the first of three chapters on other important network architectures. The classes of networks described in these chapters are unique, but in quite different aspects: one class is self-constructing, another has selective connectivity among the layers and the third builds stochastic models of the environment. We begin this chapter with a look at a new approach to the construction of feedforward networks. The networks are constructive (self-growing) in that the learning algorithm builds one or more hidden layers incrementally during the supervised training process. The networks are constructed by adding nodes and connections until the training errors are reduced to acceptable levels. Two of the network types are for general mapping applications. The other networks are suitable for general classification problems. All of the networks are multilayered, with feedforward signal propagation and trained using supervised training algorithms.

11.1 Introduction

The networks we have studied in previous chapters were handcrafted. The optimal size of the networks for a given application were generally unknown and had to be determined through a trial and error process. The process sometimes ended in failure, for example when local minima traps were encountered during training, or when the environment changed, a completely different architecture was required. Although some guidelines were given in Chapters 6 and 7 for MLFF networks in the determination of the number of hidden layers and number of nodes in the hidden layers, experimentation was still required. These problems are largely eliminated when using the networks described in this chapter. These networks are self-grown and encounter no problems with local minima. The training algorithms used for these networks build the network by adding hidden-layer nodes as required until the error rate reaches a tolerable level.

In the following sections, we study four types of self-growing networks. The first two are reviewed in detail with typical applications presented. The last two types are briefly described for completeness. We begin with a description of the reduced coulomb network, a network that has been patented. We next examine the cascade correlation network. Finally we review the operation of the Tower and Pyramid networks and the upstart algorithm.

11.2 Reduced Coulomb Energy Networks

Reduced coulomb energy networks (RCE) were developed by Leon Cooper, Douglas Reily and colleagues (Reily et al., 1982, 1987). RCE networks learn to map an arbitrary input feature vector $\mathbf{x}$ from real-valued n-dimensional space to an output category space C (among c possible categories) through an energy equation $E : \mathbf{x} \to C$, where

$$C = E(\mathbf{x})$$

The RCE name comes from the network's relation to physics where an "electrostatic" energy function E is defined based on the network's memory sites in n-dimensional space. To use a physical analogy, an input E is mapped to an output C by the mapping R, where $C = R^{-1}E$ or $RC = E$. Their definition of energy, which we omit here, has "coulomb" memory basins which have local minima only at the corresponding memory sites (unlike the Hopfield network).

The network is a reduced connection, feedforward network with three processing layers: an input layer with n cells, an internal or intermediate mapping layer consisting of m cells, and an output layer with c cells. Cells in the input layer correspond to feature or attribute values of the input stimulus pattern, whereas cells in the output layer each correspond to a different distinct class or category. Cells in the internal layer map the input feature values to the output categories. The network assigns an input vector to a category when an output node "fires" (equals 1). Feature vectors that elicit a single output response are called *unambiguous* mappings. Input vectors that elicit multiple output responses or no output response are *ambiguous* mappings. We expect a trained network to give unambiguous outputs. However, ambiguous mappings that produce some outputs might still be useful if they can give an indication of the most likely categories to which the input pattern belongs. This issue is addressed below.

Each intermediate-layer cell is fully connected to all input-layer cells through adjustable weights. Intermediate-layer cells project an output connection to only a single ouput-layer cell through fixed weights. There are no lateral connections and no feedback connections. The basic RCE network is illustrated in Figure 11.1. Note that output cells may, in general, have more than one input connection from inner layer cells.

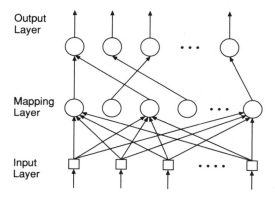

Figure 11.1   RCE Network Connections

Each inner layer cell i defines a region of "influence" in pattern space based on its input weight vector $\mathbf{w}_i$ and an associated threshold parameter θ_i. The region is defined through an activation function $F_{\theta_i}(d(\mathbf{w}_i, \mathbf{x}))$, where d is an appropriately chosen metric. For example, the metric could be Cartesian distance, Hamming distance, vector inner product or some other measure, and $\mathbf{x}$ is the input feature vector value. The threshold function $F_{\theta_i}(\cdot)$ is defined by

$$F_{\theta_i}(z) = \begin{cases} 1 & \text{if } z \leq \theta_i \\ 0 & \text{if } z \geq \theta_i \end{cases}$$

If d is Cartesian distance in n-dimensional real-valued space, the region of influence is a hypersphere of radius θ_i with center located at $\mathbf{w}_i$. To summarize, the region of influence for a given mapping layer cell i is defined by three factors: (1) a central location point in n-space determined by the cell's weight vector $\mathbf{w}_i$, (2) the size (radius) of the region as determined by the threshold parameter θ_i and (3) the topology or geometry of the region determined by the metric d. An example of a region of influence for a two-dimensional feature space with Cartesian metric is illustrated in Figure 11.2. In the figure, one pattern **x** is within the region and a second pattern **x'** is outside the region.

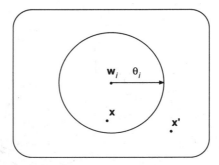

Figure 11.2   The Region of Influence for Mapping Layer Cell *i*

Inner layer cells are activated or "fired" by producing an output value of unity whenever the distance between the input feature value **x** and the corresponding weights $\mathbf{w}_i$ for the cell is less than the threshold value θ_i. Thus, referring to Figure 11.2, when pattern **x** is presented to the input layer, cell *i* in the inner layer becomes active. This would not be the case if pattern **x'** were presented at the input. The activated cell *i* sends its output to a single output unit.

Output layer cells behave like a logical OR gate. They fire whenever any of their input links are active. Weights on the connections between inner-layer and outer-layer cells are all constant with unit (+1) values. For proper operation, an RCE network will produce unambiguous outputs for every input pattern **x**, and the outputs will correctly classify the input patterns. Correct classification can often be achieved through the RCE supervised training procedure. This procedure begins with a partially constructed network which consists of *n* input nodes and *c* category nodes where *n* is the number of feature values in the input vector and *c* the number of categories. It is not necessary to start the training with any inner-layer nodes connected. They are added as needed during the training process as outlined below.

Training RCE Networks

As noted above, training in the RCE network can begin with an incomplete network, a network with no inner-layer cells. We assume the network does have *n* input cells to match the dimension of the training pattern vectors and c output cells, one for each known category. A form of supervised training is used where patterns from the different category regions are selected at random and presented to the input layer. If the output response is correct for the input pattern, no action is taken and no learning takes place. If an output cell is off (0) when it should be on (1), an error signal of $+1$ is generated and returned to the inner layer (a teacher signal). If an output cell is on (1) when it should be off (0), an error signal of -1 is returned to the inner layer. These error signals are used by the system to train the network. Training consists of two activities: committing new inner-layer cells and adjusting an existing cell's threshold value. An inner-layer cell is committed to the network by connecting a new cell's input to all n input nodes, connecting the cell's single output to an appropriate output node, setting the cell's weight vector values and setting an initial threshold value for the cell. A cell's threshold is adjusted by reducing it by a fixed amount $\Delta\theta$.

When an error signal of $+1$ is received from the kth output cell, a new internal cell i is committed (added to the network) and connected to the kth output cell. Input connections are made to the newly committed cell from all input nodes and the adjustable weights $\mathbf{w}_i$ on these connections are set equal to the input pattern vector $\mathbf{x}$. This insures that output cell k fires whenever the current input pattern $\mathbf{x}$ is presented to the network. The threshold θ_i of the new cell is set according to

$$\theta_i = \max\{\theta_{max}, \theta_{opp}\}$$

where θ_{opp} is the distance to the nearest influence field center of any cell with pattern class different from the class of the input pattern $\mathbf{x}$. In other words, θ_{opp} is the minimum distance between the weight vector $\mathbf{w}_i$ and the weight vector $\mathbf{w}_j$ of the nearest cell of different category, and θ_{max} is the maximum of any threshold value ever assigned, a value initially defined by the user. The newly committed cell guarantees that the correct output cell will fire whenever the associated input pattern is presented, correcting the state of the $+1$ error signal.

When an error signal of -1 is received by the inner layer (the teacher signal) from the kth output cell, a reduction of $\Delta\theta$ is made to the threshold θ_i of all active inner-layer cells connected to the kth cell. At least some of the cells connected to the kth cell are firing erroneously. Reducing the threshold parameter value reduces the size of the region of influence of the internal cells connected to the kth output cell, making it less likely that the wrong category is selected for the input pattern that caused the error. These training signals are summarized in Table 11.1.

In Figure 11.3, a partially trained network is illustrated. The training patterns come from two different category regions A and B which are shown together with

Table 11.1   Learning Actions Due to ±1 Type Error Signals

Error Signal from kth Output Cell	Action Taken
+1	Commit inner-layer cell and connect to kth output cell
−1	Reduce thresholds of all active inner-layer cells connected to the kth output cell
0	No change to any cells

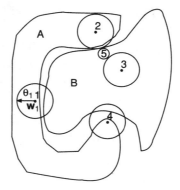

Figure 11.3   Regions of Influence for Five Inner-Layer Cells at the Start of Training

the regions of influence for five inner-layer cells (discs numbered 1 through 5). At this stage of the training, inner-layer cells 1 and 4 will produce incorrect (ambiguous) responses when patterns of category B lying within the region of influence of these cells are presented. Correct (unambiguous) responses will be given for patterns lying within the region of influence of cells 2, 3 and 5, however. Note that the region of influence of cell number 5 is much smaller than the other cells. This illustrates the result of threshold reduction on the cell during the training process. Cell number 2 could produce an incorrect result if a noisy pattern lying between regions A and B were presented. This problem can be corrected through the use of special noisy patterns in training the network as described below.

If the training set is limited or if a poor choice of the initial threshold assignment is made to the inner-layer cells, the category regions may not be fully covered by the cell's regions of influence during training. This could result in erroneous classifications for patterns not yet "seen" by the network during training. An example of spotted coverage that can result is given in Figure 11.4 where the network has been trained on patterns from two classes, A and B.

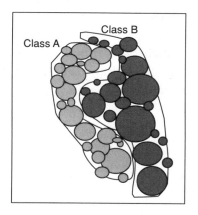

Figure 11.4   Partially Covered Regions of Influence for Category Regions A and B

Assuming that enough representative training patterns have been presented to the network and a sufficient number of internal cells committed, the network should then be capable of classifying patterns from several categories, even if the category regions are complex and overlapping, including, for example, complex disjoint nonlinearly separable regions in n-dimensional space. To learn the categories, many cell regions of influence may be required to cover each category, especially if the regions are very complex. Noisy training patterns are patterns chosen near the boundaries of regions but lying outside the category regions. They can help to sharpen the category region boundaries, since thresholds of inner-layer cells will be reduced by the noisy patterns while at the same time no cells are committed for these patterns. To prepare noisy training patterns requires some knowledge of the category boundaries. This may be difficult to determine for some applications.

Thus, to sum up, we see that any input pattern falling within the influence region of a cell will cause that cell to fire. If a pattern lies within the influence region of several overlapping cells, all of the cells will fire. If some of the firing cells represent different categories, multiple output cells will fire producing an ambiguous classification. When all firing inner-layer cells are connected to the same output cell, unambiguous classification results.

Although ambiguous classifications are erroneous, there are some cases where a form of likelihood measure for category type would be useful. For example, when category regions do overlap, it would be useful to have an estimate of a pattern's category when it lies in the overlapping region. This notion is illustrated in Figure 11.5 where a confusion zone is defined by inseparable overlapping regions for two categories A and B. In enhanced versions of the RCE network, a method of estimating probabilities of occurrence of patterns lying in each category of a confusion zone is implemented. In this case, a minimal threshold θ_{min} is used to define "probabilistic" cells which can be used to implement the classification of these nonseparable classes (Scofield et al., 1987). The details of this method are beyond the scope of our treatment here.

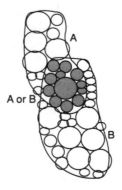

Figure 11.5   Separable Regions are Mapped Deterministically, the Confusion Zone is Mapped
Probabilistically

Dynamic Category Learning

A form of dynamic category learning is possible with RCE networks since new categories can be learned without complete retraining on old patterns. This is accomplished by simply introducing the new class patterns and training the system on these patterns together with all neighboring class patterns. The neighboring class patterns are needed to help form sharp, nonoverlapping regions of influence between the existing and newly added classes. These concepts are illustrated in Figure 11.6 where the network is being trained to classify patterns from a new category C after learning to classify patterns from categories A and B.

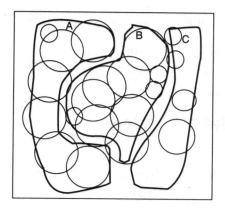

Figure 11.6   Learning a New Category C After Learning Categories A and B

RCE networks have a number of important features that other networks may lack, including:

- Self-growing to appropriate size.

- No local minima problem.

- Low computation requirements, making real time applications possible in some instances.

- High storage efficiency since only a single inner node is required to store any input pattern (recall that some networks such as Hopfield have a storage capacity of about 14% only).

- Low connectivity, the number of connections is almost linear in the number of nodes N, as compared to N^2 for many other networks.

- The ability to learn quickly from relatively few training examples only, and to learn dynamically without relearning all other categories when new ones must be learned.

Some poor qualities possessed by these networks include the following:

- Normally, they do not generalize well.

- They require a separate output node for each category.

- They may grow very large for some problems.

• they cannot perform general mapping function tasks.

Before considering RCE network applications, we introduce the use of multiple RCE networks to form a type of majority voting in difficult classification tasks.

Multiple and Cascaded RCE Networks

Multiple RCE networks have been used in combinations with a controller to solve some complicated pattern classification problems. For example, the input may consist of multiple feature sets that are generated by different sensors or partitions in the feature space as suggested by common themes in the characteristics being measured. Partitioning may also be introduced naturally as a result of new features being discovered and added to the system later in time. When the output of a single network is ambiguous for such problems, unambiguous solutions may be found through a kind of correlation or voting scheme (Rimey et al., 1986). In this case, the networks can be connected in a hierarchical structure to a controller as illustrated in Figure 11.7.

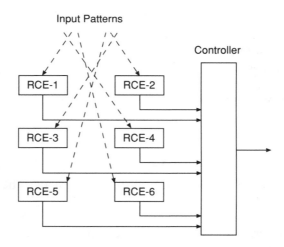

Figure 11.7   Multiple RCE Networks with Majority Voting

The use of multiple networks can sometimes improve the accuracy of classification for many applications. For example, when one network cannot distinguish between two classes A and B well and a second network cannot distinguish between classes B and C, the use of two or more networks as illustrated in Figure 11.8 may provide a solution.

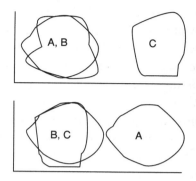

Figure 11.8   Using Multiple Networks with Majority Voting

RCE networks have been used extensively in a variety of applications. We conclude our treatment of these networks with a look at several such applications.

11.3 RCE Network Applications

In this section, we describe seven applications of RCE networks to the solution of real world problems. The applications include: invariant object recognition, counting of minnows in fish farming, diagnosis of abnormal livers from ultrasonic images, character recognition for identification of X-ray films, detection of surface defects in rolled metal products and classification of plant species. We begin with an application in computer vision, a common problem in manufacturing operations.

Invariant Object Recognition

An important computer vision application is one in which multiple objects need to be identified as they move along on a conveyor belt. This requires that they be recognized at different locations in the field of view, different scales and at different orientations. Wei Li and Nasrabadi (1990) used a cascade of three RCE networks to learn this difficult problem of invariant object recognition. To achieve the invariance, the image of 256×256 pixels with gray level intensities in the range of 0–255 is preprocessed and mapped into a 48-dimensional feature vector. The features are then processed by the networks to identify the objects.

Preprocessing of the image data consists of thresholding the image into a binary image using intensity histogram methods, computing the centroid of the binarized object, converting from Cartesian to polar coordinates and then normalizing the image. The object representation is then divided into 12 angular segments (360/30) around the origin and four descriptor codes are extracted from each segment. The four pieces of information are: (1) the number of object boundary points in the segment divided by the total number of boundary points, (2) the normalized area of the object in the segment (total number of black pixels), (3) the maximum distance of the object boundary from the centroid point for each segment, and (4) the minimum distance of the object boundary from the origin. These preprocessing computations provide the invariance to shift, scale and orientation needed. The problem of invariant recognition is illustrated in Figure 11.9 where an outline of a hammer is portrayed in three different positions. Polar coordinate plots of the corresponding normalized hammer boundaries are given on the right of the figure.

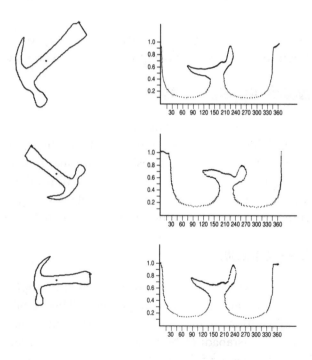

Figure 11.9   Three Different Views of a Hammer and the Corresponding Normalized Boundaries
in Polar Coordinates
(Courtesy of Professors W. Li and M. Nasrabadi.)

To achieve better generalization in learning, three cascaded RCE networks were trained using tool objects such as a hammer, pliers, wrench and so on. A total of 48 objects were used in the training set. During training, if the first network fails to correctly recognize some objects after several cycles, learning is stopped and a new network is cascaded to the first network and trained on the unclassified objects. The process is repeated until the cascade of nets correctly classifies all objects. For the present application, three networks were required. The first network learned more coarse features and the remaining two nets finer object features. The first network created 11 inner-layer nodes and learned to classify 34 of the objects. The second network created 14 inner-layer nodes and learned to classify 13 objects. The third network created only a single inner-layer node and learned to recognize the final remaining object.

During the recognition phase, 50 different views of the objects were used to test the networks using randomly selected camera settings and object orientations. The networks achieved a classification accuracy of 100%. For this application, the RCE algorithm proved to be very fast in both training and recognition as compared to other network architectures.

Fish Counting

Fish farming is a growing industry worldwide. This is an important source of high protein, low fat food. An important problem facing fish farmers is fish tracking. This is essentially a problem in counting the density of minnows in a sample drawn from specific locations. Although many automated methods have been tried, the most accurate method found to-date is human estimation, but even this method exhibits a 10% error rate.

Recent RCE network solutions also offer some promise (Collins, 1992). The network solution is based on counting the number of minnows appearing in an image taken of a minnow sample poured into a shallow plate. The total number of minnows is estimated by summing clumps of minnows appearing in mutually exclusive regions of the area. Each clump may contain from zero to five minnows.

The image is first preprocessed by binarization and erosion to eliminate small organic blobs. Connected blobs of pixels are then used to compute object features (area, perimeter, dispersion, diameter, number of "tips" and radial signing). The features serve as the input to an RCE network which outputs the number of minnows in the blob (clump).

To train the network, the computed features of the blob serve as input to the network together with the number actually observed by an operator. A video monitor is attached to the vision system frame grabber and, as each blob is detected, it is highlighted and the operator is queried for the actual number in the blob. Once a sample has been obtained, it is used to train the network as noted above.

Liver Diagnosis

Human livers can be classified as either normal or abnormal through an analysis of ultrasonic images of a human liver. Statistical and geometrical features that have been used to characterize the liver images include: mean intensity, mode intensity, maximum gray-level frequency, minimum intensity values, maximum intensity values, intensity variance and standard deviation, smoothness, skewness, kurtosis, 10% and 90% intensity percentile points, maximum probability coefficient, entropy coefficient, inverse differential coefficient, correlation coefficients, mean gradient, standard deviation of gradient and so on (Collins, 1992). Several classification methods were examined and compared including, nearest neighbor clustering, linear discriminant analysis, MLFF networks with BP, Counter Propagation networks and RCE networks. As reported, none of the methods compared achieved the 90% accuracy attained by the RCE network.

Character Recognition on X-Ray Films

The identification of patient's X-ray films is accomplished using ID numbers recorded on the bottom of the film. These numbers are used to store and transfer films in hospitals. Fast and reliable methods for character recognition are desirable to speed up the storage and transfer functions. An RCE network has been used to perform the recognition process with recognition rates of 99.4% accuracy (Hasegawa et al., 1993). Characters used to identify patients include the letters T, M, S and the ten digits 0 through 9. Patients' names are also recorded, but are not used in the ID process.

Preprocessing of the ID image includes segmentation, rotation and binarization. The preprocessed character consists of 12×15 pixels which are used as input to the network. Thus, the network has 180 binary-valued inputs and 13 outputs. The number of second layer kernal units is determined automatically during the learning phase. A modified learning scheme called Hyper-Spherical Surface Interactive Interconnections (HSII) was used for the application. This method uses a form of error backpropagation to refine the weights connected to the hidden-layer inputs. It has been found to be superior to the standard RCE learning paradigm. In general, HSII generated fewer hidden-layer nodes than standard RCE during the learning process and realized superior performance. For example, the HSII method generated a total of 31 hidden-layer nodes, compared to 55 generated by standard RCE learning. Learning time of the HSII was also shorter. It was trained on a set of 2,250 characters taken from 90 X-ray sheets. Convergence was realized after 710 iterations.

Detection of Surface Defects in Rolled Metal Products

Several types of surface defects are created during the rolling process in metal products. Conventional detection methods relied on an operator to monitor a video display or a semi-automated warning system which signaled the operator of potential flaws. This system was not able to identify the type of blemish, however. A solution to the problem was found using an RCE network trained on 19 surface features. The features used included: geometry of the defect envelope, distribution of pixel activity, and histograms of pixel intensities. The trained system learned to classify some 15 different classes of defects. Furthermore, the system is incrementally trained on new defects as they are encountered.

Classification of Iris Species

Classification of plant and other species is a common problem for biologists. Plant species can often be differentiated using distinguishing features such as size, color, texture, shape of leaves and so on. An example of a benchmark classification problem that has been used extensively to compare statistical techniques and ANN performance is the classification of Iris species. This is done using measurement data taken from samples of plant leaves.

For this application, the author trained an RCE network to classify Iris species. The three species for classification are Setosa, Versicolor, and Virginica. The features used for training and classification are four petal measurements: sepal length, sepal width, petal length and petal width. A total of 75 measurements were used in the training set and 25 in the test set. The RCE network creates 10–12 inner-layer nodes depending on the order of presentation. It achieved an accuracy of some 92% correct classifications, the same accuracy level achieved by a MLFF network with backpropagation training.

11.4 Cascade Correlation Networks—Training and Operation

The Cascade Correlation Network introduced by Fahlman and Lebiere (1990) is another network that builds its own architecture during the training process. The completed network is a feedforward network with input, hidden-layer and output nodes. Supervised training is used to incrementally build a minimal size network needed to achieve the desired error tolerance. Like RCE networks, the Cascade

Correlation Network (CCN) starts with some initially predetermined number of input and output nodes as required by the application. The input nodes are fully connected to the output nodes with adjustable weights. There is also a fixed bias input with value $+1$. There are no hidden-layer nodes at the start of training. Hidden-layer nodes are added to the network one at a time, and once added, do not change. The network can be trained using almost any supervised training method such as Perceptron, backpropagation, Quickprop, the simple Delta Rule or other appropriate method since only a single layer of weights is being adjusted at one time during the training process. Activation functions can be linear or nonlinear (sigmoid, hyperbolic tangent or other), mixed (sine, sigmoid, Gaussian) or the same throughout.

Training is carried out on the initial one-layer network until no further improvement in the error is realized. If the error is acceptable, training stops. Otherwise, a single hidden-layer node is added to the network by connecting its input to the output of all input nodes. The connections all have adjustable weights. No output connections from the new node are added at this time. The weights on the input connections are then adjusted to maximize the correlation C between the new node's output and the residual error of the output nodes where

$$C = \sum_{o} \left| \sum_{p} (V_p - \overline{V})(E_{p,o} - \overline{E}_o) \right|$$

The indices o and p range over all output nodes o and training patterns p, respectively. The V_p are the outputs from the newly added node, and the $E_{p,o}$ the residual errors from the output nodes. The $\overline{V}$ and $\overline{E}_o$ are the averages of the V_p and $E_{p,o}$, respectively. The residual error of the output nodes is the difference between the desired and computed output multiplied by the derivative of the output node. This is the quantity that would be propagated backward if the backpropagation learning algorithm were used. The correlation (actually, the absolute covariance value) is maximized by finding the partial derivative of C with respect to each of the new candidate's incoming weights, $\partial C/\partial w_i$, in a manner similar to the operation of the delta rule (Chapters 4 and 6). Once the correlation has been maximized, the node's input weights are frozen and the output of the node is connected to all output units through adjustable weight connections. These weights, as part of all output unit weights are then adjusted using the chosen training method. If the overall error is still not acceptable, another hidden-layer node is then added to the network with adjustable weight connections being made to all input nodes as before as well as to the previously added hidden-layer nodes. Effectively, this adds a second (single node) hidden layer. Training then proceeds in the same way as for the first hidden node, first training to adjust the input weights to maximize the correlation C, freezing these weights and then training newly connected weights on the output together with all output node weights. This process is continued until an acceptable error rate is realized over the training set. The network architecture for two successive stages of training are illustrated in Figures 11.10 and 11.11. These are the completed networks after the two stages of training and the nodes have been fully connected to the other nodes.

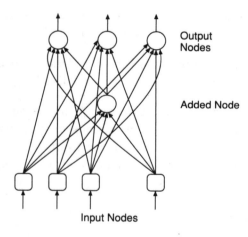

Figure 11.10   Cascade Correlation Network After Addition of One Hidden-Layer Node

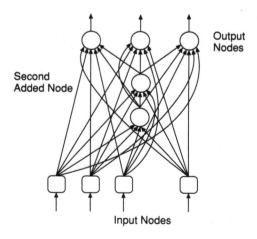

Figure 11.11   Cascade Correlation Network After Addition of Two Hidden Layers

The training algorithm for the network is summarized below.

1. Create the initial network with the required number of fully connected input and output nodes and randomize the values of all weights.

2. Train the network using the chosen method until the output error reaches a minimum. If the error is below an acceptable level, stop, otherwise go to step 3.

3. Add a hidden-layer node with input connections from the outputs of all input units and initialize the weights to small random values.

4. Adjust the weights to maximize the correlation C over the whole training set. Once the weights converge, they are fixed.

5. Connect the output of the new node to all output units and adjust the weights on all output unit's connections to minimize the error over all training patterns. If acceptable error limits have been reached, stop. Otherwise add another hidden-layer node and connect the new node's inputs to all input nodes and to the output of all other hidden-layer nodes.

6. Repeat steps 4 and 5 until acceptable error limits have been reached or until a computation time limit has been reached.

Several variations on the above training algorithm are possible. For example, rather than maximizing the correlation for a single candidate node, a pool of nodes can be used, each with a different set of initial random weight values. The pool of nodes can then be trained in parallel since they all use the same training set, see the same residual error and they do not interact with each other. When the error can be reduced no further, the one with the maximum correlation is selected for addition to the network. This approach can reduce the chance that a useless unit gets installed (stuck in a local minimum), and, for a parallel machine, can speed up training since many parts of the weight space can be explored simultaneously.

Another variation is to use standard error minimization rather than correlation maximization as the objective training function. This requires some modification to the network growing process as described by Littman et al. (1992). In this case, all of the cascaded units are trained to approximate the target output and each newly added unit becomes the network output with the previously added unit acting as virtual input to the new unit.

The Cascade Correlation Network can boast a number of advantages over many other multilayer feedforward networks. Some of the advantages cited include the following:

- There is no need to guess the network architecture in advance. The CCN automatically builds a small network size which meets the error criteria.

- Learning is fast compared to other methods such as backpropagation (BP). The training process incrementally solves the problem with no conflicting interactions among the nodes.

- Deep networks with high-order feature detectors can be built without the slowed down learning as found in BP when more than two hidden layers are used.

- Learning of new information is possible without complete retraining. Only the output weights may need retraining.

- Since only one layer of weights is being trained at any time, the training computations are simpler. Results can be cached during the training process.

- There is no need to propagate error signals backward through the network. Training requires the transmission of signals in only one direction, simplifying the computations.

- Since candidate units do not interact with each other, the limited communication makes the architecture attractive for parallel implementation.

Like feedforward networks trained with BP, CCN can learn to approximate any "reasonably well behaved" function to any desired degree of accuracy (Drago and Ridella, 1991). They show that the integrated squared error has a speed of convergence of order $O(1/n_h)$ where n_h is the number of hidden-layer nodes.

We complete this discussion of cascade correlation networks with a look at network applications.

11.5 Cascade Correlation Network Applications

In this section, we present two applications of CCNs, one a difficult pattern recognition problem and the other, a financial forecasting problem. Since in general, CCNs can be trained to solve any problem a conventional multilayer feedforward network can solve, including all problems described in Chapter 8, we limit the applications described here to only two.

Pattern Recognition

One of the most difficult benchmark problems related to pattern recognition is the two-spirals problem. The inputs to the network for this problem are continuous-valued x-y coordinate points which describe two interlocking spirals in two-dimensional space. The network has a single output node which should produce a $+1$ for all points associated with one spiral and a -1 for all points associated with the other spiral. The set of training points used for this application are illustrated in Figure 11.12.

Figure 11.12   Training Points for the Two-Spirals Problem
(Courtesy of Professor Scott Fahlman and Christian Lebiere.)

Clearly, hidden-layer nodes are required in any network that can learn to solve this nonlinearly separable problem. This problem was studied using a CCN solution developed by Fahlman and Lebiere (1990). The problem was run 100 times using sigmoidal activation functions for all nodes and a pool of eight candidate hidden-layer units. All trials were successful, requiring 1,700 epochs of training on average. The number of hidden nodes built into the final networks ranged from 12 to 19. Training times beat standard BP by a factor of ten, while building about the same complexity of network (15 hidden-layer nodes for the BP network). Other two-spiral experiments conducted with conventional BP networks required some 150,000 to 200,000 epochs for training (unpublished report from Alexis Wieland of MITRE Corp.). Experiments conducted on other problems have produced similar dramatic results.

Predicting Prepayment Rates of Mortgage Loans

One of the key components in the pricing of mortgage-backed securities is the rate at which homeowners prepay their mortgages. Mortgage-backed securities account for more than 25% of the outstanding residential debt in the U.S. which was estimated to be \$3.25 trillion at the first quarter of 1992 (Yamamoto and Zenios, 1993). Clearly then, accurate, easy-to-calibrate models of this market has profound implications for trading and portfolio management applications.

Different prediction models for mortgage prepayment have been developed, including a Cascade Correlation Network model (Yamamoto and Zenios, 1993). The performance of the CCN model compares favorably with the other approaches and has the advantages over standard MLFF network approaches noted above. The details of the network are given below.

Training data for the network consisted of the following variables:

t	—	age of the mortgage in months from its issuance
m	—	the month of the year
B	—	the outstanding balance in the mortgage pool
C/R	—	the ratio between the mortgage contract and the prevailing rate at which the mortgage can be refinanced
$(C/R)t$	—	the time history of C/R ratios

The first three variables were input as normalized real values and the remaining two were input as actual values.

The output was in actual prepayment rates given in real values:

CPR	—	actual prepayment rates

The training and test data were taken from actual time series data over a period of ten years for two different coupon rates, 9% and 12%. Two different networks were trained, one for each coupon rate. The last 12 months of data were used for testing. The networks were not trained on this data. Both linear and nonlinear activation functions were used in the models with almost equal performance reported. Typically, both networks converged after some 3,000 epochs of training. Upon completion of training, the network trained for the 9% coupon had 14 hidden nodes and the network trained for the 12% coupon had 18 hidden nodes. Training time took less than ten minutes on average on a Sun Sparc station. Plots of the two network errors during training are illustrated in Figure 11.13. One can see the sharp drop in the error curve after a new hidden node is inserted.

In addition to conventional CCN models, recurrent CCN models were constructed and trained on the mortgage data. The performance of the recurrent

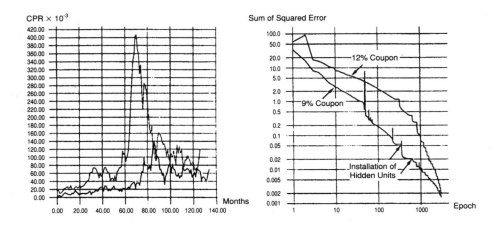

Figure 11.13   Errors Plotted Versus Training Epoch
(Courtesy of Dr Y. Yamamoto and S. Zenios.)

CCN was comparable to the standard CCN, but both performed better than an econometric model and a model based on use of the previous month's value to predict the next month's value. The results are summarized in Table 11.2 for four coupon rates.

The self-growing networks we describe in the following section are similar to the CCN in that the networks are grown as shallow multiple hidden-layer networks. They also share other similarities with the CCN.

Table 11.2   Prediction Accuracies for Four Coupon Rates Given in Standard Deviations

Coupon Rate (%)	Previous Month Projection $\times\ 10^{-1}$	Economic Model $\times\ 10^{-2}$	Cascade Correlation Algorithm $\times\ 10^{-2}$	Recurrent Cascade Correlation $\times\ 10^{-2}$
9.0	1.256	5.175	0.4801	1.320
11.0	2.757	16.29	1.500	2.566
12.0	1.654	21.91	2.459	1.984
13.0	2.161	38.39	1.776	1.445

11.6 Other Self-Growing Networks

In this section, we describe three additional self-growing networks that have some similarities to the previously described network. The first two networks are known as the Tower and Pyramid networks. They were proposed by Gallant (1986) and Gallant (1990).

The Tower Network

The tower network algorithm constructs a network incrementally by cascading hidden-layer nodes until the error is reduced to acceptable levels. The first hidden-layer node is fully connected to the input nodes and a bias input. Subsequent hidden-layer nodes are also fully connected to the input nodes and the single hidden-layer node directly below it as illustrated in Figure 11.14. The network is trained one node at a time using the pocket algorithm with ratchet (see Chapter 4). After each node is trained, the $n + 2$ weights (including bias input) are frozen and the output of the added node becomes the input to the next node. This training process is a modification of the perceptron learning algorithm which can only be applied to single layer networks. Since the weights of each added node are fixed at each stage of training, the procedure is equivalent to training a single layer network.

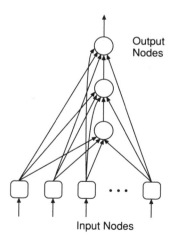

Figure 11.14   An Example of the Cascaded Tower Network

Tower networks are, of course, capable of learning to solve problems with nonlinearly separable decision regions. Gallant (1993) has given a proof of convergence for these networks.

The next network we describe, the pyramid network, is closely related to the tower network.

The Pyramid Network

The pyramid network is similar to the tower network except that each newly added node receives inputs from all other nodes and not just from the one directly below it. A proof of convergence similar to the tower proof has also been given for this network. One might conjecture that the added connections for this network would give it increased computational abilities, but this has yet to to be demonstrated.

The final constructive algorithm we discuss is the Upstart algorithm.

The Upstart Network Algorithm

Frean (1990) has proposed an interesting construction algorithm which adds nodes to correct the errors as they are found using the existing network. The inputs and activation outputs of the network nodes are linear threshold nodes (binary or bipolar -1, $+1$). Training begins with a single node u_1 connected to n input nodes. The pocket algorithm with or without ratchet is used to adjust the weights (see Chapter 4). If this node is unable to learn one or more of the training patterns, an additional node is added to correct the errors. The added node, either node u_1^+ or node u_1^- give positive and negative reinforcement, respectively, to the existing node when its output is incorrect. The added node is fully connected to the inputs and its output is connected to the initial node through a large positive weight (for u_1^+ nodes) or negative weight (for u_1^- nodes) to correct the corresponding error.

Let T_p denote the target output for the pth training pattern. Then positive training patterns for node u_j^+ are patterns defined by $T_p = 1$ and $u_j^p = 0$ where u_j^p denotes the output for node u_j^+ when T_p is the desired pattern. Negative training patterns for u_j^+ are those defined by $T_p = 0$. Other patterns are ignored. Likewise, for u_j^-, positive training patterns are defined as

$$T_p = 0 \text{ and } u_n^p = +1$$

and negative training patterns are defined by

$$T_p = 1$$

The positive and negative training patterns are used to correct errors made during training.

Training begins with the first node u_1. If this node makes any wrongly "on" errors, a u_j^- daughter node is added. This node is trained to correct the on error. If u_1 is wrongly "off" a u_j^+ daughter node is added. This node is trained to correct the off error. Once these units are trained, their weights are frozen and the output connected to the input of u_1. The weight from the u_j^- nodes is a large negative weight whose value exceeds the sum of the parent u_j positive node weights. The weight from the u_j^+ node is a large positive weight whose value exceeds the sum of the parent u_j positive node weights. This process continues with newly added nodes playing the role of parent and new positive or negative reinforcement daughter nodes added as needed. New units are only generated if the parent makes errors. Clearly, the number of errors decreases at each branching of the network. Consequently, convergence follows from an argument similar to the tower algorithm, assuming no contradictory training examples are used. The network is illustrated in Figure 11.15 after the addition of two daughter nodes, a u_1^+ node and a u_1^- node.

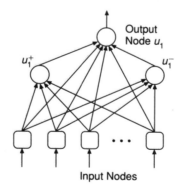

Figure 11.15   Network for the Upstart Algorithm After Two Daughter Nodes Were Added

Although only a single output was used in the above example, the algorithm can be generalized to include multiple outputs.

When the upstart algorithm was tested on the n-bit parity problem for inputs ranging up to $n = 10$, the constructed network always resulted in n units, including the output unit. For these experiments, a total of 1,000 passes over the training set was sufficient to build a minimum size network (for $n = 10$, 10,000 passes were required). The network performed well on other problem simulations besides parity.

Summary

In this chapter, we have examined five network types that build their architecture during the learning process: RCE networks, Cascade Correlation Networks, the Tower and Pyramid network algorithms and the Upstart Network. The first two networks, the RCE and Cascade Correlation Networks were studied in some detail while the remaining three were briefly reviewed. These networks have the advantage of building minimum size networks for given applications using simple learning algorithms. Typically, learning is quite fast and local minima traps are avoided. The networks also tend to use a minimal number of connections and require limited computation during operation. They should be regarded as attractive alternatives to MLFF networks for many problems. These networks can suffer from some disadvantages, namely growing extra deep or broad networks for some applications. Furthermore they do not tend to generalize very well.

12
The Neocognitron Network

In this chapter, we examine an unusual type of network architecture that was originally designed to perform image processing tasks such as character recognition. Over the years, the architecture has been refined to extend its capabilities and improve its performance to more closely model parts of the human visual system. The features that make the network unique are its selective connectivity among the hierarchical layers. Simple low-level features are detected in early layers and combined to form more global objects in subsequent layers through the expansion of the input receptive field regions. The connectivity ideas have been adapted in other networks to achieve special vision processing capabilities. The chapter contains six sections. Following an introductory section, the architecture, training algorithms and operation of the basic neocognitron is described. This is followed by a description of enhanced versions of the network which includes feedback connections. The final section presents some typical applications of the neocognitron.

12.1 Introduction

One of the most remarkable pattern recognition devices is the human vision system. Through this highly complex network of sensors and signal processing neurons, humans learn to recognize objects among varied backgrounds, independent of relative location, size or orientation. Even partially occluded objects can be recognized if only a fraction of the object is visible. It has been a real challenge to vision researchers to achieve similar levels of performance with models of the visual system. While the achievements of researchers have been modest by comparison, some preliminary results do appear promising. One particular ANN

329

architecture, the neocognitron, has been shown to be capable of limited invariant pattern recognition, that is, recognition of objects independent of their location in an image, and independent of deformations or partial occlusions to the object.

The neocognitron was introduced by the Japanese researcher Kunihiko Fukushima (Fukushima and Miyake, 1982; Fukushima et al., 1983; Fukushima, 1988; Fukushima and Wake, 1991). It is an outgrowth of an earlier multilayer self-adapting (competitive learning) neural model he called the cognitron (Fukushima, 1975). The cognitron was originally proposed as a model of visual pattern recognition in the brain. It is a feedforward network that learns without a teacher (unsupervised learning), and is capable of learning complex pattern recognition tasks. Like many other vision system architectures, the cognitron is sensitive to shift, scale and other distortions in an image. If the network is trained to recognize an object at one location in an image, it would not be recognizable at another location or if it had undergone some deformation since first being learned. The neocognitron was subsequently developed to overcome these deficiencies. The neocognitron is capable of learning shift and other deformation invariant pattern recognition tasks. Both unsupervised and supervised learning paradigms are employed in these networks. Examples of both methods are described below.

The network is composed of several hierarchical layers that process signals in a forward direction. The input-layer is responsive to features at the individual cell or pixel level. Cells in higher layers learn to integrate low-level features and hence, become responsive to more global features. The integration continues to the output layer which is used to identify full objects appearing in the image, with one cell required for each object being identified. Later versions of the neocognitron also use feedback signal paths for special processing purposes. It should be noted however, that the feedback paths in the neocognitron are not used for recurrent computations in the usual sense (i.e. there are no recurrent computations performed on the input signals as in the case of a fully connected recurrent network) nor are the paths used for learning as in backpropagation networks. In the following section, we describe the feedforward version of the network. In a subsequent section, we discuss the changes and additions needed to incorporate the feedback paths for the later version which permit the network to perform specialized tasks such as image segmentation.

12.2 Architecture of the Neocognitron

The neocognitron network is a hierarchical structure consisting of several cascaded modular units. The input layer is a rectangular array of receptor neurons of light sensitive cells. The cell outputs are either binary or real valued (gray-level) in response to an input image and the array size can range from a small number of cells (8×8) to a large number (e.g. 128×128). The most common choice of array size is in the range of 16×16 to 32×32 and cell outputs are usually binary valued.

Outputs from the sensory layer are connected to the first computation layer, an S layer ("S" for simple cells as found in the primary visual cortex) which is arranged in a long rectangular array. Connections from the input to the S layer are selectively distributed and made in a special manner as described below. The output of S layer neurons are connected to C layer cells ("C" for complex neurons as found in the visual cortex). The S-to-C-layer connections are also organized in a special way. They receive inputs from small configured regions of the preceding S layer. The remaining modules of the network are made up of pairs of S followed by C layers, with the final layer, a C layer, acting as a category layer of cells. Each cell in the final layer corresponds to a different object or class of objects. To distinguish between the different layers, we label them from input to output as U, $S1$, $C1$, $S2$, $C2$ and so on to the final C layer, the category layer. The basic architecture of the neocognitron is illustrated in Figure 12.1 where an input and four pairs of S and C layers make up the network. The actual number of layers in a network will vary, depending on the specific application. In general, more complex patterns require networks with more layers. Recognition of a greater number of objects requires layers composed of more densely populated cells.

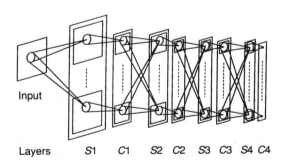

Layers $S1$ $C1$ $S2$ $C2$ $S3$ $C3$ $S4$ $C4$

Figure 12.1   Basic Structure of the Neocognitron

The input layer U is the two-dimensional array of light sensitive photoreceptor cells on the left. Succeeding layers of S cells are rectangular arrays of feature-extracting cells. Rectangular layers of C cells are inserted after the S layers to allow for positional errors in the features. The alternating layers of S and C cells with feature extraction being performed by S cells followed by compensation for shift by C cells in stages is effective for deformation-invariant pattern recognition.

In Figure 12.2, only the first three layers of a network have been presented to illustrate more details of the architecture.

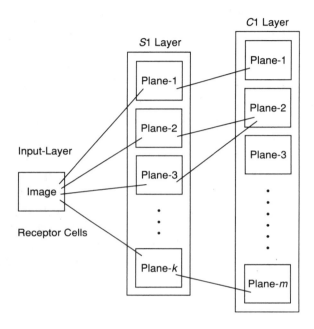

Figure 12.2   The First S and C Layers with Their Corresponding Planes of Cells

Referring to the figure, it will be noted that the $S1$ layer is composed of several sublayers or rectangular planes of cells. These planes, called S planes, play a special role in detecting low level features in the image. Each plane of cells in the layer is trained to respond to a separate, low-level pattern feature. Therefore, a network will have more planes in the $S1$ layer than the number of primitive features that need to be recognized in the input layer. Primitive features for example, might consist of short line segments occurring at different orientations as illustrated in Figure 12.3.

All cells within a single S plane are homogeneous, they respond to the same feature. This is accomplished by connecting each cell in the plane to a small group of cells from the previous layer, where each group has the same spatial configuration of elements in the previous layer, but come from a different (parallel shifted) region of the layer. Thus, to be specific, if each cell in an $S1$ plane is

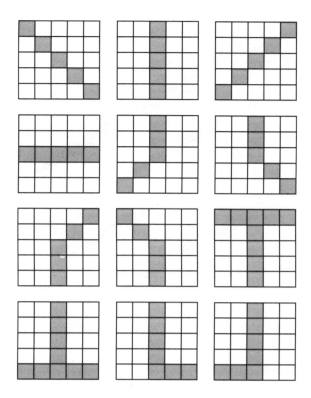

Figure 12.3   Typical Low-Level Features Detected in the Different $S1$ Planes

responsive to the same low-level feature and the connections to each cell in the $S1$ plane come from different, but covering configurations in the input layer, at least one cell in that plane will respond whenever the feature is present in the input layer, independent of its location. A cell in the following $C1$ plane receives inputs from a number of cells grouped together in a small region of the preceding $S1$ plane so that any cell in the $S1$ group producing an output stimulates the cell in the $C1$ plane. Therefore, the cell in the $C1$ plane responds to an input pattern even though the location of the pattern is shifted in the input array. In other words, the $C1$ plane cells respond to the same features as $S1$ plane cells, but they are tolerant of positional shift in the input patterns. This accounts for the network's invariance to shift and other deformations.

An example of the connections for small 4×4 square configurations of cells from the input layer to a single $S1$ layer plane of cells is illustrated in Figure 12.4. Only four groups of connections are shown for simplicity to illustrate the receptive

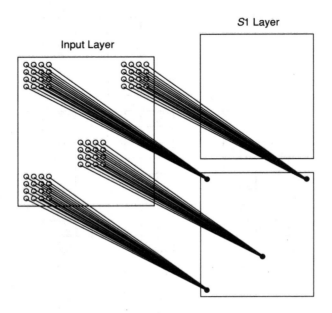

Figure 12.4   Input Connections to One of the S1 Planes

fields for different cells in one of the S1 planes. To complete the connectivity patterns in Figure 12.4, the second cell (not shown) from the upper left corner of the S1 plane would have connections from the square configuration of cells in the input layer shifted one column of cells to the right of the upper left corner. The third cell over from the upper left corner of the S1 plane would receive inputs from the upper left 4 × 4 square configuration shifted two columns to the right and so on to the final 4 × 4 group in the upper part of the input layer. The S1 plane cell directly below the upper left corner cell receives its input from the upper left 4 × 4 configuration of cells in the input layer shifted down one row and so on. The rightmost groups (bottommost groups) of configurations can be connected to "wrap around" the input layer by connecting columns (rows) of cells from the extreme right (bottom) with columns (rows) of the extreme left (top). This will give continuous input for all points in the image. Each of the other S1 planes have the same connectivity patterns as the one just described, but are responsive to different low-level features. It should be noted that the S plane cell configuration connections need not be square nor even rectangular (e.g. oval or circular). Different configurations are workable provided the input layer is completely "covered."

The connectivity patterns for subsequent C layer to S layer cells are similar to the input to $S1$ layer, but the receptive fields become successively larger so that deeper S layer cells learn to respond to more global features in the input.

As the receptive field in the input layer is increased with the layer number, the number of connections from the S layers to the C layers are gradually reduced until the final C layer is reached where each plane consists of a single cell only. The actual connectivity of the network will vary with the specific application. For purposes of illustration, an example of the network connections for a handwritten character recognition application is given in Table 12.1 (Fukushima and Wake, 1991).

Table 12.1   Network Connections for a Handwritten Character Recognition Application

Layer	Plane Array Size	Number of Planes
U	19 × 19	1
$S1$	19 × 19	12
$C1$	21 × 21	8
$S2$	21 × 21	80
$C2$	13 × 13	33
$S3$	13 × 13	97
$C3$	7 × 7	64
$S4$	3 × 3	47
$C4$	1 × 1	35

Note that the number of low-level features being recognized in the $S1$ layer is only 12. Also, unlike some networks, the connections in this one fan-out in early layers before they fan-in in the last few layers. The spatial configuration of cells from the input layer U to the $S1$ layer is a 3 × 3 square. Subsequent C-layer-to-S-layer configurations are also square with sizes of 7 × 7, 5 × 5, and 3 × 3, respectively. A total number of 70,045 cells (S, C, V, and receptor cells) were used to recognize the 36 alphanumeric characters in this application.

Suppose the network has been trained to recognize some complex objects such as one of the letters A, B or C. When one of these objects is presented at the input layer, cells in several $S1$ planes will become excited. The cells responding to the input are determined by the combination of low-level features that make up the object and the relative location at which the object is presented to the input. Only cells in those planes which are sensitive to the low-level features contained in the object are excited. These concepts are illustrated in Figure 12.5 where the letter A has been presented to the network input.

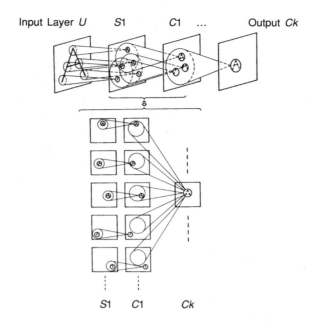

Figure 12.5   Low-Level Feature Recognition by Multiple $S1$ Planes
(From Fukushima, 1988. © 1988 IEEE. Courtesy of Professor K. Fukushima.)

In the $S1$ layer, low-level features such as the ^ (top part of the letter A) are detected in one of the top planes as illustrated. Other features are detected in other planes. When combined, these features stimulate cells in higher S layers until eventually the complete letter is recognized in the final C layer.

Weights on input connections to S layer cells are adaptable. They are trained to be responsive to pattern features. On the other hand, weights on connections from S layer to C layer cells are fixed and unmodifiable. The C cell weights are predetermined and fixed prior to the learning phase. There are actually two types of S layer cells and two types of C layer cells: excitatory and inhibitory. Excitatory cells for the S and C layers are labeled as U_S and U_C and the inhibitory cells as V_S and V_C respectively. The connectivity of the cells is illustrated in Figure 12.6. The method of combining and processing input signals by different cells is described below.

As noted above, different $S1$ layer cells respond to primitive features in their receptive field of the input layer. The responsive cells produce a positive output signal which is propagated forward to the $C1$ cells which combine and "blur" the inputs. The $C1$ layer cells responding to the inputs, also produce positive output signals which are propagated on to $S2$ layer cells which are responsive to

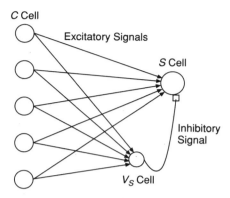

Figure 12.6   Connections from *C* Layer Plane Cells to *S* Layer Cells

combinations of the primitive features in the input image. They are trained to respond to these higher-level (combined) features. The responsive $S2$ layer cells produce positive output signals which are passed on to the $C2$ cells and so on until the final *C* layer is reached. At each stage of processing, the *S* layer cells respond to more global features and the following *C* layer cells blur the inputs adding further tolerance to shift and distortion in the image. Since the receptive field grows with each layer of processing, the number of cells in subsequent planes is correspondingly reduced.

The final *C* layer cells act as gnostic cells with only one cell per plane. These cells have receptive fields that cover the complete input layer *U*. They respond to the most global features, complete objects. To summarize, the cells in the layers are connected in a cascade and the deeper the layer, the larger the receptive field becomes for each cell in that layer. Likewise, the density of the cells in each cell plane decreases with the depth proportional to the increase in receptive field size. In the final *C* layer, the receptive field of the individual cells cover the whole input layer. The process of incrementally combining low-level features into higher-level features is illustrated in Figure 12.5 where several features of the letter A are combined.

12.3 Training the Neocognitron

Training in the neocognitron can be either supervised or unsupervised. In either case, only the *S* layer input connections are adaptable. *C* layer weights are predetermined and fixed for given applications. The training process proceeds layer by layer from the $S1$ layer to the final S layer. Initially, the weights on all S-cell connections are set to small, but different, positive values. The C-cell weights are set to fixed positive values. Training patterns are then presented to the network input in any given order. Cells in the different $S1$ planes will respond competitively to the training pattern with varying strengths depending on their initial weight values. Cells which have the strongest response to the stimulus are chosen, and at most one cell from each plane is then selected to act as a "representative" for the plane. The representative from among all the $S1$ planes with the strongest output is then selected for weight adjustment during the learning process. The selected cell then learns to become even more responsive to the stimulus. The weights of all other cells in the winning cell plane are set equal to the representative cell's weights during training.

When a new pattern is presented to the network, a cell in a different plane will become the winner since the first winning cell has been adapted to respond to a different feature. Again, the new winning cell is adapted to become more responsive to the pattern feature and other cells in the winning cell plane have their weights set equal to the winning cell's weights. The process is repeated for all the training patterns, each time selecting a different plane to become responsive to the pattern feature. In this way, all the representative cells become more sensitive to a given pattern and less responsive to other patterns, so eventually each plane will contain cells that all respond in the same way to a single, but different pattern feature. Thus, all cells in the same $S1$ plane are trained to be responsive to the same input pattern feature, but have connections from different locations in the input array.

Because of the shift in position of the input connections from the input array to different cells in an $S1$ plane, the location of a stimulus pattern does not reduce the effectiveness of the recognition process. At least some cells in a given $S1$ plane will be excited if the feature appears somewhere in the input (image) array. This special connectivity of the input-to-$S1$ layer gives the neocognitron the ability to detect patterns independent of location in the image, invariant to shift and some distortion.

The output signals from all cells employed in the neocognitron are nonnegative, real-valued. There are actually four different types of cells in the neocognitron: S cells, C cells and V_S and V_C cells. S and V_S cells are found only in S layers and C and V_C cells are found only in C layers. The S and C cells are excitatory cells and the V_S and V_C cells are inhibitory. A typical S and V_S cell is illustrated in Figure 12.6. The V_S cell receives inputs from the same C cells as the S cell, but has fixed weights on its connections.

Input signals to S cells then, are either excitatory or inhibitory. Excitatory inputs x_i tend to increase the output of the cell, while inhibitory inputs v suppress the output. The excitatory input signals are multiplied by the corresponding weights w_i and added to produce a net signal $e = \Sigma_i x_i w_i$. The single inhibitory input v is multiplied by the adjustable weight b to produce the signal $h = bv$. The e and h signals are then combined to produce the signal y, where

$$y = r\varphi \left[\frac{1 + \sum\limits_i x_i w_i}{1 + \dfrac{r}{r+1} bv} \right] = r\varphi \left[\frac{1 + e}{\dfrac{2r+1}{r+1} h} \right]$$

where r is a positive constant that determines the efficiency of the inhibition by the V_S cells. The output from the S cell is then transformed to produce the activation value $y = r\varphi(z)$, where

$$\varphi(z) = \max(0,\, z) = \begin{cases} z & \text{for } z \geq 0 \\ 0 & \text{for } z < 0 \end{cases}$$

The output from the V_S cell is given by

$$v = \left(\sum_i c_i\, x_i^2 \right)^{1/2}$$

The output function y is shaped somewhat like an S-shaped curve similar to a hyperbolic tangent function.

C cells have outputs given by

$$u = \phi \left[\sum_j d_j y_j \right]$$

where the d_j are fixed weights and y_j the input signals from the preceding S layer. The index j runs over the connections from the S-to-C-layer cells. The activation function φ for the C cell uses a saturation function ϕ, where

$$\varphi(y) = \begin{cases} \dfrac{y}{\alpha + y} & \text{for } y \geq 0 \\ 0 & \text{for } y < 0 \end{cases}$$

and α is a positive constant which determines the degree of saturation of the output.

During training, the winning cell weights, on both the excitatory and inhibitory connections are increased according to the following adaptation rule

$$\Delta w_i = q w_i x_i$$
$$\Delta b = q v$$

where q is a positive learning rate constant that determines the speed of reinforcement.

Once the $S1$ layer weights have been adapted for all low-level pattern features the $S2$ layer weights are adjusted in the same way. Due to the connectivity configurations leading up to the $S2$ cells, these cells respond to more global features, combinations of the $S1$ layer's low-level features. The weight update rule for all S layers is the same as for the $S1$ layer and the training process the same except that the features each layer learns to become responsive to become more global as the layer number increases. The learning process is complete when all S layers have been trained for all patterns. Typically, this requires several presentations of each training pattern at the input layer. The patterns can be presented in any order, including multiple presentations of the same pattern.

When training has been completed, S cells become responsive to a single feature and lose their responsiveness to other features. They receive excitatory signals indicating the existence of only the relevant feature to be extracted. If an irrelevant feature is presented, the inhibitory signal from the V_S cell becomes stronger than the direct excitatory signals from the C cells and the response of the S cell is suppressed. In this way, the V_S cells "watch" for the existence of irrelevant features. The V_S cells help the S cells differentiate between relevant and irrelevant features and increase the selectivity of feature extraction in the network.

Supervised training can take on different forms, but in general proceeds sequentially from lower to higher layers as in the case of unsupervised training. Training starts with the first adaptable layer, $S1$ and ends with the last S layer. Training for each S layer is completed before the next highest S layer is trained. Since one form of supervised training is described below under applications, we postpone that description until later. The training described later is for an application which involves handwritten character recognition. The method described is typical of all supervised training methods used.

12.4 Enhancements to the Neocognitron

Enhanced versions of the neocognitron have incorporated feedback paths from the output recognition layer to preceding layers to facilitate autoassociative recall and the sequential recognition of multiple objects in the same image. The feedback signals perform a kind of attention focusing operation so that a single learned object can be segmented and identified, following which the system becomes non-responsive to that object. It can then shift attention and become responsive to a second object, and so on until every learned object within the image has been recognized in sequence. We too perform this type of selective attentional focusing when observing multiple objects in our field of view. We concentrate on one object at a time, switching attention to other objects of interest.

As in the basic neocognitron network, the feedforward paths in the enhanced network perform the function of pattern recognition. The feedback paths perform the added functions of selective attention, associative recall and object segmentation. The overall signal flow paths are illustrated in Figure 12.7.

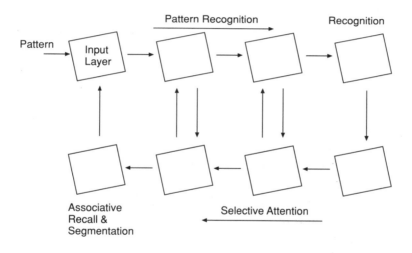

Figure 12.7   Signal Flow Paths in the Enhanced Neocognitron

A portion of a single signal path of cells from the initial and terminal arrays of cells is illustrated in Figure 12.8 where both forward and backward paths are shown. Cells denoted as Ck are the recognition cells in the final C layer, whereas cells labeled as Ws, Wc and Wv are feedback path cells that play roles similar to S, C and V cells respectively, in the forward paths. The W cells also have variable and fixed weight on their input connections and excitatory and inhibitory output signals comparable to the corresponding S, C and V cells in the forward paths with the Ws and Wc cells exchanging roles.

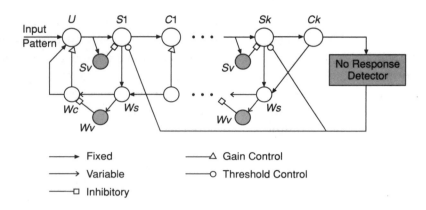

Figure 12.8   Interconnections Between Cells in Forward and Backward Signal Paths

Once an object has been recognized, the output of the recognition layer, one of the Ck cells, is propagated back to lower layers through the feedback paths stage-by-stage to the recall layer. The feedback signals follow the same route backward as the feedforward signals. This is made possible by the cells responding in the feedforward paths which then gate the feedback signals. In this way, the backward signal flow is guided by the forward signals so they reach the same starting location as the forward signals. Since backward signals are propagated back by the single activated Ck cell in the output layer, only the signal components corresponding to the recognized pattern reach the recall layer. Consequently, the recall layer signals reinforce the recognition process resulting in a form of autoassociative recall and object segmentation.

Feedback path weights are similar to feedforward path weights and the two types are reinforced together during the training process. (Actually, Ws cells have fixed and Wc cells variable weights to facilitate the signal gating process. There are also some differences in the connectivity patterns to contain and direct the feedback signals back along the same path as the forward signals as opposed to fanning out in the forward direction for shift invariance.) The net result is that objects that induce an excitatory response in the forward direction tend to induce an "expectation" response in the backward direction, resulting in mutual signal reinforcement or resonance (see Chapter 15). This process also assists in reducing noise in the image, a form of image cleaning.

The no-response detector at the far right of Figure 12.8 monitors the output of the recognition cells. When a no-response state is detected, this unit sends signals to the feature detecting S cells at all stages to lower their threshold and make them more responsive to features in the input layer. This helps to activate at least one gnostic cell in the output.

When two or more patterns are simultaneously presented to the input layer, two or more output cells may initially become activated at the start. All but one will soon stop responding, however, due to competitive lateral inhibition connections - among all the S layer cells in the forward paths. When all but the one cell stops responding, only the backward signal components corresponding to the activated cell reach the recall layer. These signals result in a segmentation of the single pattern, even if it is a deformed version of the learned pattern. The backward path signals also increase the gain of the forward path signals to enhance the selective attention paid to the one pattern. A momentary interruption of the backward signal results in switching of the selective attention to another pattern. This is due to a loss of signal gain in the C layer cells which require facilitating support from the Wc cells in the backward path. Consequently, another set of input and C cells will become activated and a' different pattern in the image recognized and segmented. Through a repetition of this process, attention is switched to each of the learned patterns in the image, even when they overlap somewhat. This selective recognition and segmentation is illustrated in Figure 12.9 where a network has been trained to recognize five characters 0, 1, 2, 3, and 4 (Fukushima, 1988).

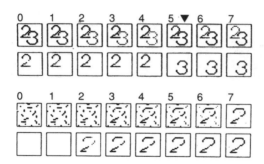

Figure 12.9   Recognition Steps for Multiple Pattern Inputs (Top Row) and Segmented Network
Output (Lower Row)
(From Fukushima, 1988. © 1988 IEEE. Courtesy of Professor K. Fukushima.)

In the top part of Figure 12.9, the two numbers 2 and 3 are presented to the input receptor simultaneously and then sequentially recognized and segmented as described above. In the lower part of the figure, a 2 is recognized and "cleaned" from among a background of random noise.

We conclude this chapter with a section on neocognitron applications.

12.5 Neocognitron Applications

Most of the published applications for the neocognitron have been related to vision or pattern recognition, including handwritten character recognition and various types of objects in specialized images. We briefly describe three such typical applications in this section.

Recognition of Edge-Junction Types of Objects

Lee and Patterson (1991) have developed a hybrid neocognitron network capable of recognizing wire frame models of office types of objects, objects that are composed of regions bounded by straight lines and junctions such as file cabinets, tables, desk lamps and so on. Examples of the objects the network learned to recognize are illustrated in Figure 12.10.

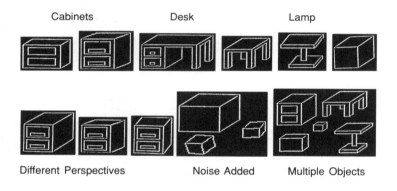

Figure 12.10   Examples of Office Furniture Objects Recognized by the Network

Low-level features learned by the network are junctions which are the structural primitives of the objects. Some 28 different junctions were used to make up the low-level features. The junctions learned and responded to by the first two layers are combined to form regions in the second pair of layers. In the third pair of layers, the regions are combined to make up enclosed spatial planes of sub-objects and the final pair of layers respond to the complete objects. These combining operations are illustrated in Figure 12.11 where a filing cabinet is recognized. The input layer consisted of 128 × 128 pixels. Subsequent layers have fewer connections with the final layer being "created" during the training phase as each new object is learned.

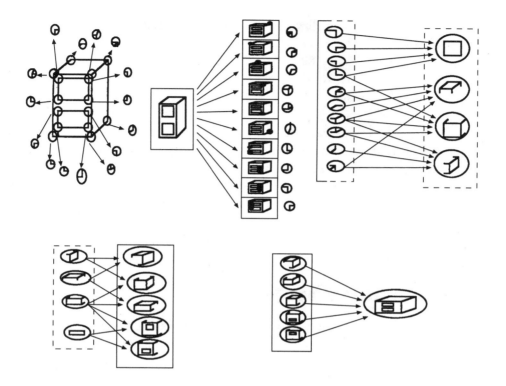

Figure 12.11   Feature-to-Object Recognition by Successive Layers

Because of the shift and deformation invariant recognition ability of the neocognitron, the network can recognize the same object at different orientations from the one used during training and also tolerate a high level of background noise. Some success in the recognition of occluded objects were also achieved in the experiments.

Object Recognition

Menon and Heinemann (1988) trained a four-level neocognitron to recognize wire frame objects (jeeps, tanks, trucks) for shift invariance. They used an input-layer consisting of 128 × 128 pixels which were connected to six planes in the $S1$ layer. The size of each $S1$ layer was 121 × 121 cells. The remaining S and C layers also had six planes each with the following sizes (number of cells):

Layer	Plane Size	Layer	Plane Size
S1	121 × 121	S3	25 × 25
C1	62 × 62	C3	13 × 13
S2	57 × 57	S4	8 × 8
C2	30 × 30	C4	1 × 1

Although this network was capable of shift invariant recognition, it was learned that there was a trade-off between classification ability and shift invariance. Shift invariance was also dependent on the overlap between adjacent regions of input. To provide more robust performance, a deeper network is required to permit a more gradual thinning of cells. To achieve reliable classification for any image location in the input, it was estimated that a network with 15 levels would be required. The network was able to tolerate up to 30% noise in the images and still accurately classify the objects, however.

Handwritten Character Recognition

Several researchers have used neocognitron networks for the recognition of alphanumeric characters, both machine and handwritten characters. In Section 12.2, the connections for a network capable of accurate recognition of 35 handwritten characters (the numbers 0 through 9 and 25 letters of the English alphabet with the letter "O" being excluded) was developed by Fukushima and Wake (1991). Examples of some deformed characters their network correctly recognized are shown in Figure 12.12. This network was trained by teacher supervision which we describe next.

The Supervised Training Process

This network was trained by supervised learning. Training proceeds from lower to higher level layers as in the case of unsupervised learning. Higher layers are trained only after lower layers are completely trained. All adjustable weights are initially set to zero. A teacher then selects the S cell plane to be trained. A training pattern is presented to the input layer U and the teacher chooses a cell within the selected plane to act as a "seed" cell. The seed cell is pointed to by the position of its receptive field center. The variable weights of the seed cell are reinforced to become responsive to the relevant connections determined by the features to be learned. The amount of reinforcement of each input connection to the seed cell is proportional to the intensity of the response of the cell from which the relevant connection is leading. As a result of this learning principle, the weights are made to grow to form a template which exactly matches the spatial distribution of the

Figure 12.12   Examples of Deformed Characters Recognized by the Neocognitron
(From Fukushima, 1988. © 1988 IEEE. Courtesy of Professor K. Fukushima.)

responses of the cells in the preceding layer. In this way, the seed cell acquires the ability to extract the feature of the stimulus during the training. All other cells in the plane with the seed cell follow the seed cell like a crystal growth. Their weights are reinforced to follow the seed cell, and hence, have the same spatial distribution as those of the seed cell. Thus, all cells in the plane learn to extract the same feature, but at different locations.

Layer $S1$ is trained to extract simple line components of different orientations similar to those of Figure 12.3. Only 12 patterns were used to train the 12 planes of $S1$ layer and each of the training patterns is presented to the network only once. The cell at the center of the cell plane to be trained is always chosen as the seed cell. Since the receptive field of each cell in this plane is 3×3, only the central 3×3 area of each training pattern is effective during training. The $S2$ layer cells have receptive fields of 9×9. There are 80 planes in this layer which correspond to various combinations of the features used to train the $S1$ layer. The $S3$ layer is trained to be responsive to more global features. This layer combines features from the $S2$ layer using 97 cell planes. The final S layer, $S4$ is trained to recognize complete characters. This layer has 47 cell planes and different copies of most characters are used to train the layer to help deformation invariant learning. One of the main advantages of supervised learning as used for this network is the short training time required. Once the training set had been created, only 13 minutes was required to train the network on a SUN SPARC station. By comparison, multilayer feedforward networks trained to do the same task using backpropagation required three days training time (le Cun et al., 1990).

Summary

We have described the architecture and operation of the neocognitron network, a hybrid hierarchical multilayer feedforward (and feedbackward) network that has been motivated by neural cells found in the visual cortex. The network consists of several stages of S and C layer pairs. The S layers act as feature detectors, while the C layers perform a type of feature blurring on the S cell outputs to make the network less sensitive to shift and deformations in the image patterns. The $S1$ layer learns to respond to low-level features while higher numbered layers respond to combinations of low-level or more global features until the final C layer where complete objects are recognized. The S and C layers are arranged in rectangular planes of cells and have connections that are specially arranged in spatial groups to achieve shift invariance in the input patterns.

The neocognitron can learn in either a supervised or unsupervised mode. In either case, only the weights on input connections to S layers are adaptable. C layer connection weights are fixed. Learning is carried out layer by layer in a competitive manner where the cell responding the most to the training pattern becomes the representative for the plane of cells and has its weights adjusted to become more responsive to the pattern. Weights on connections to C layer cells are fixed. Inhibitory cells also play a role in the learning and recognition process.

Enhanced versions of the neocognitron network permit the sequential recognition and segmentation of multiple objects in an image. These networks utilize special feedback paths to perform the segmentation and sequential associative recall operations.

These networks have been used mainly in invariant character and object recognition applications.

13
Stochastic-Based Networks

The title of this chapter should not be misinterpreted. The networks covered here perform stochastic modeling. They do not operate in a probabilistic manner, as in the case of the Boltzmann Machine described in Chapter 10. We have seen several examples of networks that build stochastic models of their environment. For example, multilayer feedforward networks with backpropagation training build nonlinear nonparametric regression models. They do so incrementally in a heuristic manner and are subject to local minima traps during the training. What sets the networks in this chapter apart from these other networks is the direct use of nonparametric estimation methods in building the network. Furthermore, the training process is direct, constructive and very fast. There are no local minima problems. This chapter is, in a sense, a continuation of Chapter 11, since the classes of network types described here are also self-growing. They grow an inner mapping layer during the supervised learning process adding a node for each training pattern or for each cluster of patterns.

13.1 Introduction

For many years, statistical techniques were the accepted approach to pattern recognition tasks. Methods based on linear regression, clustering, correlation and Bayesian classifiers were the commonly accepted standards for recognition and classification tasks. With the introduction of neural network computing, that paradigm has changed. We have already seen several instances where ANNs perform certain types of recognition through a form of statistical analysis. In this chapter, we extend these methods to include two network architectures that perform stochastic modeling of the pattern environment, but in a more direct way. In both networks, pattern training samples are used to create nonparametric estimation models of the sample distributions. The networks are constructed through the addition of inner-layer nodes that represent the statistical properties of the training patterns. The output of these nodes are then combined to produce the desired mapping of input to output. The networks both operate deterministically, and not probabilistically as in the case of the Boltzmann Machine (Chapter 10). They share the same basic connectivity and architectures. Both networks were introduced by the same researcher, Donald Specht, a student of Bernard Widrow (Chapters 2 and 4). We begin with a description of the first network proposed by Specht (1988, 1990), the probabilistic neural network.

13.2 Probabilistic Neural Network

The probabilistic neural network (PNN) was introduced by Donald Specht (1988, 1990). This network is based on concepts used in classical pattern recognition problems. In particular, the PNN models the popular Bayesian classifier (Mood and Graybill, 1962), a technique which minimizes the expected risk of classifying patterns in the wrong category. The operation of Bayesian classifiers can be described as follows. Let $\mathbf{x}$ be an n-dimensional input vector characterizing objects which belong to one of K possible classes, and let $f_1(\mathbf{x})$, $f_2(\mathbf{x})$, ..., $f_K(\mathbf{x})$ be probability density functions for the K class populations, respectively. Let $p_1, p_2, ...,$ p_K be the *a priori* probabilities that a feature vector $\mathbf{x}$ belongs to the corresponding class. We want a decision function $d(\mathbf{x}) = C_i$, $i = 1, 2, ..., K$ that classifies $\mathbf{x}$ as belonging to class C_i that is best in some sense. For example, we might define best as a function that classifies input patterns with minimal risk of incorrect classification. Let $L_1, L_2, ..., L_K$ be loss functions (possibly subjective in nature) associated with making a wrong decision such that loss L_i is incurred whenever $d(\mathbf{x}) = C_i$, $i \neq j$ and $x \in C_j$. The loss of a correct decision is taken to be zero. The Bayes' decision rule for this type of classification problem compares the product probabilities

$$p_1 L_1 f_1(\mathbf{x}), \ p_2 L_2 f_2(\mathbf{x}), \ ..., \ p_K L_K f_K(\mathbf{x})$$

and chooses the class corresponding to the largest product value. Thus, if

$$p_i L_i f_i(\mathbf{x}) > p_j L_j f_j(\mathbf{x}) \qquad \text{for } j = 1, 2, ..., K, \ i \neq j \tag{13.1}$$

the decision rule assigns $\mathbf{x}$ to class C_i. Variations of the selection criteria may also be used, including the use of a cost or other function to penalize the choice of an incorrect classification.

One of the main criticisms of Bayes' classification techniques is the lack of information about the class probability distributions. They are usually unknown and must be estimated in some way. The *a priori* probabilities p_i may be known or can easily be estimated directly from a sample of the pattern vectors, but the probability density functions $f_i(\mathbf{x})$ are generally more difficult to estimate. Of course, one could assume some distributional form (e.g. a normal distribution) and then estimate the unknown parameters using standard statistical techniques. Without any real knowledge of the distributional form it is more appropriate to use nonparametric estimation methods. One powerful nonparametric technique is based on the use of Parzen windows (Parzen, 1962) which are used to construct a family of estimates from kernals. The general form of the estimator is given by the following equation

$$f_n(x) = \frac{1}{n\lambda} \sum_{i=1}^{n} \varphi\left(\frac{x - x_i}{\sigma}\right) \qquad \cdot \qquad (13.2)$$

where the x_i are independent, identically distributed random variables with absolutely continuous distribution function. The weighting function φ must be bounded and satisfy the following conditions

$$\int_{-\infty}^{\infty} \left|\varphi(y)\right| dy < \infty$$

$$\lim_{y \to \infty} \left|y\varphi(y)\right| = 0$$

and

$$\int_{-\infty}^{\infty} \varphi(y) dy = 1$$

The function $\sigma = \sigma(n)$ must be chosen such that

$$\lim_{n \to \infty} \sigma(n) = 0, \qquad \lim_{n \to \infty} n\sigma(n) = \infty$$

Parzen has shown that these estimators are consistent. They asymptotically converge to the underlying distribution at the sample points when it is smooth and continuous. Parzen's results have also been extended to the multivariate distribution case by Cacoullos (1966). One useful form of the weighting kernal function φ is the multivariate exponential (Gaussian) function. For this case, equation (13.2) takes the form

$$f_i(\mathbf{x}) = \frac{1}{2\pi^{n/2}\sigma^n} \frac{1}{k_i} \sum_{j=1}^{k_i} \exp\left[-\frac{(\mathbf{x} - \mathbf{x}_{ij})^T(\mathbf{x} - \mathbf{x}_{ij})}{2\sigma^2}\right] \tag{13.3}$$

where n is the dimension of the random variable, k_i is the number of pattern sample points in class C_i, and $\mathbf{x}_{ij}$ is jth sample belonging to class i. The coefficient σ is a smoothing parameter which must be determined experimentally. This particular estimator is a sum or average of k_i exponential terms (Gaussian functions), one for each sample in the given class. The shape of the summed exponentials is determined by the smoothing constant σ. A large value of σ results in a flat curved surface, while a small σ produces narrow peaked curves. The choice of σ will affect the estimation error, but in general the procedure is not too sensitive to variations in the value (Specht, 1988). Examples of the estimator surface for different values of σ are illustrated in Figure 13.1.

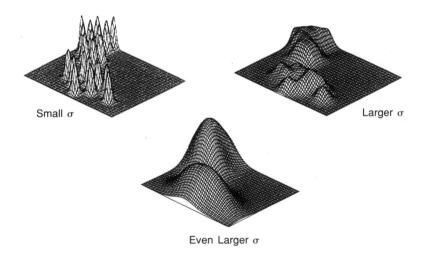

Small σ Larger σ

Even Larger σ

Figure 13.1   Plots of the Parzen Estimator for Different Values of σ
(Courtesy of Dr. William Meisel.)

The architecture of the PNN as proposed by Specht (1988, 1990) is an implementation of the Bayes' classifier using the Parzen window estimator (equation (13.3)) to estimate the probability distributions of the class samples. The use of an exponential (or other) Parzen type kernal for activation functions permit the PNN to learn to build nonlinear decision boundaries which approach the optimal Bayes' classifier decision surfaces.

The architecture of the PNN is illustrated in Figure 13.2. It consists of an input layer followed by three computational layers. For simplicity, only two summation-layer units and one output-layer unit are shown in the figure. Hence, the network shown in Figure 13.2 is a two-class classifier. For a multiclass classifier, the network will have more than one output unit and additional summation units, one for each class.

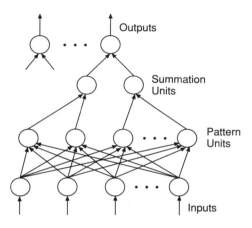

Figure 13.2   The Probabilistic Neural Network Architecture
(Courtesy of Dr. Donald Specht.)

All input patterns are normalized to have unit length before processing. The input layer is used to distribute the input patterns to the next layer, the pattern unit layer. The pattern-layer units are fully connected to the input layer through adjustable weights. The pattern-layer has K units, one for each training pattern. The weight values of units in this layer are set equal to the different training patterns and the weight vectors are also normalized to unit length. Pattern-layer units perform a dot product on the input pattern vector and the unit's weight vector. Since both are normalized to unit length, this is equivalent to performing the product operation

$$(\mathbf{x} - \mathbf{w}_i)^T(\mathbf{x} - \mathbf{w}_i)$$

which is the same form of the exponent in equation (13.3). The activation functions of the pattern-layer units are of the exponential type like those used in equation (13.3). The above argument, which is a measure of the distance between the input pattern $\mathbf{x}$ and the unit's weight vector $\mathbf{w}_i$ are exponentiated by the pattern units before passing the output to the summation layer. Thus, the output of the jth pattern-layer unit is given by

$$f(\mathbf{x}, \mathbf{w}_j) = \exp\left(\frac{\sum\limits_{i=1}^{n}(x_i - w_{ij})^2}{2\sigma^2}\right)$$

The pattern-layer outputs are selectively connected to units in the summation layer depending on the class of patterns they represent. The summation units simply sum the pattern-layer outputs to complete the computation of equation (13.3). Since each summation unit collects inputs from pattern units of the same class, their output is an estimate of the class probability density function given by equation (13.3) where the kernals are centered on the training samples (the $\mathbf{w}_i$). The output units produce a binary output signal. These units each have two input connections. The units compute the product of the summation units output and the weight coefficient C_k ($k = 1, 2$),

$$C_k = -\frac{p_2 L_2}{p_1 L_1} \cdot \frac{k_1}{k_2}$$

where k_1 and k_2 are the numbers of patterns from the two classes, 1 and 2, respectively.

One of the main advantages of the PNN is the speed with which it can be trained. No iterative procedures are used and no feedback paths are required in the training process. In a comparison made between a multilayer feedforward network using backpropagation (BP) training and a PNN, the PNN was trained 200,000 times as fast as the BP network (Specht, 1990). The application was ship hull classification for which the performance of both networks was equivalent. In training the PNN, only a single pass through the training set is needed. Thus, the decision boundaries can be modified in real-time using new data as it becomes available. PNN networks also tolerate noisy samples and they can work with sparse samples too. A PNN can work with time-varying statistics, since old patterns can be overwritten with new patterns. Finally, the network architecture is such that it can be implemented in hardware using artificial neurons that operate in parallel.

PNNs need not be used for classification tasks only. They can also be used to estimate *a posteriori* probabilities, probabilities that an input pattern **x** belongs to category C, $P[C|\mathbf{x}]$. They can also be used as associative memories and for other general mapping applications. For example, when used as an associative memory, and the category of a partially complete pattern is input, the unknown inputs can be varied to identify the values that maximize the network output.

One of the main disadvantages of the PNN is that the size of the pattern layer can grow very large when large training sets are used. To alleviate this problem, class prototype patterns can be substituted for large groups of individual patterns provided the prototypes are representative estimators of the group probabilities. In a set of experiments conducted by Burrascano (1991), learning vector quantization (see Chapter 14 for a description of LVQ) methods were used to reduce the number of pattern layer nodes by factors of 10 and 100 using the LVQ code vectors to approximate the group probability distributions. The classification performance results were less accurate by only a margin of 2–3% for the reduced nodes cases. Therefore, this alternative should be considered when very large data sets are available.

13.3 Probabilistic Neural Network Applications

One interesting application of the PNN is in the classification of vibration signatures collected from a steel manufacturing mill. Vibration monitoring and analysis of data from "laminar flow" table rolls in a sheet steel manufacturing mill makes it possible to detect impending faults, and hence, to take corrective measures beforehand. In an application carried out by Loskiewicz-Buczak and Uhrig (1993), data are collected from sensors at nine locations on each of nine machines. Signals acquired from the machines are correlated, but different due to sensor and fault locations. The spectrum of each sensor output is generated using Fast Fourier Transform techniques and the 150 coefficient points collected are stored in a database. The data set contains signatures from the 49 machines for which each type of fault has been identified. Faulty operating conditions include: misalignment, looseness wear, outboard bearing damage, improper lubrication, and some double and triple faults such as misalignment and looseness and other combinations such as misalignment, looseness and outboard bearing damage.

Multisensor fusion of the signals is used for the fault classification tasks. An illustration for the fusion and classification for two sensor signals is illustrated in Figure 13.3.

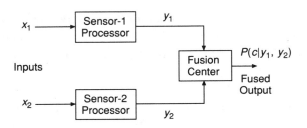

Figure 13.3   Fusion and Classification for Two Sensor Inputs

Each sensor can produce a decision based on the data from one of the input sensors. The "fusion center" of the overlapping classes is then used to make an overall classification decision. The two input vectors $\mathbf{x}_1$ and $\mathbf{x}_2$ are first transformed by the sensor processors $S1$ and $S2$. The transformed outputs $\mathbf{y}_1$ and $\mathbf{y}_2$ are then fused and the class estimate is made by the PNN according to

$$P(c|\mathbf{x}) \propto P(c|\mathbf{x}_1)P(c|\mathbf{x}_2)\left[\frac{P(c|\mathbf{y}_1, \mathbf{y}_2)}{P(c|\mathbf{y}_1)P(c|\mathbf{y}_2)}\right]$$

where $P(c|\mathbf{x}_1)$ and $P(c|\mathbf{x}_2)$ are independent classification probabilities and the term in brackets is a correction factor when correlations between $\mathbf{x}_1$ and $\mathbf{x}_2$ exist (this term has the value $1/P(c)$ in the independent case). The numerator of the correction factor is the correct Bayesian decision function for the nine sensors.

Vibration signature classification is addressed in three phases. Phase I includes the extraction of relevant features from the vibration spectra for each sensor separately and compression and transformation of the spectra using recirculation neural networks. Phase II includes classification of compressed signatures using one standard feedforward network with backpropagation (BP) (Chapter 6) per sensor and Phase III performs the fusion of decision information from the individual classifiers using a PNN. The complete system is illustrated in Figure 13.4. The recirculation networks each take a 150-point signature input from a given sensor and compresses it to a 50-point representation. This compressed signature is used as input to the feedforward BP network. There is one network for each sensor. The BP networks produce a decision on the degree a given signature belongs to each of the classes. Finally, the BP decisions are input to the fusion center, a PNN network, which performs Bayesian decision fusion and final classification.

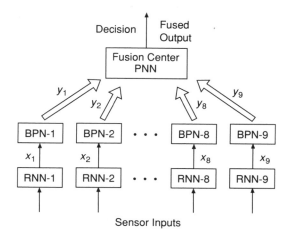

Figure 13.4   Architecture of the Complete Classification System

Classification of Electrocardiograms

Electrocardiogram analysis requires trained experts to distinguish between normal and abnormal heart conditions. The analysis amounts to a careful review of multisensor chart patterns of a patient's heart activity over a short period of time. In one study described by Specht (1967), a PNN was trained on 249 collected patterns of patients with known condition. The networks were trained to classify the patients into one of two classes: normal or abnormal. The input pattern consisted of a 46-dimensional vector. For testing, an additional 63 patterns were used. The percentage of correct classifications as a function of the smoothing parameter σ is illustrated in Figure 13.5.

Note that σ is the only parameter that must be found experimentally. Usually, a suitable value can be found from a few tests. One approach is by comparing the accuracies obtained for different values of σ when single samples are "held out" during training and then used for testing. Only a limited range of values need be tested. For example, inspection of Figure 13.5 shows that maximum diagnostic accuracy was achieved for values of σ between 4 and 6. This is a fairly wide range of values. It illustrates the relative insensitivity of the network's performance on the choice of σ, and hence, that finding a suitable value experimentally is not difficult. Indeed, it can be seen that any value in the range of 3 to 10 yields good results. Values outside this range are still much better than randomly selected classifications.

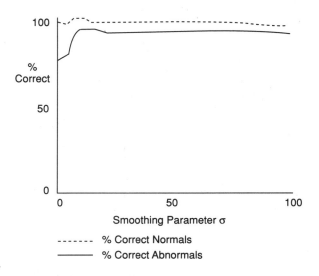

Figure 13.5   Percentage of Samples Correctly Classified by the PNN

As σ varies from 0 to ∞, the decision boundary constructed by the network changes from a nonlinear boundary representing the nearest neighbor classifier to a flat hyperplane. This gives adequate flexibility for different applications, but in general, one would normally choose a value giving good generalization, and that value can be determined experimentally.

13.4 Generalized Regression Neural Network

Statistical prediction methods are widely used for many purposes: to predict tomorrow's weather, the sales of a newly introduced product, various financial indices such as a particular stock market index, electric power consumption, the demand for durable goods and so on. Statistical regression analysis like correlation methods, is a commonly used tool for prediction. Regression analysis is used to fit a smooth curve to a number of sample data points which represents some continuously varying phenomena. The fitting technique can be used to predict the values of one or more variables on the basis of information provided by measurements on the other independent (explanatory) variables. To perform regression analysis, a functional form, which is believed to represent the relationship between the dependent and the independent variables is chosen.

The general linear model has the form

$$z_k = \mathbf{x}_k\beta + \varepsilon_k, \qquad k = 1, 2, ..., P \tag{13.4}$$

where there are P observations on the dependent variable z_k and the independent variables $\mathbf{x}_k = (\mathbf{x}_{k1}, \mathbf{x}_{k2}, ..., \mathbf{x}_{km})$ and β is an unknown vector of $m \times 1$ parameters that must be estimated. The random variable ε_k is a "disturbance" that is unobserved. The linear model given by equation (13.4) is the stochastic model assumed to hold for many prediction problems.

In performing regression analysis, the parameters defining the functional relationship must be estimated using some statistical criteria. For example, to perform a simple linear regression between two variables x and y, a straight-line functional form is assumed and the slope and intercept parameters of the line are then estimated. If the two variables are known or suspected to be linearly related, that relationship can be represented by the family of equations for a line, $y = ax + b$ where b is the y intercept and a the slope of the line. Estimates for a and b can be obtained from measured sample pairs of the variables x and y. A popular estimation criteria is least squares, that is, finding those parameter values for a line which minimize the sum of the squared differences between the observed data points and the regression line as illustrated in Figure 13.6.

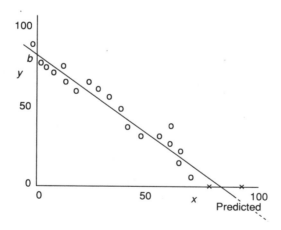

Figure 13.6   Estimating the Slope and Intercept Parameters for a Line Using Least Squares Criteria

Once estimates of the parameters are obtained, the fitted line can be used to predict values of the dependent variables for any new values of the independent variables. This is done through an interpolation between sample points or an extrapolation of the line beyond the original sample data points. An example of prediction by extrapolation is illustrated in Figure 13.6 with the dashed line extension to the fitted line. More general regression analysis includes the use of multiple independent and dependent variables and methods to accommodate nonlinear relationships among the variates. One of the flaws with the regression method, however, is the necessity to assume a functional form between the dependent and independent variables, an unknown for most problems. An incorrect assumption can result in poor, misleading predictions. The assumption of a simple linear relationship given by equation (13.4) is often unwarranted.

We are interested in performing more general, nonlinear regression analyses. For this, let $f(\mathbf{x}, z)$ be the joint probability density function of the vector random variable $\mathbf{x}$ and scalar random variable z. The regression of z on $\mathbf{x}$ is defined as the conditional mean of z given $\mathbf{x}$, that is $E[z|\mathbf{x}]$, where

$$E[z|\mathbf{x}] = \frac{\int_{-\infty}^{\infty} zf(\mathbf{x}, z)dz}{\int_{-\infty}^{\infty} f(\mathbf{x}, z)dz} \tag{13.5}$$

The joint density $f(\mathbf{x}, z)$ is usually not known, so it must be estimated from sample data points of $\mathbf{x}$ and z. Various techniques are available to estimate $f(\mathbf{x}, z)$ using measurements on $\mathbf{x}$ and z. A popular nonparametric technique is based on the Parzen (1962) window method referred to above in Section 13.2. One type of Parzen window estimator for this density function has the form given by

$$f_p(\mathbf{x}, z) = \frac{1}{(2\pi)^{(n+1)/2}\sigma^{n+1}} \frac{1}{P} \sum_{i=1}^{P} \exp\left[-\frac{(\mathbf{x} - \mathbf{x}_i)^T(\mathbf{x} - \mathbf{x}_i)}{2\sigma^2}\right] \exp\left[-\frac{(z - z_i)^2}{2\sigma^2}\right]$$

where P is the number of sample points, n is the dimension of the vector of sample points $\mathbf{x}_i$ and the argument $\mathbf{x}$, and σ is a smoothing constant. This estimator is known to be consistent, so it tends to approximate the underlying distribution closer and closer as the number of sample points P increases with convergence asymptotically under fairly nonrestrictive conditions related to continuity of the underlying distribution and σ. An interpretation of the estimator is that it is the mean of P sample probabilities, each of width σ for the sample points $\mathbf{x}_i$ and z_i. If the estimator $f_P(\mathbf{x}, z)$ is substituted for $f(\mathbf{x}, z)$ in equation (13.5), one can obtain a closed form for an estimate of the regression, denoted as $\hat{z}$. The result is given by Specht (1991) as

$$\hat{z} = \frac{\sum_{i=1}^{P} z_i \exp\left(\frac{-D_i^2}{2\sigma^2}\right)}{\sum_{i=1}^{P} \exp\left(\frac{-D_i^2}{2\sigma^2}\right)} \tag{13.6}$$

where the scalar D_i^2 is defined as

$$D_i^2 = (\mathbf{x} - \mathbf{x}_i)^T(\mathbf{x} - \mathbf{x}_i)$$

The variables z and $\hat{z}$ can both be vector valued in the above expressions with appropriate modifications being made.

The Generalized Regression Neural Network (GRNN) was introduced to perform general (linear or nonlinear) regression. As in the case of the PNN, it was also introduced by Donald Specht (1991). It is capable of performing regression analysis directly from sample data. To use this network, no assumptions are needed regarding the functional form relating the dependent and independent variables as in the case of statistical regression. The network performs the estimation directly from the underlying probability distribution of the input patterns using some of the estimation techniques described above.

Each input pattern $\mathbf{x}$ is assumed to belong to one of K clusters where the number of patterns belonging to cluster j is k_j for $k_j = 1, 2, \ldots$. Before a GRNN can be constructed, the training patterns should be grouped into known clusters. The clustering can be performed using any of several methods such as K-means, nearest neighbor or the use of an ANN such as a Kohonen SOFM or LVQ network (see Chapter 14). If the number of training patterns is not too large, each pattern can act as an exemplar, that is, each cluster contains one pattern only ($k_j = 1$ for all j). The input pattern vectors should also be scaled or normalized for better performance. Once the number of clusters and cluster centroids are known and the patterns scaled, the network can be created and trained. The network architecture and the training algorithm are designed to facilitate the regression analysis computations described above. Note that equation (13.6) applies to clusters with single patterns only. To perform regression in the general cluster case, the procedure must be modified. In that case, $\hat{z}$ is estimated by

$$\hat{z} = \frac{\sum\limits_{i=1}^{P} A_i \exp\left(\frac{-D_i^2}{2\sigma^2}\right)}{\sum\limits_{i=1}^{P} B_i \exp\left(\frac{-D_i^2}{2\sigma^2}\right)} \tag{13.7}$$

where $A_i \equiv A_i(k) = A_i(k - 1) + z_j$ and $B_i \equiv B_i(k) = B_i(k - 1) + 1$. These quantities are the values of the coefficients for cluster i after k observations. They are incremented each time a training observation z_j for cluster i is encountered.

The GRNN architecture is similar to the PNN architecture. It consists of an input-layer followed by three computational layers: pattern, summation and output-

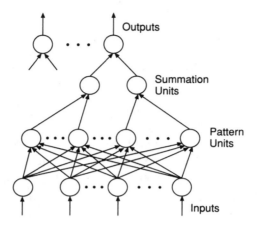

Figure 13.7 The Generalized Regression Network Architecture
(Courtesy of Dr. Donald Specht.)

layers. The basic architecture is illustrated in Figure 13.7. Compare the architecture of the GRNN in Figure 13.7 with the PNN network of Figure 13.2.

The input layer is used to distribute the input patterns to the next layer, the pattern unit layer. The pattern unit layer has K units, one for each exemplar or one for each pattern cluster. This layer is fully connected to the input layer through adjustable weights. The weight values are set equal to the exemplar patterns or to the cluster center values (centroid values). Thus, the weights on connections from the input layer to the ith pattern-layer unit has values equal to the ith (n-dimensional) cluster centroid vector.

When an input pattern $\mathbf{x}$ is presented at the input layer, the pattern-layer units compute the distance between its weight vector and the input vector. This distance is then transformed by the unit's activation function. The pattern unit's activation functions are exponential functions (Gaussian) or similar functions where the argument is the distance between $\mathbf{x}$ and the weight vector $\mathbf{w}_i$. For example, if the sum of squares of the component differences is used as the distance metric, the output of the jth pattern-layer unit is given by

$$f(\mathbf{x}, \mathbf{w}_j) = \exp\left(\frac{\sum\limits_{i=1}^{n}(x_i - w_{ij})^2}{2\sigma^2}\right) \qquad (13.8)$$

where σ is a smoothing constant. Other measures of distance besides squared Euclidean distance may also be used as well as other types of activation functions.

The output of the pattern layer is fully connected to the summation-layer units through adjustable weights. In Figure 13.7, only two summation units and one output unit have been shown for simplicity. However, additional summation and output units can be added as described below. The summation layer is composed of two types of neurons, type A and type B. If the output layer has more than one unit, say m units, there will be m type A and also m type B units in the summation layer. The summation-layer units process their inputs by performing a vector dot (scalar) product of the input from the pattern layer with their connection weight values. Type A neurons are used to represent the "desired" regression outputs for the patterns. The weights on their connections have a value equal to the sum of the samples z_i associated with cluster x_i. This gives an output from these units equal to $\hat{z}f(\mathbf{x})K$ where $\hat{z}$ is the estimate of the conditional mean of z given $\mathbf{x}$ ($E[z|\mathbf{x}]$), the regression of z on $\mathbf{x}$, $f(\mathbf{x})$ is the density function of $\mathbf{x}$ and K is a constant determined by the Parzen window used (K is not data dependent and need not be computed). The type B unit weights, on the other hand, are each equal to the number of patterns in a cluster. These units compute the quantities $f(\mathbf{x})K$ by performing a dot product on the pattern unit outputs and corresponding weights. The output layer performs a division operation on the output of the two summation-layer units to produce the estimate $\hat{z}$ of the regression of z on $\mathbf{x}$.

The smoothing parameter σ determines the decision surface boundary. It must be determined experimentally. Small values of σ give narrow peaked surfaces that fit well near sample points. Larger values of σ result in flatter, smoother surfaces. Good generalization, requires a trade-off between the two extremes. However, in general, the performance of the network is not too sensitive to changes in σ. Almost any value in the range of two to six will give good performance for many applications (Specht, 1991).

The training process for the GRNN is fast and straightforward. Only a single pass through the training set is needed. No iterative or recursive computations are required as in backpropagation or other network training algorithms since the network computes the estimates for $\hat{z}$ (equation (13.7)) directly from the samples. In fact, the network can begin to perform the regression after a single training sample has been presented and as more and more examples are presented the performance of the network will continue to improve. The computation load for the network is relatively heavy, however. Other advantages of the GRNN include the ability to work with sparse data and in real-time environments because the regression surface is defined everywhere instantly.

Having described the functioning and training of the system, we consider next an interesting modeling application of the GRNN. For other applications, see Chapter 8, since all MLFF applications given there could be applied to the GRNN.

13.5   Generalized Regression Neural Network Applications

GRNNs can be used in a variety of applications, including prediction, plant process modeling and control, and general mapping problems. In this section, we describe two representative applications. The first is an application of modeling the nonlinear dynamics of a fighter aircraft.

Modeling Aircraft Dynamics

The aerodynamics of a fighter aircraft are typically very nonlinear in nature. Significant nonlinearities occur as a result of kinematic and inertial couplings, aerodynamic nonlinearities and control deflection rate limitations. In a study conducted by Youssef (1993), simulations were carried out to see how well different ANN architectures could model the dynamics of an F-16 fighter aircraft for two highly nonlinear maneuvers: low angles of attack dynamics and deep-stalls. Five time-dependent variables were input to the network at discrete time points k and two response variables predicted. The system which uses a neural network identifier to learn to model the aircraft dynamics is illustrated in Figure 13.8.

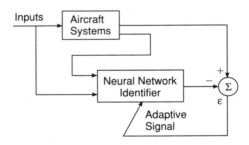

Figure 13.8   Neural Network Model of Aircraft Dynamics

The input variables to the network were control deflection command $\delta_c(k)$, angles of attack at $\alpha(k)$ and $\alpha(k-1)$, and pitch rates at $q(k)$ and $q(k-1)$. The output vector consists of the predicted angle of attack $\hat{\alpha}(k+1)$ and pitch rate $\hat{q}(k+1)$ at the next discrete time point $k+1$. Approximation errors for the angle of attack and pitch rate are given by the quantities

$$E_a = \left[\sum_k (\alpha(k) - \hat{\alpha}(k))^2 \right]^{1/2}$$

and

$$E_q = \left[\sum_k (q(k) - \hat{q}(k))^2 \right]^{1/2}$$

In this study, a comparison was made of the performance of six neural networks: a network that performs linear regression, a third-order polynomial network, an MLFF (two hidden-layer) network with backpropagation, a Cerebellar Model Articulation Controller network (CMAC), a Radial basis function network and a GRNN. Performance was based on learning speed, modeling precision, network flexibility, and complexity.

The MLFF required 50 nodes in each hidden layer and required more than 50 epochs to converge. The CMAC generated a total of 400 hypergrids and a memory of size 2,000. It converged after more than ten epochs. The RBF network used 18 basis nodes to characterize the variables. RBF and the other networks converged after a few epochs, but only the GRNN was trained in a single pass over the training patterns. For the GRNN 1,600 nodes were generated for the second experiment (200 for the first). A range of σ values was tested for best generalization and it was found that any value in the range of 0.1 to 5.0 was satisfactory.

Although the performance of all networks except linear regression was satisfactory, the overall performance of the GRNN was best. This becomes evident when errors for E_a and E_q are compared. The errors are summarized in Table 13.1.

Table 13.1 Approximation Errors E_a and E_q for the Two Aircraft Maneuvers (Courtesy of Dr. H. M. Youssef.)

Neural Network	Case 1 E_a	Case 1 E_q	Case 2 E_a	Case 2 E_q
Linear	2.4571	1.2220	10.3168	6.4562
Polynomial	2,2207	1.1490	7.4597	4.3873
Multilayer FF	2.8777	2.7712	3.7296	2.7893
Radial Basis	2.1457	1.3625	4.1159	3.2475
CMAC	2.3595	4.9421	4.3139	3.4102
GRNN	2.0910	1.2176	2.8319	2.7865

Summary

In this chapter, we have examined two related networks that are both stochastically based. The first network described is the Probabilistic Neural Network and the second, the General Regression Neural Network. They are both feedforward networks that are trained using a form of supervised learning. The networks use training sample patterns to estimate probability density functions of their environment, and both networks have the same basic architectural structure. They have an input layer that distributes the input patterns to the first computational layer, the pattern layer. The pattern layer performs the first stage of estimation by computing a part of the nonparametric Parzen window estimator. The next layer, the summation layer, sums the output of the pattern-layer units and passes this on to the output layer for final processing. The PNN learns complex decision boundaries for category classification tasks. The GRNN on the other hand, learns the general regression function relationship (linear or nonlinear) between the dependent and independent variables. It can be used in a variety of applications, including prediction, modeling and general function estimation.

Part VI

Networks Based on Unsupervised Learning

14
Self-Organizing Feature Maps and Vector Quantization

This is the first of two chapters in which unsupervised learning is used. Unsupervised learning can be divided into two classes: competitive and (Hebbian) noncompetitive. A description of the two classes is given first and their differences compared. This is followed by a look at specific implementations. In particular, we look at networks that are capable of learning an effective form of vector quantization (VQ). Quantization is the process of transforming an analog or continuous valued variable to a discrete variable. The VQ networks learn to quantize and encode input patterns from some environment, a process that is also learned in biological networks. We consider two variations of the basic VQ network which have been labeled as VQ2 and VQ3. The second type of network we look at is the self-organizing feature map (SOFM), a generalization of the VQ process. We study this architecture in some detail because of its astonishing mapping ability. We conclude the chapter with a look at some applications for both the VQ and SOM networks. In the following chapter, we look at a much different architecture based on unsupervised learning, the family of adaptive resonance theory or ART networks.

14.1 Introduction

The networks covered in this chapter are self-organizing. They learn without supervision from a teacher. During the learning process, a sequence of input patterns x are presented to the network. The patterns are generated by some (usually) unknown probability distribution $\rho(x)$. When a pattern is presented to the network, it responds by computing output activations, but there is no direct feedback given to the network on the correctness of the response to the input.

Indeed, there is no correct answer! There is not even a clue or indication of whether the output is right or wrong. The network must somehow learn by discovering and exploiting any structure found among the input examples.

What types of structure might a network discover among a set of pattern samples? The answer to this question is, of course, dependent on the source $\rho(\mathbf{x})$ and the learning paradigm used by the network. But in general, the following types of structure might be found: (1) groupings or clusters of closely related patterns, (2) frequencies of occurrence of groups of patterns, (3) relative orderings (e.g. length) among the vector inputs, (4) correlations among the patterns (in particular, a network might discover which vector component variables have the greatest variability—a form of principal component analysis), (5) mappings which transform input patterns to a lower dimension space—a form of structured coding of the inputs, and (6) feature mapping—transforming the input manifold to one of different dimension through a topological preserving process.

The unsupervised learning methods we examine fall into one of two categories: competitive and noncompetitive paradigms. Either category of network may have single or multiple layers. Our emphasis will be on the competitive type because of their popularity. Several noncompetitive classes of networks have been studied by different researchers, including Linsker (1988) and Oja (1982). These networks all use methods based on some form of Hebbian or modified Hebbian learning.

Unsupervised Noncompetitive Learning Networks

The networks based on unsupervised noncompetitive learning that we examine here, have all been based on some form of Hebbian learning. Hebbian models permit effective unsupervised learning since a unit that responds more to a given input is allowed to undergo more learning than less responsive units. When similar inputs are experienced repeatedly by such units, they become even more responsive to this clustering of similar patterns leaving other units to "discover" different pattern clusters. Through this process, units learn to respond to different clusters together without the necessity of being "told" the pattern is a member of the cluster. The simplest form of Hebbian learning, recall, has the following form

$$\Delta w_i = \alpha x_i y \tag{14.1}$$

where w_i is the weight on the connection from the input to unit i, α is a learning coefficient, x_i is the (presynaptic) input to unit i and y is the (postsynaptic) response from unit i. To be useful, this form of learning must be constrained or modified. Otherwise, the weights may grow without bound and learning may never become stable. To correct this problem, modified forms of equation (14.1) have been introduced. For example, the weight update rule may contain a renormalization factor, the weight values may be constrained to lie within limits through "clamping" or a forgetting term may be added to reduce and limit weight growth. Forgetting or decay term modifications take the following forms:

$$\Delta w_i = \alpha(x_i y - y w_i) \tag{14.2}$$

or

$$\Delta w_i = \alpha(x_i y - y^2 w_i) \tag{14.3}$$

Principal Component Analysis

A rule based on equation (14.3) was introduced by Oja (1982) who showed that the weights **w** actually converge to unit length without renormalization, that is, weights tend to satisfy the relationship $\Sigma_i w_i^2 = 1$ as they mature. Furthermore, after learning has progressed for some time, the mature weights lie in the direction of the maximal eigenvector of the correlation matrix of the input patterns, $\mathbf{C} = E[\mathbf{x}\mathbf{x}^T]$. Thus, once the weights have stabilized, the unit has actually learned to perform principal component analysis (PCA) on the inputs, a popular statistical data analysis method used for feature extraction (see Chapter 3 for a description of PCA). The weight vector **w** evolves such that the input patterns are projected onto the axis parallel to **w**, and for which case, they have maximum variance. The projection of the **x** onto the axis parallel to **w** when $\Sigma_i w_i^2 = 1$, is in fact equal to the unit's output $y = \Sigma_i x_i w_i$, and the variance of the projected distribution is the same as the variance of y. In performing PCA, the unit has learned to select those variable components of the input vectors that have the greatest effect or variability on the output y. The utility of this method is illustrated in Figure 14.1 for the case of an input vector with only two variables. In Figure 14.1, it should be noted that when the data set is viewed from the axis labeled as (a), the distribution is clearly seen to be bimodal with a large variance as opposed to the projection onto the (b) axis for which only a single mode is observable and a distribution with a smaller variance. Thus, in transforming data originally from the latter to the former form, PCA transformations help to uncover structure in the data that might otherwise be hidden.

Another aspect of PCA that can be very useful is in the reduction of the feature space dimension. By selecting those components of the vector which account for most of the variability, noncontributory variables can be eliminated, thereby reducing the dimension of the input space. Of course, for the single unit network, only the first principal component is found. To perform useful multivariate PCA,

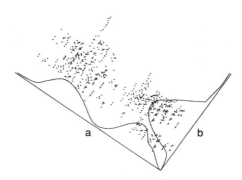

Figure 14.1   Principal Component Analysis for Two Variables

the network must have multiple outputs. Below, we describe other instances of networks that learn to perform PCA, including multivariate component identification. In particular, Oja (1989) and Sanger (1989) have both developed one-layer linear networks with multiple outputs. In addition, a linear multilayer network was developed and studied by Linsker (1988) which we consider below.

Another modified Hebbian learning rule related to the rules given by equations (14.2) and (14.3) were studied by Yuille et al. (1989). Their rule uses a decay term proportional to the norm of **w** squared rather than the output y. It has the form

$$\Delta w_i = \alpha(x_i y - w_i \|\mathbf{w}\|^2) \tag{14.4}$$

It has been shown that the weight vector for this rule also converges to a limit and in the same direction as the maximal eigenvector of **C**. The limiting value of **w** in this case is equal to the maximum eigenvalue. We omit the analysis here and refer the interested reader to the reference cited above.

As noted above, feedforward networks with multiple outputs have also been studied using modified Hebbian forms. The activation functions for these networks are also linear with output y_j given by

$$y_j = \sum_{i=1}^{n} x_i w_{ij} \qquad j = 1, 2, ..., m \tag{14.5}$$

Two similar learning rules also use decay terms. The rules consist of the products of unit outputs and weights, somewhat similar to the backpropagation learning rule (Chapter 6). One of the rules has the form given by equation (14.6) (Sanger, 1989),

$$\Delta w_{ij} = \alpha y_i \left(x_j - \sum_{k=1}^{i} y_k w_{kj} \right)$$ (14.6)

where the upper summation limit is a function of the weight being updated. The second rule is the same except that the upper summation limit in this case is n, the total number of inputs (Oja, 1989):

$$\Delta w_{ij} = \alpha y_i \left(x_j - \sum_{k=1}^{n} y_k w_{kj} \right)$$ (14.7)

Sangar (1989) extended his results to the nonlinear case where sigmoidal activation functions clamped to zero (at a threshold value) were used. The networks were used in applications for vector quantization and data compression.

Unsupervised Multilayer Networks

A somewhat different architecture was proposed by Linsker (1988) who studied multilayer feedforward networks using a form of Hebbian learning. Linsker was interested in determining if linear, self-adapting units can learn to develop useful feature analyzing capabilities similiar to those that have been discovered in the visual cortex. For example, it is known that simple low-level features such as edge and contrast orientations are processed in the early stages of the visual system, whereas higher-level features such as multiple edges and complete objects are processed in higher stages. The networks used to model this type of organization were connected as multiple layers of two-dimensional units as illustrated in Figure 14.2.

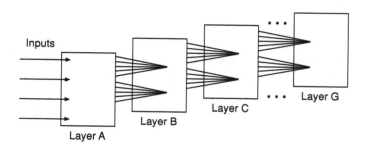

Figure 14.2   Linsker's Network with Two-Dimensional Layers of Feedforward Units

The layers are labeled successively as A, B, C, ..., G, where layer A receives external inputs from the environment and layer G produces the high-level outputs. A unit in any of the successive layers receives input from a group or neighborhood of units from the previous layer. Units in subsequent layers each have several hundred input connections from previous layer units. All units have linear activation functions of the form

$$y = \beta + \Sigma_i x_i w_i \tag{14.8}$$

where β is a constant and the x_i and w_i are the inputs and connection strengths from the previous layer, respectively. Although the output of a multiple-layer network with linear activation functions is equivalent to a single-layer, linear product transformation (see Section 5.1), the layers were allowed to develop by successively training each layer until the weights fully stabilized. The weights between layer A and layer B were trained first. When these weights stabilized, the weights between layer B and layer C were then trained until they stabilized, and so on. For the simulations conducted, the units in layer A received random input patterns from a "visual" world. Random inputs were presented to layer A so that the inputs to layer B units were the same (the input covariance matrix is proportional to the identity matrix). A form of Hebbian learning was used for all the units as defined by

$$\Delta w_i = \alpha_1 x_i y + \alpha_2 x_i + \alpha_3 y + \alpha_4 \tag{14.9}$$

where the α_i are arbitrary coefficients with the learning rate parameter $\alpha_1 > 0$. In this model, the weights are prevented from unbounded growth by clipping them, that is, by constraining their values to lie within the limits $w_- \leq w \leq w_+$, where w_- and w_+ are lower and upper constant limit values.

It is useful to know how the weights evolve according to equation (14.9) when a large number of input patterns are presented to the network. We can find the mathematical expectation or average change $E[\Delta w_i]$ by substituting the value of y (equation (14.8)) in (14.9) and finding the indicated expected value. Since the x_i are identically distributed with mean value $E[x_i] = \mu$, say, we let $x_i = z_i + \mu$. Then

$$\begin{aligned} E(\Delta w_i) &= \alpha_1 E[(z_i + \mu)(\beta + \Sigma_i(z_i + \mu)w_i)] \\ &\quad + \alpha_3 E[\Sigma_i(z_i + \mu)w_i] + k \\ &= k_1 + \Sigma_j C_{ij} w_j + \frac{k_2}{n}\Sigma_j w_j \end{aligned} \tag{14.10}$$

where k, k_1 and k_2 are constant terms taken as combinations of the α_1-α_4 and μ

and the $C_{ij} = E[(x_i - \mu)(x_j - \mu)]$ are elements of the covariance matrix $\mathbf{C}$ of the input vectors. It will be seen shortly that the matrix $\mathbf{C}$ plays an important role in the development of the units in each of the network's layers.

Given random input patterns to layer A, the C_{ij} for layer A output activities are simply 1 when $i = j$ and 0 otherwise. These values, together with the A layer unit outputs determine the developed weight values on the A-to-B connections. Likewise, the C_{ij} for the B layer activities together with the B layer unit outputs determine the developed weight values on the B-to-C connections, and so on for successive layers.

Simulations were conducted for different values of the parameters in equation (14.10). The simulations showed that B layer unit weights saturate at w_+ at which point the units compute a local average of the activity from the region in which they receive inputs from layer A. Nearby units in layer B develop correlated activity. When a B unit is high, nearby units tend to be high. This form of unit organization in B induces a form of "center-surround" type of activity in layer C units that act as a contrast-sensitive filter which responds most to circular bright spots centered at the unit's receptive field and surrounded by a dark background. Center-surround units that respond in the opposite way also develop, that is, they respond maximally to a dark spot on a bright background.

The C_{ij} for C layer units determine the behavior of the next layer which exhibit orientation-selective behaviors. The D layer units respond maximally to features such as edges or bars at particular orientations. The receptive field for such a unit is illustrated in Figure 14.3.

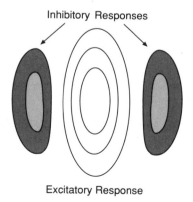

Inhibitory Responses

Excitatory Response

Figure 14.3   Receptive Field Map of Orientation-Selective Fields Used for Feature Detection

For this case, the unit's orientation is vertical, but in general, when only feedforward connections are used, the orientation development is somewhat arbitrary. On the other hand, if lateral intra-layer unit connections are used, the orientation develops in other directions as well. Points of illumination in the plane evoke output responses proportional to the contour value at that point. Units having similar orientation preferences develop to occupy irregular band-shaped regions as well. This type of selectivity has been found in the visual cortex of the cat and monkey.

Optimization Properties

Having looked at the adaptive feature analyzing aspects of these networks, we turn now to consider some other interesting properties exhibited by the Hebb-type learning rule defined by equation (14.9). In particular, we will see that the weights of individual units develop so as to maximize the statistical variance of their output activations. Under certain conditions, this is equivalent to maximizing the rate of information transfer from a unit's input to output. In other words, the learning process selects a set of weights that maximize the preservation of information.

We can analyze the behavior of a unit during the adaptive process by observing the output activations as the weights mature. For this, we define a function e consisting of two terms: one term proportional to the variance of the output activations and the other term a function of the unit's weight values. In addition, for reasons which will become apparent shortly, we would like the function e to be defined such that $-\partial e/\partial w_i = dw_i/dt$ for all i and such that e decreases along a path of locally steepest descent as the weights change. Thus, when the weights stabilize at $dw_i/dt = 0$, e will then be at a local minimum. It is known that the local minimum is actually a near global minimum (Linsker, 1988). A function e satisfying the above conditions is given by

$$
\begin{aligned}
e &= -\frac{1}{2}\left[E\left[(y - \mu)^2\right] + k_1\Sigma_i w_i + \frac{k_2}{2n}(\Sigma_i w_i)^2\right] \\
&= -\frac{1}{2}\left[\Sigma_i\Sigma_j C_{ij}w_i w_j + k_1\Sigma_i w_i + \frac{k_2}{2n}(\Sigma_i w_i)^2\right]
\end{aligned}
$$

where E is mathematical expectation, $\mu = E(y)$, with $y = \Sigma_i x_i w_i$ and the C_{ij} are the covariance terms defined above. Note that for a given set of weights, e is a minimum when the variance of the outputs is maximum. Thus, the unit matures by selecting a set of weights which maximize the variance of the output activations for the given set of input patterns.

Choosing a set of weights that maximizes the variance of a unit's output activations suggests that the unit may develop in such a way that a high rate of information transfer is preserved from input patterns to the output activations. Indeed, this can be shown to be the case for certain input pattern distributions. For example, suppose the input to a unit is corrupted with processing noise v where v is normally distributed with zero mean and variance s_v as illustrated in Figure 14.4. Suppose the output y is also normally distributed with variance s_y. Let the noise and input components x_i be uncorrelated so that $E(x_i v) = 0$ for all i. Because the noise is additive, the unit's output is also normally distributed with the random variable y given by

$$y = \Sigma_i x_i w_i + v \qquad (14.11)$$

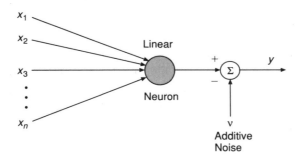

Figure 14.4   A Unit Corrupted with Processing Noise

Since we know the distributions of input and output variates, the rate of information transfer from input to output can be found directly from the mutual information between output and input (see Chapter 3 for a definition of mutual information),

$$I(y ; \mathbf{x}) = h(y) - h(y|\mathbf{x}) \qquad (14.12)$$

Note that the second term in equation (14.12), the conditional entropy of y given $\mathbf{x}$, is just distributed as v since the x_i are given (constants). Therefore, from the definition of differential entropy (see Chapter 3) we find directly

$$h(y) = \tfrac{1}{2}\left[1 + \log\left(2\pi\,\sigma_y^2\right)\right] \qquad (14.13)$$

Likewise, the conditional differential entropy of y given $\mathbf{x}$ is

$$h(y|\mathbf{x}) = h(\nu) = \frac{1}{2}\Big[1 + \log\big(2\pi\,\sigma_\nu^2\big)\Big] \tag{14.14}$$

Combining equations (14.13) and (14.14) we find the mutual information to be

$$I(y\,;\,\mathbf{x}) = \frac{1}{2}\Big[\log\big(2\pi\,\sigma_y^2\big) + \log\big(2\pi\,\sigma_\nu^2\big)\Big] = \frac{1}{2}\bigg[\log\Big(\frac{\sigma_y^2}{\sigma_\nu^2}\Big)\bigg] \tag{14.15}$$

Thus, for fixed noise input with variance σ_ν^2, we see that the mutual information or rate of information preservation is maximum when σ_y^2 is maximum. Hence, for the Hebbian rule (equation (14.9)) and assumptions of normality, each layer in the Linsker network maximize the preservation of information in an information-theoretic sense.

Other simple examples given by Linsker produce similar results. For example, if the input processing noise is distributed over the input connections so that the input to the ith unit is $x_i + \nu_i$ (and hence $y = \Sigma_i(x_i + \nu_i)w_i$) where each ν_i is independently normally distributed with common variance σ_ν^2 as depicted in Figure 14.5, one finds that the resultant mutual information is given by

$$I(y\,;\,\mathbf{x}) = \frac{1}{2}\bigg[\log\Big(\frac{\sigma_y^2}{\sigma_\nu^2\Sigma_i w_1^2}\Big)\bigg]$$

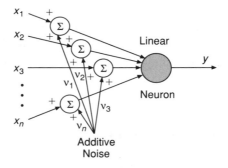

Figure 14.5   Multiple Processing Noise Inputs

For this case, again with fixed noise inputs, the mutual information is maximum when $\sigma_y^2 / \Sigma_i w_i^2$ is maximum, that is when the variance is maximum and the weights are constrained to a small value. But this is equivalent to the unit selecting a set of weights that perform principal component analysis (PCA) on the input patterns (see Chapter 3 for a description of PCA). Thus, like Oja's rule (equation (14.3)), we see another case of Hebbian learning that results in some form of adaptive organization to achieve a form of optimal performance.

To summarize the above findings, the model proposed here is a layered network with feedforward connections and linear activation functions. The simple Hebbian type of learning rule builds layers of units that have progressively more sophisticated feature-analyzing properties. These properties include the development of cells that under certain constraints:

1. maximize the variance of their output activities,

2. perform principal component analysis (feature extraction) on their inputs, and

3. preserve maximum information about the input activities.

The above properties also apply to cases where the activation functions are not necessarily linear. The overall biological implications of these findings are also consistent with the principle that the survival of organisms whose perceptual systems are best adapted to their environment is strengthened.

Unsupervised Competitive Learning Networks

Competitive networks have been studied by several researchers including Grossberg (1972), von der Malsburg (1973), Kohonen (1982) and Rumelhart and Zipser (1985). A general competitive model can be described as follows: Units may be organized into one or more functional layers with the units in a single layer grouped into disjoint clusters. Each unit within a cluster inhibits all other units within the cluster to compete for the winning position in a "winner-takes-all" competition. The unit receiving the largest input achieves its maximum output while all others are driven to zero. Units in the same cluster all receive the same inputs. A three-layer competitive network is illustrated in Figure 14.6.

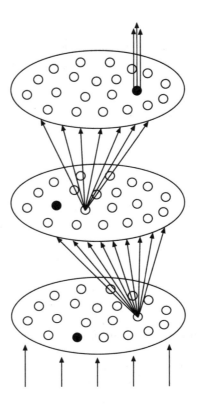

Figure 14.6   General Competitive Network Architecture

A unit learns only if it wins the competition in a cluster. Learning is achieved through the redistribution of weights on input-to-unit connections where the total amount of weight for each unit is held fixed (e.g. $\Sigma_i w_{ij} = 1$). This means that learning is accomplished by shifting quantities of weights from the inactive to the active connections of the winning unit. No learning takes place among the losers. In one common learning approach, weight values of the winner are shifted toward the input pattern vector. This process is illustrated in Figure 14.7 where the input and weight vectors are assumed to be normalized to unit vectors. As such, they represent points on a sphere of unit radius (x represents input patterns and o the weight vector values (Figure 14.7a)). In Figure 14.7a, three groups of training vectors are shown on the sphere together with three weight vectors before any training has taken place. In Figure 14.7b, after some training has been completed, the weight vectors have been shifted toward the centers of the pattern vector clusters.

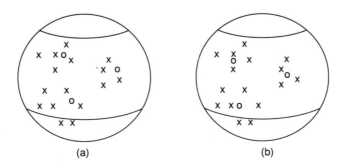

Figure 14.7   Illustration of Competitive Learning

Figure 14.8 illustrates how a weight vector **w** is updated during the learning process. The weight of the winning unit is shifted toward an input pattern vector **x** by adding a fraction of the difference vector (**x** − **w**) to the weight vector.

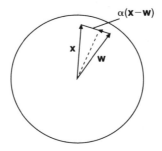

Figure 14.8   Illustration of Weight Update for Competitive Learning

One of the most amazing examples of competitive networks that learn by self-adaptation is the Self-Organizing Feature Map (SOFM) developed by Kohonen (1982, 1989). This work was inspired by earlier results published by Grossberg (1972) and work on competitive learning initiated by von der Malsburg (1973). SOFM networks self-adapt to input stimuli patterns **x** which are described by some unknown probability distribution $\rho(\mathbf{x})$. The resultant adaptation produces a network that maps input patterns to output patterns in a topologically coherent way. The mapping is continuous, order preserving, and one which reflects the probability distribution of the input population. This topology preserving property is retained even when the SOFM performs a reduction in the dimension of the feature space. SOFM networks have been used for a number of applications including vector quantization, data compression, combinatorial optimization, robotic control, and speech and pattern recognition. We examine typical applications in Section 14.5. To gain a better appreciation of the SOFM adaptation process, we describe vector quantization next. VQ networks can be regarded as a special case of SOFM networks.

14.2 Vector Quantization

In applications such as speech recognition or image processing, large quantities of data must be stored, processed, and possibly transmitted over communication channels. For example, a single high resolution image will require as much as $1,000 \times 1,000$ bytes of data, where each byte corresponds to a pixel gray-level intensity value. When many such images must be processed, the quantity of data handling can become enormous. Typically, there is much redundancy in data of this type. Large portions of an image such as a sky background or other homogeneous objects will have nearly the same intensity values or repetitive texture patterns. When contiguous data of nearly the same values occur, some form of data compression or encoding can be performed to reduce the total quantity of data processed. For example, adjacent pixels (characters or numbers) with about the same value can be grouped together and assigned a single index or codeword value. Alternatively, a pattern that can be grouped into one of a finite number of classes can be assigned the index of the prototypical vector for that class. The length of the encoding can be much smaller than the original data resulting in a compression of total data quantity. The reduction realized in bandwidth, data processing and data storage can amount to as much as thirty to eighty percent.

Some compression methods permit full recovery of the original data and other methods do not. In the latter case, there is a trade-off between the amount of resolution lost through the compression and the reduction in the quantity of data. If the total number of codewords k is small, fewer classes or intensity levels can be represented and ample recovery may be impossible. If k is large, there will be little loss of resolution, but only a small reduction of data. Clearly, the best choice of k is application dependent.

Many techniques have been developed for data compression (Devijver and Kittler, 1982), but the better methods rely on some knowledge of the probability distribution $\rho(\mathbf{x})$ from which the patterns $\mathbf{x}$ are drawn. Efficient coding schemes take advantage of the relative frequencies with which input patterns occur by assigning shorter codewords to the most frequently occurring patterns. One of the most familiar examples of such coding is the Morse code where a single "dash" is used to encode the most frequently occurring letter in the English alphabet, the letter E. With the use of information theory, it is always possible to devise a most efficient coding scheme when the statistics of the source are known. When little is known of the source distribution, and particularly when the distribution is highly nonlinear, other methods may be more effective. One compression method that has been successfully applied to ANN architectures is vector quantization. ANN data compressors may be appealing when little is known of the source distribution. The performance of this approach has been studied and has been shown to compare favorably with other comparable compression techniques (Kohonen, 1988).

Vector quantization is the process of mapping vectors $\mathbf{x}$, which are usually continuous, real-valued vectors, from some manifold $A \in \mathbf{R}^n$ onto the nearest reference weight vector $\mathbf{w}_i$ belonging to a manifold $B \in \mathbf{R}^m$. In other words, the input vectors $\mathbf{x}$ of dimension n are transformed to one of a finite number of classes where each class is represented by a codeword or prototype vector $\mathbf{w}_i$ ($i = 1, 2, ..., m$). The index i of dimension $m < n$ becomes the class label for $\mathbf{x}$. The VQ mapping $f : M \rightarrow B$ is a nearest neighbor mapping, where "nearest" can be defined in different ways. Typically, it is Euclidean distance or some cost function such as the squared error distortion $d(\mathbf{x}, \mathbf{w}_i)$ defined by

$$d(\mathbf{x}, \mathbf{w}_i) = \|\mathbf{x} - \mathbf{w}_i\|^2 = \sum_{j=1}^{n} (x_j - w_{ij})^2$$

and the nearest $\mathbf{w}_i$ to $\mathbf{x}$ is the one with the minimum distortion d.

The VQ networks we consider here all function as competitive networks where the m output units compete to represent the input patterns as described in the previous section. The unit with the weight vector closest to $\mathbf{x}$ becomes the winner in a "winner-takes-all" competition. Competing neurons reinforce their own excitations through a self-feedback connection and inhibit other competing units through lateral connections. The unit with the strongest input excitation wins the competition. A VQ network is illustrated in Figure 14.9.

The complete model takes into account external inputs $\mathbf{x}^T \mathbf{w}_j$ to the jth unit as well as internal feedback among the units. The dynamics of the system can be described by a set of differential equations in the activation values y_j for the jth unit ($j = 1, 2, ..., m$) as given by

$$\frac{dy_j}{dt} = \sum_i w_{ij} x_i + \sum_{k \in sj} v_{kj} y_k - h(y_j) \tag{14.16}$$

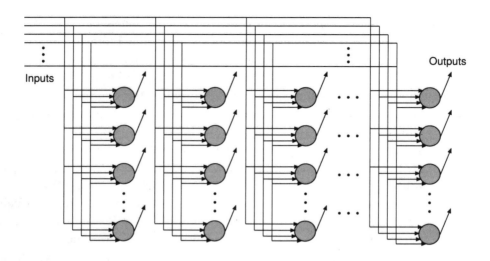

Figure 14.9   A Vector Quantization Network

where the x_i are the inputs ($i = 1, 2, ..., n$), w_{ij} is the weight on the connection between the ith input and the jth unit, v_{kj} is the weight on the internal connection from the kth unit output to the jth unit input, S_j is the set of units that have connections with unit j and $h(y_j)$ is a nonlinear leakage term that accounts for a collection of effects such as saturation, leakage, and shunting. Only the weights w_{ij} on the input connections are adaptable. The weights v_{kj} on the feedback connections are fixed. The differential equations governing the learning process are

$$\frac{dw_{ij}}{dt} = \begin{cases} \alpha(x_i - w_{ij}) & \text{if } y_j = 1 \text{ (the winner)} \\ 0 & \text{otherwise} \end{cases} \qquad (14.17)$$

where α is a learning coefficient.

When the sum of the weight values are held constant for each unit, say $\Sigma w_{ij} = 1$ and the same for all units, and when the input values $\mathbf{x}$ are normalized, $\|\mathbf{x}\| = 1$, a shortcut approximation can be used to determine the winning unit (Kohonen, 1984). It makes use of the Euclidean norm as a measure of proximity between the input vectors and the unit weights. Thus, unit c with weight vector $\mathbf{w}_c$ wins the competition when

$$\|\mathbf{w}_c - \mathbf{x}\| = \min_i \|\mathbf{w}_i - \mathbf{x}\| \qquad (14.18)$$

When the weight vector lengths are constant and the inputs normalized, the maximum scalar product $\mathbf{x}^T\mathbf{w}_j$ is equivalent to equation (14.18).

Learning in these networks is performed only by the winning unit and in such a way that the weight vector $\mathbf{w}_c$ of the winning unit c is moved in the direction of input pattern $\mathbf{x}$ (Figure 14.8). The adaptive update rule is given by

$$\begin{aligned}
\mathbf{w}_c^{new} &= \mathbf{w}_c^{old} + \alpha(\mathbf{x} - \mathbf{w}_c) && \text{for the winning unit } c \\
\mathbf{w}_i^{new} &= \mathbf{w}_i^{old} && \text{for } i \neq c
\end{aligned} \qquad (14.19)$$

where $\alpha > 0$ is a learning coefficient that may be fixed or decreased as learning progresses. The process defined by equations (14.18) and (14.19) is equivalent to k-means clustering and asymptotically, the weights $\mathbf{w}_i$ partition the pattern space into regions described by a Voronoi tessellation. A two-dimensional portrayal of the partitions and corresponding reference prototype vectors is given in Figure 14.10. In n-dimensional space, this nonlinear partition is given by bounding hypersurfaces whose interior cell densities approximates the input pattern probability distribution. Any pattern falling within a given region will be assigned an index that identifies that particular tessellation cell. Groups of one or more cells can correspond to different class assignments.

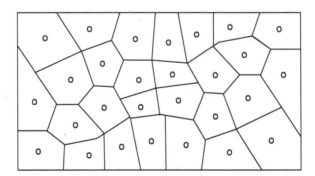

Figure 14.10 Two-Dimensional Voronoi Tessellation Partition of Pattern Space

The discrete regions in $\mathbf{R}^m$ defined by (14.18) and (14.19) amounts to a near optimal quantization of the vector space. This means that the number of misclassified patterns will be a minimum, because the distance of any point within a cell will be closer to the prototype point than to any other cell prototype. It has been noted that this form of VQ partitioning closely approximates the theoretical method based on Bayesian decision surfaces (Kohonen, 1988).

To summarize the above, learning in the VQ network can be described as follows:

1.   Initialize the weights w_{ij} to small random numbers (alternatively, to the first m pattern values). Repeat steps 2 and 3 until the network weights stabilize.

2.   Find the prototype unit to represent $\mathbf{x}$ by computing

$$\|\mathbf{w}_c - \mathbf{x}\| = \min_i \|\mathbf{w}_i - \mathbf{x}\|$$

3.   Update the weight vectors according to

$$\mathbf{w}_c^{new} = \mathbf{w}_c^{old} + \alpha(\mathbf{x} - \mathbf{w}_c) \qquad \text{for the winning unit } c$$
$$\mathbf{w}_i^{new} = \mathbf{w}_i^{old} \qquad\qquad\qquad \text{for } i \neq c$$

The above form of vector quantization is a form of unsupervised learning or self-adaptation. There was no target prototype given for each input. Supervised forms of learning have also been studied. We distinguish these from the unsupervised VQ with the label LVQ (learning vector quantization). Two such forms are described in the following section.

14.3 Modified Forms of Vector Quantization

The simple form of VQ described in the preceding section has a weakness. If the initial distribution of weight vectors and input patterns are not somewhat uniformly distributed, some of the weight vectors may never be selected as a winner and therefore never learn. If a few weight vectors are clustered together away from the patterns, one may be selected during the early learning stages and be drawn toward the input vectors. Subsequent inputs will select the same vector for learning, leaving the other vectors behind to never learn. To alleviate this discrimination, a form of "conscience" mechanism can be included in the learning equations (DiSieno, 1988). Units that win frequently can be penalized by adding a bias term that effectively increases the distance computation in proportion to the frequency with which the unit wins. Let p_i be the fraction of time that a unit i wins the competition. Then we define p_i as follows:

$$p_i^{new} = p_i^{old} + b(y_i - p_i^{old})$$

where b is a constant such that $0 < b < 1$. If z_i represents the winning unit, then a bias term B_i is introduced to modify the competition,

$$z_i = \begin{cases} 1 & \text{if } |\mathbf{w}_i - \mathbf{x}|^2 - B_i \leq |\mathbf{w}_j - \mathbf{x}|^2 - B_j \forall j \neq i \\ 0 & \text{otherwise} \end{cases}$$

The penalty term B_i has the following form

$$B_i = C(1/n - p_i)$$

where the constant C is a bias factor and n is the number of units in the network. C establishes the distance a losing unit can reach in order to enter the solution. Finally, the weights of the unit winning the competition are updated in accordance with

$$\mathbf{w}_i^{new} = \mathbf{w}_i^{old} + \alpha(\mathbf{x} - \mathbf{w}_i^{old})z_i$$

The constant α is the learning rate. It is the fraction of the distance that the winning unit moves toward the input vector.

The conscience mechanism described above is an effective method in developing equiprobable features of prototypes of the input environment. It has been shown to improve the performance of different networks that use a form of competitive learning.

Next, we briefly examine other variations of VQ including those labeled as LVQ2 and LVQ3. We consider LVQ2 first.

Supervised Learning Vector Quantization (LVQ)

Supervised forms of VQ are denoted by LVQ. The basic difference between unsupervised (VQ) and supervised (LVQ) learning is the use of known target output classifications $t(\mathbf{x}) = t$ for each input pattern $\mathbf{x}$. Let $C(\mathbf{x})$ denote the class of $\mathbf{x}$ computed by the network. Then $C(\mathbf{x})$ is found as in the case of VQ using

$$\|\mathbf{w}_c - \mathbf{x}\| = \min_i \|\mathbf{w}_i - \mathbf{x}\|$$

When the class is correct ($C(\mathbf{x}) = t$), the weight vector of the winning unit is shifted toward the input vector as in the case of VQ learning. When an incorrect prototype is selected ($C(\mathbf{x}) \neq t$), the weight vector is shifted away from the input vector. The update rule for LVQ can therefore be described as

$$\mathbf{w}_c^{\text{new}} = \mathbf{w}_c^{\text{old}} + \alpha(\mathbf{x} - \mathbf{w}_c) \qquad \text{if } C(\mathbf{x}) = t$$
$$\mathbf{w}_c^{\text{new}} = \mathbf{w}_c^{\text{old}} - \alpha(\mathbf{x} - \mathbf{w}_c) \qquad \text{if } C(\mathbf{x}) \neq t$$
$$\mathbf{w}_i^{\text{new}} = \mathbf{w}_i^{\text{old}} \qquad\qquad\quad \text{for all } i \neq c$$

We will review two variations to the above rule next.

Learning Vector Quantization-2 (LVQ2)

LVQ2 functions the same as LVQ in determining the class of the input vector (equation (14.18)). However, learning is applied only if the following conditions hold:

1. The class of the input vector is chosen incorrectly, $C(\mathbf{x}) \neq t$.

2. The second closest prototype weight vector $\mathbf{w}_{c*}$ is the correct class.

3. The input vector is close to the bounding hyperplane separating the two closest prototype weight vectors $\mathbf{w}_c$ and $\mathbf{w}_{c*}$.

When these conditions are satisfied, the weights associated with the correct class, $\mathbf{w}_{c*}$ are shifted toward the input vector and the weights of the incorrect class are shifted away from the input vector according to

$$\mathbf{w}_{c*}^{\text{new}} = \mathbf{w}_{c*}^{\text{old}} + \alpha(\mathbf{x} - \mathbf{w}_{c*})$$
$$\mathbf{w}_c^{\text{new}} = \mathbf{w}_c^{\text{old}} - \alpha(\mathbf{x} - \mathbf{w}_c)$$
$$\mathbf{w}_i^{\text{new}} = \mathbf{w}_i^{\text{old}} \qquad\qquad \text{for all } i \neq c, c*$$

This rule has been shown to have good performance properties (Kohonen, 1988).

Further refinements to LVQ have also been proposed. They have been labeled as LVQ2.1 and LVQ3. Both refinements involve weight updates to the winning and second place unit when the ratio of the distances between input and winner and input and second winner weight vectors falls within a narrow window. (The reader is referred to descriptions given by Kohonen (1990a) and Kohonen (1990b) for more details on these refinements to LVQ.)

We turn next to a more general class of networks that have also been used successfully for vector quantization in both speech and vision applications (Nasrabodi, 1988). These are the class of self-organizing feature map networks.

14.4 Self-Organizing Feature Map Networks

The cerebral cortex of the human brain is perhaps the most complex of all biological systems. On a micro level, it is organized into several layers of neurons of varying densities and types. On a macro level, it is organized into spatial regions by body function, as illustrated in Figure 14.11.

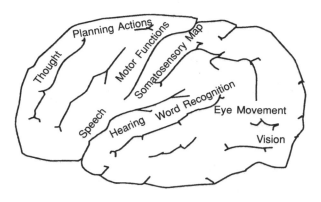

Figure 14.11   Specialized Areas of the Cerebral Cortex

Each region consists of a large number of similar neurons that cooperate when carrying out the specific functions they have become specialized to handle. Each of the regions corresponds to a mapping from some functional group of sensory inputs such as the visual cortex, auditory or hearing receptors, motor functions, the somatosensory cortex (touch), thought, and so on. Groups of neuron cells within each region respond jointly to excitations from the sensory cells they service. For example, neurons in the visual cortex respond to certain light patterns falling on the retina. Somatosensory cortex region cells become excited by inputs from sensory cells beneath the skin and auditory or tonotopic map cells respond in localized groups to different sounds based on frequency or pitch. The receptive fields of these spatially organized neurons are associated directly with the sensory neurons. There is a mapping of the features from sensory neurons to the associated spatial regions of the cortex. This biological feature mapping of the brain has been modeled reasonably well with ANNs.

The self-organizing feature map ANN is a simplified model of the feature-to-localized-region mapping of the brain from which it derives its name. It is a competitive, self-organizing network which learns from the environment without the aid of a teacher. The architecture is quite simple. It consists of a group of geometrically organized neurons in one, two, three, or even higher dimensions. The one-dimensional network is a single layer of units that are arranged in a row. In the two-dimensional network case, the units are arranged as a lattice array, and so on for higher dimensions. A two-dimensional lattice of units is illustrated in Figure 14.12. The only connections shown in the figure are inputs, outputs and connections among immediate neighbors. Interconnections to more distant units are omitted for simplicity.

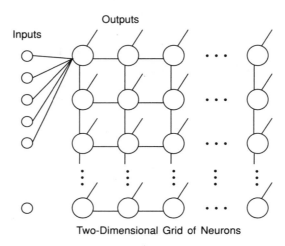

Figure 14.12   A Two-Dimensional Array SOFM Network

The input feature vector $\mathbf{x}$ of dimension n is fully connected to each of the network's units through adaptable weight vectors $\mathbf{w}_j$, $j = 1, 2, ..., m$. As in the case of VQ networks, the unit with a weight vector that is closest to the input pattern wins the competition. The winner responds maximally and drives all other units to zero output. The competitive action is implemented through lateral (fixed-weight) connections between neighboring units where both excitations and inhibitions are generated.

Unlike VQ networks, the winning unit is not the only beneficiary of learning following a competition. The winning unit shares the learning experience with its closest neighbors and the learning process is executed in such a way that nearby elements tend to align their weights in the same direction as the input pattern while more distant units have their weights aligned in opposing directions.

In later sections, we concentrate on the two-dimensional SOFM architecture. For this, it is convenient to index each unit with an x-y coordinate position vector $\mathbf{r}$. Thus, the input to the $\mathbf{r}$th unit is the external excitation $\mathbf{x}^T\mathbf{w_r}$ plus the internal feedback from units $\mathbf{r}'$ connected to unit $\mathbf{r}$ through fixed weights $\mathbf{v_{rr'}}$. The input from internal units connected to unit $\mathbf{r}$ is given by $\mathbf{y}_{\mathbf{r}'}^T\mathbf{v_{rr'}}$. Units may also have an excitation threshold θ. The single output activation from unit $\mathbf{r}$ is given by $y_{\mathbf{r}}$, where

$$y_{\mathbf{r}} = f\left(\sum_i w_{ri}x_i + \sum_{\mathbf{r}'}\mathbf{v_{rr'}}\mathbf{y_{r'}} - \theta \right) \tag{14.20}$$

The summations in equation (14.20) range over the indices of all input connections and internal units connected to unit $\mathbf{r}$ and the function f is some nonlinear activation function such as a sigmoid.

The complete dynamics of the SOFM system can be described by differential equations similar to those given above for VQ networks (equations (14.16) and (14.17)) taking into account scaling of the variables and the nonlinear activation functions f of the units. The learning stimulus generated by a winning unit behaves like an "on-center off-surround" excitation that resembles a "Mexican hat" shape as illustrated in Figure 14.13. Units close to the winning unit are excited more than units further away, and units some distance away are inhibited. Their weights are shifted away from the direction of the input vector. After learning has progressed for some time, the weight vectors in the array of units collectively tend to model the probability distribution of the input patterns through a topological feature preserving mapping.

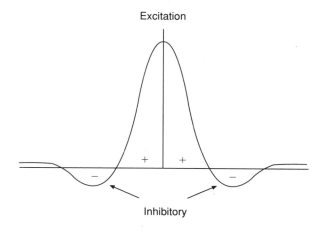

Figure 14.13   Lateral Interaction Strengths Resemble the Shape of a "Mexican Hat"

As in the case of VQ networks, a simplified form of SOFM operation can be used to approximate the system dynamics. Assuming the input patterns are all normalized to be unit length and the input weight vectors are of constant length, $\|\mathbf{w_r}\| = c$, we can write the simplified activation equations as

$$\|\mathbf{w_r} - \mathbf{x}\| = \min_{\mathbf{r'}}\|\mathbf{w_{r'}} - \mathbf{x}\|$$

where unit $\mathbf{r}$ is the winner of the competition and has weight vector nearest to the input pattern x. Learning then follows according to the rule given by

$$\mathbf{w_r}^{new} = \mathbf{w_r}^{old} + \alpha h_{\mathbf{rr'}}(\mathbf{x} - \mathbf{w_{r'}}^{old})$$

where $h_{\mathbf{rr'}}$ is a "neighborhood" function with maximum value centered at the winning unit $\mathbf{r}$ and becomes zero as the distance between $\mathbf{r}$ and neighboring units $\mathbf{r'}$ increases, that is, $h_{\mathbf{rr'}}$ is defined in terms of the distance between $\mathbf{r}$ and $\mathbf{r'}$. We use $N_{\mathbf{r}}$ to denote the neighborhood of unit $\mathbf{r}$ so that $h_{\mathbf{rr'}} > 0$ for all units $\mathbf{r'}$ within the neighborhood. The positive learning coefficient α is a function of the learning step and decreases toward zero as learning progresses. For simplicity, the form of $h_{\mathbf{rr'}}$ is sometimes taken to be a flat top shaped function of the distance over a geometrical region such as a square or hexagonal shape as illustrated in Figure 14.14.

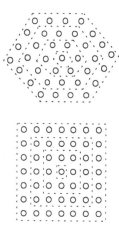

Figure 14.14   Square and Hexagonal Neighborhood Adaptive Regions
(Adapted from Kohonen, 1987. © 1987 Springer-Verlag. Courtesy of Professor T. Kohonen.)

Units within the neighborhood all have their weights adjusted in the direction of the input pattern and those outside receive no adjustment. As more and more input patterns are presented to the network, the size of the neighborhood is reduced until eventually it includes only the winning unit or the winning unit and a few of the nearest neighbors.

Initially, the values of the weights are more or less random. As learning progresses, regions of activity form over the winning unit like bubbles. A simulation of the activity formation over the winning unit is illustrated in Figure 14.15a where "activation bubbles" are formed over the two-dimensional network during learning. In Figure 14.15b, the simulation shows how the activity region shifts as the input patterns undergo a shift in location. The dark circles are units with heightened activity in the array and the size of the circles indicate the activity level. The "tail" on the right side of Figure 14.15b shows the direction of motion in the input patterns.

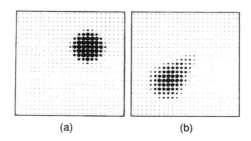

(a)   (b)

Figure 14.15   Activity Bubbles Over a Two-Dimensional Network. (a) A Region of Stable Activity, (b) Slowly Changing Input with a Moving Bubble
(From Kohonen, 1987. © 1987 Springer-Verlag. Courtesy of Professor T. Kohonen.)

Rather than use a sharp neighborhood boundary for $N_\mathbf{r}$, we might choose $h_{\mathbf{rr}'}$ to be a smooth Gaussian function of the form

$$h_{\mathbf{rr}'} = e^{-((\mathbf{r}\cdot\mathbf{r}')^2/2\sigma^2)} \tag{14.21}$$

where σ defines the radius of the neighborhood. Initially, the parameter σ is chosen to be large so that a larger number of neighboring units share in the learning experience with the winner. As the number of learning steps is increased, the value of σ is gradually decreased to a small constant value making the neighborhood region become more selective. The form of the Gaussian neighborhood function for different values of σ is illustrated in Figure 14.16. With σ also decreasing, the weights tend to converge and form a topological image of the input pattern space.

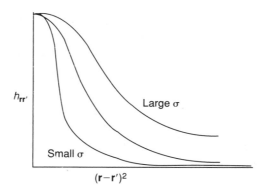

Figure 14.16   Gaussian Neighborhood as a Function of σ

The learning process for the SOFM can be summarized as follows:

1. Initialize the weights $\mathbf{w_r}$ by some suitable means (such as small random numbers) and set the learning rate and topological neighborhood parameters. Repeat steps 2 through 4 until the network weights stabilize.

2. Select a vector $\mathbf{x}$ from the input pattern distribution for input to the network.

3. Determine the array unit $\mathbf{r}$ with weight vector closest to $\mathbf{x}$ by computing

$$\|\mathbf{w_r} - \mathbf{x}\| = \min_{r'}\|\mathbf{w_r} - \mathbf{x}\|$$

4. Update the weight vectors on the $(t + 1)$th iteration according to

$$\mathbf{w_r}(t + 1) = \mathbf{w_r}(t) + \alpha(t)h_{\mathbf{rr'}}(\mathbf{x} - \mathbf{w_r}(t)) \qquad \text{for units } \mathbf{r} \in N_r$$
$$\mathbf{w_r}(t + 1) = \mathbf{w_r}(t) \qquad\qquad\qquad\qquad \text{for units } \mathbf{r} \notin N_r$$

   where, as noted above, N_r is the neighborhood of unit $\mathbf{r}$.

5. Reduce the neighborhood and learning rate parameters.

Note that if N_r is reduced to include the winning unit only, the SOFM performs vector quantization; it essentially becomes a VQ network as described in Section 14.2, and decision regions are formed by the adapted weights $\mathbf{w_r}$ with the boundaries defined by Voronoi polygons. Every point within a given region is closer to the reference weight vector $\mathbf{w}_r$ for that region than to any other weight vector and the hyperplane boundaries of the regions are orthogonal to lines connecting adjacent region weight vectors.

Once learning has progressed sufficiently so that the weights have stabilized, the trained SOFM performs a mapping from a manifold $\mathbf{X}$ of the input pattern space to an excitation center c in the network which resembles a continuous map of the input formed over the network as determined by the relative values of the network weights. The location of the maximum excitation center depends on the direction of the input vector $\mathbf{x}$ which gets mapped to a position $\mathbf{r}$ in the two-dimensional array. By allowing the parameter $\alpha(t)$ to decrease with learning, but still remain positive, the network can retain its plasticity and continue to adapt to changes in the environment. The pattern-to-weight space mapping is illustrated in Figure 14.17 where Φ is the mapping from $\mathbf{X}$ to the SOFM array.

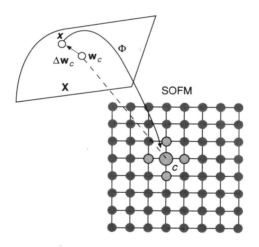

Figure 14.17   Pattern to Weight Space Mapping

The mappings performed by different network configurations for different input distributions are best illustrated by pictorial representations of the weight values for some network simulations. Two examples given by Kohonen (1989) are illustrated in Figures 14.18 and 14.19 where the input patterns are drawn from a uniform probability distribution.

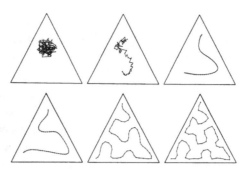

Figure 14.18   Feature Mapping from a Uniformly Distributed Pattern Space
to a Linear Row SOFM
(From Kohonen, 1987. © 1987 Springer-Verlag. Courtesy of Professor T. Kohonen.)

Referring to the figures, the assignment of a unit's receptive field (weight values) to (x, y) positions is indicated by the intersection of lines with adjacent units being connected by lines. In Figure 14.18 for example, the network is structured as a linear row of neurons and the weights were initialized to a small cluster of random values. As learning progresses, the weight cluster begins to open up and some structure is evident. The six snapshots from left to right, top to bottom correspond to learning iterations of 0, 20, 100, 1,000, 10,000 and 25,000, respectively. Eventually, the receptive fields of the units become arranged in the shape of a "Peano curve." In Figure 14.19, the SOFM is organized as a rectangular array and the weights were initialized to small "circular" random values. In this figure, the six snapshots from left to right, top to bottom correspond to learning iterations of 0, 20, 100, 1,000, 5,000 and 100,000, respectively.

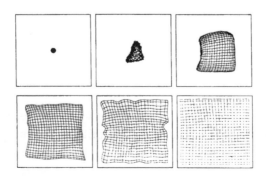

Figure 14.19   Feature Mapping from a Uniformly Distributed Pattern Space to a Rectangular
SOFM Array
(From Kohonen, 1987. © 1987 Springer-Verlag. Courtesy of Professor T. Kohonen.)

A third example of SOFM mapping is presented in the following section in connection with some interesting applications of SOFM and VQ networks.

14.5 Applications of VQ and SOFM

As noted above, VQ networks have found application in the areas of vector quantization for data compression, error correction and the generation of codewords. Since SOFM networks are a generalization of VQ networks, they can also be used for these applications. In addition, SOFM networks have been used effectively for optimization, control, speech recognition and sensory mapping. We describe four typical examples of these applications next.

The Phonetic Typewriter

Teuvo Kohonen and colleagues at the Helsinki University of Technology have been developing a "phonetic typewriter" since the early 1980s. The phonetic typewriter is a recognition system that can transcribe unlimited speech into orthographically correct text. When perfected well enough for multi-language industrial strength fielding, such a system would have tremendous impact on information handling. Automated speech-to-typewritten text would revolutionize the office environment, not to mention the publishing business. The Kohonen group in Helsinki have realized a high degree of success for phonemic languages like Finnish and Japanese, but it is not yet clear how easily their results can be extended to other, less phonetic languages such as English or Russian, or to Chinese where intonation must also be considered. Experiments conducted using three average speaking male Finns have shown that accuracy rates of about 91 to 96% are achievable when four repetitions of a set of 311 words were used. Each set of words contained 1,737 phonemes. In the benchmark experiments conducted, three of the experiments were used for training and one for testing. The coprocessor board for the system is illustrated in Figure 14.20. A conventional LVQ network is used to map phonemes to reference (codebook) classes.

Input to the LVQ network are cepstral components computed from the speech spectrum. The cepstral feature set is a nonlinear combination of two cascaded Fourier transformations (derived from a 256-point transform and then compressed). The resultant feature vectors are then classified into one of 26 phonemic classes of the Finnish language. Supervised learning using the LVQ1, LVQ2 or LVQ3 have been used for the quantization with results that are comparable in accuracy to the best nonlinear statistical decision methods. A new pattern vector is computed from the spectrum every 10 ms and classification of the pattern vector can be performed in real-time using commercially available PC hardware components.

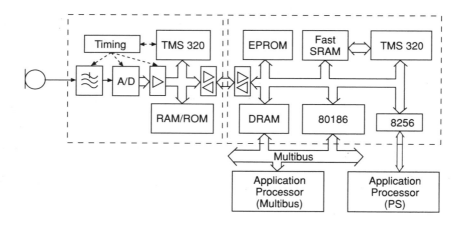

Figure 14.20   Components of the Speech Processing System
(From Kohonen, 1988. © 1988 IEEE. Courtesy of Professor T. Kohonen.)

The above classification results in a sequence of symbols or quasiphonemes which must be merged into segments, each representing a phoneme of speech. This requires some statistical analysis which is achieved through a voting scheme. A method which uses thousands of rules called Dynamically Focusing Context (DFC) is used to complete phoneme merging and segmentation. Other well-known methods are used for the decoding process including Hidden Markov Model (HMM) and then symbolic Dynamically Expanding Context to correct phonemic errors.

Speech-to-text recognition is an extremely complicated problem. It has been estimated that true speaker identification of continuous speech using a 20,000 word vocabulary as a base will require computing power of some 100,000 MIPS, the equivalent of 100 supercomputers connected in parallel (Reddy and Zue, 1983). It is not suprising then that such a task does not come easily.

We next look at an optimization application using the SOFM network to solve one of the benchmark types of hard problems.

Optimization

One-dimensional SOFM networks have been used to successfully solve optimization problems such as the traveling salesman problem (TSP). The TSP can be described (see Chapter 10) as a search for the shortest path passing once and only once through every city in a given set. Other network solutions such as the Hopfield network require in the order of N^2 nodes and N^4 connections, whereas

Boltzmann machine with simulated annealing solutions require in the order of N^2 nodes and N^3 connections. Both of these network solutions also require precomputation of network parameters for their solutions. The SOFM solution we describe in this section grows only linearly with the number of cities and requires no precomputation of network parameters or teacher supervision. It therefore seems to offer some advantages over the recurrent network solutions.

The TSP solution as formulated by Angeniol et al. (1988), uses a one-dimensional ring of SOFM nodes that "move freely" in the plane during the iterative adaptation process until the nodes are "caught" by the fixed cities. At each iteration step, a city is presented to the network and the node with weights nearest the city is adapted to move closer. The winning node's neighbors are also adapted to move closer, but as a decreasing function $f(\ )$ of the distance from the winning node. Inducing the neighbors to also move closer tends to minimize the distance between two neighbors reducing the tour distance. A new city is then selected and the process repeated until all M cities have been presented. This constitutes a complete iteration.

Nodes and cities are characterized by their Cartesian coordinates in the plane. Starting with one node at location $(0, 0)$, the number of nodes N, grows by duplication of a node when it is chosen as the winner for two different cities. The newly created node is inserted in the ring as a neighbor of the winner node and both twins are then inhibited for one iteration step. This ensures that the twin nodes get separated on the next iteration through the influence of other neighbors winning the distance competition on at least one iteration step.

During the city selection process, a gain parameter G is reduced from high to low in steps after each complete city iteration. This parameter determines the relative distance a node and its neighbors move toward the nearest city, starting with large values and becoming small until the network stabilizes. When G is large, all nodes move toward the city with near equal strength and when G is very small, only the winning node moves toward the city. The weight adjustment made to node k following a city presentation is given by

$$w_k^i \leftarrow w_k^i + f(G, d)(x_k^i - w_k^i)$$

where w_k^i is the weight identifying node k for city i, d is the distance from node k and the winning node, and x_k^i is the location of city i. The distance function f is defined as

$$f(G, n) = \frac{1}{\sqrt{2\pi}} \exp(-d^2/G^2)$$

The only parameter that requires adjustment during the adaptation process is G where it is reduced after each complete iteration by

$$G \leftarrow (1 - \alpha)G$$

A number of simulations carried out for small and medium size sets of cities confirmed that the network solutions were good (less than 3% greater than optimum). A solution for a 1,000-city problem produced a tour length of 18,036 as illustrated in Figure 14.21. The cities were assigned randomly to points in the plane rectangle of size $1,000 \times 500$ units. A value of $\alpha = 0.01$ required 12 hours of computation time to stabilize to this tour length. A value of $\alpha = 0.2$ required only 20 minutes to stabilize to tour lengths ranging between 18,200 to 18,800. The optimum tour for this set is not known.

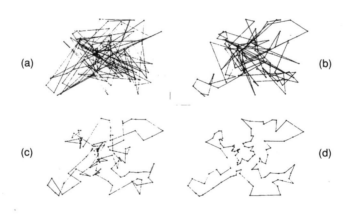

Figure 14.21   SOFM Solution to a 1,000 Randomly Placed City TSP

Pattern Recognition

Web-process inspection is an on-line inspection method used for the detection of faults on the surface of sheet material such as plated steel. Due to the large surface area and material speed of travel, vast amounts of data must be inspected for on-line operation. In an application described by Gruber et al. (1993), an LVQ2 network was trained to detect flaws in the surfaces of coated sheet steel taken from the production line of a canned food manufacturer. Three types of steel samples were inspected: tin plated and two different qualities of chromium-dioxide coated steel which have characteristic scratches in the roll direction. The surface characteristics of these samples makes inspection using intensity based methods difficult because texture must be taken into account to obtain good results. Typical defects include rust, lamination, rollmark, scratch, weld, and stain.

The training and test sets each contained 135 feature vectors: 45 vectors for good surfaces and 15 feature vectors for each of the six types of surface defects. The system was trained on each of the feature vectors and training and test sets used no common data. Training was done for both fault-no-fault classification as well as for fault-class classification. Class training used the seven fault types listed above. The performance of the two methods were similar in spite of the fact that the fault-class training was more extensive.

The inspection system consisted of several components: a rotating mirror which sweeps a helium neon laser beam over the surface at high speeds in the crossweb direction, a CCD camera which collects the scattered light from the surface of the material, mirrors to direct the light beam and the neural network detector. The overall accuracy of the system in detecting various types of defects is illustrated in Figure 14.22.

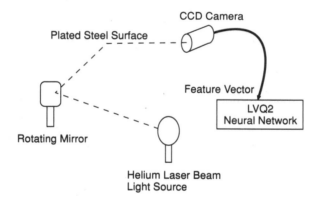

Figure 14.22   Fault Recognition Using the Hybrid Feature Set

The CCD array camera was segmented so that each segment could observe a portion of angular distribution of the scattering. The output of each segment, which is proportional to the scattered light intensity integrated over the surface of the segment, is then used as a feature. The set of features derived from all the segments at one position of the laser beam defines the complete feature vector. The segmented pixel arrangement of the CCD array is illustrated in Figure 14.23.

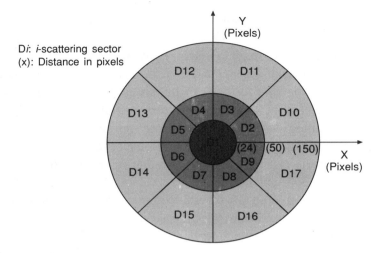

Figure 14.23   Seventeen Features from the Segmented CCD Array
(From Gruber et al., 1993. Courtesy of the authors.)

The 17 segments define the 17 features noted above. Statistical analyses of the data showed that a significant number of the features were not used by the network because, even though they may carry useful information, their low values are obscured by larger valued features. Consequently, two reduced feature sets were determined, one with seven and one with nine components. The classification accuracies for the two reduced feature sets are illustrated in Figure 14.24b. The classification accuracies given as bars in the figure are, from left to right: good, rust, laminations, rollmark, scratch, weld, stain, and overall classification, respectively. Similar accuracies were obtained for the 17 feature set (Figure 14.24a).

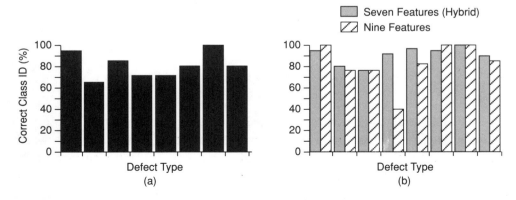

Figure 14.24   LVQ2 Network Fault Classification Accuracies for (a) a 17-Dimensional Feature
Vector and (b) Seven and Nine Feature Component Vectors
(From Gruber et al., 1993. Courtesy of the authors.)

In addition to the LVQ network, which was used to perform the actual classification, an ART 2 network was used to assess and improve the feature space. This led to the dimensional reduction in the feature space noted above.

Handwritten Signature Authentication. Perhaps the most widely used method for authenticating a person's identity is from a personal handwritten signature. This act is the basis for the daily transfer of billions of dollars using checks and other financial transaction instruments. Clearly, reliable methods of automated signature verification are important. One interesting application of automated authentication makes use of a hybrid ANN system.

The system uses two SOFM networks for initial signature classification and three multilayer feedforward nets trained with backpropagation for final authentication. The SOFM networks were used for initial classification since it was difficult to devise a set of supervised training data which accurately classified signatures into distinct sets. The signature classes are too ambiguous for human grouping and classification. The complete three level system of networks for authentication is illustrated in Figure 14.25.

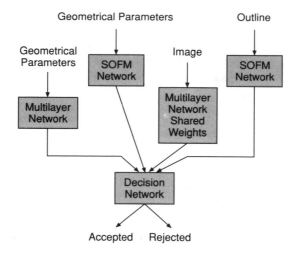

Figure 14.25   Three-Level Signature Authentication System of Neural Networks

Raw CCD camera images of the document containing the signatures consist of 1,024 × 512 pixels of 256 gray levels. Because of this, the full image could not be used for direct pixel input unless an unwieldy network size was used. Consequently, it was decided that authentication should be done in stages, the first stage being used to preclassify the signatures into similarity groups. This was the role of the two SOFM networks which used geometrical parameters and outline as inputs. Subsequent stages were specific to each signature. They were used to determine if the signature was authentic or a forgery. These roles were given to the MLFF networks which used image and geometrical parameters as input.

Inputs to one of the Kohonen SOFM networks was a 29 component feature vector computed from images of the signature. The features were size, orientation of the strokes and inertia moments. These features were believed to be both discriminant and stable as a source for reduced feature characteristics. Input to the second SOFM network was the signature outline consisting of some 400 inputs (two times the width of the outline). Both SOFM networks were square (25, 36, 49, 64) with the size being chosen by experimentation. The networks were trained using a database of 6,000 digitized checks obtained from the French Post Office. The forgeries used for training were signatures randomly taken from the same database belonging to the same siganture class as the genuine signature used in the training. A separate SOFM network was used to develop the training set by classifying the signatures into similarity sets.

Inputs to the two intermediate stage MLFF networks were the same as the SOFM inputs, the 29 geometrical features described above and the signature image respectively. In the latter case, weight sharing was used for input to the first and second hidden-layer connections (see Chapter 8 for a description of weight sharing). Both second stage networks had a single output node. The final stage of the system consisted of a single-layer network with the four previous stage networks providing inputs to the network. This network was used to make the final decision to accept or reject the signature. The network was trained with backpropagation to output a binary value, accept or reject.

With a goal of industrial strength applicability, an acceptable system must be able to accurately classify millions of signatures from hundreds of thousands of signatories. The present system required only some 300 samples from each signatory to achieve accuracies of about a 5% false reject rate, and a 2% false accept rate. Although the system described was not of industrial strength quality, the approach shows some promise in realizing the intended objectives.

Robot Control

To illustrate the ability of an SOFM network to perform nonlinear mappings we consider a complicated robotic arm application. Suppose the arm has three degrees of freedom as illustrated in Figure 14.26. The goal is to map the position of the target as sensed by the two cameras to three drive motor outputs that position the gripper at the desired target position. Because of their spacial separation, the two

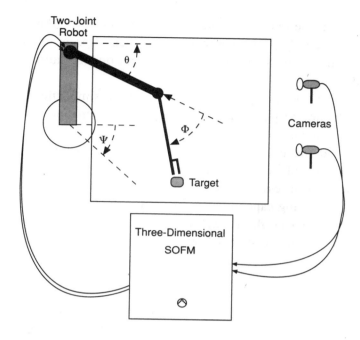

Figure 14.26   Robotic Control Application

cameras provide stereo information to the network.

Each target location corresponds to a point in the image plane of each of the two cameras. The cameras implicitly record the Cartesian coordinates of the target. When taken together, the two-dimensional vector coordinate outputs from the two cameras provide three-dimensional positioning information on the target. This information is conveyed by the cameras as four inputs to the SOFM. The SOFM is a three-dimensional lattice of units that must learn to map the four-dimensional camera inputs to the appropriate responding unit. The unit with weight values nearest the input vector is responsible for all target points in its neighborhood. This unit responds by sending a three-dimensional vector output (Ψ, Θ, Φ) to the robot drive motors to position the robot gripper at the target position. Clearly, the mapping is highly nonlinear since three different coordinate positions and two coordinate representations are involved.

During the training phase, target positions are chosen randomly. The target position is then viewed by the cameras and fed to the SOFM network. The unit with weight vector $\mathbf{w}_r$ that most closely matches the camera input vector is adapted (neighboring units are also adapted) and the unit sends its output to the drive motors. Initially, the untrained network will not position the arm correctly. The network must then use the arm-to-target error to improve its response. This can be achieved with a weight update rule that uses gradient descent to reduce the errors. The network must discover the mapping relationship autonomously in an unsupervised manner.

The system as portrayed here is actually very simplistic. The network as described could not respond very accurately as the mapping is from a four-dimensional continuous space to a discrete three-dimensional space. To position the gripper exactly at the target requires that the network learn offset distances in addition to selection of the responsible unit. After initial positioning of the arm, further refinement is necessary as sensed from the target-to-gripper-error. This also poses additional learning capabilities on the network. The more refined model has been derived by Ritter et al. (1992). A full description of the robotic problem is beyond the scope of our treatment here.

Summary

In this chapter, we have examined networks that adapt to their environment through different forms of unsupervised learning. We first looked at the behavior of single layer networks that adapt using a form of Hebbian learning. It was shown that these networks can perform a type of principal component analysis (PCA) on the input patterns. We also looked at multilayer linear networks that are trained layer by layer to acquire feature extraction capabilities similar to those found in the visual system of mammals. These networks also performed a type of PCA as well as other forms of optimization on the input patterns. We also examined competitive forms of unsupervised learning, the type of adaptation methods used in two additional types of networks: learning vector quantization (LVQ) and the self-organizing feature maps (SOFM). The learning paradigms studied for LVQ were both supervised and unsupervised. Variations on the basic LVQ networks were also examined. We then studied the unusual properties of SOFM which was introduced and studied extensively by Teuvo Kohonen. Various applications were also described for both LVQ and SOFM networks, including speech recognition, optimization, pattern recognition and control.

15
Adaptive Resonance Theory

In this chapter, we look at another important class of recurrent networks that have been named Adaptive Resonance Theory (ART) networks. These networks were largely the product of Stephen Grossberg and his associates, especially Gail Carpenter and other members of the Center for Adaptive Systems, Boston University who developed and studied initial ART architectures during the mid-1970s through the 80s. Since that time the class of ART networks have been generalized, studied extensively, and have been used in a broad range of applications. We begin the chapter with an introductory section, and go on to describe the basic theory and operation of the simplest class of ART networks, ART 1. We then look at a generalized version of ART 1, namely the ART 2 network and corresponding learning algorithms for both types of networks. We also look at some further generalizations of ART networks and finally, we describe some typical applications.

15.1 Introduction

In developing neuronal network models of biological systems, we would expect that some of the basic properties exhibited by the networks would be comparable to their biological counterparts. In particular, we would like our networks to have the ability to continually adapt in a changing environment. This means being able to retain useful facts and information in memory while at the same time learning new, important facts. New facts learned should not "wash away" old useful information. At the same time, we would like our model to be able to ignore irrelevant information and even forget outmoded or unimportant information. In other words, we would like our networks to exhibit a high degree of stability when adaptively learning new categories or concepts. We would not want the network to forget (or otherwise lose) or even alter useful facts previously stored in memory in order to accommodate the newly learned knowledge. On the other hand, we would want the network to be adaptable and hence, plastic (non-rigid) enough to be able to recognize and learn new useful concepts or categories. Such a network must, of course, be able to discriminate between useful and irrelevant information. These two conflicting traits, stability and plasticity, are what Grossberg calls the *stability-plasticity* dilemma: how can a network retain its stability while still being plastic enough to gainfully adapt in a changing environment. We would also hope that a network would not need to be unduly large to retain both the stability and plasticity characteristics during adaptation over an extended period of time.

Adaptive resonance theory was developed over some period of time as an extension to competitive/cooperative learning systems. It was developed in an attempt to overcome the stability-plasticity problem and other unstable learning characteristics associated with competitive networks. The resultant networks have a number of important traits that other architectures lack, including: real-time (on-line) learning, self-organization (unsupervised learning) capability, self-stabilizing memory in response to arbitrarily many input patterns, fast adaptive search for best match of input-to-stored patterns, fast (or slow) learning ability, rejection of *unfamiliar* input patterns when memory capacity has been reached, variable error criteria which permits the variable regulation of category groupings, and successful retention of the stability and plasticity characteristics throughout the operational life of the system. Some limitations of ART networks include the general complexity of the networks, the ability to process binary patterns only (ART 1 networks), difficulty in setting the error criteria parameter appropriately for some applications and the relatively inefficient use of output neurons (one neuron required for each category learned).

ART networks map n-dimensional input patterns to output categories or classes based on the input pattern's features. Similar (nearest-neighbor) input patterns are grouped into the same class and dissimilar patterns into separate, distinct classes. The degree of similarity required for intraclass pattern groupings is adjustable so that many class groupings of highly similar patterns are created when a similarity threshold value is set to a high level. At the other extreme, fewer classes are created when the threshold is set to a low value. In this latter case, class members may possess a lesser degree of similarity. The threshold setting can be adjusted manually or dynamically during operation of the network depending on the specific application. This permits an ART network to become more or less selective of pattern groupings as it continues to adapt.

Learning in ART networks occurs naturally in real-time during normal operation of the network. This is a form of continuous, unsupervised adaptive learning where a new category is automatically formed whenever a novel input pattern is presented to the network. New categories will continue to be formed from novel inputs until the network exhausts its pool of uncommitted output category neurons at which time it will reject any further new novel input patterns. Input patterns that are similar to already established categories are promptly "recognized" by producing a high output at the selected category neuron. Inputs that match existing categories also initiate some degree of learning for the given category, without at the same time upsetting the stability of the learned categories.

We first describe the operation and dynamics of the simplest version of ART, ART 1, and then proceed to describe some generalizations of the basic network including ART 2 and other variations on the ART architectures.

15.2 The ART 1 Network Architecture

ART 1 is designed for binary inputs only. These networks perform a mapping from n-dimensional binary input patterns to a single output category. The network consists of two fully connected layers with adaptive (adjustable) weights on all connections linking the bottom layer nodes, the F1 layer, to the top layer nodes, the F2 layer, and adaptive weights on all feedback connections linking the top layer nodes back to the bottom layer nodes. In addition, there are connections between both the F1 and F2 layer neurons to special neurons that perform control functions. The basic architecture is illustrated in Figure 15.1.

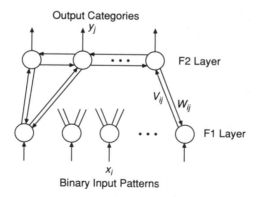

Figure 15.1   The Basic ART 1 Network Architecture

When an input pattern is presented to the F1 layer neurons, an output activation is generated by each of the neurons. The F1 layer output signals are then passed on to the F2 layer through synoptic weights v_{ij}. The F2 neuron that has a closest match between the signal vector arriving from the F1 layer and its corresponding weight vector **V** becomes the winner in a "winner-takes-all" competition among the F2 neurons. The winning F2 neuron then produces an output activation signal, a stored top-down memory *expectation* that is propagated back to the F1 layer through the feedback weights w_{ji}. The outputs of all other F2 layer neurons are driven to zero through the competitive process, and hence, prevented from producing output signals. The weighted signal fed back to the F1 layer is compared to the input signal at the F1 layer. If the match between the two signals is close, the activation output from the F1 layer is strengthened. (Note that the signal fed back by the winning F2 neuron may alter the activation levels of the F1 neurons.) The strengthened F1 output signal in turn reinforces the signal fed back from the F2 winner and a form of resonance occurs between the two layers. When this process stabilizes, the winning F2 neuron produces a high output signal signifying the selected category for the input pattern.

When the match between the input pattern and the recalled signal from the F2 layer is not "close enough," a reset signal forces the winning F2 neuron to deactivate for the duration of the cycle. Following the reset, the input signal at F1 again reactivates the F2 layer neurons and a new F2 neuron may then become the winner in a second winner-takes-all contest. Again, if the match between the input pattern and signal pattern fedback from the new F2 winner is not close enough, another reset occurs, deactivating the second F2 winner. This hypothesis testing process continues until a good match is found or until all committed neurons in F2 have been deactivated. In the latter case, a new, uncommitted neuron is selected to become a newly created category. The new category is created by setting both the feedforward and feedback connection weights to the same pattern values as the (binary) input pattern.

Given a new input pattern, if all of the available neurons in the F2 layer have been previously committed to categories and an acceptable bottom-up to top-down match is not found, the input pattern is rejected. None of the output F2 neurons will become active and no learning occurs. In fact, the *adaptive* learning only occurs whenever a good match is found and resonance has been established (of course, a type of direct pattern learning does occur whenever a newly committed neuron is selected). Learning is accomplished through an adjustment of the weights in both the feedforward and feedbackward paths to shift the values in the direction of the input pattern, a pattern that is already close to the stored category prototype pattern. The name "adaptive resonance theory" was given to these networks to signify that normal adaptive learning only occurs during resonance between F1 and F2.

ART networks have two additional subnetworks that perform control functions.

One such subnetwork, called the Short Term Memory reset (STM reset) is a part of the Orienting Subsystem (node denoted A in Figure 15.2).

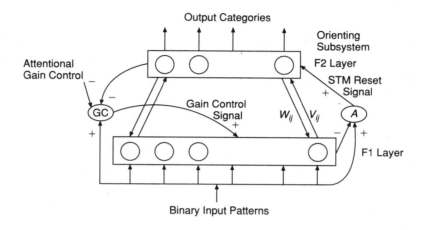

Figure 15.2   ART 1 Pattern and Control Signal Flow Paths

STM reset sends a signal to inhibit the active F2 layer node when the match between the input pattern and the F2 layer activation pattern is not close enough. The degree of mismatch tolerated before a reset signal is generated depends on an adjustable threshold value ρ called a *vigilance* parameter.

The second subnetwork is called the Attentional Gain Control (AGC) as illustrated in Figure 15.2. The function of this subnetwork is to regulate the category hypothesis testing process and self-stabilization of learning. It provides the mechanism needed whereby the F1 layer can differentiate between the bottom-up and top-down signals received. The subnetwork has three inputs: an excitatory bottom-up input signal, an inhibitory top-down expectation signal and an inhibitory intermodal signal (input pattern switching control signal). The AGC becomes activated and produces an output to F1 nodes when an input pattern $\mathbf{I}$ is presented at F1. The output excites equally each node in the F1 layer permitting F1 nodes to become active enough to send output signals to the F2 layer. When the F2 layer becomes active, the AGC is shut off by the inhibitory signal from F2. Consequently, the F1 nodes must receive a reinforcing (expectation) input from the F2 layer in order to sustain an output. In other words, the F1 layer must receive two of its three inputs to remain active. Otherwise, the total output from F1 is decreased. The requirement that two of the three inputs be active for an output to be generated is known as the 2/3 Rule. Clearly, this subnetwork interacts with the operation of the Short Term Memory Reset process. We describe the operation of the subnetwork in more detail below.

ART 1 Dynamics

The adjustable weights in ART are referred to as long term memory (LTM) since they change or adapt slowly relative to the presentation of input patterns over time. Neuron activations caused by input signals on the other hand are referred to as short term memory (STM) since they are usually short lived, lasting for only a single processing cycle. From Figures 15.1 and 15.2, we see that F1 collectively denotes the *feature* field layer of neurons and F2 collectively refers to the *category* field or output layer of neurons. To understand the dynamics of ART 1 networks and how the layers interact, we need some further notation. We let $\mathbf{I}$ denote the external binary input vector $\mathbf{I} = (I_1, I_2, ..., I_n)$ where I_i is the input bit to node i of F1. Let x_i be the activity signal value received at node i, $i = 1, 2, ..., n$. (The vector $\mathbf{X}$ of activity signals, the so-called short term trace of F1, will initially be equal to the input $\mathbf{I}$, but in general may differ due to feedback signals from the F2 layer.) The output activation x_i from node i is filtered (multiplied) by v_{ij}, the LTM component (weight) on the feedforward connection between node i of F1 and node j of F2 to give $R_i = x_i v_{ij}$. This signal is transmitted on to node j in the F2 layer where it is combined with other signals from F1. Let S_j ($j = 1, 2, ..., m$) be the total signal received at node j of the F2 layer, where

$$S_j = \sum_{i=1}^{n} x_i v_{ij} = \sum_{i=1}^{n} R_i \qquad (15.1)$$

The output signal generated by node j of the F2 layer is the result of a competitive exchange among the F2 nodes. The F2 node receiving the largest net input wins. The output from the jth node is given by y_j, the STM trace at F2, where

$$y_j = f(S_j) = \begin{cases} 1 & \text{if } S_j = \max\{S_k\} \\ 0 & \text{otherwise} \end{cases} \qquad (15.2)$$

The F2 layer output activation signal $\mathbf{Y} = \{y_1, y_2, ..., y_m\}$ is fed back to layer F1 nodes through top-down LTM weights w_{ji}. These weights filter the signal fedback from node j in F2 to give $T_j = y_j w_{ji}$. These signals are combined with other signals from F2 and passed on to node i in the F1 layer. The net activation signal value received at node i of the F1 layer from the F2 layer is U_i where

$$U_i = \sum_{j=1}^{m} y_j w_{ji} = \sum_{j=1}^{m} T_j \qquad \qquad (15.3)$$

The vector **U** is combined with the input pattern signal **I** at F1 to produce a new output vector $\mathbf{X}^* = \{x_1^*, x_2^*, \ldots, x_n^*\}$ from the F1 layer. The input signal **I** is also *compared* to the feedback signal **U** in the F1 layer to see how closely they match. The comparison is used to determine if a reset is initiated or not. The complete (roundtrip) transformation of signals from binary input **I** received at F1 to receipt of the feedback signal **U** (from F2) back at F1 is:

$$\mathbf{I} \rightarrow \mathbf{X} \rightarrow \mathbf{R} \rightarrow \mathbf{S} \rightarrow \mathbf{Y} \rightarrow \mathbf{T} \rightarrow \mathbf{U}$$

A reset signal is generated by node A of the Orienting Subsystem whenever the the match between the top-down expectation and the input pattern is not close enough. This occurs whenever the net input to A is less than the threshold parameter value ρ. This will be the case whenever the top-down components from F2 differ from the input signal by a prescribed amount. One input to A is excitatory $(+)$. It is proportional to the input signal **I**, that is, $\pi|\mathbf{I}|$, where $|\mathbf{I}|$ denotes the number of positive components (one bit) in the input **I** and π is a positive constant. The other input to A is an inhibitory signal $(-)$. It is proportional to the output of the F1 layer signals, that is $\theta|\mathbf{X}|$ where again $|\mathbf{X}|$ denotes the number of positive components in the vector **X** and θ is a positive constant. The inhibitory signal is chosen to be larger than the excitatory signal $(\pi \le \theta)$ so that no reset is generated when the F2 layer is inactive (then $|\mathbf{X}| = |\mathbf{I}|$). The vigilance parameter ρ is therefore appropriately defined to be the ratio given by $\rho = \pi/\theta \le 1$ and reset occurs whenever $|\mathbf{X}|/|\mathbf{I}| < \rho$. Likewise, the match/reset criteria prevents a reset signal from occurring whenever the proportion of positive top-down to input signals exceeds the threshold, that is whenever

$$\frac{|\mathbf{X}|}{|\mathbf{I}|} = \frac{|\mathbf{U} \cap \mathbf{I}|}{|\mathbf{I}|} \ge \rho$$

In this case, resonance will occur whenever enough of the specific active nodes in F2 match the same active input signal components of **I** at F1.

The 2/3 Rule requires that two of the three inputs to the F1 layer be active in order that the F1 layer nodes be supraliminally activated. Any output from F2 sends an inhibitory signal to the Attentional Gain Control subnetwork node thus preventing F1 layer nodes from becoming very active unless *specific* matching excitatory signals are also received at the F1 layer from the F2 layer through the LTM paths. Thus, in order for resonance to occur, the top-down signal must match the input signal to the extent required by the vigilance threshold level. We see that the 2/3 Rule thereby permits the network to differentiate between matching and nonmatching input and top-down expectation signals and supports the reset criteria. Note that the third input to the Gain Control node is an inhibitory signal (an intermodality input) which prevents an input **I** alone from overly activating F1 layer nodes.

The activity of node i in the F1 layer is governed by the differential equation

$$\delta \frac{dx_i}{dt} = -x_i + (1 - a_1 x_i) J_i^+ - (b_1 + c_1 x_i) J_i^- \tag{15.4}$$

where $J_i^+ = I_i + U_i$ is the total excitatory input to node i and $J_i^- = \sum_j f(y_j)$ is the total inhibitory input to node i (the Attentional Gain Control signal input described above). The parameters δ, a_1, b_1, and c_1 are all nonnegative. Similar equations govern the behavior of the F2 layer node activities from which the application of equation (15.2), the winner-takes-all criteria, is then applied. The activation equations for F2 layer nodes are given by

$$\delta \frac{dy_j}{dt} = -y_j + (1 - a_2 y_j) J_j^+ - (b_2 + c_2 y_j) J_j^- \tag{15.5}$$

where the parameters δ, a_2, b_2, and c_2, are nonnegative and $J_j^+ = g(y_j) + S_j$, is a positive self-feedback signal to node j. The input quantity $J_j^- = \sum_{k \neq j} g(y_k)$ is the sum of negative feedback signals from all other nodes in the F2 layer. The parameters in the above equations are chosen such that the F2 node receiving the largest net input S_j becomes the winner among all *nondisabled* nodes in F2, that is, node j is the winner, with

$$y_j = f(S_j) = \begin{cases} 1 & \text{if } S_j = \max\{S_k : k \in J\} \\ 0 & \text{otherwise} \end{cases} \tag{15.6}$$

where we have modified equation (15.2) by adding the F2 layer node index set J which includes only the node indices in F2 that have not been disabled by a reset signal.

ART 1 Learning

Learning occurs in LTM whenever a match is found and resonance has occurred or whenever a newly committed category node in F2 is chosen. The equations governing learning in both the bottom-up and top-down LTM paths follow the Weber Law and Associative Decay rules which require that LTM weights learned during encoding of an F1 pattern **X** having a smaller number of positive inputs be made larger than the weights for a signal **X** with more positive components. This condition is required to be able to distinguish pattern **a** from pattern **b** by the F2 category nodes when **a** is a proper subset of **b** (**a** $\subset$ **b**). Consistent with this requirement, the implementation presented here allows for competitive interactions among the F1 layer nodes. The details of the combined Weber Law and Associative Decay rules used in the implementation of ART 1 presented here are discussed in detail in Grossberg (1988).

Either fast or slow learning can be implementd in ART networks. In what follows, we concentrate only on fast learning. For this, the bottom-up/top-down LTM learning equations are of the same basic form, but the bottom-up path equations are somewhat more complicated to account for the competition during learning. For the bottom-up paths we have weight adjustments according to

$$\frac{dv_{ij}}{dt} = \kappa f(S_j)\left[(1 - v_{ij})\lambda h(x_i) - v_{ij}\sum_{k \neq i} h(x_k)\right] \tag{15.7}$$

where κ and λ are constants, $f(S_j) = y_j$ is the output of node j in F2 and $h(x_j)$ is the output emitted by node i in F1.

The top-down learning equations are somewhat simpler. They are given by

$$\frac{dw_{ji}}{dt} = f(S_j)\left[-w_{ji} + h(x_i)\right] \tag{15.8}$$

The simplicity of equation (15.8) over (15.7) is due to a simplification of constants equivalent to κ and λ in equation (15.7). For the implementation described here, they have both been set equal to 1 in equation (15.8).

A consequence of the application of both the Weber Law and Associative Decay rule is that LTM learning will only take place when either a proper match is found between bottom-up pattern and top-down memory expectation or when a new novel pattern is recognized and uncommitted F2 nodes are available. The LTM equations (15.7) and (15.8) can then be expressed in the succinct forms given below. Note that bottom-up learning occurs when node i in F1 and node j in F2 are both active since then both $f(S_j) = y_j = 1$ and $h(x_j) = 1$; on the other hand v_{ij} quickly decays to zero when node i in F1 is inactive, but node j in F2 is active; and finally, no learning takes place in v_{ij} if node j in F2 is inactive.

$$\frac{dv_{ij}}{dt} = \begin{cases} \kappa[(1 - v_{ij})\lambda - v_{ij}(|\mathbf{X}| - 1)] & \text{if node } i \text{ in F1 and node } j \text{ in F2 are active (1)} \\ -\kappa|\mathbf{X}|v_{ij} & \text{if node } i \text{ in F1 is inactive and node } j \text{ in F2 is active (1)} \\ 0 & \text{if node } j \text{ in F2 is inactive (0)} \end{cases}$$

$$(15.9)$$

A similar equation for top-down LTM learning can be derived for the three cases cited above. Thus, some learning occurs in w_{ji} whenever node i in F1 and node j in F2 are both active since then both $f(S_j) = y_j = 1$ and $h(x_j) = 1$ and increases exponentially toward 1 (node j tries to learn the activity pattern across F1); but, v_{ij} quickly decays (exponentially) to zero when node i in F1 is inactive, but node j in F2 is active (the 2/3 Rule ensures that node i remains inactive unless there is a supporting input $\mathbf{I}$); and no learning takes place in v_{ij} if node j in F2 is inactive, thus

$$\frac{dw_{ji}}{dt} = \begin{cases} -w_{ji} + 1 & \text{if node } i \text{ in F1 and node } j \text{ in F2 are active (1)} \\ -w_{ji} & \text{if node } i \text{ in F1 is inactive and node } j \text{ in F2 is active (1)} \\ 0 & \text{if node } j \text{ in F2 is inactive (0)} \end{cases} \qquad (15.10)$$

To ensure that the hypothesis search process proceeds orderly in the F2 layer and to ensure that uncommitted F2 nodes do not learn from input patterns unless they are actually selected for a new category, it is necessary to preset the values of the bottom-up and top-down weights v_{ij} and w_{ji} respectively. It can be shown that the initial values for the bottom-up weights should satisfy the requirements

$$0 < v_{ij}(0) < \frac{\lambda}{\lambda - 1 + m} \qquad (15.11)$$

where m is the number of F2 layer nodes. This is known as the *direct access inequality*.

The initial top-down weight values should satisfy the *template learning inequality*

$$\frac{b_1 - 1}{d} < w_{ji}(0) \leq 1 \qquad (15.12)$$

where b_1 is defined in equation (15.4) and d is a positive constant multiplier for active F2 node outputs.

Furthermore, it can be shown that during the (fast) learning process the weight values approach limiting asymptotes according to the following

$$v_{ij} \cong \begin{cases} \dfrac{\lambda}{\lambda - 1 + |\mathbf{X}|} & \text{if } i \in \mathbf{X} \\ 0 & \text{if } i \notin \mathbf{X} \end{cases} \qquad (15.13)$$

and

$$w_{ji} \cong \begin{cases} 1 & \text{if } i \in \mathbf{X} \\ 0 & \text{if } i \notin \mathbf{X} \end{cases} \qquad (15.14)$$

on each learning trial.

Grossberg (1988) has proven a number of theorems which demonstrate that learning in response to an arbitrary list of binary input patterns to ART 1 is self-stabilizing and that all patterns directly access their categories after the recognition learning process stabilizes.

15.3 The ART 2 Network Architecture

ART 2 networks are generalizations of ART 1 networks. They are capable of learning and recognizing real-valued (and binary-valued) input patterns. The connectivity of ART 2 networks is similar to that of ART 1 except that the input nodes are somewhat more complicated. Input layer F1 nodes in ART 2 actually consist of a small subnetwork of six nodes that serve as a buffer between the input signal and the top-down expectation signal. These nodes also carry out normalization and matching functions on both the input signals and the signals fedback from F2. The category layer F2 is the same in ART 2 as in ART 1.

ART 2 Dynamics

The architecture of ART 2 is illustrated in Figure 15.3 where a single input F1 layer node has been expanded to expose the function of the subnetwork nodes contained within the ith F1 layer node. The bottom-up path of the input signal I_i to the jth node in layer F2 is

$$I_i \rightarrow t_i \rightarrow x_i \rightarrow s_i \rightarrow u_i \rightarrow p_i \rightarrow S_j$$

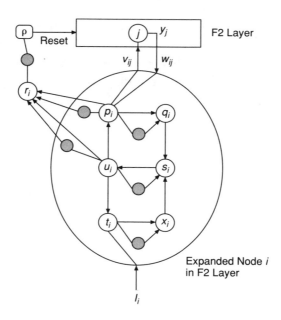

Figure 15.3   ART 2 with Expanded View of a Single Node i in the F1 Layer
(Courtesy of Professor Stephen Grossberg)

where

$$S_j = \sum_{i=1}^{n} p_i v_{ij}$$

is the sum of all weighted inputs to node j from the F1 layer.

The top-down signal path from the output (y_j) of the jth F2 layer node to the ith node in layer F1 is

$$y_j \rightarrow p_i \rightarrow q_j \rightarrow s_i \rightarrow u_j$$

Note that the signal received at u_i will, in general, be changed as a result of the return path signal. Also, it should be noted that the Attentional Gain Control (AGC) function described for ART 1 has been distributed over several nodes in ART 2. AGC is carried out through the links passing through the smaller shaded nodes (Figure 15.3), the GC nuclei which inhibit their target nodes in proportion to the L2 norm of the activation source node outputs.

The output activity of node i ($i = 1, 2, ..., n$) o_i in the F1 layer can be written in the same general form as that for ART 1, that is

$$\varepsilon \frac{do_i}{dt} = -Ao_i + (1 - Bo_i)J_i^+ - (C + Do_i)J_i^- \tag{15.15}$$

where, as in the ART 1 case J_i^+ is the total excitatory input and J_i^- is the total inhibitory input to node i and ε is a small positive constant, the ratio of the STM and LTM relaxation times. For ART 2 (in conformance with Figure 15.3), equation (15.15) can be simplified by setting $B = C = 0$, and letting $\varepsilon \to 0$. The singular form of (15.15) can then be written as

$$o_i = \frac{J_i^+}{A + DJ_i^-} \tag{15.16}$$

Using this form, the equations governing the dynamics of node i in F1 (the expanded subnetwork of Figure 15.3) can now be given. They are, in order from bottom-up signal flow

$$t_i = I_i + au_i \tag{15.17}$$

$$x_i = \frac{t_i}{e + \|\mathbf{t}\|} \tag{15.18}$$

$$s_i = f(x_i) + bf(q_i) \tag{15.19}$$

$$u_i = \frac{s_i}{e + \|\mathbf{s}\|} \tag{15.20}$$

$$q_i = \frac{p_i}{e + \|\mathbf{p}\|} \tag{15.21}$$

$$p_i = u_i + \sum_j g(y_j)w_{ji} \tag{15.22}$$

where $0 < a < 1$, $b > 0$, and $e > 0$ are constants, $\|\mathbf{x}\|$ is the norm of the vector $\mathbf{x}$, and $f(x)$ is the continuously differentiable function

$$f(x) = \begin{cases} \dfrac{2\theta x^2}{x^2 + \theta^2} & \text{if } 0 \leq x \leq \theta \\ x & \text{otherwise} \end{cases} \tag{15.23}$$

Since x_i and q_i are always between 0 and 1, the value of f is also bounded by 0 and

1. (Note that the constant e is included as a safeguard in case the norms in equations (15.18), (15.20) and (15.21) become very small. In practice, equations (15.17) to (15.22) can be simplified by setting e to zero and then $\|\mathbf{x}\| = \|\mathbf{q}\| = \|\mathbf{u}\| = 1$.) The function $g(y_j)$ in (15.22) is the competitive selection function which makes a choice among the F2 layer nodes, depending on the relative strengths of the S_j signals at the F2 layer, that is

$$g(y_j) = \begin{cases} d & \text{if } S_j = \max\{S_k : \text{the } k\text{th node has not been reset}\} \\ 0 & \text{otherwise} \end{cases} \qquad (15.24)$$

where y_j is the activity of the jth node in F2 and $0 < d < 1$ is a constant. Note that from (15.24), equation (15.22) reduces to the simple form

$$p_i = \begin{cases} u_i & \text{if F2 is inactive} \\ u_i + dw_{Ji} & \text{if node } J \text{ in F2 is active} \end{cases} \qquad (15.25)$$

The match and reset operation in ART 2 is performed in the Orienting Subsystem with the vector $\mathbf{r} = (r_1, r_2, ..., r_n)$ where

$$r_i = \frac{u_i + cp_i}{\|\mathbf{u}\| + \|c\mathbf{p}\|} \text{ and } c > 0 \text{ is a constant.} \qquad (15.26)$$

A reset is performed in F2 whenever the match between the input STM and stored LTM is not close enough as determined by the vigilance parameter (where $0 < \rho < 1$), that is, whenever

$$\frac{\rho}{e + \|\mathbf{r}\|} > 1$$

It can be shown that $\|\mathbf{r}\| = 1$ when the STM pattern $\mathbf{u}$ exactly matches the LTM pattern of the selected node in F2 (say node J with LTM pattern w_{Ji}). Thus, since reset occurs only if $\rho \leq \|\mathbf{r}\|$, no reset will occur in F2 when $\mathbf{u}$ and $\mathbf{w}_J$ match closely (i.e. $\cos(\mathbf{u}, \mathbf{w}_J)$ is near 1). This will be the case whenever a top-down expectation pattern matches the input pattern well. A reset must also be prevented from occurring when none of the committed nodes match $\mathbf{u}$ well since then a new uncommitted node must be selected to represent (learn) the new unrecognized input pattern. This can be accomplished by assigning the weights of all uncommitted nodes initial values near zero (for all uncommitted nodes $\mathbf{J}$, $\|\mathbf{w}_\mathbf{J}\| \cong 0$). Like ART 1, we see that a reset is prevented whenever some learning is needed.

ART 2 Learning

Although the architecture of ART 2 is more complex than ART 1, the learning process is essentially the same. In fact, the LTM learning equations are somewhat simpler. The bottom-up and top-down LTM learning equations for ART 2 are given by

$$\frac{dv_{ij}}{dt} = g(y_j)[p_i - v_{ij}] \qquad \text{bottom-up} \qquad (15.27)$$

$$\frac{dw_{ji}}{dt} = g(y_j)[p_i - w_{ij}] \qquad \text{top-down} \qquad (15.28)$$

If, for a given input, the STM pattern **u** matches one of the stored F2 node LTM patterns closely enough, that node (say node J) is selected as the winner and some learning takes place. In that case, because of (15.24), equations (15.27) and (15.28) can be written as

$$\frac{dv_{iJ}}{dt} = d(1 - d)\left[\frac{u_i}{1 - d} - v_{iJ}\right] \qquad (15.29)$$

$$\frac{dw_{Ji}}{dt} = d(1 - d)\left[\frac{u_i}{1 - d} - w_{Ji}\right] \qquad (15.39)$$

For all other F2 nodes ($j \neq J$), $dv_{ij}/dt = 0$ and $dw_{Ji}/dt = 0$ so no learning takes place in these nodes.

It was noted above that the weights of all uncommitted nodes in F2 must have initial values near zero (for uncommitted nodes J, $\|\mathbf{w}_J\| \cong 0$) to prevent reset from occurring when a poor match results between **u** and $\mathbf{w}_J$. The bottom-up LTM traces $\mathbf{v}_i$ must also be initialized near zero, but for a different reason. From (15.28) it can be shown that for the bottom-up weights connecting to the Jth node in F2, say $\mathbf{v}_J$, $\|\mathbf{v}_J\| \rightarrow 1/(1 - d)$ during learning. Thus, if the initial value of the $\mathbf{v}_J$ were chosen greater than $1/(1 - d)$ an input that chose an uncommitted node during a trial could switch to other uncommitted nodes during the trial. Consequently, it is necessary to set bottom-up weights initially to values of $1/(1 - d)n^{1/2}$ or to small random numbers.

The details related to the derivations of ART 2 equations and required constraints needed to fulfill the stability/plasticity trade-off are given in Carpenter and Grossberg (1987).

15.4 Other ART Networks

Modifications to the basic ART networks can be made for specific applications or for added stability. For example, by adding a preprocessing buffer stage to ART 2, the input vector **I** can be used directly as an input to the Orienting Subsystem rather than the vector **u**. The buffer mimics the upper and lower loops of the F1 layer (Figure 15.4). The advantage of this modification is that **I** does not change when F2 becomes active, thereby giving a more stable input to the orienting subsystem throughout the cycle. The complete details of this modification as well as other variants are described in Carpenter and Grossberg (1987).

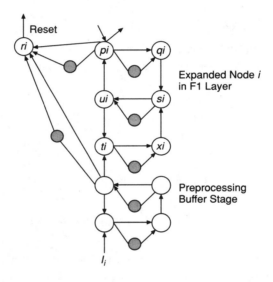

Figure 15.4   Modified ART 2 with Buffered Input in the F1 Layer
(Courtesy of Professor Stephen Grossberg)

Another more interesting variation on ART 2 is Fuzzy ARTMAP (Carpenter et al., 1991). We present a simplified version of this modification to real-valued ART, one that is based on supervised learning (Kasuba, 1993). The basic architecture is that of a simplified ART 2 with two additional layers: a Complement Coder (CC) layer and a Category layer (Figure 15.5). The Complement Coder takes an input n-dimensional feature vector, where each component has been normalized to values in [0, 1] and produces $2n$ outputs, where the additional n output values are the ones complement of the original n inputs respectively. For example, if the normalized input is the three-dimensional vector [0.2, 0.5, 0.7], the output of the

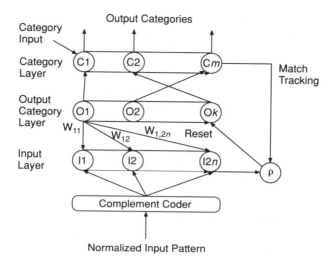

Figure 15.5   Simplified Fuzzy ARTMAP

CC to the Output Category (OC) layer is the six-dimensional normalized vector consisting of the original inputs plus their concatenated complements [0.2, 0.5, 0.7, 0.8, 0.5, 0.2]. The added input components are provided to make it easier for the network to form decision regions. Note that the sum of the CC output components is just the input dimension n, that is, $\Sigma_i I_i + \Sigma_i(1 - I_i) = n$. This feature of CCs can be used to normalize raw input data vectors.

The top category layer has m nodes, the maximum number of categories the network can learn, each to be labeled as a unique category or class. This layer serves as a storage repository for up to m different categories the network can learn. It receives category input information only during the supervised learning process and produces a single, labeled category output for any given input pattern, as determined by the OC layer's classification of the input pattern.

When an input $\mathbf{I}$ is presented to the network, the OC layer node J having the largest activation value T_J becomes the winner ($T_J = \max_j\{T_j\}$) in a competitive learning contest. The maximum activation comparison is actually based on the fuzzy conjunction of the input and the OC node weight vectors (see Chapter 3 for definition of fuzzy conjunction). The activation for the jth node is given by

$$T_j(\mathbf{I}, \mathbf{W}) = \frac{|\mathbf{I} \wedge \mathbf{W}_j|}{|\mathbf{W}_j| + e} \tag{15.31}$$

where we use the notation $|\mathbf{I} \wedge \mathbf{W}_j| = \Sigma_i(\min_j\{I_i, W_{ji}\})$: summation over the pairwise minimums of the input and corresponding weight vector components. The constant e is a small positive number, $0 < e \ll 1$, and the denominator term $|\mathbf{W}_j| = \Sigma_i W_{ji}$ is used as a normalization factor.

The match function M_j is similar to the OC node activation function, but normalized with a denominator of $|\mathbf{I}| = n$. It measures the degree to which the CC output $\mathbf{I}$ is a *member* of the fuzzy subset of $\mathbf{W}_j$, the jth OC node weights,

$$M_j(\mathbf{I}, \mathbf{W}) = \frac{|\mathbf{I} \wedge \mathbf{W}_j|}{|\mathbf{I}|} = \frac{|\mathbf{I} \wedge \mathbf{W}_j|}{n} \qquad (15.32)$$

The match function value of the winning node in the OC is compared to the vigilance parameter ρ and a reset is triggered whenever the match between the input vector and the selected OC node's LTM (weights) is not close enough, that is whenever

$$\frac{|\mathbf{I} \wedge \mathbf{W}_j|}{n} < \rho \qquad (15.33)$$

The details of the match function operation are given below.

As with other supervised learning paradigms, there are two phases of operation: the learning phase and classification phase. We describe the learning process first. The training set consists of labeled input pattern/category pairs. During training, whenever a pattern for a new category is input to the network, a new output node is committed in the OC layer by setting its weights equal to the input pattern $\mathbf{I}$ (equal to the CC output) and connecting the output of the node to the appropriately labeled category node. If the input pattern is known (labeled with a *committed* output node category), a match comparison is made between the OC winning node weights (node with the largest T_j value) and the input (equation (15.32)). The match is compared to an initial vigilance value ρ_0. If there is a mismatch ((15.33) holds), a reset is initiated to the OC layer inhibiting the current winner for the duration of the cycle, and no learning takes place. Also, the node with the largest T_j among the remaining uninhibited nodes becomes the new winner. This process is continued until no reset occurs or all committed nodes have been inhibited. If no nodes are found with a close enough match as determined by the vigilance parameter, a new uncommitted node in the OC layer is selected to represent (encode) the input $\mathbf{I}$ as the new category.

If, during the training, the input category has been seen and a node is found with a match value greater than or equal to the vigilance parameter (no reset occurs), but the *category does not match* the training pattern label, a new category node is committed as described above. In addition, ρ is set equal to the match value M_j of the OC node plus a small positive value ε ($\rho = M_j + \varepsilon$). If the category does match (and $M_j \geq \rho$), resonance occurs and some learning then takes place. The weights of the winning node J in the OC are changed to include a portion of the fuzzy intersection of the input pattern and existing weights, according to the following update equation (15.34)

$$\mathbf{W}_J^{\text{new}} = \alpha(\mathbf{I} \wedge \mathbf{W}_J^{\text{old}}) + (1 - \alpha)\mathbf{W}_J^{\text{old}} \tag{15.34}$$

where $0 < \alpha \leq 1$ is a learning coefficient that determines the rate of learning. (Note that larger values of α result in faster learning since then the selected node weights are more heavily influenced by the input pattern.)

Training of the network continues for several passes through the training set (several epochs) until the weights stabilize. Once training with a representative set of patterns has been completed, and the weights stabilized, the network is ready for operation, that is, the classification of new patterns. During operation, category assignment for an input pattern is always made on the basis of the node in the OC that wins the competition.

Fuzzy ARTMAP networks can learn cluster groupings or general mappings from n-dimensional space to m-dimensional space, much like the MLFF networks described in Chapters 6–8.

15.5 Applications Using ART Networks

In this section, we describe a few applications that are typical of the ways ART networks are being used to carry out experiments and to solve practical problems. We describe three diverse applications in some detail (fault diagnosis, sensor data fusion, and stock market analysis) and list a few other important published results.

High Resolution Fault Diagnosis in Digital Circuits

ART networks can be used to detect and locate faults in digital circuits during design, fabrication and operation of the circuits. The network is first trained to recognize faults and possibly their location, from a training set of input vectors that represent known fault and fault-free signature patterns consisting of inputs concatenated from control points and test measurements across the circuit network (cuts). The training data can be generated by algorithms (Fugiwara and Shimono, 1983), by circuit board simulations, or manually by introducing known faults (short circuiting pins). Once the network has been trained on a large number of input pattern/fault-type pairs, it can be placed in operation while continually learning new fault types whenever unknown faults are encountered.

Both ART 1 and FuzzyARTMAP are candidates for digital circuit fault diagnosis. In some cases, a more effective diagnosis can be achieved using two ART networks, one to learn fault and fault-free patterns and the other to learn fault-type/location associations (Kalkunte et al., 1992).

Radar Sensor Data Fusion and Tracking

Sensor data fusion using neural networks is described briefly in Chapter 3. In such applications, data from multiple sources are presented to a network for the purpose of combining the data and performing tasks such as identification/classification, monitoring, or control. The application described here, makes use of an ART 2 network to combine kinematic data (x, y, z coordinate positions) originating from two different radar sources. The two radars track multiple aircraft targets in real-time and the target data is "fused" by the network to determine which radar-target pairs belong to the same track. In this way, target tracks become more credible and accurate. In addition, other fusion tasks become more feasible with multisource inputs (e.g. target identification, situation and threat assessment).

The ART 2 network used in this application has 30 input nodes in the F1 layer to accept ten input samples each of x-y-z position data from the two radars. The position data presented to the network is actually the normalized *difference* in x-y-z position reported by two radar types for ten samples over a ten-second interval. The output nodes correspond to radar-track categories. For example, if the radars are jointly tracking five targets where radar-1 (R-1) tracks targets T-1, T-2, and T-5 and radar-2 (R-2) tracks T-1, T-2, T-3, and T-4, the network should properly classify the pair {(R-1, T-1), (R-2, T-1)} as a single track (one ART output category), the pair {(R-1, T-2), (R-2, T-2)} as another single track and T-3, T-4, T-5 as separate categories (Figure 15.6).

The input to the network is 30 real numbers which correspond to the normalized differences between the radar coordinate position data (azimuth, elevation and range data converted to x-y-z coordinate data). The vigilance parameter was adjusted using known tracks until the network could produce the right categories. After a brief training exercise, the network correctly classified all target tracks for both simulated and real target track data. The results were then compared to another more conventional statistical fusion method.

Let $\mathbf{Y}_i(k)$ and $\mathbf{P}_i(k)$ denote the ith ($i = 1$, 2) actual track state vector and covariance matrix at time k respectively (R-1 and R-2), and let $\mathbf{E}_{12}(k) = \mathbf{Y}_1(k) -$

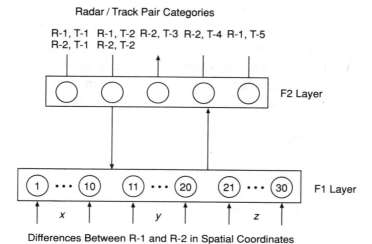

Figure 15.6   Radar Track Classification from Position Difference Data

$Y_2(k)$. Also, let $Y_i'(k)$ denote the *estimated* state vector and $E_{12}'(k) = Y_1'(k) - Y_2'(k)$. Define $E_{12}^*(k) = E_{12}(k) - E_{12}'(k)$. Now the covariance matrix of $E_{12}^*(k)$ is just $P_1(k) + P_2(k) = \Sigma_{12}$ (the two radars are independent). Therefore, the hypothesis test is

$$H0 : E_{12} = 0 \text{ (same targets)}$$
$$H1 : E_{12} \neq 0 \text{ (different targets)}$$

using the test statistic for H0 of

$$e = E_{12}' \Sigma_{12}^{-T} E_{12}'^T < \alpha$$

where, as usual, superscript T denotes transpose. Using a threshold probability of false correlation $P_\alpha = 0.01$, a Chi-squared statistic (**e** is distributed as Chi-squared) with 30 degrees of freedom is used to test H0. As in the case of ART, the classical hypothesis test results give correct pairings of radar tracks: {(R-1, T-1), (R-2, T-1)} as a single track, the pair {(R-1, T-2), (R-2, T-2)} as another single track and T-3, T-4, T-5 as separate categories.

The experiments here showed that although both methods correctly predicted the aircraft tracks, the computation times were significantly different. The simulated ART network produced correct predictions almost instantly, whereas the statistical test required more computation time since the test statistic must be computed at each point along the track and compared with the level of significance. Also, as the number of targets change, ART can quickly form new categories. The classical approach, on the other hand, requires knowledge of the target distributions and different threshold values may be needed (leading to possible misclassifications) for different targets. Finally, unlike the classical approach, it was not necessary to calculate the accuracy of the sensors for ART. This can be accomplished indirectly through adjustment of the vigilance parameter during training (using known target track data). Although the adjustment was done manually for these experiments, they could be done dynamically using an appropriate algorithm.

Stock Market Analysis

The Taiwan Stock Exchange (TSE) is one of the youngest and most volatile markets in the world. From a base level of 100, the index rose to over 9,000 in less than 30 years' time and frequently saw gains or losses of more than 50% within a few months' time. This made it difficult to apply conventional prediction methods for analysis and modeling. The same patterns of movement may never repeat in such a market. Thus, a method of fast learning is suggested for this problem.

ART 1 was applied to the problem of determining if, and to what degree, a relationship exists between the TSE index and other economic indices. In particular, five factors were studied each together with the TSE index: currency exchange rate, volume of imports, volume of exports, money supply, and consumer price index. These factors were first studied pairwise with the TSE using conventional regression analysis to determine correlation coefficient values. The same relationships were then examined using an ART 1 network with three input nodes for each input variable and a variable number m of output nodes (pattern clusters). The inputs were the TSE index normalized to three-bits of accuracy and the five economic factors, each normalized to three-bits of accuracy for six sets of weekly data. The vigilance parameter was varied over a range of values near zero to one and the results tallied and compared to the correlation coefficient data. It was shown that there is a strong relationship between the two.

To predict the TSE index trend, an MLFF network was used where the output of the ART 1 served as input to the MLFF network. It was claimed that more accurate predictions were possible when the pair of networks were used in tandem (Szu et al., 1992).

Neural Information Retrieval System

Companies that manufacture a large number of customized systems such as the Boeing Airplane Company tend to generate hundreds or even thousands of different part designs. Without a well-coordinated (and used) design indexing scheme, the same parts are often redesigned either by different design groups located at different sites or by the same group after some time lapse. This inadvertent waste of resources is pervasive throughout the manufacturing sector (Smith et al., 1991). It is an unnecessary waste of time and money.

Conventional retrieval systems that rely on indexing or coding of part features are cumbersome to create and difficult to maintain and use. This has led Boeing Computer Services to create a neural network solution that automatically groups and retrieves part designs based on geometric data extracted directly from computer aided design (CAD) drawings. They use an ART 1 based retrieval system to classify and store designs for some 20,000 different aircraft parts. The system is organized as a hierarchy of three levels of ART network modules where each level corresponds to a group of features. The lowest of networks is used to select stored designs that had been clustered into groups on the basis of shape. The next level of networks select on the basis of bends in the parts and the final layer selects on the basis of holes in the parts. This architecture gives the user the ability to discriminate on shape alone, on shape and holes, on shape and bends, or shape, holes and bends. The Neural Information Retrieval System (NIRS) architecture is illustrated in Figure 15.7.

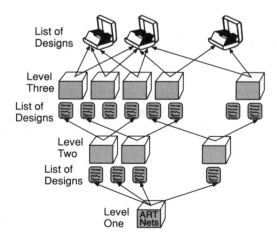

Figure 15.7   The Neural Information Retrieval System Architecture

Each box in the figure represents an ART 1 module. Collections of ART modules make up a macrocircuit (level). Each macrocircuit corresponds to a functional feature. For example, the lowest level macrocircuit selects on the basis of part shape. The next highest level selects on the basis of "holes" and the highest level on the basis of "bends." Combinations of shape, holes and bends can also be chosen as the criteria for selection and appropriate lists are generated from the descriptions input to the networks. The vigilance parameters permit the user to vary the degree of match chosen on each of the features selected. Thus, a range of designs can be retrieved from a large number of loosely similar ones to a small set of highly similar designs.

When a query is made, the lowest module puts the design into one of its clusters. Clusters at this level represent the most general abstraction of designs stored. When a winning cluster is selected at the first level, the module in the next highest level associated with this group is activated. This module places the design into one of its clusters and the process repeats.

The network is trained with the same three levels of detail. At the lowest level is a CAD data parser that constructs a binary vector from a silhouette view of the part as a two-dimensional binary image of 400×400 pixels. This vector is input to the network for clustered classification. Similar inputs are used for silhouettes of hole positions and bends in the part.

Training time takes approximately 12 hours with most of the time spent in generating representations of the CAD designs. Retrieval time for a query on a PC is between 30 and 45 seconds. The return of manufacturing data is also optional. Graphical sketches of the returned part designs can be viewed for comparison and analysis. Five levels of vigilance let the user choose the number of parts returned.

Process Monitoring and Control (Stirred Tank Recycle Reactor)

Monitoring, control, and optimization of modern chemical plants can be improved significantly with the use of knowledge-based pattern recognition technology. A successful example of the use of this technology is demonstrated by Whiteley and Davis (1993) in the application of ART 2 networks as part of a hybrid system that performs a type of qualitative interpretation (QI) through numeric-to-symbolic sensor data transformation. The temporal evolution of process variables are monitored from numeric multisensor plant data. A QI-Map of known pattern classes is learned by the ART network through pattern clustering. Inputs to the network include temporal sensor data, product quality data and other contextual data for a simulated stirred tank recycle reactor system. The reactor is used to carry out a highly exothermic, second order reaction. A shell-and-tube heat exchanger removes the heat of reaction via an external recycle loop. The QI problem is to identify the state (normal or abnormal) of the coolant flow to the external heat exchanger. Normal coolant flow corresponds to situations where the objectives of the reactor system are being met and product purity is on specification.

Unsupervised learning was performed with the ART 2 network from a pattern database of 25 hours of simulated process behaviors. Individual simulations were generated for 30 minutes of operation with disturbances injected at $t = 10$ minutes. Both normal and abnormal simulations were run starting from 25 different steady-state operating points. All simulations included measurement of noise, first order temperature measurement lags, and approximation of incomplete reactor mixing as dead time. Pattern slices of 8.1 minutes each were labeled to represent an evolving view of the process in time. Each 30-minute simulation contributed 75 labeled pattern slices. The complete pattern database included 3,750 pattern slices.

A quantitative analysis of the similarity between the normal and abnormal pattern slices was performed to determine the clustering criteria. This corresponded to an extreme similarity value of 0.99996 in ART terms. With this setting, the structure of the QI-Map was formed after one random pass through the 3,750 pattern slices. Subsequent refinement of five additional passes gave a stable set of clusters with only 0.5% of the patterns relocated to different clusters from the previous pass.

In testing of the system, normal/abnormal classification performance was perfect for all patterns that were within the range of the learning set. The system also identified all novel sensor patterns, that is, patterns that were outside the range of learning set. When testing using sequential patterns evolving in time, the system correctly duplicated the expert's ability to identify transition from normal-to-uncertain-to-normal/abnormal states. Timing of transition recognition also mimicked that of the experts. Based on this success of process monitoring, further applications of ART networks are being explored, including control and interpretation of analytical data.

In addition to the above applications, ART networks have been used in image and speech processing, control, risk assessment and other interesting applications too numerous to describe here.

Summary

In this chapter, we have studied the family of adaptive resonance theory or ART networks. These networks are two-layer, dynamic recurrent networks that adapt automatically through a form of unsupervised training. The networks satisfy the stability-plasticity problem since they are able to learn new facts and concepts in a changing environment without washing away relevant facts that have been learned previously. At the same time, they can forget old unimportant facts. This ability is made possible through the ART learning paradigm. New novel patterns that do not match previously learned patterns are stored as new facts until the capacity of the memory is reached. When that happens, the new patterns are rejected. Patterns that do resemble previously stored patterns recall the stored pattern and some learning occurs. The long term memory weights are shifted in the direction of the input pattern. A vigilance parameter controls the degree on match required to form new clusters and recall patterns.

ART 1 networks store binary patterns, while ART 2 networks store real-valued patterns. The patterns are grouped into nearest-neighbor clusters with the cluster centroid acting as the stored prototype pattern. Training can be very fast compared to other networks, but a single node is required in the F2 layer for each category learned. There is no "stored pattern sharing" among the weights as in the case of some other networks.

Several variations of ART networks have been explored, including buffered input for special applications and the Fuzzy ARTMAP.

ART networks have been used in a number of important applications, including sensor data fusion, diagnosis, control, and database indexing of design drawings.

16
Neuro-Fuzzy Systems, Soft Computing, Genetic Algorithms and Neuro-Logic Networks

In this final chapter, we deviate from the pattern of earlier chapters. Instead of considering specific ANN architectures or applications, we consider topics that have a close relationship to neural networks. In particular, we look at the relationship of fuzzy logic to ANNs and the combination of the two in building neuro-fuzzy systems. We also examine another paradigm of self-adaptation, that of genetic algorithms. We look at ways in which genetic algorithms can be applied to the construction of ANNs and fuzzy systems. Finally, we describe a completely different class of neural networks known as neuro-logic networks, networks of parallel "logic processors." In the final section of the chapter, we "crystal ball" the future direction of ANN development. We make some predictions on where this important field is heading.

16.1 Introduction

In the previous 15 chapters, our interest has focused on conventional ANN architectures and applications. We progressed from an understanding of simple adaptive neurons such as the perceptron and ADALINE to multiple neural memory systems and multilayer feedforward networks such as the MADALINE and the popular MLFF networks with backpropagation training. We studied variations of the feedforward networks such as the reduced coulomb energy network, the cascade correlation network, the general regression network, the neocognitron and so on. We also studied various network architectures with feedback connections, networks which perform recurrent computations on the inputs. These included the simple recurrent networks with one or more context layers, Hopfield networks, ART networks, the Boltzmann machine and general recurrent networks. Various learning

431

algorithms were also studied for both supervised and unsupervised adaptation. Throughout the text, we saw diverse examples of ANN applications.

In this concluding chapter, we depart from the previous pattern, and instead, look at a few topics related in a more general way to neural networks. We see how neural networks are related to fuzzy logic (see Chapter 3) and soft computing systems and how neural networks and genetic algorithms share some commonalities. Finally, we briefly examine a class of networks that help bridge the gap between symbolic computation using formal logic as a representation and neural network computing methods to perform "commonsense" reasoning.

16.2 Soft Computing Systems

One of the main goals of artificial intelligence researchers has been to build computer systems that mimic the ability of humans to perceive, reason, and solve "real-life" problems. Curiously, traditional artificial intelligence approaches in solving these problems have been based on the application of formal knowledge representations such as predicate (two-valued) logic and symbolic computations. This is a form of "hard" computing which is based on precision, certainty and rigor. It is in sharp contrast to real human reasoning or what is known as commonsense reasoning, reasoning which is based on approximate, rather than precise, computing methods. Human reasoning is typically shrouded in vague, incomplete facts accompanied with a myriad of uncertainties. Modeling this form of reasoning accurately requires a representation scheme that captures the real, natural semantics of the process. This is where fuzzy logic (see Chapter 3) can play a role since it provides a flexible and natural basis for "uncertain" knowledge representation.

Fuzzy logic links language with computing (reasoning) through linguistic variables and quantifiers. Linguistic variables such as "age" or "tall" can assume word values such as "young" or "average," which are quantifiable through fuzzy membership functions. Likewise, linguistic quantifiers such as "some" or "many" or "less than half" are quantifiable as fuzzy subsets of the real line which correspond to imprecise values of amount. The variables and quantifiers are mapped to fuzzy membership functions (possibility distributions) which assume values in the range of [0, 1].

Suppose U, V and W are linguistic variables and X, Y and Z the corresponding universe of values they each can assume. A standard type of fuzzy expert system rule R is given by the following:

R: If U is A and V is B, then W is D.

where A, B and D are fuzzy subsets of X, Y and Z, respectively. This type of statement conveys knowledge that the value of the variables U, V and W lie in the fuzzy sets A, B and D. For example, if U corresponds to Adrian's age, V to his dexterity and W to his ability to dress himself, then the universe X is the set of integers from 0 to 110, Y is the set of integers from 1 to 10 (a dexterity index) and Z the set of integers from 1 to 10 (a dressing score). The knowledge that Adrian is an infant with a certain dexterity and therefore capable of "limited" dressing is conveyed in the conjunctive proposition "U is A and V is B" with the conclusion of his ability to dress in the implication "W is D." A complete expert rule base will consist of many such rules:

R_1: If U is A_1 and V is B_1, then W is D_1.

R_2: If U is A_2 and V is B_2, then W is D_2.

...   .

...   .

...   .

R_k: If U is A_k and V is B_k, then W is D_k.

(For more examples of fuzzy rules, see Section 3.5 where fuzzy expert systems were used to perform approximate or fuzzy reasoning tasks.)

While fuzzy logic provides a close link between natural language and "approximate computational reasoning," fuzzy computing methods do not include the ability to learn adaptively, to perform associative memory feats, and tolerate high levels of noise and pattern deformations, capabilities that are needed for tasks like perception, learning, and predictive behavioral response. This is where neural networks can play a role. Putting the two capabilities together, we have the power of a *neuro-fuzzy* computing system. This is what Zadeh (1994) has termed as "soft" computing. Soft computing methods make it possible for us to describe a difficult concept or to park an automobile with ease. A sufficient description of the concept is an approximate one, and the position and orientation of the parked car need not be precisely fixed. The traits of these two fields complement each other in creating intelligent systems since they model human forms of representation and reasoning more closely than the "hard" approaches. Therefore, it is only natural that they be used jointly and even combined in a type of neuro-fuzzy system.

Several proposals have been made for neuro-fuzzy systems, including Teow et al. (1993), Hsu et al. (1990), and Yager et al. (1994). The proposed methods differ in both representations and network architectures. We briefly outline one approach which also forms the basis for the design specifications for a neuro-fuzzy shell. In fact, complete neuro-fuzzy shells have been developed at the Institute of Systems Science, National University of Singapore as early as 1991. Neuro-fuzzy shells are general systems which facilitate the creation of a neuro-fuzzy system for a specific application. Only the knowledge needs to be coded and added to the system.

The neuro-fuzzy system we describe has five layers of neurons with selected feedforward interconnections as illustrated in Figure 16.1 (compare the fuzzy expert system described in Section 3.5). The first layer neurons (A and B nodes) are linguistic input variable values which correspond to conjuncts in the antecedents of fuzzy rules. Each of these units are connected to a few units in the first hidden layer. The first hidden-layer neurons are divided into subgroups, each corresponding to a fuzzy domain. Units from these subgroups are connected to the second hidden-layer units, the fuzzy-rule neurons. Each input connection to a rule neuron corresponds to a conjunct in the rule's antecedent. The rule unit outputs are the consequents of the rules. They are connected to the third hidden-layer neurons in fuzzy domain groups similar to the first hidden-layer units. The final layer is the conclusion, the output fuzzy variable value.

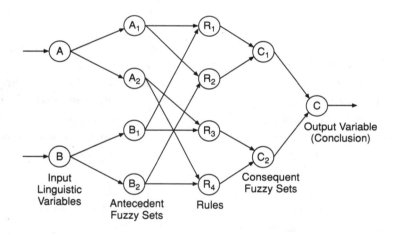

Figure 16.1   A Simple Neuro-fuzzy Network

The four fuzzy rules R_1 to R_4 in Figure 16.1 can be interpreted as follows:

R_1: If A is A_1 and B is B_1, then C is C_1.

R_2: If A is A_1 and B is B_2, then C is C_2.

R_3: If A is A_2 and B is B_1, then C is C_1.

R_4: If A is A_2 and B is B_2, then C is C_2.

The fuzzy inference method used for this system is Truth Value Flow Inference (TVFI) as described in Chapter 3 and by Wang (1993). This method uses a simplified fuzzification step at the output of the network without the need to perform the aggregation step. It is equivalent to the more complicated Mamdani (1974) (centroid of combined sets) method for some cases. The inputs to the network are convex, normalized fuzzy sets A, that is, they have at least one point x with membership value $\mu_A(x) = 1$ and for some interval [1, r] for which $\mu_A(x) = 1$, we define the midpoint $P_A = (1 + r)/2$ as the *representative point* of the fuzzy set A.

The normalized inputs are passed to the different antecedent set units through the input to antecedent unit connections. The output of the antecedent units are the corresponding singleton membership values for the input fuzzy sets. Each rule unit has weight values equal to $1/k$ where k is the number of inputs to the rule. With these weights, they perform the MIN operation (as described below) which is the standard operation for fuzzy intersection. Likewise, each consequent set unit has weight values set equal to 1, which, using the activation function defined below, results in a computation of the MAX operation, the standard operation for set union. The output units then compute the final defuzzified result in accordance with the following:

$$\text{out} = \frac{\sum_i P_i z_i}{\sum_i z_i}$$

where z_i is the activation value of the ith consequent set connected to the output unit and P_i the representative point as defined above.

The complete algorithm for the neuro-fuzzy network is as follows:

1. Sort the inputs x_i in ascending order giving $x_i' \leq x_{i+1}'$, and compute the differences $b_i = x_{i+1}' - x_i'$ with $x_0' = 0$.

2. Associate weights with the b_i inputs to obtain $\{w_1, w_2, ..., w_n\}$

3. Compute the output activation value

$$\text{output} = \sum_{i=1}^{n} b_i \cdot F\left(\sum_{j=1}^{n} w_j\right)$$

where

$$F(x) = \begin{cases} 0 & \text{for } x \le (1 - 1/n) \\ n(x + 1/n - 1) & \text{for } (1 - 1/n) < x < 1 \qquad (16.1) \\ 1 & \text{for } x \ge 1 \end{cases}$$

In training the network, a form of gradient descent error backpropagation is used to "fine-tune" the two layers of weights (initially set to $1/k$ and 1, respectively) to soften the MAX and MIN operations. The backpropagation equations are based on the generalized delta rule described in Chapter 6, but with a "heuristic" derivative term based on the activation equation (16.1).

Simulations of the neuro-fuzzy network were conducted to evaluate its performance in learning a fuzzy version of the classical gas law $PV = nRT$ where P is the pressure, V the volume, T the temperatue and n and R are arbitrary constants. The network was constructed using a tool called Flexi-Net developed at the Institute of Systems Science. For this system, some 18 rules were learned. A typical rule learned is:

If the **volume** is very large and ***pressure*** is very high, then ***temperature*** is T9.

The Tk (T9) quantities in the conclusion of the rule are the consequent sets for temperature.

The network was trained with 1,000 examples for ten iterations. Only ten iterations were needed to fine-tune the weights because the training examples were from rules given by "experts."

Networks of this type have several advantages over conventional systems. For example, they are able to encode expert knowledge given in imprecise linguistic terms and still improve the accuracy of the knowledge through training examples. Furthermore, the network is not a black box; its operations can be understood from the rules it encodes.

Neural networks and fuzzy logic expert systems have also been used in a complimentary rather than combinational way. For example, neural networks have been used to speed up the design of fuzzy systems and improve their performance through higher accuracy in: (a) determining the optimal number of fuzzy rules for a system, (b) determining the best membership functions, and (c) in the adjustment of membership functions adaptively when environmental changes occur. Neural networks can also be used to modify the fuzzy reasoning results of a fuzzy expert system.

In summary, neural networks and fuzzy logic can be applied concurrently within the same system to achieve different, but complimentary objectives or separately as tools to improve the performance of a system. They compliment each other in the following ways:

- Fuzzy logic can express qualitative "values" of human logic well and provide smooth actions through continuous membership functions (good for control and other applications).

- Fuzzy logic rules can express a wide range of condition/action relationships thereby requiring fewer rules than conventional logic-based expert systems.

- Neural networks are good for unstructured tasks such as pattern recognition and they can determine membership relations.

- Neural networks can learn to formulate complex nonlinear functions from training examples such as multidimensional membership function surfaces which are difficult to design (e.g. temperature, humidity, wind velocity).

- Neural networks can learn various tasks from training examples (adaptive reasoning) including temporal pattern sequences.

Systems employing fuzzy logic have been on the market for several years now. Japanese companies were quick to utilize fuzzy logic during the 1980s in a variety of consumer products as well as in numerous industrial systems, including "smart" controllers for subway trains. Applications of neuro-fuzzy systems too have begun to appear on the market. In the January 6, 1995 edition of the *Malaysian Star* newspaper, a full page advertisement for a Goldstar neuro-fuzzy controlled refrigerator appeared. Among other things, the advertisement claimed this was the largest six-door refrigerator in the world which employed "a human brain-like intelligent system that can learn and memorize the user's behaviors and its surroundings to keep the interior temperature constant at all times." It is almost certain that this is just the beginning of a long list of sophisticated neuro-fuzzy system applications.

16.3 Genetic Algorithms

Genetic algorithms (GAs) were first introduced and studied by John Holland (1975) and his students at the University of Michigan. They are search algorithms that are based on the mechanics of natural selection and natural genetics. They perform a global, random, parallel search for an optimal solution using simple computations. Starting with an initial population of genetic structures, genetic inheritance operations based on selection, mating, and mutation are performed to generate "offspring" that compete for survival ("survival of the fittest") to make up the next generation of population structures.

GAs are characterized by robust performance using the secrets of adaptation and survival as patterned after biological evolution. They have been theoretically and empirically proven to provide robust search in complex spaces, because they are not limited by restrictive assumptions of continuity, existence of derivatives, unimodality and other restrictions. They have found wide applicability in business, scientific, and engineering areas including pattern recognition, function optimization, scheduling, machine learning, clustering, engineering design, expert system design, process control and many others.

In the GA paradigm, knowledge is represented as a population pool $\Pi(t)$ of M genetic structures at time t:

$$A_1 \ A_2 \ A_3 \ \dots \ A_n$$
$$B_1 \ B_2 \ B_3 \ \dots \ B_n$$
$$\dots$$
$$\dots$$
$$\dots$$
$$M_1 \ M_2 \ M_3 \ \dots \ M_n$$

Genotypes [A], [B], ..., [M] each represented by n alleles $X_1, X_2, ..., X_n$

The genetic structures can represent:

- Fuzzy membership function parameters

- "If ... Then ..." rules

- Connections or weight values in a neural network

- The response surface of a nonlinear control system

- Moves in a board game (e.g. checkers or chess)

- A function value

and so on. The structures are most commonly chosen to be character strings such as binary bit strings or real numbers. The operations to model natural genetics are most commonly chosen as either crossover, mutation or inversion. They are most simply described by example as illustrated below.

Crossover: "Mating" Between Two Strings

<u>Before Crossover</u>		<u>After Crossover</u>

$\downarrow$ Crosspoint

$A_1\ A_2\ A_3\ A_4\ A_5\ A_6\ A_7 \qquad \Rightarrow \qquad A_1\ A_2\ A_3\ B_4\ B_5\ B_6\ B_7$

(Parent Genotype 1)   (Offspring 1)

$B_1\ B_2\ B_3\ B_4\ B_5\ B_6\ B_7 \qquad \Rightarrow \qquad B_1\ B_2\ B_3\ A_4\ A_5\ A_6\ A_7$

(Parent Genotype 2)   (Offspring 2)

The crossover operation is applied to two parent structures selected probabilistically from the population. A crossover point is then selected randomly as a position between two of a parent's allelles (bits or characters) and the allelles following the crossover point of one parent are concatenated to the allelles preceding the crossover point of the other parent and conversely. The two strings resulting from the concatenations are the offspring of the parents.

The mutation operator is a simple one-character (one-bit) operation on a single population member. A member is chosen with some small probability and a character position (bit position) is selected randomly. The character at that position is then changed. In the case of a binary string parent, the bit selected is simply flipped (from one to zero or zero to one). This operation is applied less frequently than other operations, typically less than 1% of the time. It is useful in breaking search paths that get trapped or when the population members have become stagnated. The mutation operation is illustrated below where a member of the population is assumed to be a seven-bit binary string.

Mutation: Random Mutation Operator

$\downarrow$ Selected mutation bit

$A_1\ A_2\ A_3\ A_4\ A_5\ A_6\ A_7$ Before Mutation

$A_1\ A_2\ A_3\ B_4\ A_5\ A_6\ A_7$ After Mutation

The inversion operation is also a single parent operation. As in the previous case, a parent is selected on the basis of a probability distribution and a character position in the parent is selected at random. The resultant offspring structure is formed as a concatenation of the characters after the inversion point followed by the characters preceding the inversion point. The inversion operation is illustrated below.

Inversion:

$\downarrow$ Selected Inversion Point

$A_1 \; A_2 \; A_3 \; A_4 \; A_5 \; A_6 \; A_7$ Before Inversion

$A_4 \; A_5 \; A_6 \; A_7 \; A_1 \; A_2 \; A_3$ After Inversion

With these three basic operations (and possibly other operations not considered here), the GA search process is carried out according to the algorithm depicted in Figure 16.2.

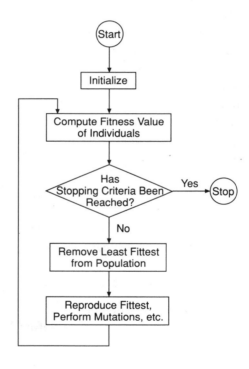

Figure 16.2   A Flowchart of the Basic Genetic Algorithm

To begin the search cycle, a fitness or performance measure must be defined as a function of the population members. Secondly, several parameters must be set. These include as a minimum: the population size, and frequency of mutation and crossover. An initial population is then generated (randomly, possibly with constraints), and the fitness of each individual is computed. If the fitness of any individual satisfies the stopping criteria, the search is terminated and the solution returned. Otherwise, a new generation is created through reproduction, crossover, mutation and possibly other operations.

One of the reasons for the success of GAs is their ability to exploit the better building blocks of an individual. They tend to generate high performance, short-defining-length, low order schemata at an ever increasing (exponential) rate in successive generations. Schemata are similarity templates that describe a subset of strings with similarities at certain positions. For example, a k-bit binary schemata acts as a pattern matching structure for any k bits where each bit position value can be 0, 1, or * (don't care). The five-bit schema *0*10 matches four strings, 00010, 10010, 00110, and 10110. This exploitation is possible because reproduction allocates more copies to the best schemata and crossover does not disturb these short-defining schema with high frequency.

It has been shown that GAs operate like the k-armed bandit problem. They give more than exponentially increasing numbers of trials to the observed best of the "k arms" (schema) in search of a minimal expected loss solution (Goldberg, 1989). We briefly describe the two-arm ($k = 2$) bandit problem which is illustrated in Figure 16.3. A slot machine with two separate arms has unknown payoff probabilities. It is known that the probabilities for the arms are different, but the higher payoff arm is not known. Of course, one would play only the higher payoff arm if it were known. The problem then is to try to determine the best arm as quickly as possible. The k-arm bandit is a direct generalization of the two-arm bandit problem.

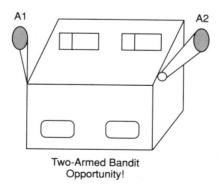

Two-Armed Bandit
Opportunity!

Figure 16.3   A Two-Armed Bandit Example of GA Operation

For GAs, the k-arm bandit analogy can be used to show that schema grow at the rate of

$$m(H, t + 1) = m(H, t)\frac{f(H)}{\bar{f}}$$

where $m(H, t)$ is the number of examples of a given type H of schema at time t, $f(H)$ is the average fitness of strings representing schema H, and $\bar{f}$ is the average fitness of the entire population of strings. If the schema H remain above the average by $c\bar{f}$ (with $c > 0$), then the number of H schema at time t is given by

$$m(H, t) = m(H, 0)(1 + c)^t$$

In the two-armed bandit version, let

> Arm A_1 has reward: r_1 with variance σ_1

> Arm A_2 has reward: r_2 with variance σ_2

where $r_1 \geq r_2$ and both r_1 and r_2 are unknown. Then it can be shown that the expected loss L is given by

$$L(N, n) = |r_1 - r_2|[(N - n)q + n(1 - q)]$$

where N is the total number of trials, n is the number of trials for each arm, and q is the probability of error after $2n$ trials. From this, one can find the optimum trials n^* from the relation:

$$N - n^* \cong N \cong (8\Pi b^4 \ln N^2)^{1/2} \exp(n^*/2b^2)$$

where $b = \sigma_1/(r_1 - r_2)$.

To illustrate some of the above concepts, we close this section with an example of a GA application in fuzzy logic system design. The example illustrates how a GA-designed fuzzy logic controller system outperforms a more conventional, trial and error designed system (Karr, 1991). The system consists of a cylindrical tank of a certain liquid chemical fluid which is drawn from the tank by a process plant. The problem is to control the level of the fluid such that from any initial starting point the level h is quickly brought to the set point (at the centerline CL) and maintained there with as little deviation as possible. Control is provided using a fuzzy logic flow control system. The system is illustrated in Figure 16.4.

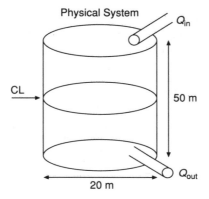

Figure 16.4   A Fuzzy Logic Controlled Liquid Supply System

The membership functions for the controller system were designed both by an experienced engineer and through the use of genetic algorithms. A comparison of the performance was then made for the two different approaches. To better illustrate the application of GAs to a problem such as this, we describe the details of the GA design optimization process. The physical system is governed by the following equation:

$$h^{t+1} = h^t + [(Q_{in} - Q_{out})/A_{tank}]\Delta t$$

where h is the liquid-level height, A_{tank} is the cross-sectional area of the vessel, Δt is the incremental time step, and Q_{in} and Q_{out} are the volumetric flow rates into and out of vessel. Inflow and outflow rates were allowed to vary between 0.0 and 200.0 m^3s^{-1} with a time step of 1 s. The decision variables used by the controller are h (four fuzzy sets—high, med-high, med-low, low), dh/dt, the time-rate of change of the liquid height (five fuzzy sets—positive-big, positive-small, near-zero, negative-small, negative-big), and liquid flow in and out Q_{in} and $Q_{out,}$ respectively. The membership functions used for the four decision variables are the standard triangular shaped functions as illustrated in Figure 16.5. The five membership functions for dh/dt (not shown) are similar in shape to the Q_{in} and Q_{out} functions, but with values ranging from -0.635 to 0.635.

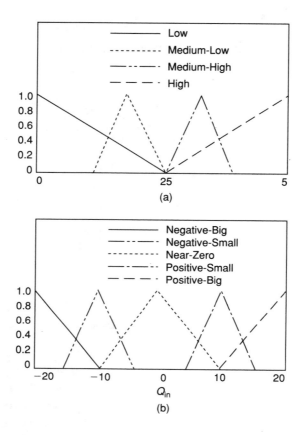

Figure 16.5   Membership Functions for (a) h and (b) Q_{in} (Q_{out})

The objective function f used to assess the fitness of individuals is a function of the squared difference in level from the centerline (25 m),

$$f(h,\ t) = \sum_{i=\text{case1}}^{\text{case4}} \sum_{j=0\text{s}}^{20\text{s}} (25 - h_{ij})^2$$

Note the summation limits in the objective function. A time index is included to penalize the system for a slow response and four cases of initial conditions. The cases were chosen to insure that the system could raise and lower the liquid level with equal effectiveness. The levels chosen are:

Number	h	dh/dt
1	00.0	0.6366
2	50.0	−0.6366
3	10.0	−0.3183
4	40.0	0.3183

Other parameters used for the GA design include:

Crossover probability: 0.8
Mutation probability: 0.01
Population size: 500
Maximum Generations: 80
String length: 132 bits (6 bits for each parameter as described below)

The population consists of 500 binary strings, each of length 132 bits. A single string represents 22 parameters, each of length 6-bits. Each of the variable parameters corresponds to an x-axis location of a membership function base. For example, a total of 6 × 6 bits are required to define the four membership functions for the liquid height h, 6-bits are used to define the x-axis position of the *low* membership function, 6-bits for the *high*, 12-bits for the two base positions for *medium-low* and 12-bits for *medium high*. Likewise, the five membership functions for dh/dt and Q_{in} (Q_{out}) each require 6 × 8 parameter values.

Simulation results comparing GA with conventional trial and error solutions show that the GA solutions for the membership function designs were superior in all cases. The GA designed controllers drove the liquid height to the set point faster and maintained the level there more stably than the other approach.

Genetic Algorithms and Neural Networks

Genetic algorithms and neural networks are both optimization algorithms. GAs seek to find one or more members of a population that represents a solution to the objective function and ANN learning algorithms seek to find a set of synapses (weights) that minimize the number of incorrect classifications. The two are also related in the sense that both are models of natural processes, processes which adapt to improve their performance, and hence, their chance of survival. While they share these common traits, their joint use in applications has been more related to the use of GAs in constructing better ANN architectures or in refining and improving the performance of given architectures. In this regard, GAs have been used with neural network designs to: (1) find an optimal set of weights for (smaller) MLFF networks (Montana and Davis, 1989; Whitley et al., 1993), (2) construct optimal networks for given applications (Bornholdt and Graudenz, 1992; Mandischer, 1993), (3) find optimal network parameters (learning rate, momentum term rate, number of nodes) for given applications (Murray, 1994), and (4) to even find a set of rules that "describe" the behavior of a trained network (Mitchell et al., 1993). In most of the cases cited above, the real problem is in finding an appropriate representation for the variables and translating it into a constrained solution space, one which is tractable for a GA solution. Although some results are encouraging, still much work remains to be done before the full benefits of GAs are realized in supporting ANN development efforts.

16.4 Overview of Neural Logic Networks

Neural logic networks (NLNs) are networks of simple processors that use a three-valued logic representation: true, false and unknown (yes, no, don't-know). These networks combine the salient features of parallel processing, adaptation and formal logic. They were developed by Professor Teh Hoon Heng and associates (Teh and Tan, 1989; Chan et al., 1991) at the Institute of Systems Science, National University of Singapore beginning in the late 1980s. Since their initial introduction, the theory has been extended to include a variety of network architectures and learning algorithms, the incorporation of fuzzy logic in neuro-fuzzy-logic systems, and neuro-logic-probabilistic reasoning. In this section, we give only a brief description of the basic concepts and some of the building blocks used to develop more sophisticated networks.

In combining neural computing with Boolean logic, one gains some of the power of pattern processing and logical reasoning within the same framework. In using three-valued, rather than two-valued logic, one gains more expressiveness in the representation of knowledge and a simplification in the reasoning process.

The basic operations of NLNs can be summarized as follows: NLNs are directed graphs consisting of input, output and hidden nodes (vertices) with directed connections (edges). Inputs and node activation values are all three-valued with the following ordered pair representations:

> (1, 0) for true
> (0, 1) for false
> (0, 0) for don't-know

Connections between nodes have ordered pairs of real-valued (positive, negative or zero) weights (v, w) which can be learned adaptively or can be directly computed for specific applications. Positive weights are excitatory and negative weights inhibitory.

Inferencing is performed by the propagation of signals in a feedforward direction and is based on the following computations:

Let S be a node with inputs (α_i, β_i) from nodes V_1, V_2, ..., V_k with corresponding connection weights (v_i, w_i) and activation threshold equal to one:

1. compute $net = \sum_{i=1}^{k}(\alpha_i v_i - \beta_i w_i)$

2. set the activation function of node S according to

$$(\alpha_s, \beta_s) = \begin{cases} (1, 0) & \text{if } net \geq 1 \\ (0, 1) & \text{if } net \leq -1 \\ (0, 0) & \text{otherwise} \end{cases}$$

As an example of the above concepts, consider the NLN network depicted in Figure 16.6. For this simple network, the activation function is computed as

$$\begin{aligned}
(0, 1) \times (-1, 2) &= (0, 2) \\
(1, 0) \times (2, 1) \ \ &= (2, 0) \\
(0, 0) \times (3, -1) &= (0, 0) \\
(1, 0) \times (2, 1) \ \ &= \underline{(2, 0)} \\
&\quad\ \ (4, 2)
\end{aligned}$$

Thus, $net = 4 - 2$, and hence, the activation function of S is $(1, 0)$.

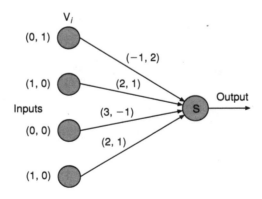

Figure 16.6 Example of a Simple Four Input NLN

Using the above propagation rules, simple NLNs that compute basic Boolean functions are easily constructed. For example, the operations of OR, AND, Negation and Implication are illustrated in Figure 16.7 and the XOR and Majority are illustrated in Figure 16.8. Note the duality between OR and AND. Other NLN operations have this duality feature (XOR and XAND and so on).

There are a total of 2^8 basic operations for NLNs. They can be combined to give a wide range of expressions. For example, the simple NLNs of Figure 16.7 can be combined into more complex networks to form a rule for an expert system. Consider a rule with an antecedent consisting of two disjuncts, one a negated expression and the other two conjuncts and a single conclusion. Such a rule, which can be written as

If (expression-1 AND expression-2) OR (NOT expression-3) Then expression-4

can be constructed from the building blocks of Figure 16.7 as illustrated in Figure 16.9. Using these and other basic building block networks, compound rules expressing many different facts and relations can be created.

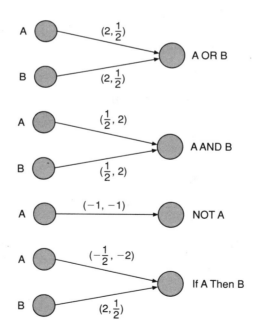

Figure 16.7   Simple NLNs that Compute Basic Boolean Functions

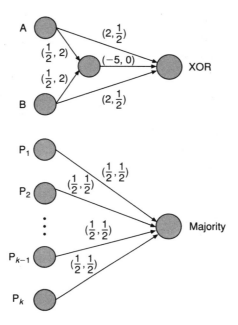

Figure 16.8   NLNs That Compute XOR and Majority Wins Functions

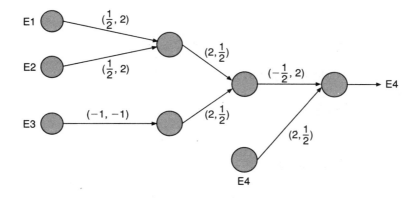

Figure 16.9   The Expert System Rule "If (E1 AND E2) OR (NOT E3) Then E4"

A number of such rules containing facts related to a given domain of expertise can be created to form the complete knowledge base for an expert system. For example, a diagnostic expert system for complex electronic circuits may be constructed from these rules where the premises contain conditional fault symptoms and the rule conclusions give the faults corresponding to the symptoms. If the knowledge relating to the many possible faults are unknown, but examples of symptoms and faults are available, the networks can be trained as in the case of other ANNs studied in previous chapters.

Uncertain reasoning can also be accommodated in NLNs by extending their operation to include probabilistic values. The simplest approach is to assign probability values a and b to the true and false conditions, that is (a, b) is the probability activation pair corresponding to true and false, where $0 \leq a \leq 1$, $0 \leq b \leq 1$, $0 \leq a + b \leq 1$. Hence, the probability of unknown is $1 - (a + b)$. We omit the details here.

Finally, NLNs have been combined with fuzzy logic to build neuro-logic fuzzy networks. In this case, the ordered pair (a, b) with $0 \leq a + b \leq 1$ is used to represent "evidence" for or against a condition or lack of evidence regarding the condition. The "a" value denotes evidence for the condition, "b" denotes evidence against the condition and $1 - (a + b)$ is the lack of evidence regarding the condition. For example, if the opinion of 100 experts is obtained regarding some situation, and 75 of them agree it is true, 15 regard it as untrue and 10 say they don't know, then $(a, b) = (0.75, 0.15)$.

To train an NLN, one can use any of the conventional ANN methods, including backpropagation, the perceptron or simple delta rule.

A complete treatment of the theory of NLNs is well beyond the scope of this section. Indeed, it would require several volumes to completely describe the topic well. In recognition of this seminal work, the Japanese government has awarded the Institute of Systems Science a research grant as part of the Real-World Computing project supported by MITI of Japan.

16.5 Future Directions

It is obvious that many of the new, forthcoming advances in ANN performance will come from the hardware side. Over the past 30 years, the size of hardware components have been reduced by a factor of about 1/2 every three years. At the same time, the speed has almost doubled in this period of time. Costs have been reduced dramatically as well over this period. Presently, tens of millions of transistors can be fabricated on a single VLSI (very-large-scale integrated) chip. It is likely that further advances in size reductions and computing speeds will continue at this rate until the physical limits have been reached. Thus, it will soon be possible to build artificial neural networks with millions of silicon neurons and thereby, truely begin to mimic some intelligent human processing functions.

Along with the increase in size will be an increase in complexity. We will see new ANN architectures being built, including hybrid networks which incorporate low-level pattern recognition units connected to higher level processing units that perform multifunction tasks similar to, but much simpler than, human vision processing. However, the real advances will most likely come from the "fabrication" of commercial, biomolecular components, natural cells which will begin to appear on the market before the end of this century. Such components are needed to match the immense storage capacities and massively parallel computing capabilities of parts of the human brain. This is a formidable challenge to the neural network research community, but not beyond realization.

There are several laboratories in the United States, Japan and Europe where active work is underway in building biomolecular processing and storage devices. Some astonishing successes in the development of these components have already been realized. Therefore, it is not unreasonable to believe we will see some *natural* neural networks being fabricated before the end of this century. To be sure, these networks will be microscopic by comparison with the human brain and their functions will be more limited. Nevertheless, powerful networks that can be grown, and hence, scale up to minibrain sizes will become a reality.

Since the initial successes in biomolecular advances have been well researched and compiled in a recent book by Freedman (Brainmakers, 1994) we refrain from giving an account of them here. Instead, we leave it to the interested reader to convince himself/herself of the inevitable direction ANN research will take and lead us in the not-too-distant future.

Summary

In this chapter, we have looked at systems that combine the salient features of neural networks and fuzzy logic. Such neuro-fuzzy systems are able to closely model the way humans reason, that is, commonsense reasoning. This is achieved by combining language with fuzzy logic, a knowledge representation scheme that can deal with uncertainty and vagueness. Such systems also possess the characteristics of neural networks: self-adaptation, generalization and robust, parallel computation. This type of information processing has been termed "soft computing" or "soft information processing."

We also considered the relationship of genetic algorithms and neural networks and fuzzy logic and genetic algorithms in this chapter. It was shown that GAs, which are based on the laws of natural selection and survival of the fittest, have been used successfully to construct and refine neural networks as well as fuzzy expert systems.

We have also examined a new type of neural network, one based on three-valued logic. These networks have been labeled as neurologic networks. The theory underlying these networks has been thoroughly developed and the networks applied to a number of practical problems. This research is now being partially funded through the Real-World Computing project of Japan. Finally, in the concluding section we have made some general predictions regarding the future direction neural network research will take.

REFERENCES

Aarts, E. and J. Korst, 1989, *Simulated Annealing and Boltzmann Machines: A Stochastic Approach to Combinatorial Optimization and Neural Computing*, Wiley, New York.

Ababarbanel, H. D. I., Reggie Brown and L. S. Tsimring, 1993, The Analysis of Observed Chaotic Data in Physical Systems, unpublished document preprint.

Abe, Shigeo, M. Kayama and H. Takenaga, 1991, Synthesizing Neural Networks for Pattern Recognition, *Proceedings of the IJCNN-91*, Singapore, pp. 1105–10.

Abu-Mostafa, Y. S., 1989, The Vapnik-Chervonenkis Dimension: Information Versus Complexity in Learning, *Neural Computation*, Vol. 1, pp. 312–7.

Ackley, D. H., 1987, *A Connectionist Machine for Genetic Hillclimbing*, Kluwer Academic Publishers, Boston.

Ackley, D. H., G. E. Hinton and T. J. Sejnowski, 1985, A Learning Algorithm for Boltzmann Machines, *Cognitive Science*, Vol. 9, pp. 147–69.

Almeida, L. B., 1987, A Learning Rule for Asynchronous Perceptrons with Feedback in a Combinatorial Environment, *Proceedings of the First IEEE International Conference on Neural Networks*, San Diego, Vol. 2, pp. 609–18.

Amari, S-i, 1967, A Theory of Adaptive Pattern Classifiers, *IEEE Transactions on Electronic Computers*, Vol. EC-16, pp. 299–307.

Amari, S-i, N. Fujita and S. Shinomoto, 1992, Four Types of Learning Curves, *Neural Computation*, Vol. 4, pp. 605–18.

Anderson, J. A., 1968, A Memory Model Using Spatial Correlation Functions, *Kybernetik*, Vol. 5, pp. 113–9.

Anderson, J. A., 1970, Two Models for Memory Organization, *Mathematical Biosciences*, Vol. 8, pp. 137–60.

Anderson, J. A., 1983, Cognitive and Psychological Computation with Neural Models, *IEEE Transactions on Systems, Man, and Cybernetics*, Vol. SMC-13, No. 5, pp. 799–815.

Anderson, J. A., J. W. Silverstein, S. A. Ritz and R. S. Jones, 1977, Distinctive Features, Categorical Perception, and Probability Learning: Some Applications of a Neural Model, *Psychological Review*, Vol. 84, pp. 413–51.

Andes, D., B. Widrow, M. Lehr and E. Wan, 1991, MRIII: A Robust Algorithm for Training Analog Neural Networks, *Proceedings of the International Joint Conference on Neural Networks*, Seattle, WA, Vol. I, Erlbaum, Hillsdale, NJ, pp. 533–6.

Angeniol, B., G. De La Croix Vaubois and J.-Y. Le Texier, 1988, Self-Organizing Feature Maps and the Traveling Salesman Problem, *Neural Networks*, Vol. 1, pp. 289–93.

Asakawa, Kazuo and Hideyuki Takagi, 1994, Neural Networks in Japan, *Communications of the ACM*, Vol. 37, No. 3, pp. 106–12.

Atiya, A. F., 1988, Learning on a General Network, in *Neural Information Processing Systems*, D. Z. Anderson (ed.), American Institute of Physics, New York.

Ballard, D. H. and C. M. Brown, 1982, *Computer Vision*, Prentice-Hall, Englewood Cliffs, NJ.

Barr, D. S. and G. Mani, 1994, Using Neural Nets to Manage Investments, *AI Expert*, Vol. 9, No. 2, pp. 16–21.

Battiti, R., 1992, First- and Second-Order Methods for Learning: Between Steepest Descent and Newton's Method, *Neural Computation*, Vol. 4, No. 2, pp. 141–66.

Baum, E. B. and D. Hausler, 1989, What Size Net Gives Valid Generalization? *Neural Computation*, Vol. 1, pp. 151–60.

Bilbro, G., R. Mann, T. K. Miller, W. E. Snyder, D. E. Van den Bout and M. White, 1988, Optimization by Mean Field Annealing, in *Advances in Neural Information Processing Systems*, I. D. S. Touretzky (ed.), Morgan Kaufmann, San Mateo, CA, pp. 91–8.

Bishop, C., 1992, Exact Calculation of the Hessian Matrix for the Multilayer Perceptron, *Neural Computation*, Vol. 4, pp. 494–501.

Block, H. D., 1962, The Perceptron: A Model for Brain Functioning, *Reviews of Modern Physics*, Vol. 34, pp. 123–35.

Blum, E. B., 1989, A Proposal for More Powerful Learning Algorithms, *Neural Computation*, Vol. 1, pp. 201–7.

Blum, A. and R. Rivest, 1988, Training a Three-Node Neural Network is NP-Complete, *Proceedings of the Computational Learning Theory (COLT) Conference*, Morgan Kaufmann, San Mateo, CA, pp. 9–18.

Blumer, A., A. Ehrenfeucht, D. Haussler and M. Warmuth, 1989, Learnability and the Vapnick-Chervonenkis Dimension, *Journal of the Association for Computing Machinery*, Vol. 36, pp. 929–65.

Bornholdt, S. and D. Graudenz, 1992, General Asymmetric Neural Networks and Structure Design by Genetic Algorithms, *Neural Networks*, Vol. 5, pp. 327–34.

Broomhead, D. and D. Lowe, 1988, Multivariate Function Interpolation and Adaptive Networks, *Complex Systems*, Vol. 2, pp. 321–55.

Burr, D. J., 1988, An Improved Elastic Net Method for the Traveling Salesman Problem, *Proceedings of the IEEE International Conference on Neural Networks*, San Diego, Vol. 1, pp. 69–76.

Burrascano, P., 1991, Learning Vector Quantization for the Probabilistic Neural Network, *IEEE Transactions on Neural Networks*, Vol. 2, No. 4, pp. 458–61.

Cacoullos, T., 1966, Estimation of a Multivariate Density, *Annals of Institute of Statistical Mathematics*, Vol. 18, No. 2, pp. 179–89.

Cardot, H., M. Revenu, B. Victorri and M. J. Revillet, 1993, An Artificial Networks Architecture for Handwritten Signature Authentication, *Proceedings of the SPIE Applications of Artificial Neural Networks IV*, Orlando, FL.

Carpenter, G. A. and S. Grossberg, 1987, A Massively Parallel Architecture for a Self-Organizing Neural Pattern Recognition Machine, *Computer Vision, Graphics, and Image Processing*, Vol. 37, pp. 54–115.

Carpenter, G. and S. Grossberg, 1988, A Massively Parallel Architecture for a Self-Organizing Neural Pattern Recognition Machine, in *Neural Networks and Natural Intelligence*, S. Grossberg (ed.), MIT Press, Cambridge, MA, pp. 54–115.

Carpenter, G. A. and S. Grossberg, 1988, ART 2: Self-Organization of Stable Category Recognition Codes for Analog Input Patterns, *Applied Optics*, Vol. 26, No. 23, pp. 4919–30.

Carpenter, G. A. and S. Grossberg, 1988, The ART of Adaptive Pattern Recognition by a Self-Organizing Neural Network, *Computer*, Vol. 21, pp. 77–88.

Carpenter, G. A., S. Grossberg and D. B. Rosen, 1991, Fuzzy ART: Fast Stable Learning and Categorization of Analog Input Patterns by an Adaptive Resonance System, *Neural Networks*, Vol. 4, pp. 759–71.

Chan, S. C., L. S. Hsu, K. F. Loe and H. H. Teh, 1991, *Neural Logic Networks*, internal publication of the National University of Singapore, Singapore, pp. 1–54.

Chang, C. F., B. J. Sheu and J. Thomas, 1993, Multilayered Backpropagation Neural Networks for Financial Analysis, *Proceedings of the INNS Meeting, World Congress on Neural Networks*, Portland, OR, Vol. I, pp. 445–50.

Chen, C. L. and R. S. Nutter, 1991, Improving the Training Speed of Three-Layer Feedforward Nets by Optimal Estimation of the Initial Weights, *Proceedings of the IJCNN-91*, Singapore, Vol. 3, pp. 2063–8.

Chester, D. L., 1990, Why Two Hidden Layers are Better Than One, *Proceedings of the IJCNN-90*, Washington, DC, pp. 265–8.

Chiuh, T. D., T. T. Tang and L. G. Chen, 1993, Vector Quantization Using Tree-Structured Self-Organizing Feature Maps, *Proceedings of the International Workshop on Applications of Neural Networks to Telecommunications*, J. Alspector, R. Goodman and T. X. Brown (eds.), Lawrence Erlbaum Associates, Hillsdale, NJ, pp. 259–65.

Chong, H. L. and K. C. Park, 1992, Prediction of Monthly Transition of the Composition Stock Price Index Using Recurrent Backpropagation, *Artificial Neural Networks*, Vol. 2, pp. 1629–32.

Chow, M. Y., G. Bilbro and Sui Oi Yee, 1991, Application of Learning Theory to an Artificial Neural Network that Detects Incipient Faults in Single-Phase Induction Motors, *International Journal of Neural Systems*, Vol. 2, pp. 91–100.

Cleeremans, A., D. Servan-Schreiber and J. L. McClelland, 1989, Finite-State Automata and Simple Recurrent Networks, *Neural Computation*, Vol. 1, pp. 372–81.

Cohen, M. A. and S. Grossberg, 1983, Absolute Stability of Global Pattern Formation and Parallel Memory Storage by Competitive Neural Networks, *IEEE Transactions on Systems, Man and Cybernetics*, Vol. 13, pp. 815–26.

Cohn, D. and G. Tesauro, 1992, How Tight are the Vapnik-Chervonenkis Bounds? *Neural Computation*, Vol. 4, pp. 249–69.

Colombi, J. M., T. R. Anderson and S. K. Rogers, 1993, Auditory Model Representation for Speaker Recognition, *Proceedings of the SPIE Applications of Artificial Neural Networks IV*, Orlando, FL, pp. 9–14.

Croall, I. F. and J. P. Mason (eds.), 1991, Industrial Applications of Neural Networks, in *Project ANNIE Handbook*, Springer-Verlag, Berlin.

Cybenko, G., 1988, Approximation by Superpositions of a Sigmoidal Function, *Mathematics of Control, Signals, and Systems*, Vol. 2, pp. 303–14.

Dahl, E. D., 1987, Accelerated Learning Using the Generalized Delta Rule, *Proceedings of the First IEEE International Conference on Neural Networks*, San Diego.

Denker, J., D. Schwartz, B. Wittner, S. Solla, R. Howard, L. Jackel and J. Hopfield, 1987, Large Automatic Learning, Rule Extraction, and Generalization, *Complex Systems*, Vol. 1, pp. 877–922.

Denueux, T., R. Lengelle and S. Canu, 1991, Initialization of Weights in a Feedforward Neural Network Using Prototypes, *Proceedings of the ICANN-91*, Espoo, Finland, pp. 623–8.

DeSieno, D., 1988, Adding a Conscience to Competitive Learning, *Proceedings of the IEEE International Conference on Neural Networks*, San Diego, Vol. 1, pp. 117–24.

Drago, G. P. and S. Ridella, 1991, An Optimum Weights Initialization for Improving Scaling Relationships in BP Learning, in *Artificial Neural Networks*, Vol. 1, T. Kohonen, K. Makisara, O. Simula and J. Kangas (eds.), North-Holland, Amsterdam, pp. 1519–22.

Drago, G. P. and S. Ridella, 1991, Cascade Correlation: An Incremental Tool for Function Approximation, in *Neural Information Processing Systems*, Vol. 2, R. P. Lippman, J. E. Moody and D. S. Touretzky (eds.), Morgan Kaufmann, San Mateo, CA, pp. 750–6.

Elman, J. L., 1991, Distributed Representations, Simple Recurrent Networks, and Grammatical Structure, *Machine Learning*, Vol. 7, pp. 195–225.

Fahlman, S. E., 1988, An Empirical Study of Learning Speed in Backpropagation Networks, Carnegie Mellon Report No. CMU-CS-88-162.

Fahlman, S. E. and C. Labiere, 1990, The Cascade-Correlation Learning Architecture, Carnegie Mellon Report No. CMU-CS-88-162.

Fernando, S., F. Islam, P. Utama and K. Watson, 1992, High Impedance Fault Detection Using Recurrent Networks, *Artificial Neural Networks*, Vol. 2, I. Aleksander and J. Taylor (eds.), North-Holland, Amsterdam, pp. 1615–18.

Filippidis, A., 1993, Multisensor Data Fusion, M.Sc. Thesis, Department of Electrical and Electronic Engineering, University of Adelaide, South Australia.

Fogelman-Soulie, F., 1991, Neural Network Architectures and Algorithms: A Perspective, in *Artificial Neural Networks*, Vol. 1, T. Kohonen, K. Makisara, O. Simula and J. Kangas (eds.), North-Holland, Amsterdam, pp. 605–15.

Frean, M., 1990, The Upstart Algorithm: A Method for Constructing and Training Feedforward Neural Networks, *Neural Computation*, Vol. 2, pp. 198–209.

Freedman, D. H., 1994, *Brainmakers*, Simon & Schuster, New York.

Freisleben, B., 1992, The Neural Composer: A Network for Musical Applications, in *Artificial Neural Networks*, Vol. 2, I. Aleksander and J. Taylor (eds.), North-Holland, Amsterdam, pp. 1663–6.

Fukushima, K., 1975, Cognitron: A Self-Organizing Multilayered Neural Network, *Biological Cybernetics*, Vol. 20, pp. 121–36.

Fukushima, K., 1988, A Neural Network for Visual Pattern Recognition, *IEEE Computer*, Vol. 21, No. 3, pp. 65–75.

Fukushima, K. and S. Miyake, 1982, Neocognitron: A New Algorithm for Pattern Recognition Tolerant of Deformation and Shifts in Position, *Pattern Recognition*, Vol. 15, No. 6, pp. 455–69.

Fukushima, K. and N. Wake, 1991, Handwritten Alphabetic Character Recognition by the Neocognitron, *IEEE Transactions on Neural Networks*, Vol. 2, No. 3, pp. 355–65.

Fukushima, K., S. Miyake and T. Ito, 1983, Neocognitron: A Neural Network Model for a Mechanism of Visual Pattern Recognition, *IEEE Transactions on Systems, Man, and Cybernetics*, Vol. SMC-13, pp. 826–34.

Gallant, S. I., 1990, A Connectionist Learning Algorithm with Provable Generalization and Scaling Bounds, *Neural Networks*, Vol. 3, pp. 191–201.

Gallant, S. I., 1993, *Neural Network Learning and Expert Systems*, MIT Press, Cambridge, MA.

Gallant, S. I. and H. White, 1989, There Exists a Neural Network that Does Not Make Avoidable Mistakes, *Proceedings of the IEEE International Conference on Neural Networks*, San Diego, Vol. 1, pp. 657–64.

Garey, M. and D. Johnson, 1979, *Computers and Intractability: A Guide to the Theory of NP-Completeness*, W. H. Freeman, San Francisco.

Geman, S. and D. Gemen, 1984, Stochastic Relaxation, Gibbs Distributions and the Bayesian Restoration of Images, *IEEE Transactions on Pattern Analysis and Machine Intelligence*, PAMI-6, pp. 721–41.

Geman, S. and C. R. Whang, 1986, Diffusions for Global Optimization, *SIAM Journal of Control and Optimization*, Vol. 24, pp. 1031–43.

Geman, S., E. Bienenstock and R. Doursat, 1992, Neural Networks and the Bias/Variance Dilemma, *Neural Computation*, Vol. 4, No. 1, pp. 1–58.

Geva, S. and J. Sitte, 1991, Networks of Exponential Neurons for Multivariate Function Approximation, *Proceedings of the IJCNN-91*, Singapore, pp. 2305–10.

Giles, C. L. and T. Maxwell, 1987, Learning, Invariance, and Generalization in High-Order Neural Networks, *Applied Optics*, Vol. 26, No. 23, p. 4972.

Girosi, F. and T. Poggio, 1989, Representation Properties of Networks: Kolmogorov's Theorem is Irrelevant, *Neural Computation*, Vol. 1, pp. 465–9.

Goldberg, D. E., 1989, *Genetic Algorithms*, Addison-Wesley, Reading, MA.

Grefenstette, J. J., 1986, Optimization of Control Parameters for Genetic Algorithms, *IEEE Transactions on Systems, Man, and Cybernetics*, Vol. SMC-16, No. 1, pp. 122–8.

Grenender, U., 1981, *Abstract Inference*, Wiley, New York.

Grossberg, S., 1969, Embedding Fields: A Theory of Learning with Physiological Implications, *Journal of Mathematical Psychology*, Vol. 6, pp. 209–39.

Grossberg, S., 1972, Neural Expectation: Cerebellar and Retinal Analogs of Cells Fired by Learnable or Unlearned Pattern Classes, *Kybernetik*, Vol. 10, pp. 49–57.

Grossberg, S., 1987, Competitive Learning: From Interactive Activation to Adaptive Resonance, *Cognitive Science*, Vol. 11, pp. 23–63.

Grossberg, S., 1988, Nonlinear Neural Networks: Principles, Mechanisms, and Architectures, *Neural Networks*, Vol. 1, No. 1, pp. 17–61.

Gruber, S., L. Villalobos and J. Olsson, 1993, Neural Networks for Webb-Process Inspection, *Proceedings of the SPIE Applications of Artificial Neural Networks IV*, pp. 491–503.

Gutzwiller, M. C., 1992, Quantum Chaos, *Scientific American*, January, pp. 78–84.

Haario, H. and P. Jokinen, 1991, Increasing the Learning Speed of Backpropagation Algorithm by Linearization, in *Artificial Neural Networks, Proceedings of the ICANN-91*, Espoo, Finland, Vol. 1, T. Kohonen, K. Makisara, O. Simula and J. Kangas (eds.), North-Holland, Amsterdam, pp. 629–34.

Hamilton and Hufnagel, 1992, Early Detection of Epileptic Attacks, in *Applications of Neural Networks*, H. G. Schuster (ed.), VCH Verlagsgesellschaft, Weinheim, pp. 173–8.

Hartman, E. J., J. D. Keeler and J. M. Kowalski, 1990, Layered Neural Networks with Gaussian Hidden Units as Universal Approximations, *Neural Computation*, Vol. 2, pp. 210–5.

Hasegawa, A., K. Shibata, K. Itoh, Y. Ichioka and K. Inamura, 1993, Adapting-Size Neural Network for Character Recognition on X-ray Films, *Proceedings of the International Workshop on Applications of Neural Networks to Telecommunications*, J. Alspector, R. Goodman, and T. X. Brown (eds.), Lawrence Erlbaum Associates, Hillsdale, NJ, pp. 139–46.

Hebb, D. O., 1949, *The Organization of Behavior*, Wiley, New York.

Hecht-Nielsen, R., 1987, Kolmogorov's Mapping Neural Network Existence Theorem, *Proceedings of the First IEEE International Conference on Neural Networks*, San Diego, Vol. 3, pp. 112–4.

Hecht-Nielsen, R., 1989, Theory of the Backpropagation Neural Network, *Proceedings of the International Joint Conference on Neural Networks*, Washington, Vol. 1, pp. 593–605.

Herz, J. A., A. Krogh and R. G. Palmer, 1991, *Introduction to the Theory of Neural Computation*, Addison-Wesley, Redwood City, CA.

Hinton, G. E., 1986, Learning Distributed Representations of Concepts, *Proceedings of the Eighth Annual Conference of the Cognitive Science Society*, Amherst, MA, pp. 1–12.

Hinton, G. E., 1989, Connectionist Learning Procedures, *Artificial Intelligence*, Vol. 40, pp. 185–234.

Hinton, G. E. and T. J. Sejnowski, 1983, Analyzing Cooperative Computation, *Proceedings of the Fifth Annual Conference of the Cognitive Science Society*, Rochester, NY, pp. 448–53.

Hirose, Yoshio, Koichi Yamashita and Shimpei Hijiya, 1991, Backpropagation Algorithm Which Varies the Number of Hidden Units, *Neural Networks*, Vol. 4, No. 1, pp. 61–6.

Hirsh, M. W., 1989, Convergent Activation Dynamics in Continuous Time Networks, *Neural Networks*, Vol. 2, pp. 331–49.

Holland, J. L., 1973, Genetic Algorithms and the Optimal Allocation of Trials, *SIAM Journal of Computing*, Vol. 2, No. 2, pp. 88–105.

Holland, J. L., 1975, *Adaptation in Natural and Artificial Systems*, University of Michigan Press, Ann Arbor.

Hopfield, J. J., 1982, Neural Networks and Physical Systems with Emergent Collective Computational Abilities, *Proceedings of the National Academy of Science*, Vol. 79, pp. 2554–8.

Hopfield, J. J., 1984, Neurons with Graded Response Have Collective Computational Properties Like Those of Two-State Neurons, *Proceedings of the National Academy of Science*, Vol. 81, pp. 3088–92.

Hopfield, J. J. and D. W. Tank, 1985, Neural Computation of Decisions in Optimization Problems, *Biological Cybernetics*, Vol. 52, pp. 141–52.

Hornik, K., 1991, Approximation Capabilities of Multilayer Feedforward Networks, *Neural Networks*, Vol. 4, pp. 251–7.

Hornik, K., M. Stinchcombe and H. White, 1989, Multilayer Feedforward Networks are Universal Approximators, *Neural Networks*, Vol. 2, pp. 359–66.

Hornik, K., M. Stinchcombe and H. White, 1990, Universal Approximation of an Unknown Mapping and its Derivatives Using Multilayer Feedforward Networks, *Neural Networks*, Vol. 3, pp. 551–60.

Hoshino, T., M. Kano and T. Endo, 1991, Optimal Control with a Recurrent Network and a priori Knowledge of the System, *Proceedings of the IJCNN-91*, Singapore, pp. 226–31.

Hsu, L. S., H. H. Teh, S. C. Chan and K. F. Loe, 1989, Fuzzy Decision Making Based on Neural Logic Networks, *Proceedings of the Inter-Faculty Seminar on Neuronet Computing*, Technical Report DISCS No. Tra-6/89, National University of Singapore, Singapore.

Imai, K., 1991, Simple Recurrent Neural Networks Applied to the Recognition of a Lateral String of Letters, private communication with author of unpublished paper.

Ito, Y., 1991, Representation of Functions by Superpositions of a Step or Sigmoid Function and Their Applications to Neural Network Theory, *Neural Networks*, Vol. 4, pp. 385–94.

Jacobs, R. A., 1988, Increased Rates of Convergence Through Learning Rate Adaptation, *Neural Networks*, Vol. 1, No. 4, pp. 295–307.

Jordan, M., 1989, Generic Constraints on Underspecified Target Trajectories, *Proceedings of the IJCNN-89*, New York, pp. I-217–25.

Judd, S., 1987, Learning in Networks is Hard, *Proceedings of the IEEE International Conference on Neural Networks*, Vol. 2, pp. 685–92.

Kalkunte, S. S., J. M. Kumar and L. M. Patnaik, 1992, A Neural Network Approach for High Resolution Fault Diagnosis in Digital Circuits, *Proceedings of the IJCNN-92*, Beijing, Vol. I, pp. I-83, I-88.

Kanade, T., M. L. Reed and L. E. Weiss, 1994, New Technologies and Applications in Robotics, *Communications of the ACM*, Vol. 37, No. 3, pp. 58–67.

Karr, Chuck, 1991, Applying Genetics to Fuzzy Logic, *AI Expert*, March, pp. 38–43.

Kasuba, T., 1993, Simplified Fuzzy ARTMAP, *AI Expert*, Vol. 8, No. 11, pp. 18–25.

Keeler, J. D., D. E. Rumelhart and W. K. Leow, 1992, Integrated Segmentation and Recognition of Hand-Printed Numerals, in *Neural Information Processing Systems*, Vol. 3, R. P. Lippman, J. E. Moody and D. S. Touretzky (eds.), Morgan Kaufmann, San Mateo, CA, pp. 557–63.

Kim, Y. K. and J. B. Ra, 1991, Weight Value Initialization for Improving Training Speed in the Backpropagation Network, *Proceedings of the IJCNN-91*, Singapore, Vol. 3, pp. 2396–401.

Kohonen, T., 1972, Correlation Matrix Memories, *IEEE Transactions on Computers*, Vol. C-21, pp. 353–9.

Kohonen, T., 1977, *Associative Memory: A System Theoretic Approach*, Springer, New York.

Kohonen, T., 1982, Self-Organized Formation of Topologically Correct Feature Maps, *Biological Cybernetics*, Vol. 43, pp. 59–69.

Kohonen, T., 1984, *Self-Organization and Associative Memory*, first edition, Springer-Verlag, Berlin-Heidelberg.

Kohonen, T., 1987, *Self-Organization and Associative Memory*, second edition, Springer-Verlag, Berlin-Heidelberg.

Kohonen, T., 1988, The "Neural" Phonetic Typewriter, *IEEE Computer*, Vol. 21, No. 3, pp. 11–22.

Kohonen, T., 1991, Self-Organizing Maps: Optimization Approaches, in *Artificial Neural Networks*, *Proceedings of the ICANN-91*, Vol. 2, T. Kohonen, K. Makisara, O. Simula and J. Kangas (eds.), North-Holland, Amsterdam, pp. 981–90.

Kohonen, T., 1992, How to Make a Machine Transcribe Speech, in *Applications of Neural Networks*, H. G. Schuster (ed.), VCH Verlagsgesellschaft, Weinheim.

Kolmogorov, A. N., 1957, On the Representation of Continuous Functions of Many Variables by Superposition of Continuous Functions of One Variable and Addition, *Doklady Akademii Nauk SSR*, Vol. 114, pp. 953–6; English translation, 1963, *Mathematical Society Translation*, Vol. 28, pp. 55–9.

Kosko, Bart, 1987, Adaptive Bidirectional Associative Memories, *Applied Optics*, Vol. 26, No. 23, pp. 4947–60.

Kosko, Bart, 1988a, Bidirectional Associative Memories, *IEEE Transactions on Systems, Man, and Cybernetics*, Vol. SMC-18, pp. 49–60.

Kosko, Bart, 1988b, Feedback Stability and Unsupervised Learning, *Proceedings of the IEEE International Conference on Neural Networks*, San Diego, Vol. 1, pp. 141–52.

Kosko, Bart and J. S. Lim, 1985, Vision as Causal Activation and Association, *Proceedings SPIE: Intelligent Robotics and Computer Vision*, Vol. 579, September, pp. 104–9.

Kreinovich, V. Y., 1991, Arbitrary Nonlinearity is Sufficient to Represent All Functions by Neural Networks: A Theorem, *Neural Networks*, Vol. 4, pp. 381–3.

Kurkova, V., 1991, Kolmogorov's Theorem is Relevant, *Neural Computation*, Vol. 3, pp. 617–22.

Kurkova, V., 1992, Kolmogorov's Theorem and Multilayer Neural Networks, *Neural Networks*, Vol. 5, pp. 501–6.

Lapedes, A. and R. Farber, 1988, How Neural Nets Work, in *Neural Information Processing Systems*, D. Z. Anderson (ed.), American Institute of Physics, New York.

le Cun, Y., 1987, Modeles Connexionnistes de l'apprentissage, Doctoral Dissertation, University of Pierre and Marie Curie, Paris.

le Cun, Y., B. Boser, J. S. Denker, S. Solla, R. Howard and L. Jackel, 1990, Backpropagation Applied to Handwritten Zipcode Recognition, *Neural Computation*, Vol. 1, pp. 541–51.

Lee, Y., 1991, Handwritten Digit Recognition Using K Nearest-Neighbor, Radial-Basis Function, and Backpropagation Neural Networks, *Neural Computation*, Vol. 3, pp. 440–9.

Lee, H. and Y. Park, 1991, Nonlinear System Identification Using Recurrent Networks, *Proceedings of the IJCNN-91*, Singapore, pp. 2410–3.

Lee, C. H. and K. C. Park, 1992, Prediction of Monthly Transition of the Composition Stock Price Index Using Recurrent Backpropagation, *Artificial Neural Networks*, Vol. 2, pp. 1629–32.

Lee, C. M. and D. W. Patterson, 1991, Occluded Object Recognition: An Approach Which Combines Neurocomputing and Conventional Algorithms, *Proceedings of the IJCNN-91*, Singapore, Vol. 2, pp. 2612–7.

Levin, E., N. Tishby and S. Solla, 1989, A Statistical Approach to Learning and Generalization in Layered Networks, *Proceedings of the Second International Workshop on Computational Learning Theory* (COLT '89), pp. 245–60.

Li, Liang and S. Haykin, 1993, A Cascaded Recurrent Neural Network for Real-Time Nonlinear Adaptive Filtering, *Proceedings of the IEEE International Conference on Neural Networks*, San Francisco, pp. 857–62.

Li, Wei and M. Nasrabadi, 1990, Invariant Object Recognition Based on a Neural Network of Cascaded RCE Nets, *Proceedings of the IJCNN-90*, San Diego, Vol. 2, pp. 845–54.

Light, L. W. and P. Anderson, 1993, Designing Better Keyboards via Simulated Annealing, *AI Expert*, September, pp. 20–7.

Linsker, R., 1988, Self-Organization in a Perceptual Network, *IEEE Computer*, Vol. 21, No. 3, pp. 105–17.

Lippman, R. P., 1987, Introduction to Computing with Neural Nets, *IEEE ASSP Magazine*, April, pp. 4–22.

Littman, E. and Ritter H., 1992, Cascade Network Architectures, *Proceedings of the International Joint Conference on Neural Networks*, Baltimore, Vol. II, pp. 398–404.

Lorenz, E. N., 1989, Computational Chaos—A Prelude to Computational Instability, *Physica D*, Vol. 35, pp. 299–317.

Loskiewicz-Buczak, A. and R. E. Uhrig, 1993, Vibration Data Analysis Using Probabilistic Neural Network-Based System, *Proceedings of INNS Meeting, World Congress on Neural Networks*, Portland, OR, Lawrence Erlbaum Associates, Hillsdale, NJ, Vol. I, pp. 273–8.

Lui, Ho Chung and M. Cheong, 1989, Graphical Visualization of Multilayer Neural Network, *Proceedings of the Inter-Faculty Seminar on Neuronet Computing*, Technical Report DISCS No. Tra6/89, National University of Singapore, Singapore.

Mamdani, E. H., 1974, Application of Fuzzy Algorithm for Control of Simple Dynamic Plant, *Proceedings of the IEEE*, Vol. 121, pp. 1585–9.

Mandischer, M., 1993, Representation and Evolution of Neural Networks, *IEEE Proceedings of the International Conference on Artificial Neural Networks and Genetic Algorithms*, Innsbruck, Springer-Verlag, Wien, pp. 643–8.

Mane, R., 1981, *Dynamical Systems and Turbulence, Warwick, 1980*, Lecture Notes in Mathematics No. 898, D. Rand and L. S. Young (eds.), Springer, Berlin, pp. 230–42.

Martin, G. L. and J. A. Pittman, 1991, Recognizing Hand-Printed Letters and Digits Using Backpropagation Learning, *Neural Computation*, Vol. 3, pp. 258–67.

Matsuoka, K. and J. Yi, 1991, Backpropagation Based on the Logarithmic Error Function and Elimination of Local Minima, *Proceedings of the IJCNN-91*, Singapore, Vol. 2, pp. 1117–22.

McCulloch, W. S. and W. Pitts, 1943, A Logical Calculus of the Ideas Immanent in Nervous Activity, *Bulletin of Mathematical Biophysics*, Vol. 5, pp. 115–33.

McInerney, M. and A. P. Dhawan, 1993, Use of Genetic Algorithms with Backpropagation in Training of Feedforward Neural Networks, *IEEE Proceedings of the International Conference on Artificial Neural Networks and Genetic Algorithms*, Innsbruck, Springer-Verlag, Wien, pp. 203–8.

Menon, M. M. and K. G. Heinemann, 1988, Classification of Patterns Using a Self-Organizing Neural Network, *Neural Networks*, Vol. 1, pp. 201–15.

Minai, A. A. and R. D. Williams, 1990, Backpropagation Heuristics: A Study of the Extended Delta-Bar-Delta Algorithm, *Proceedings of the IJCNN-90*, San Diego, Vol. 1, pp. 595–600.

Minsky, M. and S. Papert, 1969, *Perceptrons*, MIT Press, Cambridge, MA.

Mitchell, R. J., J. M. Bishop and W. Low, 1993, Using a Genetic Algorithm to Find the Rules of a Neural Network, *IEEE Proceedings of the International Conference on Artificial Neural Networks and Genetic Algorithms*, Innsbruck, Springer-Verlag, Wien, pp. 664–9.

Moallemi, C., 1991, Classifying Cells for Cancer Diagnosis Using Neural Networks, *IEEE Expert*, December, pp. 8–12.

Montana, D. and L. Davis, 1989, Training Feedforward Networks Using Genetic Algorithms, *Proceedings of the IJCAI-89*, Vol. I, pp. 762–7.

Mood, A. M. and F. A. Graybill, 1962, *Introduction to the Theory of Statistics*, Macmillan, New York.

Mori, H. and T. Ogasawara, 1993, A Recurrent Neural Network Approach to Short-Term Load Forecasting in Electric Power Systems, *Proceedings of the World Congress on Neural Networks*, Portland, OR, Vol. I, pp. 342–5.

Morose, R. A., 1990, A Financial Neural-Network Application, *AI Expert*, May, pp. 50–3.

Morose, R. A., 1993, A Financial Neural-Network Application, in *Neural Networks in Finance and Investing*, R. R. Trippi and E. Turban (eds.), Probus Publishing, Chicago, pp. 75–83.

Murase, K., Y. Matsunaga and Y. Nakade, 1991, A Backpropagation Algorithm Which Automatically Determines the Number of Association Units, *Proceedings of the IJCNN-91*, Singapore, Vol. 1, pp. 783–8.

Murray, D., 1994, Tuning Neural Networks with Genetic Algorithms, *AI Expert*, June, pp. 27–32.

Ng, G. S. and D. Patterson, 1993, Reducing Memory Requirements of Bidirectional Associative Memory, *Proceedings of the International Conference on Neural Network Applications to Signal Processing* (NNASP-93), Singapore, pp. 318–23.

Ng, T. K. and D. Patterson, 1993, Object Recognition by Correlation of Image Subparts, *Proceedings of the International Conference on Neural Network Applications to Signal Processing*, Singapore, pp. 78–83.

Nowlan, S. J. and G. E. Hinton, 1992, Simplifying Neural Networks by Soft Weight-Sharing, *Neural Computation*, Vol. 4, pp. 473–93.

Oja, E., 1982, A Simplified Neuron Model as a Principal Component Analyzer, *Journal of Mathematical Biology*, Vol. 15, pp. 267–73.

Oja, E., 1989, Neural Networks, Principal Components, and Subspaces, *International Journal of Neural Systems*, Vol. 1, pp. 61–8.

Park, J. and I. W. Sandberg, 1991, Universal Approximation Using Radial-Basis-Function Networks, *Neural Computation*, Vol. 3, pp. 246–57.

Parker, D. B., 1985, Learning Logic, Technical Report TR-47, Center for Computational Research in Economics and Management Science, Massachusetts Institute of Technology, Cambridge, MA.

Parzen, E., 1962, On Estimation of a Probability Density Function and Mode, *Annals of Mathematical Statistics*, Vol. 33, pp. 1065–76.

Patterson, D. W. and H. J. Zhang, 1993, Motion Detection and Tracking Using a Hybrid Vision Connectionist System, *Proceedings of the International Conference on Neural Network Applications to Signal Processing* (NNASP-93), Singapore, pp. 150–4.

Patterson, D. W., K. H. Chan and C. M. Tan, 1993, Time Series Forecasting with Neural Networks: A Comparative Study, *Proceedings of the International Conference on Neural Network Applications to Signal Processing* (NNASP-93), Singapore, pp. 269–74.

Pavlidis, T. and S. Mori (eds.), 1992, Special Issue on Optical Character Recognition, *Proceedings of the IEEE*, Vol. 80, No. 7.

Pearlmutter, B. A., 1988, Dynamic Recurrent Neural Networks, Report CMU-CS-88-191, School of Computer Science, Carnegie Mellon University, Pittsburgh, PA.

Peters, Edgar E., 1991, *Chaos and Order in the Capital Markets: A New View of Cycles, Prices and Market Volatility*, Wiley, New York.

Pineda, F. J., 1988, Dynamics and Architectures for Neural Computation, *Journal of Complexity*, Vol. 4, pp. 216–45.

Pineda, F. J., 1989, Recurrent Backpropagation and the Dynamical Approach to Adaptive Neural Computation, *Neural Computation*, Vol. 1, pp. 161–72.

Platt, J., 1991, A Resource-Allocating Network for Function Interpolation, *Neural Computation*, Vol. 3, pp. 213–25.

Rao, S. S. and V. Rammamurti, 1993, A Hybrid Technique to Enhance the Performance of Recurrent Neural Networks for Time Series Prediction, *Proceedings of the IEEE International Conference on Neural Networks*, San Francisco.

Reily, D. L., L. N. Cooper and C. Elbaum, 1982, A Neural Model for Category Learning, *Biological Cybernetics*, Vol. 45, pp. 34–51.

Reily, D. L., L. N. Cooper, and C. Elbaum, 1987, Learning System Architectures Composed on Multiple Learning Modules, *Proceedings of the IEEE International Conference on Neural Networks*, Vol. 2, pp. 495–503.

Ritter, H. and K. Schulten, 1988, Kohonen's Self-Organizing Maps: Exploring Their Computational Capabilities, *Proceedings of the IEEE International Conference on Neural Networks*, San Diego, Vol. 1, pp. 109–16.

Ritter, H. J., T. Martinetz and K. J. Schulten, 1992, *Neural Computation and Self-Organizing Maps: An Introduction*, Addison-Wesley, Reading, MA.

Rochester, N., J. H. Holland, L. H. Haibt and W. L. Duda, 1956, Test on a Cell Assembly Theory of the Action of the Brain, Using a Large Digital Computer, *IRE Transactions on Information Theory*, Vol. IT-2, pp. 80–93.

Rock, D., D. Malkoff and R. Stewart, 1993, AI and Aircraft Health Monitoring, *AI Expert*, February, pp. 28–35.

Rosenblatt, F., 1958, The Perceptron: A Probabilistic Model for Information Storage and Organization in the Brain, *Psychological Review*, Vol. 65, pp. 386–408.

Rosenblatt, F., 1961, *Principles of Neurodynamics: Perceptrons and the Theory of Brain Mechanisms*, Spartan Books, Washington, DC.

Rumelhart, D. J. and D. Zipser, 1985, Feature Discovery by Competitive Learning, *Cognitive Science*, Vol. 9, pp. 75–112.

Rumelhart, D. E., G. E. Hinton and R. J. Williams, 1986, Learning Internal Representations by Error Propagation, in *Parallel Distributed Processing: Explorations in the Microstructures of Cognition*, Vol. 1: Foundations, D. E. Rumelhart and J. L. McClelland (eds.), MIT Press, Cambridge, MA.

Rumelhart, D. and J. McClelland (eds.), 1986, *Parallel Distributed Processing*, Vol. 1, MIT Press, Cambridge, MA.

Sanger, T. D., 1989, An Optimality Principle for Unsupervised Learning, in *Advances in Neural Information Processing Systems I*, D. S. Touretzky (ed.), Morgan Kaufmann, San Mateo, CA, pp. 11–9.

Sato, A., 1991, An Analytical Study of the Momentum Term in a Backpropagation Algorithm, *Proceedings of the ICANN-91*, Espoo, Finland, pp. 617–22.

Schwartz, D. B., V. K. Samalam, S. A. Solla and J. S. Denker, 1990, Exhaustive Learning, *Neural Computation*, Vol. 2, pp. 374–85.

Servan-Schreiber, D., A. Cleeremans and J. L. McClelland, 1991, Graded State Machines: The Representation of Temporal Contingencies in Simple Recurrent Networks, *Machine Learning*, Vol. 7, pp. 161–93.

Shannon, C. E., 1948, A Mathematical Theory of Communication, *Bell System Technical Journal*, Vol. 27, pp. 379–423, 623–56.

Shigeo, A., M. Kayama and H. Takenaga, 1991, Synthesizing Neural Networks for Pattern Recognition, *Proceedings of the IJCNN-91*, Singapore, Vol. 2, pp. 1105–10.

Sietsma, J. and R. J. F. Dow, 1991, Creating Artificial Neural Networks that Generalize, *Neural Networks*, Vol. 4, pp. 67–79.

Smith, S. D. G., R. Escobedo and T. P. Caudell, 1993, An Industrial Strength Neural Network Application, *Proceedings of INNS Meeting, World Congress on Neural Networks*, Portland, OR, Lawrence Erlbaum Associates, Hillsdale, NJ, Vol. I, pp. 490–4.

Sone, Tadashi, 1993, Using Distributed Neural Networks to Identify Faults in Switching Systems, *Proceedings of the International Workshop on Applications of Neural Networks to Telecommunications*, J. Alspector, R. Goodman and T. X. Brown (eds.), Lawrence Erlbaum Associates, Hillsdale, NJ.

Specht, D. F., 1967, Generation of Polynomial Discriminant Functions for Pattern Recognition, *IEEE Transactions on Electronic Computers*, Vol. EC-16, pp. 308–19.

Specht, D. F., 1988, Probabilistic Neural Networks for Classification, Mapping or Associative Memory, *Proceedings of the IEEE International Conference on Neural Networks*, San Diego, Vol. 1, pp. 525–32.

Specht, D. F., 1990, Probabilistic Neural Networks, *Neural Networks*, Vol. 3, pp. 109–18.

Specht, D. F., 1991, A General Regression Neural Network, *IEEE Transactions on Neural Networks*, Vol. 2, No. 6, pp. 568–76.

Staib, W. E., 1993, The Intelligent Arc Furnace: Neural Networks Revolutionize Steel-Making, *Proceedings of INNS Meeting, World Congress on Neural Networks*, Portland, OR, Vol. I, pp. 466–9.

Staib, W. E. and R. B. Staib, 1992, The Intelligent Arc Furnace Controller: A Neural Network Electrode Position Optimization System for the Electric Arc Furnace, *Proceedings of the International Joint Conference on Neural Networks*, New York.

Steinbuch, K. and U. A. W. Piske, 1963, Learning Matrices and Their Applications, *IEEE Transactions on Electronic Computers*, Vol. EC-12, pp. 846–62.

Sterzing, V. and B. Schurmann, 1993, Recurrent Neural Networks for Temporal Learning of Time Series, *Proceedings of the IEEE International Conference on Neural Networks*, San Francisco, Vol. 2, pp. 843–6.

Stone, G., 1986, *Parallel Distributed Processing*, Vol. 1, MIT Press, Cambridge, MA.

Szu, H. and E. Hartley, 1987, *Physics Letters*, pp. 157–62.

Szu, H., K. W. Liu, C. C. Chao, K. F. Lin, K. T. Hsu and L. Medsker, 1992, *Proceedings of the IJCNN-92*, Beijing, pp. I-333, I-339.

Takens, F., 1981, Detecting Strange Attractors in Turbulence, in *Dynamical Systems and Turbulence, Warwick, 1980*, Lecture Notes in Mathematics No. 898, D. Rand and L. S. Young (eds.), Springer, Berlin, pp. 366–81.

Tamura, S., 1991, Capabilities of a Three-Layer Feedforward Neural Network, *Proceedings of the IJCNN-91*, Singapore, pp. 2757–62.

Tan, A. H., Q. Pan, H. C. Lui and H. H. The, 1989, INSIDE: A Neuronet Based Hardware Fault Diagnostic System, Technical Report TR90-16-0, Institute of Systems Science, National University of Singapore, Singapore.

Teh, H. H. and A. H. Tan, 1989, Connectionist Expert Systems—A Neural-Logic Models' Approach, *Proceedings of the Inter-Faculty Seminar on Neuronet Computing*, Technical Report DISCS No. Tra-6/89, National University of Singapore, Singapore, pp. 16–32.

Teow, L. N., H. C. Lui, P. Z. Wang, H. H. Teh, Z. Shen and T. H. Goh, 1993, Truth Value Flow Inference (TVFI) Neural Network, private communication (in press).

Tesauro, G., 1986, Simple Neural Models of Classical Conditioning, *Biological Cybernetics*, Vol. 55, pp. 187–200.

Thorpe, C., M. Hebert, T. Kanade and S. Shafer, 1991, Toward Autonomous Driving: The CMU NavLab, *IEEE Expert*, August, pp. 31–42.

Tishby, N., E. Levin and S. A. Solla, 1989, Consistent Inference of Probabilities in Layered Networks: Predictions and Generalizations, *Proceedings of the International Joint Conference on Neural Networks*, Washington, Vol. II, pp. 403–10.

Tollenaere, Tom, 1990, SuperSAB: Fast Adaptive Backpropagation with Good Scaling Properties, *Neural Networks*, Vol. 3, pp. 561–73.

Valiant, L. G., 1984, A Theory of the Learnable, *Communication of the ACM*, Vol. 27, pp. 1134–42.

van Ooyen, A. and B. Nienhuis, 1992, Improving the Convergence of the Backpropagation Algorithm, *Neural Networks*, Vol. 5, pp. 465–71.

Vapnick, V. N. and A. Chervonenkis, 1971, On the Uniform Convergence of Relative Frequencies of Events to their Probabilities, *Theory of Probability and its Applications*, Vol. 16, pp. 264–80.

von der Malsburg, C., 1973, Self-Organization of Orientation Sensitive Cells in the Stirate Cortex, *Kybernetik*, Vol. 14, pp. 85–100.

Wai, Gang and Yang Ou, 1991, On the Bound of the Approximation Capacity of Multilayer Neural Network, *Proceedings of the IJCNN-91*, Singapore, pp. 2299–304.

Wang, P. Z., 1993, Truth-Valued Flow Inference Theory and its Application, in *Advances in Fuzzy Systems: Application and Theory*, P. Z. Wang and K. F. Loe (eds.), World Scientific, Singapore.

Wang, S. D. and C. H. Hsu, 1991, A Self-Growing Learning Algorithm for Determining the Approximate Number of Hidden Units, *Proceedings of the IJCNN-91*, Singapore, Vol. 2, pp. 1098–104.

Weigend, A. S. and N. A. Gershenfeld, 1994, *Time Series Prediction: Forecasting the Future and Understanding the Past*, Addison-Wesley, Reading, MA.

Wenocur, R. S. and R. M. Dudley, 1981, Some Special Vapnik-Chervonenkis Classes, *Discrete Mathematics*, Vol. 33, pp. 313–8.

Werbos, P. J., 1974, Beyond Regression: New Tools for Prediction and Analysis in the Behavioral Sciences, Ph.D. Thesis, Harvard University.

Werbos, P. J., 1988, Generalization of Backpropagation with Application to a Recurrent Gas Market Model, *Neural Networks*, Vol. 1, No. 4, pp. 339–56.

White, H., 1989, Learning in Artificial Neural Networks: A Statistical Perspective, *Neural Computation*, Vol. 1, pp. 425–64.

White, H., 1989, Some Asymptotic Results for Learning in Single Hidden-Layer Feedforward Network Models, *Journal of the American Statistical Association*, Vol. 84, No. 408, Theory and Methods, pp. 1003–13.

White, H., 1990, Connectionist Nonparametric Regression, Multilayer Feedforward Networks Can Learn Arbitrary Mappings, *Neural Networks*, Vol. 3, pp. 535–49.

Whitley, J. R. and J. F. Davis, 1993, Qualitative Interpretation of Sensor Patterns, *IEEE Expert*, April, pp. 54–63.

Whitley, D., S. Dominic and R. Das, 1991, Genetic Reinforcement Learning with Multilayer Neural Networks, *Proceedings of the Fourth International Conference on Genetic Algorithms*, Morgan Kaufmann, San Mateo, CA.

Widrow, B. and M. E. Hoff, 1960, Adaptive Switching Circuits, 1960 IRE WESCON Convention Record, New York.

Widrow, B. and S. D. Stearns, 1985, *Adaptive Signal Processing*, Prentice-Hall, Englewood Cliffs, NJ.

Widrow, B. and R. Winter, 1988, Neural Nets for Adaptive Filtering and Adaptive Pattern Recognition, *IEEE Computer*, Vol. 21, No. 3, pp. 25–39.

Widrow, B., R. G. Winter and R. A. Baxter, 1987, Learning Phenomena in Layered Neural Networks, *Proceedings of the First IEEE International Conference on Neural Networks*, San Diego.

Widrow, Bernard, David Rumelhart and Michael Lehr, 1994, Neural Networks: Applications in Industry, Business and Science, *Communications of the ACM*, Vol. 37, No. 3, pp. 93–105.

Williams, R. J. and J. Peng, 1990, An Efficient Gradient-Based Algorithm for On-Line Training of Recurrent Network Trajectories, *Neural Computation*, Vol. 2, pp. 490–501.

Williams, R. J. and D. Zipser, 1989, A Learning Algorithm for Continually Running Fully Recurrent Neural Networks, *Neural Computation*, Vol. 1, pp. 270–80.

Willshaw, D. J., O. P. Buneman and H. C. Longuet-Higgins, 1969, Non-Holographic Associative Memory, *Nature*, Vol. 222, pp. 960–2.

Yager, R. R., 1994, Modeling and Formulating Fuzzy Knowledge Bases Using Neural Networks, *Neural Networks*, Vol. 7, No. 8, pp. 1273–83.

Yamamoto, Y. and S. A. Zenios, 1993, Application of Neural Networks to Mortgage-Backed Securities, *Proceedings of the World Congress on Neural Networks*, Portland, OR, Lawrence Erlbaum Associates, Hillsdale, NJ, pp. 646–9.

Yanicoglu, B. A. and P. A. Sandon, 1993, Off-Line Cursive Handwriting Recognition Using Neural Networks, *Proceedings of the SPIE Applications of Artificial Neural Network IV*, Orlando, FL, pp. 102–6.

Yeung, D. Y., 1991, Automatic Determination of Network Size for Supervised Learning, *Proceedings of the IJCNN-91*, Singapore, pp. 158–64.

Youssef, H. M., 1993, Comparison of Neural Networks in Nonlinear System Modeling, *Proceedings of the World Congress on Neural Networks*, Portland, OR, pp. IV5–9.

Yu, X. H., 1991, On the Nonexistence of Local Minima of the Backpropagation Error Surfaces, *Proceedings of the IJCNN-91*, Singapore, Vol. 2, pp. 1272–7.

Yuille, A. L., D. M. Kammen and D. S. Cohen, 1989, Quadratic and the Development of Orientation Selective Cortical Cells by Hebb Rules, *Biological Cybernetics*, Vol. 61, pp. 183–94.

Zadeh, L. A., 1994, Fuzzy Logic, Neural Networks, and Soft Computing, *Communications of the ACM*, Vol. 37, No. 3, pp. 77–84.

Zak, M., 1991, An Unpredictable-Dynamics Approach to Neural Intelligence, *IEEE Expert*, August, pp. 4–10.

Zipser, D., 1989, A Subgrouping Strategy that Reduces Complexity and Speeds Up Learning in Recurrent Networks, *Neural Computation*, Vol. 1, pp. 552–8.

INDEX